Postcolonial English

The global spread of English has resulted in the emergence of a diverse range of postcolonial varieties around the world. *Postcolonial English* provides a clear and original account of the evolution of these varieties, exploring the historical, social, and ecological factors that have shaped all levels of their structure. It argues that while these Englishes have developed new and unique properties which differ greatly from one location to another, their spread and diversification can in fact be explained by a single underlying process, which builds upon the constant relationships and communication needs of the colonizers, the colonized, and other parties. Outlining the stages and characteristics of this process, it applies them in detail to English in sixteen different countries across all continents as well as, in a separate chapter, to a history of American English. Of key interest to sociolinguists, dialectologists, historical linguists, and syntacticians alike, this book provides a fascinating new picture of the growth and evolution of English around the globe.

EDGAR W. SCHNEIDER is Professor and Chair of English Linguistics in the Department of English and American Studies, University of Regensburg. His most recent books include *Degrees of Restructuring in Creole Languages* (2000), and *A Handbook of Varieties of English* (2004).

Cambridge Approaches to Language Contact

General Editor
Salikoko S. Mufwene, University of Chicago

Editorial Board
Robert Chaudenson, *Université d' Aix-en-Provence*
Braj Kachru, *University of Illinois at Urbana*
Rajend Mesthrie, *University of Cape Town*
Lesley Milroy, *University of Michigan*
Shana Poplack, *University of Ottawa*
Michael Silverstein, *University of Chicago*

Cambridge Approaches to Language Contact is an interdisciplinary series bringing together work on language contact from a diverse range of research areas. The series focuses on key topics in the study of contact between languages or dialects, including the development of pidgins and creoles, language evolution and change, world Englishes, code-switching and code-mixing, bilingualism and second-language acquisition, borrowing, interference, and convergence phenomena.

Published titles

Salikoko Mufwene, *The Ecology of Language Evolution*
Michael Clyne, *The Dynamics of Language Contact*
Bernd Heine and Tania Kuteva, *Language Contact and Grammatical Change*

Further titles planned for the series

Guy Bailey and Patricia Cukor-Avila, *The Development of African-American English*
Maarten Mous, *Controlling Language*
Clancy Clements, *The Linguistic Legacy of Spanish and Portuguese*

Postcolonial English

Varieties around the world

Edgar W. Schneider

University of Regensburg

CAMBRIDGE
UNIVERSITY PRESS

CAMBRIDGE UNIVERSITY PRESS
Cambridge, New York, Melbourne, Madrid, Cape Town, Singapore, São Paulo

Cambridge University Press
The Edinburgh Building, Cambridge CB2 8RU, UK

Published in the United States of America by Cambridge University Press,
New York

www.cambridge.org
Information on this title: www.cambridge.org/9780521539012

First published 2007

Printed in the United Kingdom at the University Press, Cambridge

A catalogue record for this publication is available from the British Library

ISBN 978-0-521-83140-6 hardback
ISBN 978-0-521-53901-2 paperback

Contents

List of maps, figures, and tables	*page* ix
Series editor's foreword	xi
Preface and acknowledgments	xiii
List of abbreviations	xvi

1 Introduction — 1

2 Charting the territory: Postcolonial Englishes as a field of linguistic investigation — 8
2.1 Ancestry — 8
2.2 Approaches — 11
2.3 Alternative perspectives and issues — 17

3 The evolution of Postcolonial Englishes: the Dynamic Model — 21
3.1 Transforming selves in migration: theoretical background — 21
3.2 The Dynamic Model of the evolution of Postcolonial Englishes — 29
3.3 Variations on the basic pattern — 55
3.4 Wider applicability — 68

4 Linguistic aspects of nativization — 71
4.1 Structural nativization: characteristic features — 72
4.2 Tracing structural nativization: methodological and conceptual issues — 90
4.3 The road to nativization: linguistic processes — 97

5 Countries along the cycle: case studies — 113
5.1 Fiji — 114
5.2 Australia — 118
5.3 New Zealand — 127
5.4 Hong Kong — 133
5.5 The Philippines — 140
5.6 Malaysia — 144
5.7 Singapore — 153
5.8 India — 161
5.9 South Africa — 173

5.10 Kenya   189
5.11 Tanzania   197
5.12 Nigeria   199
5.13 Cameroon   212
5.14 Barbados   219
5.15 Jamaica   227
5.16 Canada   238

6   The cycle in hindsight: the emergence of
    American English   251
    6.1   "Assembled in America from various quarters": Phase 1
          (ca. 1587–1670)   254
    6.2   "English with great classical purity": Phase 2 (ca. 1670–1773)   264
    6.3   "That torrent of barbarous phraseology": Phase 3
          (ca. 1773–1828/1848)   273
    6.4   "Our honor requires us to have a system of our own": Phase 4
          (1828/1848–1898)   282
    6.5   "We know just who we are by our language": Phase 5 (1898–) 291
    6.6   Summary and outlook   307

7   Conclusion   309

    Notes   318
    References   331
    Index of authors   360
    Index of subjects   363

Maps, figures, and tables

Maps

5.1: SW Pacific (Fiji, Australia, New Zealand)   *page* 114
5.2: Hong Kong and the Philippines   134
5.3: Malaysia and Singapore   144
5.4: India   162
5.5: South Africa   173
5.6: East Africa (Kenya and Tanzania)   190
5.7: West Africa (Nigeria and Cameroon)   200
5.8: The Caribbean (Barbados and Jamaica)   219
5.9: Canada   239

Figures

2.1: Kachru's "Three Circles" model   13
2.2: Charting the territory: approaches to PCEs   15
4.1: Sources and processes leading to PCEs   100

Tables

3.1: The evolutionary cycle of New Englishes: parameters of   56
     the developmental phases
4.1: Features which are highly characteristic of specific regions   75
4.2: Pronunciation tendencies by language types   77

Series editor's foreword

The series *Cambridge Approaches to Language Contact* was set up to publish outstanding monographs on language contact, especially by authors who approach their specific subject matter from a diachronic or developmental perspective. Our goal is to integrate the ever-growing scholarship on language diversification (including the development of creoles, pidgins, and indigenized varieties of colonial European languages), bilingual language development, code-switching, and language endangerment. We hope to provide a select forum to scholars who contribute insightfully to understanding language evolution from an interdisciplinary perspective. We favor approaches that highlight the role of ecology and draw inspiration both from the authors' own fields of specialization and from related research areas in linguistics or other disciplines. Eclecticism is one of our mottoes, as we endeavor to comprehend the complexity of evolutionary processes associated with contact.

We are very proud to add to our list Edgar W. Schneider's *Postcolonial English: varieties around the world*. This is, to my knowledge, the most comprehensive uniformitarian account of how English has spread around the world and diversified into a multitude of varieties (including creoles) thanks both to England's important participation in the European colonization of the world since the seventeenth century and to the American and British leadership role in the recent wave of economic globalization. If the spread of English has before been compared to that of Latin, Schneider has easily produced the only book that makes this comparison obvious. He also highlights the ways in which its prevalence over numerous indigenous and other European vernaculars in former settlement colonies, as well as over alternative lingua francas in the rest of the world, has been only a pyrrhic victory. Having been appropriated by new speakers in diverse contact ecologies, English has been adapted to different communicative practices and indigenized to express local and novel cultures. Schneider proposes a Dynamic Model which articulates various ecological factors bearing on the same general language-restructuring equation in order to account for the setting-specific ways in which English has evolved.

This new approach also makes obvious who have been the actual agents of the spread of English, not always the former colonists and colonizers from the United Kingdom, or Americans and Australians since the independence of former exploitation colonies, but often the local intellectual elite and political leaders. Paying attention to the actual ethnographic functions of English in various places, Schneider also makes it obvious why the spread of this language as a vernacular in former settlement colonies, as an official language in former exploitation colonies, but only as an international lingua franca in the rest of the world has not been a uniform threat to the vitality of indigenous languages around the world. *Postcolonial English* thus provides useful information to rethink the recent common characterization of English as the agent of globalization and the "killer language" *par excellence*, while indirectly also raising an issue out of the use of a by-now established discourse of language competition that is too lopsidedly based on tropes of power, prestige, violence, and war.

This is a brilliant application of the ecological approach to language evolution, highlighting a host of factors that account for the speciation of English into a host of novel varieties. The distinction between the "settler," "adstrate," and the "indigenous strands" in the ways that English has been transmitted from one generation to another in (former) settlement and exploitation colonies goes a long way to account for the extent to which particular postcolonial Englishes have been influenced by adstrate and substrate influence. He provides an alternative way to speak about the significance of founder effects and the ongoing competition between, on the one hand, target structures and, on the other, adstrate and substrate alternatives in language evolution, identifying the particular cultural domains where adstrate and substrate contributions (especially lexical) are not only favored but also almost unavoidable. Schneider takes us a long way toward understanding the correlation not only between language spread and colonization (including the population genetics sense of "relocation to a new place," also identified as *colony*), but also between, on the one hand, language evolution and, on the other, language imposition or willful appropriation, patterns of interaction, nature of the target variety, means of appropriation, communicative function, and power and identity, all as ecological factors. Specialists and non-specialists alike will find this book informative and thought-provoking, as it questions the traditional view that has misguidedly made the emergence of especially creoles and indigenized Englishes somewhat exceptional.

SALIKOKO S. MUFWENE, *University of Chicago*

Preface and acknowledgments

The evolution of Postcolonial Englishes is a most fascinating subject. Having worked on English-language dialectology, sociolinguistics, creolistics, and historical linguistics before, I was fully attracted to this field when I took over the editorship of the journal *English World-Wide* and the book series *Varieties of English Around the World* in 1997. The role as an editor is demanding and time-consuming, but it is also a privilege in many ways. It not only forces me to keep up to date with current discussions and writings in the field but it also brings me in touch with colleagues all around the globe, with young scholars with fresh ideas, and with new concepts, perspectives, and data. Luckily, it also provides excellent excuses to travel to all kinds of places, to present my own research and to get first-hand exposure to different language ecologies. So, what I have ended up with is a bird's-eye view of this exciting process of the globalization and, at the same time, local diffusion of English in all of its forms and functions.

It was this perspective that suggested to me that there are more similarities between individual processes of the emergence of indigenized Englishes in various localities than has hitherto been recognized. From there, it is only a short step to the uniformitarian hypothesis that has informed the present book, the claim that there is a single, coherent process which underlies the evolution of Postcolonial Englishes. The thesis was presented for the first time about five years ago in Sydney, and since then it has met with a lot of interest and supportive response. The present book builds upon ideas and facts published in my article "The dynamics of New Englishes: from identity construction to dialect birth," in *Language* 79 (2003): 233–81, but it goes substantially beyond what was discussed there. It presents a wide range of new data and case studies, and a version of the core thesis which has been developed further, modified, and expanded in a few aspects, and spelt out in greater detail.

Over the years I have benefited immensely from contacts and conversations with many friends and colleagues who have shared their views and, in some cases, their more intense familiarity with specific countries and situations with me. This book would not be conceivable without them, and I want to say a big thank you to all of them. At the same time, of course, they are not at all responsible for any errors or weaknesses in this text: while I have profited enormously from advice, sometimes I am stubborn and have resisted it. So for all errors and shortcomings I am solely responsible.

In the genesis of this book Salikoko Mufwene, the Series Editor, has been most influential and helpful. From the beginning, he has been the most astute and supportive editor one could hope for. He has read the entire manuscript extremely carefully and has suggested numerous improvements. I have also enjoyed the continuous support and interest of Andrew Winnard and Helen Barton at Cambridge University Press. I am most grateful to them.

Raj Mesthrie, Dani Schreier, and Udo Hebel also read select chapters and gave me valuable comments. Many others have influenced my thinking through their discussions with me and their reactions to other writings of mine on global Englishes, including earlier stages of the present work: Laurie Bauer, Maria Lourdes S. Bautista, Kingsley Bolton, Jack Chambers, Chng Huang Hoon, Peter Collins, Saran Kaur Gill, Manfred Görlach, Anthea Fraser Gupta, Braj and Yamuna Kachru, Thiru Kandiah, Joybrato Mukherjee, Peter Mühlhäusler, Aloysius Ngefac, Pam Peters, Jeff Siegel, Jan Tent, Peter Trudgill, and many more. Many friends in American sociolinguistics, most notably Guy Bailey, Ron Butters, Bill Kretzschmar, Michael Montgomery, and Walt Wolfram, have been very important for me and have influenced me more than they may have realized. I am grateful to all of them and look forward to further exchanges!

Portions of the ideas and the material discussed in this book have been presented at several conferences and universities: the Australian Style Council in Sydney in April 2001; the Universiti Kebangsaan Malaysia in Bangi in December 2003; the "Methods in Dialectology" conference in Moncton, New Brunswick, in August 2005; the "Studies in the History of the English Language" conference in Flagstaff, Arizona, in September/October 2005; the University of Stockholm, Sweden, in October 2005; and the "International Conference on Language, Literature and Education in Multicultural Societies" in Yaoundé, Cameroon, in May 2006. I thank the audiences for their interest and their valuable feedback. Thanks are also due to Noboyuki Honna and ALC Press for permission to use parts of an article published in *Asian Englishes* 2003 in section 5.5.6, and to Brian Joseph and the Linguistic Society of America for permission to reproduce select parts of the 2003 *Language* article quoted above.

What remains to be acknowledged is the foundation, the network of human relations without which I couldn't thrive and enjoy life and write a book. My team in Regensburg, including students, assistants, and colleagues, are a part of this. My friends, in Burgweinting and elsewhere, give me the down-to-earth human touches that make me feel comfortable and that I need as grounding in real life. And my family – well, they know they are my sunshine anyhow. Their smiles with which they tolerate my occasional absence or absent-mindedness are just wonderful to see. So I dedicate this book to Jutta, who has always stood by my side in so many ways without giving up her own path, and to Berit and Miriam, who are flying high but continue to have roots with us.

Abbreviations

AAVE	African-American Vernacular English
ADS	Adstrate speech community
ANZAC	Australia and New Zealand Army Corps
"BSAE"	Black South African English
CCR	consonant cluster reduction
EFL	English as a Foreign Language
ENL	English as a Native Language
ESL	English as a Second Language
ICE	International Corpus of English
IDG	Indigenous speech community
L1	first language
NCS	Northern Cities Shift
p.c.	personal communication
PCEs	Postcolonial Englishes
RP	Received Pronunciation (standard British pronunciation)
SAfE	South African English
SGEM	Speak Good English Movement (Singapore)
STL	Settlers speech community

1   Introduction

One of the most remarkable, and perhaps unexpected, sociocultural changes of the modern period, culminating in the late twentieth century, has been the global spread of the English language, a major component of a "language revolution" postulated by David Crystal (2004). For centuries scholars have dreamt of a single, universal language which would allow all of mankind to communicate with each other directly, but all attempts at constructing such a code artificially have failed in practice. Now, it seems, one has emerged quite naturally. The English language has spread into precisely this role without any strategic planning behind this process – it is the world's lingua franca and the language of international communication, politics, commerce, travel, the media, and so on. However, at the same time, and contrary to expectations, English has diversified, developing into homegrown forms and uses in many locations. It has also become an indigenized language, even a mother tongue, in several countries around the globe. In some countries, the descendants of former colonists or colonizers have retained the language to the present day; in others, interestingly enough, it was the local, indigenous population who have adopted and appropriated the English language for themselves, thus contributing to its diversification and the emergence of new varieties.

Certainly this state of affairs is the product of colonial and postcolonial history, most notably the spread of the British Empire. Crystal (1997) explains the role of English as the leading world language through a series of subsequent but rather coincidental processes: English happened to be the language of the British Empire and colonial expansion between the seventeenth and nineteenth centuries, of the industrial revolution thereafter, and in the twentieth century of the USA as the leading economic and military superpower and the main agent of today's economic and cultural globalization. That is certainly true, but it is only part of the story. In many countries English was a language imposed by foreign, colonial masters. Intuitively one could have expected it to be abandoned as fast as possible after independence. Indeed, some countries, like Tanzania or Malaysia, attempted to do so and proposed the removal of English as their political goal. After all, it was a foreign tongue, alien to a substantial proportion of the indigenous population, and an unwelcome reminder and heritage of colonialism, which meant, among other things, foreign dominance and loss of political and cultural sovereignty.

However, in most cases something strange, exactly the opposite, has happened, in bits and pieces, and in several countries independently of each other: English has managed to stay, not only in formal and official functions; it has indigenized and grown local roots. It has begun to thrive and to produce innovative, regionally distinctive forms and uses of its own, in contact with indigenous languages and cultures and in the mouths of both native populations and the descendants of former immigrants, making ever deeper inroads into local communities. Its pull and attractiveness are immense. From Barbados to Australia, from Kenya to Hong Kong a traveler will today get along with English, but he or she will also realize that the Englishes encountered are quite different from each other – pronounced with varying accents, employing local words opaque to an outsider, and even, on closer inspection, constructing sentences with certain words in slightly different ways. What is perhaps even more interesting is that our virtual traveler will encounter native speakers of English not only in Canada and New Zealand, where this would be expected, but also in Nigeria and Singapore, and in many more parts of the world in which English is not an ancestral language. English has become a local language of everyday communication in many countries and new environments; it is developing indigenous forms; it appears to be fragmenting, breaking up into regional varieties so that intelligibility may be compromised. And, interestingly enough, this process has intensified substantially during the latter part of the twentieth century and into the new millennium.

No doubt this global spread and concurrent indigenization of English is a phenomenon with many different facets and components, of concern to various people and disciplines. It raises issues of language policy and pedagogy, of cultural evaluation and sociopsychological integration, and, of course, for a linguist also of structural and pragmatic evolution. A new sub-discipline within (English) linguistics, somewhat fuzzily known as the study of "World Englishes" or English as a world language, has emerged since the early 1980s, with journals, textbooks, collective volumes, and conference series of its own, and the topic is becoming ever more popular (see Bolton and Kachru 2006). This is not surprising given that it is highly vibrant, with the changes happening to English going on at an undiminished pace and being relevant to all kinds of theoretical and practical questions.

As in many young fields, terminology is still somewhat unsettled, and there are alternative labels for the phenomenon under consideration emphasizing slightly different aspects. When in 1980 Manfred Görlach founded the first scholarly journal exclusively devoted to these processes, he considered choosing *Englishes* as its title but refrained from doing so because the plural form was still felt to be unacceptable, and he opted for *English World-Wide* instead. The books by Pride (1982) and Platt, Weber and Ho (1984) introduced the label *New Englishes*, which gained quite some currency but was also opposed by some scholars who argued that the label *new* reflected primarily a shift of attention in western, Anglocentric scholarship. Braj Kachru and his followers have employed the term *World Englishes*, introduced by a journal of that name founded in 1982 and disseminated also by an active scholarly organization, known as *IAWE*, the *International Association of World Englishes*. This label is useful, customary, and widespread today, though associated with a specific school in the discipline and its programmatic agenda of "decolonising English . . . outside the 'Western World' " (Hickey 2004b:504). In this book I use the term *Postcolonial Englishes*, not only because it is more neutral but also because it focuses precisely on the aspect which I intend to emphasize: the varieties under discussion are products of a specific evolutionary process tied directly to their colonial and postcolonial history. I am concerned with developmental phenomena characteristic of colonial and the early phases of postcolonial histories until the maturation and separation of these dialects as newly recognized and self-contained varieties; hence, the term is taken to encompass all forms of English resulting and emerging from such backgrounds.

By and large, the relevant linguistic developments are products of the colonial expansion of the British Empire from the late sixteenth to the twentieth century. During the Elizabethan Age, Britain began to develop global ambitions and to challenge the dominance of the Spanish, Portuguese, Dutch, and French as colonial powers. In the seventeenth century North America was settled, and, importantly, economically prosperous possessions were colonized throughout the Caribbean. At the same time firm trading connections were built with coastal locations in Africa and with the Far East. In the late eighteenth and early nineteenth centuries, British ships explored the Pacific, substantial numbers of British settlers moved to Australasia and South Africa, and the Empire became the leading colonial power in South and South-East Asia. The late nineteenth and early twentieth centuries, finally, brought with them colonial authority in further parts of Africa and also the emergence of the United States of America as a colonial power, mainly in the Philippines.[1]

Note, however, that what counts here is not the colonial history or the former colonial status of a given country per se, and also not the specifically British connection, but rather the type of contact situation caused by these historical circumstances, the expansion and relocation of the use of a single language to new territories where a characteristic type of language-contact situation evolves.

This book proposes a unified systematic approach of the emergence of Postcolonial Englishes (henceforth PCEs): it describes their general characteristics in the light of a uniform theory and looks at many of their individual manifestations, with all their bewildering variability. PCEs have emerged in a wide variety of sociohistorical circumstances, throughout the history of colonialism and on all continents. Hence, it is necessary to look closely into the sociohistorical contexts of their emergence, their "ecologies" (Mufwene 2001b). Different scenarios emerged, and they account for persistent differences from one variety to another. But one thing that all these varieties have in common is that they have originated in contact settings, involving intercultural encounters: contact between immigrants of various social and regional backgrounds (including speakers of different English dialects), and contact between English-speaking immigrants and indigenous populations.

It is natural to expect that differences in extralinguistic backgrounds have resulted in the far-reaching differences between the individual varieties that we find today in their respective forms and functions. Indeed, this is the position that scholarship has typically taken: it has been customary to view individual PCEs in isolation, independently of each other, as unique cases shaped by idiosyncratic historical conditions and contact situations. So far, theory formation in this emerging field has not proceeded beyond categorizations of the countries concerned into types according to the roles English plays in them (to be discussed briefly in chapter 2). In contrast, the present book points out that a uniform underlying process has been effective in all these situations and explains a wide range of parallel phenomena from one variety to another.[2] Thus, it presents the first unified, coherent theory to account specifically for the evolution of PCEs around the globe.

A closer look at what is going on in many English-speaking countries reveals strange, perhaps surprising similarities despite all obvious differences in their regional and sociocultural settings, illustrating the fact that a transnational perspective is required in understanding global English(es) today. Why is it that "nation building" was a major political issue typically associated with linguistic matters in many countries on different continents? Why is it that Singaporeans just like US Southerners or Nigerian Pidgin speakers keep resisting their politicians' and educational gatekeepers' pronouncements to speak "proper" English and to avoid "bastardized" dialects of the language (whatever the fashionable discourse convention at any given location might be)? Why do South African, Indian, and Caribbean writers employ local idioms to entertain their audiences, although this may restrict international accessibility to (and commercial success of) their literary products? Why are so many nations in Africa, Asia, and in the Caribbean struggling with the issue of which norm of English to prescribe in education, officially promoting a British speech type that obviously is not a realistic (and perhaps not even a desirable) target? Why are conservative language critics lamenting "falling standards" of English in so many different countries, from New Zealand to Tanzania? Why were observers and visitors surprised about the putative "homogeneity" of English as spoken in nineteenth-century North America or twentieth-century New Zealand, while currently we get reports of regional speech differences emerging in locations as far apart as Canada or Australia? Why are words borrowed from indigenous languages into local forms of English typically from specific semantic domains? Aren't the similarities between the kinds of structural innovations to be observed in a great many different varieties of English around the globe (like local "accents," specific borrowings, the coinage of new compounds, or slight variations in the uses of prepositions or the constructions which verbs allow) linguistically remarkable, even stunning? Obviously, PCEs have more in common than one might think at first sight.

It is the core thesis of this book that, despite all obvious dissimilarities, a fundamentally uniform developmental process, shaped by consistent socio-linguistic and language-contact conditions, has operated in the individual instances of relocating and re-rooting the English language in another territory, and therefore it is possible to present the individual histories of PCEs as instantiations of the same underlying process. More specifically, it is posited that evolving new varieties of English go through a cyclic series of characteristic phases,[3] determined by extralinguistic conditions. Individual countries in which PCEs are spoken are regarded as positioned at different phases along this cycle, an explanation which accounts for some of the differences observed in the shapes and roles of PCEs.

At the heart of this process there are characteristic stages of identity reconstructions on the side of the parties involved, which are to some extent determined by similar parameters of the respective contact situations. Comparable constellations of communities in migration contact settings (between indigenous population and immigrant groups, respectively) have resulted in analogous processes of mutual accommodation and, conse-quently, in similar sociolinguistic and structural outcomes. In essence, the process consists of a gradual and mutual cultural and linguistic approxima-tion of the two parties in a colonization process: in the early phases of colonial expansion settlers consider themselves outpost representatives of a distant homeland, and the burden of linguistic adaptation and, sometimes, language shift rests largely upon the indigenous population. In the long run, this process entails structural nativization, understood as the emergence of locally characteristic linguistic patterns and thus the genesis of a new variety of English. In the course of this process both groups tend to rewrite their identities, based upon permanently shared territory, and in the end they emerge as a new nation with hybrid roots and new linguistic norms.

Chapter 2 situates the approach pursued here in its scholarly context. I will briefly survey the disciplines that have influenced the study of PCEs methodologically and conceptually, the various approaches that have dominated the field over the last few decades, and a few general issues that need to be considered.

In chapter 3 the theoretical framework behind this book, which I call the "Dynamic Model" of the evolution of PCEs, is outlined. Before going into the model itself, some foundations will be addressed, notably a taxonomy of language contact settings and colonization types, and the theories of social identity and linguistic accommodation. This is followed by a thorough presentation of the components of the model itself. I suggest that in a typical developmental scenario, the history of PCEs can be described as a sequence of five distinct phases, labeled "Foundation," "Exonormative stabilization," "Nativization," "Endonormative stabilization," and "Differentiation." Each of these is characterized by specific ecological and linguistic characteristics, so at each stage a mutually dependent set of factors needs to be considered, relating to the respective sociopolitical background, the identity constructions of the parties involved in a contact setting, the resulting sociolinguistic conditions, and the linguistic effects of these factors. Finally, I discuss a few important parameters of variation within the model, and I consider its wider applicability, e.g. to the global diffusion of Romance languages.

Chapter 4 elaborates on the strictly linguistic side of the central thesis. It asks which structural phenomena on the levels of phonology, lexis, and grammar are widespread in PCEs; it looks into the methodological and conceptual basis behind our familiarity with, and perception of, differences between varieties of English; and it investigates the linguistic processes which have produced the similarities between them. Given that, quite naturally, much attention in the literature is devoted to extralinguistic conditions and sociolinguistic parameters, it is the intention of this chapter to redress the balance and to develop a strictly linguistic, structurally descriptive perspective on PCEs that goes beyond a conventional, somewhat anecdotal listing of individual examples.

Subsequently, in chapter 5, the concepts developed up to then are applied to a wide range of case studies. The histories and present-day situations and characteristics of English in as many as sixteen countries from all continents, ranging from Fiji to Canada, from New Zealand via Malaysia to Kenya and Barbados, are discussed in the light of the Dynamic Model. This chapter can be read as the first-ever global history of PCEs, paying attention to both the underlying uniformity and the remarkable diversity of this process. It strikes a balance between emphasizing common, underlying traits shared by substantially different locations and historical settings on the one hand and respecting differences between such varieties on the other. These differences can be either of an idiosyncratic nature or determined by colonization types (e.g. between communities where European settlers predominated, as in Australia; where English was deliberately selected by the indigenous community, as in Nigeria; and where creoles developed, as in Jamaica). Overall, a rich texture of the evolution of English and Englishes around the world, paying attention to their political and cultural contexts, sociolinguistic settings, and structural characteristics, emerges.

Chapter 6 approaches the topic from a complementary perspective, namely by describing in some detail the emergence of a variety that has passed all the way through the evolutionary cycle (and thus allows us to evaluate it in hindsight) but is not typically discussed as one of the PCEs, American English. Apart from the fact that the Dynamic Model is found to apply quite convincingly in this case as well, this chapter presents a history of American English as such, one which in its coherence, explanatory power, and also attention to detail goes considerably beyond earlier historical surveys of this variety.

Finally, the conclusion considers a few general aspects of, and insights derived from, the previous chapters. Based upon the earlier discussions and the input of the case studies, it evaluates the applicability of the Dynamic Model and its theoretical and practical consequences.

2 Charting the territory: Postcolonial Englishes as a field of linguistic investigation

2.1 Ancestry

First and foremost, PCEs are varieties of English, shaped and determined by the sociohistorical conditions of their origins and by the social nature of man. Human beings usually associate closely with other humans nearby and have considerably less contact with people who live far away or in different social circumstances, whom they are less likely to encounter. Hence, they accommodate and adjust their speech forms to those of their friends and neighbors to express solidarity, which is the reason why there are dialects and varieties of languages. The study of PCEs builds upon some precursor disciplines which have investigated such variation and developed methodologies to probe into regional, social, and other types of language variation. Obviously, the popular idea that there is only one "standard" variant, a "correct," monolithic form of English, with all other realizations being somehow "deviant," "dialectal," or "broken," is misguided. Rather, with Mufwene (2001b) we need to accept that every language consists of an enormously large "pool" of features, linguistic options to choose from if one wishes to express one and the same idea. Choices are possible in vocabulary, pronunciation, word forms, and also the syntactic arrangement of sentence constituents. Which of these choices are made, and how precisely we speak, depends upon and at the same time signals an individual's background. In most instances, as soon as a person starts to speak, listeners will be able to roughly assess where the speaker grew up, in which social circumstances, and how formal or casual is the speech situation being framed.

By implication, the same applies to speakers of PCEs. These parameters of variation have been studied by linguistic disciplines which can be regarded as precursors of the field of studying PCEs: dialect geography, sociolinguistics, and pidgin and creole studies (or contact linguistics, more generally). These disciplines have provided methodological tools, are driven by similar research goals, and are interested in comparable applications of their results.

The first parameter of language variability linguists turned their attention to, originally because of its implicit significance for the understanding of outcomes of language history, was *regional variation*, investigated by dialect geography (Francis 1983; Davis 1983; Chambers and Trudgill 1998). It is a trivial fact that speakers from different countries, regions, or, at times, even villages speak differently and can be recognized by their "accents," by regionally marked words, and (although this is less well known popularly) by regional features of grammar. Beginning in the late 1920s in the USA and in the 1940s in England, dialect geographers have systematically collected evidence of such differences to establish "linguistic atlases," both in Britain and in North America (as well as in non-English-speaking countries, of course).

Differences between New Englishes can be regarded as a continuation of such regional differences: comparing English as spoken in, say, Australia, Nigeria, or India essentially entails looking at regional language differences. Provided that the listener has an ear for such differences and has had exposure to the respective varieties before, the regional origin of a speaker can usually be identified on the basis of his or her accent and other features of language use. In the case of PCEs, the assignment of a speaker to a certain location on the basis of such differences has usually operated on an inter-regional or even international basis, i.e. by broadly comparing the Englishes of one country to another, and not intranationally, with an eye to internal regional differences. This is a consequence of the time depth of the respective varieties: it takes a very long time – generations or even centuries – for regional speech differences to emerge, stabilize, and become recognizable in the public mind. In most PCE-speaking countries, therefore, a dialectology with a "traditional" orientation and methodology has not yet been initiated, also because internal regional differences tend not to be as pronounced and conspicuous as in "older" English-speaking countries. However, in the case of some communities where conditions for the emergence of regional differences (internal group coherence being more important than outside contacts for an extended period of time) have prevailed, we do find regional differences and scholarly documentations of such variation, e.g. with respect to dialects of American English, inter-island differences in the Caribbean, or emerging regional speech differences in Australia and New Zealand. I will return to some of these topics in the case studies below. A most interesting case in point, for instance, is Bryant's (1989, 1997) work on the regional lexis of Australian English, which has produced dialect maps along the lines of earlier word geographies to describe regional variation in a new variety of English.

In the 1960s linguists began to emphasize the fact that speech differences are motivated not only by regional differences but also by an individual's social background, i.e. parameters such as social class, education, sex, ethnicity, and that in general it is necessary to understand the way competing languages and language varieties are used in increasingly complex societies. Accordingly, as is well known, the discipline of *sociolinguistics* can be subdivided into two major branches. "Macro-sociolinguistics" (e.g. Fishman 1972) is broadly concerned with the functions of languages and language varieties in a society, i.e. questions of language policy, multilingualism, diglossia, language uses, educational policies. "Micro-sociolinguistics," as developed by William Labov (1972; Chambers 2003), employs quantitative methods to work out detailed correlations between individual language variants (features of pronunciation, morphology, and syntax) on the one hand and language-internal constraints and extralinguistic (social) users' groupings on the other, frequently motivated by a fundamental interest in principles of language variation and language change (Chambers, Trudgill and Schilling-Estes 2002). Clearly, both approaches are of immediate concern to and have greatly influenced investigations of PCEs. Macro-sociolinguistic problems show and have been documented most clearly in multilingual societies, many of which frequently, precisely because the language situation is so complex, have resulted in the emergence of new varieties of English. Micro-correlational sociolinguistics has been applied to Australia (Horvath 1985), to New Zealand (most vigorously and successfully in the 1990s and after in work by Laurie Bauer, Allan Bell, Elizabeth Gordon, Janet Holmes, Peter Trudgill, and many others; see Bell and Kuiper 2000, which includes a survey of earlier research, and Gordon et al. 2004), the Caribbean (in work by Peter Patrick, John Rickford, Don Winford, and others) and to Singapore (by John Platt and his associates).

At about the same time, during the late 1950s and the 1960s, *pidgin* and *creole* linguistics evolved as a field of study, with various linguists working on creole languages having recognized unexpected structural similarities across creoles based on different lexifiers (see Holm 1988/89; Arends, Muysken, and Smith 1995). Consequently, in its early phase creole linguistics was strongly concerned with fairly general, theoretical questions, like theories of creole genesis and the roles of universals, substrates, and superstrates, respectively (see Muysken and Smith 1986). More recent research tendencies have included a broader documentation of early creole texts (e.g. Rickford 1987 for Guyanese, Winer 1993 for Trinidadian, D'Costa and Lalla 1989 for Jamaican, or Huber 1999 for West African Pidgin English), the recognitions that some creoles have emerged gradually rather than abruptly (Arends 1993) and that creoles come in different degrees of "depth" (Schneider 1990; Neumann-Holzschuh and Schneider 2000), and, in fact, that it seems impossible to delimitate them precisely as a class of languages. While early creolist theory (and also some recent contenders, e.g. McWhorter 2000) argued for the fundamental distinctness of creoles from English (and other lexifiers), recent scholarship has recognized that the distinction is in fact a gradual one (see Neumann-Holzschuh and Schneider 2000), and some scholars, like Mufwene (2000a, 2001b, 2005a), claim that creoles are actually dialects of their lexifiers. Obviously, this debate has consequences for the relationship between creoles and PCEs. The close relatedness between both types of language varieties is immediately apparent: both derive from contact situations; many pidgins and creoles are spoken in regions and countries where English is an official language (like throughout the Caribbean and West Africa, in the southwest Pacific, and also in Australia), so both contribute to the sociolinguistic complexity in such nations; and, in fact, the relationship between local varieties of English and creoles is not always clear.

Whatever the outcome of this debate, or one's individual position in it, may be, it is undisputed that both creoles and so-called "New Englishes" are largely products of *language contact*, albeit to varying degrees, which provides a common framework for them to be investigated (see Thomason and Kaufman 1988; Thomason 1997; Kachru et al. in Prendergast 1998; Mufwene 2001b). Historical linguists have for a long time tended to overemphasize the purity of languages in their historical transmission from one generation to another and to underestimate the impact of contact between languages, but more recent scholarship has recognized contact to be almost ubiquitous and of primary importance in the development of languages and language varieties (see Goebl et al. 1996/97; Mufwene 2001b; Thomason 2001; Winford 2003).

2.2 Approaches

As was stated in the introductory chapter, an awareness of the study of PCEs constituting a coherent field of scholarly investigation goes back to the early 1980s. Obviously, individual scholars have brought their own experiences and perspectives, both personal and scientific, into this endeavor, and by now a few research traditions, perhaps to be called paradigms, have evolved. Bolton (2003:7–36) provides a competent survey and a critical evaluation of a variety of approaches to the new discipline of "World Englishes." He lists the following, in each case together with their best-known practitioners and further references: English studies; English corpus linguistics; sociology of language; "features-based" sociolinguistic studies; Kachruvian studies; pidgin and creole studies; applied linguistics; lexicography; popularizers; critical linguistics; and linguistic futurology. This overview is useful and commendable for its comprehensiveness, even if it compiles sub-disciplines which are not really on a par. All of these approaches have contributed to our understanding of PCEs, but some of them are central to this line of thinking and have emerged together with it, while other categories represent sub-disciplines of linguistics in general which have employed data drawn from PCEs in addition to other languages, and others, again, are quite narrowly circumscribed.

Two comprehensive models of PCEs have been suggested to categorize the varieties of worldwide English into broader types, with both looking at the functional and political role of English in a given country, and both assuming three classes.

The first of these models builds upon a distinction of "*ENL*" (English as a Native Language) countries from "*ESL*" (English as a Second Language) countries and "*EFL*" (English as a Foreign Language) countries. McArthur (1998:42) traces the model back to a suggestion made by the late Barbara Strang in her *History of English* of 1970 which was imbued with authority and spread by its adoption in Quirk et al.'s *Grammar of Contemporary English* of 1972, the forerunner of the most authoritative grammar of English, the *Comprehensive Grammar of the English Language* (Quirk et al. 1985). It was also promoted by Görlach (1991b:12–13). In ENL countries, even if multilingualism may play an important role in the society at large, English is the vernacular language of almost all or at least a significant majority of the population (like Britain, the USA, or Australia). In ESL countries, English exists side by side with strong indigenous languages, is widely spoken, and assumes prominent intranational, sometimes official functions, as the language of politics, the media, jurisdiction, higher education, and other such domains (as in Ghana, Nigeria, India, Singapore, Papua New Guinea, etc.). In EFL countries, English, acquired almost exclusively by formal education, performs no official internal function but is still strongly rooted and widely used in some domains (like the press or tertiary education) because of its special international usefulness in business, the sciences, technology, etc. (as in Israel, Egypt, or Taiwan). Of course, the status of English in any given country may change in the course of time. For instance, certain ESL countries have deliberately reduced the role of English to an EFL status.

This model has been found useful and has been adopted widely, but like all models it ignores certain facets of complex realities. For example, it fails to acknowledge the presence of non-native-speaking groups, whether indigenous or immigrant, in ENL countries: there is no room reserved in this framework for, say, French Canadians, Native Americans, Australian Aboriginals, or Pakistani communities in Britain. Conversely, native speakers of English, whether expatriates or, more importantly, indigenous people, in ESL countries are equally sidestepped: Hong Kong people of

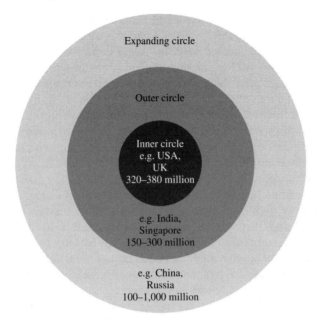

Figure 2.1: Kachru's "Three Circles" model (from Crystal 1997:54)

English origin or native speakers of English in, say, Sri Lanka, Singapore, or Nigeria appear as an anomaly. An officially multilingual country like South Africa cannot be categorized clearly as either ENL or ESL. In general, the framework fails to account for the fact that recent realities seem to be rendering the ENL – ESL distinction increasingly obsolete: in many so-called ESL countries, in a "grassroots" movement English is being adopted as a first language by some families and groups. The model also fails to offer a clear delimitation between ESL and EFL, and it deals with complex language situations like that in the Caribbean only inadvertently if at all (as "ESD" or "English as a Second Dialect," for instance; see Görlach 1991b:12).

The second widespread categorization is Kachru's "*Three Circles*" model, presented for the first time in Kachru (1985). Kachru's classification (see Figure 2.1 or McArthur 1998:100) distinguishes countries of an "Inner Circle," an "Outer Circle," and an "Expanding Circle." While the exact criteria for inclusion in any of these categories are not always clear, and individual countries are assigned essentially to function as examples, it is obvious that in terms of their membership countries the three circles largely correspond to the ENL – ESL – EFL distinction. The difference between the two models is primarily one of their broader goals and political implications. Kachru rejects the idea that any special prominence or a superior status should be assigned to ENL countries and "native language" status, and, accordingly, he is less concerned with the Inner Circle countries but places greatest emphasis on the Outer Circle (see Kachru 1992), and also the Expanding Circle. The implication is that norms and standards should no longer be determined by Inner Circle/ ENL contexts; instead, Kachru emphasizes that the English language belongs to all of those who use it, and that the most vigorous expansions and developments of the language can be observed in Outer and Expanding Circle countries. Kachru is less interested in microlinguistic and descriptive approaches (in fact, he rather doubts the possibility of "objective" scholarship; p.c. 2002) but rather pursues a quasi-political mission, that of fighting existing inequalities in scholarly and public perceptions of and attitudes toward varieties of English. In that respect, he has been extremely influential, mostly in Applied Linguistics, influencing perspectives on language policies and language teaching.

Both of these models have remained rather superficial and fuzzy in their capacity for establishing categories of linguistic description and classification. Both have listed criteria for the inclusion of nations into one category or another, but in neither case has a listing of features been provided that convincingly serves to fit problematic cases (like South Africa or Malaysia), and neither one has attempted to list all countries in a given category exhaustively.

Melchers and Shaw (2003:29–40) propose a scheme of classification which is more complex than earlier ones but also more flexible, because it explicitly pays attention to relevant dimensions and criteria to categorize distinct aspects of the field. They classify varieties by standardization (discussing the standard vs. nonstandard dimension) and degree of codification (including prescriptive attitudes); varieties by type of prestige (overt vs. covert; acrolect – mesolect – basilect); texts by degree of standardization (i.e. editorial interference in production); countries by domains of English use and proportion of efficient speakers of some variety); and speakers by type and scope of proficiency. Perhaps most interestingly, they also distinguish ideological frameworks of scholarship, by political stance, namely conservatives (who regard the assimilation of less powerful groups to the language practices of more powerful groups as a necessary step in gaining respect and credibility), liberals (who emphasize the equality of all language varieties in their respective contexts) and radicals (who view English as a tool in the creation of global inequalities and wish to fervently fight this development by political action).

In a broader perspective, the above classifications and attempts at finding delimitations obviously do not exhaust the range of possible

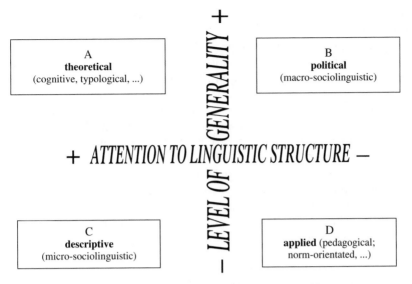

Figure 2.2: Charting the territory: approaches to PCEs

approaches to PCEs in scholarship, although as in any discipline there is a tendency for scholars and investigations to cluster around established notions and paradigms. Figure 2.2 provides an attempt to chart the territory, to relate relevant directions of scholarship to more general approaches to linguistic inquiry. These approaches have been arranged along two dimensions. The first one, "attention to linguistic structure," distinguishes investigations which focus primarily upon the structural properties of given languages and language varieties on the levels of phonology, lexis, and grammar from those which are interested in non-structural correlates and conditions of language use in a society. The second dimension, "level of generality," accounts for the observation that in some cases individual details and case studies are the goals of an investigation while in others scholars aim at broader generalizations of some kind. Consequently, I suggest that, on account of the possible combinations of these parameters, the existing approaches to PCEs can be broadly assigned to four major types which at the same time illustrate the relationship between PCEs as objects of inquiry and the discipline of linguistics in general.

Category A, "theoretical" approaches, applies when PCEs are analyzed to yield insights of a more fundamental nature, concerning linguistic theory and the nature of human language in general. It is clear that the sociolinguistic and linguistic scenarios in which PCEs have evolved should lend themselves to investigations of general questions of language variation and change, second-language acquisition, language shift, language change under specific types of contact conditions, the impact of language attitudes, and the like – although it has to be admitted that such inquiries have been the exception rather than the rule so far. "Political" questions (category B), on the other hand, with little interest in linguistic structure but a tendency to posit sweeping generalizations, have been a frequent concern in discussions of PCEs, given that in these countries macro-sociolinguistic issues concerning the uses of language(s) in society (like which language policy to adopt, whether or not to develop and support a new "national language," whether to tolerate certain linguistic variants in public and official domains, and the like) can be immediately pressing. Such questions may be employed to create a sense of nationhood, but they may also be instrumentalized in intranational power struggles, with linguistic issues masking group tensions. Studies in category C are driven by an interest in language description in detail, including micro-sociolinguistic correlational investigations – a type of approach that, in my view, should constitute a prerequisite for generalizations and applications of all kinds. Finally, in an applied perspective (category D), questions of language pedagogy and other practical needs, like which forms to strive for and accept as correct, figure prominently. Understandably enough, given their practical relevance in many societies, questions of "How to teach English in X" are frequently discussed in the literature, though not always with sufficient empirical grounding.

Of course, the choice of topics considered worthy of investigation in this field is also determined by the sociology of its practitioners: certain schools and individuals promote certain approaches and find less interest in others, and there are tides of fashion in addition to the gradual advancement of knowledge achieved by a growing consensus among the members of the scientific community. There are also assumptions and positions, linguistic and political, which are at odds with each other and on which there is heated debate at times. It is interesting to observe that scholars who originate from or live in developing countries, and who are thus more directly exposed to the immediate practical needs of a society, tend to be more interested in questions of an applied or political nature, whereas scholars from other countries tend to be more interested in general, comparative and theoretical questions and objective description: an outside perspective in this case may be an undeserved privilege of those who are not exposed to a society's daily and urgent needs. Still, it should be clear that both positions are perfectly legitimate and need to complement each other for each to be effective.

2.3 Alternative perspectives and issues

In this section I raise a few more questions that have been brought up in the context of PCEs and that need to be addressed, if only briefly, to achieve a more comprehensive understanding of the complexity of the issues involved.

The first of these concerns the notion of *nativeness*. Central as it may seem (to the ENL – ESL distinction, for instance), the importance of being a native speaker of English has been questioned in recent years (Kachru 1986; Singh 1998). The traditional view holds that only native speakers fully command a language and have proper intuitions on its structural properties. On the other hand, it has been pointed out that in many parts of the world, especially in ESL/Outer Circle contexts, reality has turned out to be much more complicated than this simplistic assumption implies. Competence in a language is tied to its constant use, and in such countries we find both indigenous native speakers of English in the narrow sense (like minorities of Indians or Sri Lankans who grew up speaking English), whose intuitions may differ significantly from those of British or American people, and speakers who, after having acquired an indigenous mother tongue, have sooner or later shifted to using English only or predominantly in all or many domains of everyday life. Such speakers can be classified as "first-language (or vernacular) English" speakers, although they do not qualify as native speakers in the strict sense.[1] It is undisputed, however, that their importance in their respective cultures, as linguistic models and as users and owners of PCEs, is paramount. Accordingly, Kachru (1997:4–5) has convincingly made a point in arguing that what he calls "functional nativeness" is just as important as "genetic nativeness."

Secondly, there is the issue of establishing *norms of correctness*. Typically, PCEs emerge and are spoken in sociolinguistically complex circumstances, and they are therefore characterized by a high degree of linguistic variability, including linguistic forms which are hybrid (English modified by contact with indigenous languages) or nonstandard (English not accepted as socially adequate in formal circumstances). In many contexts, especially spoken and informal ones, such variation is functional: it signals characteristics of the speaker (such as his or her social status) or the context of situation (such as a relaxed atmosphere). There are other contexts, however, which, by common understanding, require the use of a formal linguistic norm, a standard variety. The notion of "Standard English" is commonly taken to refer to such a norm, usually understood to designate a non-regional vocabulary core and the grammar of the written language. For pronunciation, there is no international norm, but in the majority of communities under discussion the historical origins of the immigrants have meant that the spoken norm is the standard British type of pronunciation, known as RP (see Upton 2004) – irrespective of whether that is what the majority of a population really speak.

Hence, not infrequently there is a clash between the reality of everyday speech performance and the expectations resulting from linguistic norm orientations. Formal contexts, including teaching, require norm orientations as to which linguistic forms count as acceptable or as targets in education and speech production, but the question is which and whose norms are accepted; not surprisingly, in this context emotional opinions and strong attitudes frequently prevail. Descriptive and theoretical linguists fundamentally believe that all language varieties are functionally adequate in their respective contexts and internally well structured, but frequently this is difficult to bring home to conservative observers and decision-makers in the educational and political arena. From a strictly linguistic perspective, it would make sense to establish the careful usage of the educated members of a society as the target and as an indigenous language norm; obviously, a micro-sociolinguistic description of usage correlated with sociostylistic parameters needs to be a starting point. But in practice, this cleavage frequently results in emotional debates between conservative and more liberally minded language observers. In the long run, every society needs to make its own decisions with respect to required and desirable political and pedagogical actions, and observed usage needs to be interpreted in the light of the tension between these norms and the range of local performance realities.

In a broader perspective, the topic of norm-setting needs to be discussed in the light of a more versatile understanding of the notion of "linguistic norm," not only in the sense of "conforming to a standard of correctness accepted in a society" but also as "pragmatically appropriate for a given social setting as judged by the participants in a given speech event." In other words, the notion of a linguistic norm touches upon the distinction (and tension, for that matter) between public norms and written language on the one hand and private and spoken performance on the other, epitomized by the notions of overt and covert prestige in sociolinguistics (Labov 1972:249; Chambers 2003:241–4). Correspondingly, all observations of language developments in PCEs need to be judged also as situated on the cline between formal and informal, written and spoken, educated and vernacular usage. Some of the phenomena I will point out in chapter 3 have an effect predominantly or exclusively on one end of this dichotomy, leaving the other largely untouched. For example, koinéization or structural nativization, as discussed below, affect some people's speech behavior but not others' attitudes; conversely, the tradition of complaining about a perceived decrease in the "quality" of linguistic usage or the codification of a variety characterize the top end of the sociostylistic continuum, with limited, delayed, or no effects on the other end. Clearly, this parameter of variation is closely related to that of social class and associated speech differences (like, for example, the continuum between "Broad," "General," and "Cultivated" varieties posited by Mitchell and Delbridge 1965 for Australian English).

Thirdly, the global spread of English has triggered political debates on how to evaluate this process and on how it is being represented in the scholarly literature. Inspired by postcolonial theory (see Loomba 1998) and in the wake of "Critical Discourse Analysis" (e.g. Phillipson 1992; Pennycook 1998; for some thoughtful and healthy reactions see Conrad 1996, Lucko 2003 and Mufwene 2004b), it has recently been pointed out that many seemingly descriptive statements (including the ENL – ESL – EFL categorization mentioned above) entail culturally biased value judgments, and some scholars doubt whether any language description can be devoid of ideological baggage (Kachru, p.c. 2002). In many statements on global Englishes there is an inherent hidden tendency to regard and portray Britain and other ENL countries as the "centers," thus entitled to establishing norms of correctness, and, conversely, PCEs as peripheral, thus in some sense deviating from these norms and, consequently, evaluated negatively. Obviously, there are political questions and orientations behind this, and, as in political matters in general, opinions are likely to be divided. On the one hand, English is accused of "linguistic imperialism" or "linguicism," of being a "killer language" which oppresses and sometimes eradicates indigenous languages, dialects, and cultures (see Crystal 2004:ch. 2). On the other hand, many speakers hail it as the road to economic prosperity, an unavoidable prerequisite in the struggle for improved life conditions for themselves and their children. Consequently, in many countries there is an unbroken tendency to acquire English, and for many parents such considerations cause them to pass on English to their children.

These are difficult and sensitive issues, mostly because for so many individuals they touch upon potentially painful personal decisions that need to be made. In many PCE-speaking countries parents need to decide whether to give priority to a preservation of a cherished cultural and linguistic legacy or to what is perceived as the "pursuit of happiness" on an economic basis. Personally, I strongly believe that we should try to keep scholarly investigation separate, as far as reasonably possible, from taking a political stand: the evolution of language follows principles of its own, and a preconceived mind, set upon pursuing some sociopolitical agenda, is likely to be barred from recognizing such principles, directing one's attention elsewhere. But that does not imply that alternative positions, with different goals, do not deserve respect and are not worthy of discussion – they are just different in their goals and orientations, and interpretations of facts (Melchers and Shaw 2003:30).[2] Certainly I agree that disguised value judgments must be avoided. Most importantly, it is mandatory that the concerns and the dignity of the communities involved be respected.

It seems difficult to steer clear of moral and political judgments in discussing the history and emergence of PCEs. After all, in many instances this process has indeed been accompanied by military invasion, occupation, and oppression, by cruelties like slavery and genocide. I do not wish to ignore or play down these parts of colonial history. All I need to state is they are not my primary concern in focusing upon linguistic developments. Even while I describe macro-sociolinguistic processes this book is not meant to address the issue of the politics of language usage at all. I argue that the process which I am interested in, and which I describe in chapter 3, is largely independent of questions of right and wrong, and of the moral or political evaluation of the fact that typically settlers occupy a territory that indigenous groups used to regard as their own (and that this has frequently happened by force). Of course the type and quality of the relationship between indigenous and immigrant groups, whether or not military actions took place or legal titles were obtained peacefully, made a difference and determined the speed and many aspects and details of the process of linguistic evolution. However, my claim is that the dynamic process which has resulted in the emergence of PCEs kept running nevertheless, modified but not determined in its core by the details of its implementation. In essence, as I will be pointing out below, this process is triggered by an immigrant group's decision to stay in the new land for good, and by the social consequences of this decision itself for all parties involved, whether voluntarily or not. It is a process caused solely by sociocultural and psycholinguistic realities.

3   The evolution of Postcolonial Englishes: the Dynamic Model

3.1   Transforming selves in migration: theoretical background

In section 3.2 of this chapter I introduce the Dynamic Model of the evolution of PCEs, which claims that despite all surface differences there is an underlying uniform process which has driven the individual historical instantiations of PCEs growing in different localities. In the present section I outline some theoretical prerequisites which have informed this model. It operates within the confines of language contact theories in general, for instance as surveyed by Thomason (2001), and, more specifically, it adopts an evolutionary perspective emphasizing the importance of linguistic ecologies and the idea of new language varieties emerging in a competition-and-selection process between features available to speakers in a "feature pool" of possible linguistic choices (Mufwene 2001b, 2005a). In particular, it rests upon the assumption that, in selecting from this pool, speakers keep redefining and expressing their linguistic and social identities, constantly aligning themselves with other individuals and thereby accommodating their speech behavior to those they wish to associate and be associated with.[1]

3.1.1   Language contact: processes, perspectives, scenarios

PCEs have emerged in language contact situations, so a theory of language contact provides a necessary frame of reference. While some branches of linguistics, in particular historical linguistics in models like the family tree, have emphasized the purity and homogeneity of languages, the ubiquity of language contact in almost all cultures around the globe has recently been recognized and established, and language contact theory has come to be a growing sub-discipline of linguistics. Thomason (2001) outlined a coherent and convincing perspective on language contact, so I am adopting that here. Thomason surveys processes, scenarios, and characteristic outcomes of language contact, including a typology of mixed languages (see also Winford 2003). The following aspects of her theory are most directly relevant for my line of thinking:

- There is a correlation between social and linguistic clines of contact intensity, respectively: the closer the contact and the higher the degree of bi- or multilingualism in a community, the more likely are strong contact effects. Broadly speaking, light contact readily leads to lexical borrowing; stronger contact may result in morphosyntactic transfer; and highly intense contact of some kind may cause creolization or the birth of truly mixed languages (or also, in extreme cases, language attrition and death).
- The structural effects of language contact depend to a strong extent upon social conditions: external history plays an important role, and linguistic changes are to a considerable extent dependent upon and reflect the fates of their speaker communities.
- Contact-induced change and interference can be achieved by a variety of mechanisms, all of which I hold to have been effective also in the shaping of PCEs: code-switching, code alternation, passive familiarity, "negotiation," second-language acquisition strategies, bilingual first-language acquisition, and deliberate decision.
- All generalizations in the area of language contact, in particular the correlation between linguistic predictors and structural effects, are essentially probabilistic in nature. As predictions they are relatively robust, i.e. they account for the majority of observable cases, but at the same time they are not firm rules, likely to face a counterexample somewhere. In that sense, it is admitted that any theory of language contact is bound to be only a rough approximation to a messy reality, leaking somewhere, as all models do.

Mufwene's (2001b, 2005a) theory of the "ecology" of language evolution, with its focus on contact-induced restructuring and creolization, provides another important frame of reference which, I believe, is in line with my proposal in essential ways. Ingeniously, his theory adopts ideas drawn from population genetics and biology to linguistics, disciplines between which he sees important parallels (see Mufwene 2005b). The following of Mufwene's ideas are essential and apply directly to contact situations which result in PCEs:

- Language evolution, and the emergence of contact-induced varieties, can be regarded as speakers making selections from a pool of linguistic variants available to them in a contact setting. This "feature pool" consists of the sum total of the individual forms and variants that each of the speakers involved, with different language backgrounds and varying linguistic experiences, brings to the contact situation.
- Which variants from this pool are chosen as stable elements of the newly emerging variety depends upon the complete "ecology" of the contact situation, the set of relevant conditions and circumstances, both

extralinguistic and intralinguistic. All these parameters enter a complex "contact equation," which is too complex to be spelled out explicitly and allows for some degree of chance impact (ecology "rolls the dice," it is stated). They include the following components at least: the numerical (demographic) and social relationships (including mutual attitudes and power distributions) between the participants in a contact situation, the amount and types of communicative events, the nature of the linguistic input elements, surface similarities and typological degrees of relatedness between the languages involved, and so on.

- A continuous "competition of features" (a notion also discussed by Thomason 2001:86–9) goes on between the variants in the pool of linguistic options, so in individual instances an emerging new variety of English consists of elements of both "diffusion," continuously transmitting elements of the (typically nonstandard) English input, and "selection," innovations adopted from an indigenous language form (Schneider 2000b).
- The precise nature of such a mixture of features is typically decided on largely in the early phase of contact, while things are still in flux, so a "founder effect" (Mufwene 1996b, 2001b) can be expected to play a role: inspired by the notion of a "founder principle" in biology, Mufwene suggests that characteristics of the vernaculars of the earliest populations in an emerging colony predetermine the structural features of the resulting variety to a strong extent.
- Mufwene employs the metaphor of a language as a species parasitic upon its host population, a community of human speakers. This particular aspect is in line with an important constituent of Thomason's framework, the priority of social determinants.
- The diffusion of these linguistic forms proceeds through "imperfect replication," i.e. speakers potentially copy each others' linguistic choices (if these are found to be communicatively successful); in so doing they reproduce, transmit, and at the same time continuously recreate and "appropriate" elements of a language variety. This replication operates not only vertically (i.e. with an offspring generation copying their parent generation's usage) but also horizontally (with speakers who interact with each other continuously influencing each other). Idiolects are therefore regarded as the primary loci of linguistic change and evolution, with idiolectal grammars being continuously influenced by the linguistic performances of other individuals around and speakers striving to accommodate their modes of speaking to each other.

Mufwene explicitly applies his line of thinking to both "New Englishes" and to creoles. He argues that these varieties, like mixed dialects resulting from koinéization, are products not of a "special" type of restructuring but

of essentially the same competition-and-selection process that characterizes most languages in their historical evolution, a principle which explains
why heterogeneity and hybridity are fundamental properties of practically
all human languages. The only difference between other colonial dialects
and these types of varieties, he argues, is a quantitative one, caused by
different settings of some parameters of the restructuring equation: creoles
emerge by the selection of relatively more "xenolectal" features while
so-called "dialects" select a larger number of "lexifier" features, but there
is no difference in principle between both processes.

Given that contact effects depend to a considerable extent upon sociohistorical conditions, it makes sense to ask whether these conditions can be
categorized somehow, and to what extent the various cases of transplanting
English to new countries are similar to each other. The process of colonial
expansion was driven by a variety of motives, among them economic,
political, military, and religious ones, and its agents were the state, business
companies, religious communities, missionary and colonization societies,
and also individuals. Consequently, different types of contact scenarios
arose. Thomason (2001:17–21) provides a useful survey of types of contact
onsets, many of which we also find realized in the present framework,
including "the movement of one group into another group's territory,"
"immigration of small groups or scattered individuals," "importing a labor
force," or cultural contacts through long-term neighborly relations. Useful
as this is, it is possible to go beyond this classification of reasons for contact
to begin: history tells us that processes and outcomes of colonial endeavors
can be categorized under a small number of headings.

Mufwene (2001b:8–9, 204–6; see also 2004b) distinguishes three fundamentally different types of colonization, and the differences between them
determined the regularity and kinds of linguistic contacts, the power
stratification and amount of integration versus segregation between the
parties involved, etc.:

- Trade colonization was marked by sporadic contacts intended primarily
  for the exchange of commodities; so limited access for local populations
  to the lexifier typically resulted in pidgins. Typically, trade colonies were
  not permanent but "generally evolved into settlement or exploitation
  colonies" (Mufwene 2004a:212).
- Exploitation colonies were larger territories under European administrative control, typically established in the nineteenth century. They
  were marked by clear social segregation with an unequal power stratification. The European lexifier was introduced in a scholastic form to a
  local elite of colonial and missionary auxiliaries only, essentially for
  them to serve as a managerial group sandwiched between the colonizers
  and the colonized. In the long run, the indigenization of English in such

communities resulted from its appropriation by this group, under decreasing influence of native speakers, with the indigenous elite expanding its range of uses to new, internal communicative functions, originally unintended by the Europeans.

• Settlement colonization led to interactions between several varieties of a European source language, integrating speakers of different backgrounds, and produced varying patterns of segregation, regional or social, between select speaker groups; in plantation settlement colonies restricted contacts between Europeans and farm hands in such contexts led to creolization. Hence, in settlement colonies continua of varieties marked by different degrees of restructuring can be found, but it is characteristic of such developments that variants of the lexifier were adopted as the vernacular by coexistent communities.

Mufwene's category of settlement colonies masks a distinction which is important in the present context. In some cases, large numbers of Europeans migrated to new continents to settle there, typically carrying out manual, mostly agricultural, labor themselves, and due to their ever-increasing numbers and their military and economical superiority they established themselves as the dominant power and marginalized indigenous peoples. Other colonies were founded deliberately as sites of plantations, i.e. the European settlers imported laborers from elsewhere and reserved ownership and managerial roles to themselves. I will reserve the label "settlement colony" for the former type, with a demographic dominance of Europeans, and will refer to the latter context, which typically leads to creolization, as "plantation colonies."[2]

Gupta (1997) has developed a related set of distinctions that describe relocation types of English and their sociolinguistic consequences. She distinguishes five patterns: "monolingual ancestral English" (e.g. in Australia); "monolingual contact variety" (e.g. in Jamaica); "multilingual scholastic English" (e.g. in India); "multilingual contact variety" countries (e.g. Singapore); and "multilingual ancestral English" (e.g. in South Africa).

Such distinctions provide for variations within the framework outlined below, and determine distinctive subtypes, so I will get back to them when appropriate. But the interesting thing is that these distinctions are clear-cut and important mostly for the early phases of settlement, but they tend to get increasingly blurred in the course of time, with the complexity of societies and the amount of population mixing increasing, especially so, in many cases, after independence. Therefore, my main point is that in the long run these settlement and transmission types, important as they are, are not prime determinants of the outcome of the process of new dialect emergence. How or why two groups were brought together and what their relationship was like in the early phases of contact turns out to be less important in the long run than the recognition that once the settler group stays for good they will have to get along together, for better or for worse. This insight forces all the parties involved in a contact setting to reconsider and rewrite their perceptions of themselves, their social identities – a process with direct linguistic consequences.

3.1.2   Social identity and linguistic accommodation

Central to the model which I am advocating is the notion of social identity and its construction and reconstruction by symbolic linguistic means – a topic which has gained some prominence in recent sociolinguistic theorizing (see Gumperz and Cook-Gumperz 1982; LePage and Tabouret-Keller 1985; Woodward 1997; Wodak et al. 1999; Eckert 2000; Norton 2000; Schneider 2000b; Kroskrity 2001; Hazen 2002; Joseph 2004). Identity is defined as "the systematic establishment and signification, between individuals, between collectives, and between individuals and collectives, of relationships of similarity and difference" (Jenkins 1996:4; Woodward 1997). The basic tension of the concept encompasses the relationship between individual and group identity (Joseph 2004). Humans are social beings. To survive and to enjoy life they need to associate themselves with others, and they form groups because in a world which is potentially hostile and threatening group membership offers a higher degree of safety and comfort. Such groups define and delimitate themselves by a shared set of beliefs and values, by a shared history, and usually by some form of common outward appearance, a symbolic code that typically includes clothing, sometimes objects of possession, and, invariably, the form of linguistic expression. In this rather broad sense, one's identity is "one's 'meaning in the world'" (Eckert 2000:41). For an individual as well as a community, defining one's identity implies a need to decide on who one is and, more importantly, wishes to be: a line is drawn between "us" (those who share essential parts of a common history and value orientation, those we wish to socialize and be associated with) and "others" (who are just perceived as different, and don't share these qualities). Identity definitions entail both individual identification and social classification (Jenkins 1996:164–71).

These attitudes, socialization patterns, and group alignments usually find forms of symbolic expression, including, and perhaps most readily and rapidly, manifestation by means of linguistic variability. While other means of expressing solidarity and identity boundaries may be costly and sometimes difficult or impossible to achieve (because, for example, not everybody can afford the symbolic signposts of a certain lifestyle), choosing in-group specific language forms is a relatively simple and often achievable goal; it is always available and immediately perceptible in what it is all about, daily interaction and communication – hence, a natural choice as a means of identity expression and group loyalty (Jenkins 1996:113–4).

Many sociolinguistic studies have documented the recycling of certain linguistic forms, e.g. pronunciation details, as symbols of group identities. Classic and widely known cases in point, documented by American sociolinguists, include the centralization of diphthong onsets on Martha's Vineyard or the backing of the /aɪ/ diphthong to yield [ɔɪ] on Ocracoke (among the so-called *hoi toiders* on the Outer Banks of North Carolina) as emphasizing orientations toward traditional island lifestyles threatened by recent developments like the growth of tourism (Labov 1972; Wolfram and Schilling-Estes 1996) or the use of certain predication types (like *be + Vin'* or *be done*) as markers of African-American identities (Labov 1998). It is noteworthy that not all forms acquire symbolic meaning – but some do (Eckert 2000). Language use is thus perceived as social action, whether strategically manipulated or acted out below the level of awareness (Kroskrity 2001:108). It is so effective in this enacting process because it seems so inconspicuous, comes so naturally, but nevertheless is so powerfully laden with hidden symbolic meaning (see Wolfram and Schilling-Estes 1998:17).

The linguistic mechanism through which the symbolic expression of group identities is achieved is accommodation (Giles 1984; Winford 2003:119–21). Speakers who wish to signal a social bond between themselves will minimize any existing linguistic differences as a direct reflection of social proximity: they will tend to pick up forms used by the communication partner to increase the set of shared features and avoid forms which they realize are not used by their partner and might thus function as linguistic separators.[3] Thomason (2001:142) calls this mechanism, when speakers deliberately approximate their language to somebody else's, "negotiation." Of course, in practice the process takes time and proceeds one small step after another, and it also allows for changing degrees of mutual alignment, social and linguistic. But in the long run it results in the crystallization of a newly emerging, more focused compromise variety: the set of features shared in the feature pool increases, and those features which are identified as being shared within the group (and possibly not outside of it) will be used more regularly and become habitualized. Thomason's description of such a negotiation process (2001:142) can be taken to directly relate to the emergence of PCEs as conceived of in the Dynamic Model described below. More broadly speaking, accommodation theory can account for a range of processes of mutual linguistic approximation, including koinéization, borrowing, and mixing, or even language shift.

Furthermore, identities are not normally stable or clear-cut: creating and recreating one's identity is a constant, dynamic process. It requires continuous rethinking and repositioning of oneself in the light of changing parameters in one's surroundings, possibly to be followed by the substitution of one symbolic form of expression by another. This is by no means a simple process. In modern societies individuals are members of varying social groups, so they assume different social roles and identities. These can be based upon a variety of parameters; social anthropologists distinguish between "national, ethnic, racial, class and rank, professional, and gender identities" (Kroskrity 2001:106). Identities can be primordial (i.e. essential and unchanging) or situational (i.e. manipulable, depending upon circumstances) (Jenkins 1996:65). In fact, it is less obvious than might be assumed to which of these types any given category belongs. Even a category like ethnicity, which seems biologically based, is a social construct, open to negotiation, definition, and change (LePage and Tabouret-Keller 1985:207–34). Furthermore, it is quite natural for any individual's multiple identities to be overlapping, hybrid, and at times even conflicting with each other (Woodward 1997:16; Wodak et al. 1999:16; Joseph 2004:6–8).

It is the central claim of this book that identity constructions and realignments, and their symbolic linguistic expressions, are also at the heart of the process of the emergence of PCEs. The individual parties who came into cultural and linguistic contact with each other in the social contexts of colonial expansion needed to define and redefine themselves and their social roles in the light of the presence of the other group(s) around, of their own historical roots and cultural traditions, and in their relationship to territories and distant centers of political and military power. As these relationships changed in the course of time, so did their identities, their images of themselves in relation to others and the world, and, in turn, their language usage as an expression of these changing identities (though this correlation need not have worked consciously). I argue that these changes were neither random nor idiosyncratic; rather, a common underlying schema of historical evolution provided for a certain degree of uniformity of the sociopsychological as well as linguistic processes, a schema shaped by factors constant across many territories. The political and economic interests, personal goals, sources of power, and choices of action of the "homeland," the colonizers, and the colonized were all constrained by similar conditions and thus proceeded along similar paths in partly predictable and parallel ways. Obviously, the number of similarities across territories is a matter of degree, and room must be provided for a great deal of variation within the basic pattern (as I will point out later). I am not advocating a gross generalization that should ignore all the important differences from one historical context, territory, culture, and also individual to another: hybridity, and hence a broad range of variability and differences, is characteristic of both identity construction and linguistic evolution in the contexts considered here. But at the same time I am claiming that there is a common core behind all these processes, presented more fully in section 3.2.

3.2   The Dynamic Model of the evolution of Postcolonial Englishes

3.2.1   Rationale and overview

Research into PCEs has tended to focus upon individual varieties, their features and conditions of use (in addition to problems of language teaching). Some authors (e.g. Platt, Weber, and Ho 1984; Kachru 1986) have pointed out far-reaching similarities between certain countries and varieties, but even in these cases the primary emphasis has mostly been on one particular world region (like South or South-East Asia), and the predominant tendency has been to regard these varieties as individual linguistic entities, independent of each other and products of unique circumstances determined by geography and history. As was stated earlier, I certainly agree that differences caused by colonization types and historical accidents and idiosyncracies cannot be ignored; all these provide for the great amount of variability that we find in comparing PCEs. Yet the model which I am proposing here is more ambitious in claiming that there is a shared underlying process which drives their formation, accounts for many similarities between them, and appears to operate whenever a language is transplanted. I follow Thomason and Mufwene's arguments by devising a model which abstracts essential information from complex realities and thus provides new insights, although at the same time, as is the very nature of a model, it is not intended to account for all observable details, nor does it apply equally well to all individual instances of the process it describes. In what follows, I will therefore describe a typical developmental process and its constituent elements, emphasizing those aspects which are most widely shared and observable but also at times suggesting characteristic modifications.

Fundamentally, the evolution of PCEs is understood as a sequence of characteristic stages of identity rewritings and associated linguistic changes affecting the parties involved in a colonial-contact setting. Ultimately, the force behind this process is the reconstruction of the group identities as to who constitutes "us" or the "other" by both settlers and indigenous residents in a given territory, reflected by associated sociolinguistic and linguistic processes. In the beginning, a group of settlers in a foreign land consider themselves as an extension of the "us" of their country of origin, clearly separated from the "other" of the indigenous population of their country of destination. In the course of time, however, for one reason or another, in the settler community bonds with the former homeland weaken and are gradually dissolved, so that in their eyes the country of origin turns into an "other," while a new, regionally based construction of "us," gradually incorporating the indigenous population, is being developed. Conversely but in some ways similarly, from the perspective of the indigenous population the group of immigrants, or occupants, is initially clearly distinguished from their own as an "other" community, but once they have been around for a long time and it becomes clear that they are staying for good, typically the erstwhile "other" reading of the colonists is gradually modified and ultimately integrated into an "us" relationship of permanent residents, those who will (have to) live together, for better or for worse.[4] It is the form of linguistic expression through which much of this negotiation, definition, and expression of changing identities operates: linguistic usage and, ultimately, emerging language varieties signify associated identity changes. Hence, I propose that to a considerable extent the emergence of PCEs is an identity-driven process of linguistic convergence (which, as I will point out below, is followed by renewed divergence only in the end, once a certain level of homogeneity and stability has been reached).

Naturally, this is a highly complex process, in which a multitude of parameters and dimensions play a role, some more important and characteristic than others. In order to be able to grasp and describe it systematically, I will organize the constituent and characteristic elements of this process along two major descriptive and analytical dimensions: first, a diachronic succession of five subsequent stages, each marked by a set of characteristic properties, and, second, the two complementary communicative perspectives as experienced by the major parties of agents in this process.

First, and most importantly, identity rewritings and associated linguistic changes are described as a characteristic diachronic sequence of five progressive stages. Roughly speaking, the process leads from the transplanting of English to a new land through a period of vibrant changes, both social and linguistic, to a renewed stabilization of a newly emerged variety. I posit five stages, the characteristics of which I will discuss in greater detail below: (1) foundation, (2) exonormative stabilization, (3) nativization, (4) endonormative stabilization, and (5) differentiation.[5] At each of these stages, manifestations of four different parameters can be observed and will be pointed out, with a monodirectional causal relationship operating between them: (1) Extralinguistic factors, like historical events and the political situation, result in (2) characteristic identity constructions on the sides of the parties involved. These, in turn, manifest themselves in (3) sociolinguistic determinants of the contact setting (conditions of language contact, language use, and language attitudes), which, consequently, cause specific (4) structural effects to emerge in the form(s) of the language variety/-ies involved.

It goes without saying that, as with all analyses built upon periodizations and correlated parameters, this model describes an ideal constellation, and in reality room must be provided for variation, fuzzy transitions, and overlapping parameter realizations. In exceptional cases there are historical events which may be taken to mark the transition from one phase to another (like the Norman Conquest of 1066 symbolizes the transition from Old English to Middle English), but normally consecutive stages overlap (as did Middle English and Early Modern English as periods), as it takes time for innovations to spread through a society. Similarly, it must be expected that not all characteristics of a certain stage coexist simultaneously in a given region, given that some changes proceed more vigorously than others. It is also worth observing that situating an ongoing change on a temporal cycle allows us to compare different PCE-speaking regions with each other. Viewed in that light, certain synchronic differences between different countries can be regarded as coexistent but independent manifestations of subsequent stages of the same underlying diachronic process.

The second factor of major importance is the ethnographic ecology of the sociopolitical and, consequently, communicative relationship between the parties involved in a colonization process, a factor which I call the "strands" of communicative perspective. The entire process of the re-rooting of English in a foreign land can be viewed, and has been experienced, from two complementary perspectives: that of the colonizers, and that of the colonized. Any convincing model of the emergence of PCEs needs to cover both.[6] It is one of the strong claims that I am making that to a considerable extent the histories of PCEs can be viewed as processes of convergence between these two groups, despite all the initial and persistent differences between them. By labeling these two competing but also complementary perspectives, observable in each of the five developmental stages (though with changing degrees of different or shared features), two "strands" of development, I wish to signal that they are interwoven with each other like twisted threads. I call the settlers' perspective the "STL strand" and the experience and situation of the indigenous populations the "IDG strand."

In a sense, these two perspectives are related to the notions of "ENL" and "ESL," respectively, given that typically the immigrants were native speakers of English and the indigenous population acquired it as a second language. However, these two labels have traditionally been applied to entire countries and their respective political situations, while I wish to apply my notions of the STL and IDG strands to speech communities, frequently defined along ethnic lines, as agents in an ongoing dynamic process. In the settlers' (or colonizers') group, i.e. (mostly) British emigrants and their descendants and, in my model, the agents of "STL strand" evolution, English is continuously transmitted from one generation to the next, without a radical break of linguistic continuity or an experience of language shift. In the course of time, however, their speech behavior undergoes substantial modification and evolution through contact, at first either between dialects of English or with indigenous tongues, and later with IDG strand usage. The IDG strand represents quite a different experience initially, namely that of being exposed to a politically dominant foreign language which is gradually being acquired and adopted by the native community. Its first stages involve second-language acquisition on an individual and a community basis, possibly to be followed by language shift later on.

Yet the essential point of my model of two intertwined "strands" is that both groups who share a piece of land increasingly share a common language experience and communication ethnography, and thus the forces of accommodation are effective in both directions and in both communities, and result in dialect convergence and increasingly large shared sets of linguistic features and conventions. Ideally, the end result is the emergence of a single, over-arching language community with a set of shared norms. In practice, especially in large and complex, heterogeneous societies such a high degree of uniformity is usually not reached. In some styles and for some social contexts, smaller, socially and ethnically defined speech communities coexist and allow for internal variability under a common roof. Again, in that respect identity theory and linguistic observations are in line with each other: individuals are members of several social communities at the same time and thus construct several, partially overlapping, identities for themselves, each of which may manifest itself in linguistically slightly different ways. In any society it would be unrealistic to expect absolute uniformity, but the overall trend of linguistic development is manifestly toward increasing convergence.

Thus, in essence I propose what I call the

3.2.1.1 Dynamic Model of the evolution of Postcolonial Englishes
(1) In the process of the English language being uprooted and relocated in colonial and postcolonial history, PCEs have emerged by undergoing a fundamentally uniform process which can be described as a progression of five characteristic stages: foundation, exonormative stabilization, nativization, endonormative stabilization, and differentiation.

(2) The participant groups of this process experience it in complementary ways, from the perspective of the colonizers (STL strand) or that of the colonized (IDG strand), with these developmental strands getting more closely intertwined and their linguistic correlates, in an ongoing process of mutual linguistic accommodation, approximating each other in the course of time.

(3) The stages and strands of this process are ultimately caused by and signify reconstructions of group identities of all participating communities, with respect to the erstwhile source society of the colonizing group, to one another, and to the land which they jointly inhabit.

In what follows I discuss the characteristics of the five main evolutionary stages, from both communicative perspectives whenever the distinction applies. In each case, I distinguish the four constitutive parameters mentioned earlier: extralinguistic (sociopolitical) background; identity constructions; sociolinguistic conditions (contact settings and participants' use of specific varieties; norm orientations and attitudes); and typical linguistic consequences (structural changes on the levels of lexis, pronunciation, and grammar).

3.2.2 Phase 1: Foundation

3.2.2.1 Sociopolitical background
In the initial stage English is brought to a new territory by a significant group of settlers, and begins to be used on a regular basis in a country which was not English-speaking before. Typical contexts include the foundation of military forts and/or trading outposts (e.g. in Singapore after 1819), or emigration settlements (e.g. in New Zealand in the 1940s, organized by a colonization society), resulting from various political or economic motivations at home. The number of migrants is relatively small in the cases of trade and exploitation settlements but considerably larger, and growing in the course of time, in settlement colonization contexts. Relationships between STL and IDG groups may be anything from friendly to hostile. In some cases (like in Singapore or, mostly, India), legal titles are obtained by the settlers, and the settler groups cooperate reasonably well with the local population. In other cases, as in America or Australia, friendly relations are soon overshadowed by persistent violence, military dominance, and, largely, hostility, alongside periods of rather peaceful though rarely collaborative coexistence.

3.2.2.2 Identity constructions
As a consequence of the migration process, both groups simply become aware of the other's existence, which establishes the starting point of the subsequent modifications. Both the IDG and the STL group see themselves as clearly distinct from the "other,"

respectively. The STL population regard themselves as full members, and representatives, of the source society (Britain in the default case). Many will regard their stay in a foreign land as temporary, intending to return after a certain period of time; others hope to build a cultural copy, perhaps even an improved one, of their homeland. IDG people regard themselves as the only rightful residents, perhaps owners, of the territory under discussion, as those who "belong" there, unlike the newcomers.

3.2.2.3 Sociolinguistic conditions In almost all cases, wherever settlers move to, indigenous languages are spoken, so a complex contact situation emerges. In fact, at this stage contact operates on two levels, independently of each other at first, in two different types of linguistic ecologies. The first type, strictly within the STL stream, is dialect contact, resulting from the fact that in migration speakers from different regions in Britain get in touch with each other. The second type originates from the interaction between the settlers and the indigenous population and gets the language-contact process rolling. In plantation colonies other groups (slaves or contract laborers) are affected in much the same way as the IDG strand, with the settlers' language being imposed upon them.

In fact, in the beginning contact between the settlers and speakers of indigenous languages serves exclusively utilitarian purposes and therefore tends to remain restricted, impeded by the inability to understand each other and by different concerns and needs: each group remains, operates, and continues to communicate predominantly within its own confines. Cross-cultural communication is required, but only to a limited extent and for specialized purposes (like trading, and negotiating territorial and other mutually relevant rights and obligations). These tasks are the responsibility of some, not all, members of both communities, so the need for mutual understanding is confined to some individuals and topics.

Usually, most members of immigrating, invading, and occupying groups, who tend to be dominant in political, military, and economic terms, do not bother to learn indigenous languages (the notable exception typically being missionaries). For whatever inter-group communication is required, the task of acquiring the necessary linguistic skills tends to be left to individual members of the indigenous population. Conditions of how this happens in detail vary. In some cases, when the settlers seek to build seemingly egalitarian relationships with the natives by signing treaties, they privilege members of the local elite by teaching them their language. In others this does not happen voluntarily: in several contact situations natives are taken captive to be trained as interpreters. Certainly some knowledge of the language simply diffuses through daily interactions and natural L2 acquisition. In any case, in the IDG strand marginal

bilingualism develops, predominantly among a minority of the local population, with speakers who interact with the immigrants as traders, translators, or guides, or in some political function. A well-known example is
the Australian Aboriginal Bennelong, who after a few years in England
served as a translator and intercultural agent (see section 5.2).

3.2.2.4 Linguistic effects Three processes are worth observing at this
stage: koinéization, incipient pidginization, and toponymic borrowing.

Typically, settlers come from different regional backgrounds, and are
therefore native speakers of different regional and/or social dialects: even
if they are all speakers of "English," linguistically they do not behave in a
homogeneous way, and the notion of "English" in practice denotes a set of
nonstandard dialects. Accommodation theory predicts that forms which are
widely used and shared by many will be communicatively successful and will
therefore be used increasingly, while forms which are not likely to be widely
understood, i.e. strong regionalisms or group markers, will frequently result
in communication failure and will thus tend to be avoided. Thus, in
the course of time speakers will mutually adjust their pronunciation and
lexical usage to facilitate understanding – a process generally known as
"koinéization," the emergence of a relatively homogeneous "middle-
of-the-road" variety, as it were (described in some detail for Australia by
Trudgill 1986 and, pointing out process-internal stages based upon a case
study of New Zealand, Trudgill et al. 2000 and Trudgill 2004; for references
to a classic discussion of this process in North America, see chapter 6). STL
strand development at its initial stage is therefore characterized by a trend
toward linguistic homogeneity, and by processes including leveling, "focusing," simplification, and the occurrence of phonetically or grammatically
intermediate "interdialect" forms (Trudgill 1986; see section 4.3). This effect
is largely confined to informal, oral contexts, the spoken vernacular, and it is
strongest in settlement colonies, where large numbers of speakers predominantly from the lower social strata are involved. In trade and exploitation
colonies, on the other hand, the number of English speakers residing abroad
is considerably smaller, and the skills required by these people (largely
tradesmen, colonial administrators, military officers, missionaries, clerks,
and managerial staff in a broad sense) suggest that many of them (with
exceptions, including traders, soldiers, and the like) are higher in status and
somewhat better educated, i.e. not necessarily vernacular speakers to the
same extent as those in the settlers' colonies. Both of these factors significantly reduce the need for and the strength of koinéization in such contexts
but do not rule it out altogether.

Newly emerging contact between people who do not share a language
requires a lingua franca, and if none is available and the contact remains

restricted and relatively short lived, a reduced code is likely to emerge. Thus, in trade colonies in particular, incipient pidginization is an option.

At this early stage indigenous languages usually do not influence the English spoken by the settler community much, with one notable lexical exception: names for places are amongst the earliest, most frequent, and most persistent borrowings in such situations. It is a sad and surprising story which has repeated itself several times in history, however: even if indigenous peoples are violently subdued, frequently facing marginalization and isolation, cultural extinction, or even genocide, and leave hardly any other linguistic traces in the language of their conquerors, names which they gave to places in their natural environment tend to be adopted, linguistically adapted (sometimes reshaped by folk etymology) and retained.[7] We find heavy toponymic borrowing in a variety of situations which geographically and historically are quite far apart but which have resulted in outcomes which in that respect are astoundingly similar – native American toponyms in North America, Aboriginal names in Australia, Maori place names in New Zealand, and so on.[8] Why this is so, and how it may have happened, is easy to imagine and understand: anybody who is new to a region will ask for names of places and landmarks and accept them as naturally true, as the names which these localities simply "have."[9] Actually, the adoption of these names testifies beyond doubt that some collaborative communication between old residents and new immigrants must have taken place.

3.2.3   Phase 2: Exonormative stabilization

3.2.3.1   Sociopolitical background After a while, colonies or settlers' communities tend to stabilize politically, normally under foreign, i.e. mostly British, dominance. Colonies (or dependent territories varying in legal status) are established. English is now regularly spoken in a new environment, and it is formally established as the language of administration, education, the legal system, etc., at least in some regions and strata of society. Usually a resident community of expatriate native speakers provides for most of this stable usage (STL strand). For an extended period of time the colony simply serves the purposes for which it was founded – accommodating new settlers and providing agricultural lands; serving as an outpost for trading activities, for the military, or for missionary activities; securing political control and naval routes; providing a dumping ground for criminals and other folks unwanted at home; and the like. Frequently these activities require a growing consumption of land and result in an expansion of the region under foreign dominance, and typically they entail an ever-increasing range of contacts with members of the indigenous population. A growing number of natives have regular contacts with the Europeans, and in many cases a significant proportion of them seek and expand these contacts deliberately as a means of securing or advancing their status or economic prosperity.

3.2.3.2 Identity constructions Whether the English-speaking residents come as settlers for good or as short-term colonial agents providing support and supplies to the homeland (to which they plan to return after an extended period overseas) is largely immaterial at this stage – they perceive themselves as outposts of Britain, deriving their social identity primarily from their common territory of origin and a feeling of culturally belonging there. At the same time, it can be assumed that at this stage the identity of the local British community expands to encompass something like "British plus": genuinely British no doubt, but seasoned with the additional flavor of the colonial experience which those who stayed "home" do not share. And it may be assumed that this emerging "British-cum-local" identity carries a positive attitude, is construed as an enriching experience in the service of the less challenging, distant home country. While "home" and, most likely, the intention to return there remain the main source of identity for these British expatriates, in reality for many of them this notion increasingly turns into an "imagined territory of a myth of return" (Jenkins 1996:27).

Children of British lineage and also, in certain regions and contexts and increasingly so, children of mixed ethnic parentage are born. Quite naturally, such locally born generations develop a hybrid cultural identity. Children of fully British ancestry align themselves also with their country of birth, and the growing number of those with genetically mixed parentage unavoidably construe a mixed identity encompassing both lines of heritage for themselves.

The identity of the English-knowing locals is enriched in a fashion not unsimilar to that of the British immigrants they associate with: certainly their self-perception at this stage remains that of members of the local community, but at the same time their ability to communicate with the Europeans opens their eyes to aspects of another worldview and gives them an extra edge of experience and competitiveness within their own native group. A knowledge of English will therefore be a source of some pride, and at least amongst the higher echelons of the indigenous society at this stage we find the beginnings of the segregational elitism that characterizes English in some PCE-speaking countries to the present day. Work by Siegel (1987) on Fiji and Gupta (1996) on Singapore suggests that people of mixed descent play a particularly important role in that diffusion process.

3.2.3.3 Sociolinguistic conditions Consequently, the IDG strand development is typically marked by the fact that bilingualism, i.e. familiarity with
English in addition to competence in at least one of the indigenous
languages, spreads among the indigenous population, through education
or increased contacts with speakers of the colonial language (especially
in trade and exploitation colonization). It is frequently associated
with a relatively higher social status (as, for example, in the case of
pre-independence Malaysia in the mid-twentieth century; see Asmah
1996:515). For the indigenous population a command of English gradually
turns into an asset, opening roads to higher status or specific commercial
options. Especially in exploitation colonies schools are established to train
an indigenous elite in English and European manners, to produce a stratum of indigenous people expected to assist the British in maintaining their
dominance and in ruling the country. This does not entail uninhibited
spread of the language, however. As Brutt-Griffler (2002) has shown,
colonial authorities sought to constrain access to English amongst the
natives to a relatively small proportion of the population only, in line
with Macaulay's doctrine developed in India or Lugard's policy in
Nigeria (see sections 5.8.2 and 5.12.2, respectively). This stratification
may have ambiguous consequences – from a positive attitude toward the
use of English, promoting its further expansion, to a critical distance
toward it because of its association with and (especially later) exploitation
for the maintenance of internal power inequalities.

The notion of linguistic norms, the kind of English striven for, is not
much of an issue – it may safely be assumed that the question of what is
right or wrong in matters linguistic is but of limited interest to most people
in a settlers' community. Members of the STL community encounter
various types of learners' interlanguage, enriched by indigenous vocabulary and interference patterns. In teaching matters, and to the extent that
reflection is spent upon questions of language correctness at all, they share
a conservative and unaltered, though increasingly distant cultural and
linguistic norm orientation, unsupported by local realities: the external
norm, usually written and spoken British English as used by educated
speakers, is accepted as a linguistic standard of reference, without much
consideration given to that question.

Of course, the growing need for interethnic contacts gradually affects a
wider range of immigrants as well, who thus get in touch with local people
with some command of English and have some exposure to indigenous
languages or learners' forms of English as used by the locals.

3.2.3.4 Linguistic effects The "British-plus" identity of the STL strand
and the "British-cum-local" identity construed in parts of the IDG strand,

as well as the broader range of cross-cultural language contacts, trigger more fundamental changes in the linguistic system(s) of English as used by the two communities – largely on the lexical level initially, but beginning to affect syntactic and morphological structures later.

In the STL strand, underneath the assumption of being representatives of British culture on foreign soil, changes and adjustments to the local environment start to creep in and slowly but gradually modify the nature of English as spoken in a new country: English in its spoken form begins to move toward a local language variety. Borrowing names, as recorded in the previous stage, may be taken to affect language elements which function merely referentially and are thus not structurally relevant in the narrow sense. This is different, however, as soon as meaningful words are borrowed: this is a significant step, the onset of linguistic transfer. The first reason to adopt elements of a local language is, quite obviously, the need to refer to things local: the English-speaking settlers begin to adopt indigenous vocabulary, at first predominantly for objects which they encounter for the first time in the new territory. Their "British-plus" identity finds a formal expression in the adoption of indigenous words.

Given that the most direct exposure to unfamiliar objects of some immediate practical relevance concerns "strange" plants and animals (and, consequently, simple questions as to whether these are edible, useful, or potentially dangerous), it is not surprising that this is the semantic field from which many of the first loan words stem. Characteristically, the earliest and the most numerous borrowings from indigenous languages (as well as new coinages with English morphemes) designate the local fauna and flora, soon followed by words for cultural terms, customs and objects found to be peculiar to the indigenous community.[10] We may safely assume that at first these become passively familiar to resident English speakers and are subsequently used by them as well to designate locally important plants, animals, and things, thus being gradually incorporated into indigenous English usage. In this way an English vocabulary segment of local significance, largely consisting of loans, develops. Some of these words remain strictly local and are thus opaque to a user from outside; others diffuse into the general, international English vocabulary. It is characteristic of such early local varieties of English to develop -isms, words of local coinage or significance: cf. the notions of Americanisms (Mathews 1951), Australianisms (Ramson 1966), Indianisms (Yule and Burnell 1986, originally 1886), Ghanaianisms (Dako 2001), etc.

Conversely, in the IDG strand it may safely be assumed that this is also the kick-off phase for the process which is linguistically the most important and interesting one, viz. structural nativization, the emergence of structures which are distinctive to the newly evolving variety. As soon as a population group starts to shift to a new language, some transfer phenomena on the levels of phonology and structure are bound to occur, so in this phase the earliest structural features typical of local usage emerge, if only slowly. At this stage, grammatical innovations, even if they are consistent and systematic, are likely to pass largely unnoticed and unrecorded, being restricted to spoken vernaculars in the beginning. Europeans classify the English spoken by locals as more or less "good" or "broken," depending upon its communicative effectiveness. But beyond doubt several of the mechanisms by means of which contact-induced change occurs, listed by Thomason (2001:ch. 6), are effective at this stage, including code-switching, code alternation, passive familiarity, second-language acquisition strategies, and, most importantly, "negotiation." In line with the S-curve which sociolinguists use to describe and explain the emergence and spread of changes (C. J. Bailey 1974), innovations are likely to spring and unfold slowly and inconspicuously, without being consciously observed as yet.

In sum, what happens during this phase is not unlike the early stages of some routes leading to creolization. In fact, in some contexts, notably in plantation colonies (e.g. in the Caribbean), ecological conditions are such that already at this stage stable and expanded pidgins develop and creolization occurs. Within the Dynamic Model this is regarded as one pole of a continuum of contact-induced effects of varying intensities.

3.2.4   Phase 3: Nativization

The third phase, nativization, is the most interesting and important, the most vibrant one, the central phase of both cultural and linguistic transformation. Both parties involved realize that something fundamental has been changing for good: traditional realities, identities, and sociopolitical alignments are discerned as no longer conforming to a changed reality. The potentially painful process of gradually replacing them by something different, a new identity reflecting the current state of affairs, combining the old and the new, is in full swing. This process has immediate linguistic consequences, for language use now, with drastically increased ranges of communication between the parties involved, becomes a major practical issue.

3.2.4.1 Sociopolitical background In the STL strand, this implies the transition from the acceptance of a distant mother country as the source of both political power and linguistic and cultural guidance to increasing independence – or at least a phase of striving toward it. When the "mother country" is gradually not felt that much of a "mother" any longer, the offspring will start going their own ways, politically and linguistically – slowly and hesitantly at first, gaining momentum and confidence as time passes by. In the course of time, different experiences and circumstances of life cause the ties between residents in a colony and those in the mother country – personal, economic, political – to weaken, and the number of those who feel themselves equally at home in both worlds decreases. Characteristically, at this point independence and the relationship to the mother country are big issues in the political arena, with the usual clash to be expected between those who want changes imposed as soon as possible and those for whom any change of status seems unthinkable. At this stage many countries affected ultimately gain political independence, and others work toward it. On the other hand, all retain a close bond of cultural and psychological association with the mother country, at the very least among a significant proportion of the STL strand, for whom a permanent separation is not easy to accept. In the former British Empire, this stage has found a conventional political expression, useful to both sides and conforming to the perception of their mutual relationship, in the form of the "Commonwealth of Nations," especially in its early phase. On the individual level, the political status of a territory has ramifications for questions concerning the citizenship of the indigenous population, who may or may not be granted full or partial rights of (British) citizenship or residence.

3.2.4.2 Identity constructions The movement toward psychological, political, and economic independence and its consequences significantly affects the identity constructions of the parties involved, resulting in a kind of "semi-autonomy." The gap between immigrant and indigenous population groups is significantly reduced at this stage: both parties consider themselves permanent residents of the same territory. Of course, differences in cultural backgrounds, ethnicity, language, prosperity, and lifestyle, and also status and political power are not wiped away all of a sudden, but they are gradually reduced in importance. Both population groups realize and accept the fact that they will have to get along with each other for good, and therefore, for the first time, the STL and IDG strands become closely and directly intertwined. The boundary between "us" and "others" is gradually redrawn by individuals in both groups, so that more and more members of the other group, respectively, are accepted as approaching or actually belonging to "us."

3.2.4.3 Sociolinguistic conditions Linguistic developments and orientations reflect social and political changes, in line with Greenbaum's (1996a:11) statement that "Political independence is a precursor of linguistic independence." By this time, contacts between both groups will occur commonly and on a regular daily basis, involving not only certain individuals but significant portions of both groups in various situations, roles, and contexts. Some degree of mutual accommodation is required by both parties for the contacts to be effective and successful.

However, the two communities are unlikely to be equal partners in the approximation and acculturation process: while the STL strand group also incorporates some elements of local culture in its identity construction and symbolization (including select linguistic elements), the labor of approximating each other tends to rest predominantly upon the IDG strand group. As Schumann (1978) points out, the major causal variable in second-language acquisition is "acculturation," the degree to which an individual is socially and psychologically integrated into the target language group: "the learner will acquire the language only to the extent that he acculturates" (29). This degree of acculturation and linguistic assimilation varies along a continuum from one individual to another, and it certainly also varies from one territory and colonization type to another. In settlement colonies like North America, Australia, and New Zealand numerical and power relationships are such that any assimilation, however slow and reluctant, is always also "a site of struggle" (Norton 2000:128; see Gumperz and Cook-Gumperz 1982). In former exploitation colonies in South and South-East Asia, the STL strand is often demographically weakened, or even almost completely removed, with the return of colonial administrators after independence, but the effects and attitudes generated by them linger on and remain effective. Factors like the appreciation of English, its persistent presence with important functions, and the desire to maintain contacts with the former colonial power and to participate in international communication have the same effect as the physical presence of large numbers of English speakers. In any case, the pressure to accommodate to English usually affects primarily the IDG strand people, leading to widespread second-language acquisition of English, and sometimes an almost complete language shift or even language death (as in the cases of the Maoris, many Aboriginal communities, and Native American tribes).

In the STL community linguistic usage is likely to be divided between innovative and conservative speakers. People with wide-ranging contacts with indigenous speakers are more likely to accommodate to the special features of local people's English, i.e. to borrow native words and also other features, into their own way of speaking. Certainly social class and situation will play a major role here. The adoption of IDG strand features by STL strand speakers is more likely to occur in the lower social strata and in informal communication. Communicative effectiveness, the greater likelihood of being understood, may be one factor promoting the use of such features, but certainly that is not all. Localisms are unavoidably also a display of an increasingly locally based identity, an expression of STL strand speakers' identification with their current country of residence, their future rather than their past, gradually supplanting their loyalty to the country of origin. On the other hand, the STL strand comprises also those with a conservative norm orientation, who reject the idea of linguistic innovation and local adjustment altogether and keep believing and insisting that the only acceptable way of using English is the metropolitan, conservative linguistic norm, which by this time is clearly an external one. Obviously, such a position is also a pronounced identity manifestation, held by people who still see themselves as extensions of their country of origin and who prefer and attempt to seclude indigenous people from a new "us" definition. In addition, both positions are essentially poles on a continuum, with a range of intermediate stages of attitudes and performances in between.

In any case, an awareness of the deviance of some local linguistic usage from old norms of correctness grows and is bound to result both in a clash of opinions and in community-internal discussions of the adequacy of linguistic usage. During this phase we can frequently observe what has come to be known as the "complaint tradition" (see Milroy and Milroy 1985), the stereotypical statement by conservative language observers that linguistic usage keeps deteriorating, that in the new country "corrupt" usage can be heard which should be avoided.[11] "Letters to the editor" in quality papers are a characteristic outlet of such complaints (see the rich documentation in Hundt 1998 regarding New Zealand). Such discussions indicate insecurity about linguistic norms: is the old, metropolitan norm still the only "correct" one, as conservative circles tend to hold, or can local usage really be accepted as correct simply on account of being used by a significant proportion of the population, including educated speakers? Such questions are typically raised in public, and the process of transition is marked by some discussion of these issues. In essence, these discussions are not primarily linguistic in nature, even if they appear to be, but rather class struggles in disguise. Such issues are typically raised among the educated echelons of a society, and of but limited concern to working-class people. They are also symptomatic of the tension between spoken and written norms in literate societies in general; it may be doubted whether they affect vernacular speech forms (and vernacular speakers, for that matter) at all. The characteristic occurrence of such statements in the phase under discussion reflects also a heightened awareness on the side of some upper-class members of a society of the increasing alienation of their own orientations and linguistic behavior from that of their grassroots compatriots.[12] In any case, in the course of time the readiness to accept localized forms, gradually also in formal contexts, increases inexorably.

3.2.4.4 Linguistic effects As was implied in the previous statements, the changed state of affairs and the new identity constructions increasingly find linguistic expression and turn into markers of this new identity. Kachru confirms: "The 'acts of identity' ... are not only a matter of perception, but they have formal realization in lexicalization, in syntax, and in discourse, styles, and genres" (in Prendergast 1998:227). Largely in line with Thomason's "borrowing scale" (2001:70–1), this stage results in the heaviest effects on the restructuring of the English language itself; it is at the heart of the birth of a new, formally distinct PCE. The spread of changes typically follows the "S"-curve pattern mentioned in section 3.2.3.4 and identified by language historians and sociolinguists, a " 'slow-quick-quick-slow" pattern in the adoption of an innovation. Indigenous usage starts as preferences, variant forms used by some while at the same time a majority of others will stick to the old patterns; then it will develop into a habit, used most of the time and by a rapidly increasing number of speakers, until in the end it has turned into a rule, constitutive of the new variety and adopted by the vast majority of language users, with a few exceptions still tolerated and likely to end up as archaisms or irregularities.

The ongoing changes are perhaps most conspicuous on the level of vocabulary, with a substantial proportion of words being used increasingly which are unknown to outsiders of the community, predominantly loans from indigenous languages. Heavy lexical borrowing continues, mainly but not exclusively for further culture-specific notions; loan words permeate the entire vocabulary and tend to be widely used and noted.

Phonology is another obvious case in point. IDG strand speakers will consistently show a marked local accent, which frequently can be identified as transfer phenomena from the phonology of indigenous languages. In many communities we find quite a range of sociolinguistic accent variation in the IDG strand, with proximity to native speakers' pronunciation forms increasing in correlation with status, education, and frequency of interaction with them. In the course of time, however, the amount of variability gets reduced, and in a "focusing" process some local pronunciation forms are adopted more widely and begin to develop into a local form (not necessarily accepted as a formal norm!) of pronunciation.

Most interestingly, however, the English language now changes also on those levels of its organization which do not carry referential meaning, namely morphology and syntax: it undergoes structural nativization by developing constructions peculiar to the respective country, for example *us two's bread* in Fiji or *Instead of him to travel home* in Nigeria. This is a stage which is of great interest to theories of language change, because it illustrates how in the process of linguistic evolution a linguistic system may get modified. Grammatical features of PCEs emerge when idiosyncracies of usage develop into indigenous and innovative patterns and rules. It is noteworthy that in this process speakers are not merely passive recipients of linguistic forms drawn from the input varieties, exposed to processes of contact-induced change such as "interference"; in contrast, they function as "language builders" (Heine and Kuteva 2005:35) actively involved in the creation of something new.

Perhaps the most interesting aspect of the birth and growth of structurally distinctive PCEs, seen in this light, is the fact that the gap between erstwhile first-language and second-language forms of language diminishes gradually. The difference between the STL and IDG strands is reduced to a sociolinguistic distinction in many countries, and it will all but disappear with some individuals. Certainly social class plays a major role here: the convergence of varieties within a country will proceed more rapidly and effectively between the colonial and indigenous elites (with many members of the latter having had the benefit of better schooling and possibly an extended stay in Britain or the US) than at the bottom of the social scale, where there may be resistance to elite forms of English. But as long as an emerging PCE is not associated with elitism, lower-status members of the STL community are quite likely to become active agents in the transfer of features from the IDG strand, diffusing local, transfer-based innovations into native-language dialects. For example, the White South African progressive construction with *busy* (*I'm busy relaxing*) may be a product of transfer from Afrikaans.

Where innovations in a given PCE originate from, whether in the STL strand (as products of koinéization, focusing, or simply internal change) or in the IDG strand (as transfer phenomena or innovations caused by second-language acquisition processes) is not of primary importance in the long run, and to some extent is likely to depend upon the colonization type. In settlement colonies the former type predominates, while in trade and exploitation colonies innovations of the second type stand a better chance of prevailing. What is more important and decisive, however, is the fact that the two communities are moving closer toward each other. Mutual negotiation results in a shared variety which is a second language for some and a first language, incorporating erstwhile L2-transfer features, for others.

Such convergence processes have been analyzed by some theoreticians of language change in ways which correspond strongly to the above model. Thomason (2001:75) describes in some detail the process of mutual accommodation which she calls "negotiation." She argues that integration of the indigenous speakers into the target-language speech community will ultimately result in the negotiation of a shared new community language, an amalgam of the STL group's original language and the variety developed by the shifting group in their approximation process, including transfer phenomena. Hock and Joseph (1996:395) develop a diagram model of convergence between two languages in prolonged bilingual contact which keep interacting with and approximating each other and building mixed and increasingly similar interlanguages. These are processes of consensus building, starting out from the agency of individual speakers and the occurrence of specific speech acts which then, through repetition, growing entrenchment and thus accommodation in speech habits, translates into an emergent systemic convention.

In descriptive terms, it is interesting to observe that in its early stages this indigenization of language structure mostly occurs at the interface between grammar and lexis, affecting the syntactic behavior of certain lexical elements.[13] Individual words, typically high-frequency items, adopt characteristic but marked usage and complementation patterns. When words co-occur increasingly frequently, locally characteristic collocations and "lexical bundles" as described by Biber et al. (1999:987–1036) will emerge, as groups of words which operate jointly as phraseological "chunks." In the long run this typically results in the development of fixed expressions or idioms. Similarly, grammatical patterns characteristic of one word or class of words may spread to another class of words (most likely initially in IDG strand usage, where intuitions as to a pattern's acceptability are less strictly circumscribed) and become firmly rooted. Thus, the emerging new variety is gradually enriched with additional structural possibilities, and ultimately parts of its grammatical make-up (i.e. its lexicogrammatical constraints) are modified. Hence, grammatical nativization in PCEs typically sets out with a specific set of patterns which appear to occur more frequently than others. Chapter 4 will provide a closer look at some of these phenomena. Here is just a short listing of some interesting categories likely to be found frequently in PCEs, for illustrative purposes:

- new word-formation products, like derivations or compounds, hybrid compounds which consist of elements of the STL and IDG stocks, e.g. from South Asian English *rice-eating ceremony* (Kachru 1986:41); from Pakistani English *Bhuttocracy, autorickshaw lifters*, etc. (Baumgardner 1998); from Fiji English *bula smile* 'welcoming smile' (Tent 2001a);
- localized collocations and set phrases, e.g. the Australianism *no worries* (Ramson et al. 1988:436);
- varying prepositional usage, e.g. *different than/from/to*, known to vary between national varieties of English (Hundt 1998:105–8); *resemble to someone* (Tongue 1974:55);
- innovative assignments of verb complementation patterns to individual verbs, e.g. *screen* used intransitively, *protest* used with a direct object in New Zealand English (Hundt 1998:109–12 and 115–18); or *pick* used

transitively and not as a phrasal verb *pick up*, as in *to pick someone* in East African, Singapore, and Fiji English (Platt, Weber and Ho 1984:82, Tent 2000b:376; Schneider 2004b:240);

- alternative morphosyntactic behavior of certain, semantically defined word groups, e.g. a tendency for static verbs to occur in the progressive (e.g. I *am seeing the sky*; *she is owning*) or for noncount nouns to adopt a plural ending (e.g. *furnitures*, *equipments*), both found in many PCEs in Africa and Asia (Kortmann et al. 2004).

Clearly, the above processes are not unique to PCEs, but they seem to occur more frequently than in "older" varieties which have not been subject to the same degree of contact-induced dynamism. It remains to be investigated to what extent, and possibly why, there are differences in the productivity of these processes from one language phase or evolutionary type to another.

While such surface structure phenomena may be the easiest elements to perceive in the process(es) of the nativization of English in new environments, they need to be supplemented by a broader perspective, encompassing also the pragmatics of language use. There is a tendency for cultural and communicative conventions to be modified, possibly transferred from indigenous cultures, in such contact situations. Gumperz and Cook-Gumperz (1982:6) rightly observe that in language shift, discourse conventions are likely to persist and be transferred. Little research has been carried out in this area, but we should expect to find regionally distinctive conventions for greetings, the expression of politeness and status differences or, conversely, the lack of such, rules for turn-taking, the organization of discourse in general, and so on – searching for specific traits of the ethnography of communication in PCEs is certainly a topic which deserves closer investigation. For example, it is certainly no coincidence that Singlish, the "basilectal" form of colloquial English in Singapore, is remarkably rich in discourse markers. For the Caribbean, a recent book edited by Mühleisen and Migge (2005) represents a notable beginning. In Indian English, Sridhar (1991) analyzes different ways of expressing a request.

A final factor frequently to be observed at this stage is the emergence of mixed codes. In many localities young people express their multicultural orientations by playing with the languages which they command and by generating and using mixed varieties. This is closely related to code-switching, a process known to be widespread in many bilingual communities. Code-switching represents a performance phenomenon, however; the emergence of mixed codes appears to be a qualitatively distinct phenomenon. The interesting thing is that these mixed codes are not only recognized and commented on as such but may adopt the role of an identity carrier that is otherwise associated with a newly emerging variety of

English. Cases in point are the Philippines, Hong Kong, and Malaysia (see Thompson 2003, Bolton 2003:103–4; and Schneider 2003a:59, 61–2). Mixed codes apparently originate when the native language of the IDG strand is still strongly rooted in the community (and possibly receives official support) and English also enjoys high prestige (but access to it is limited).

It is difficult to predict at this point whether this phenomenon will be transitional or will lead to the stabilization of genuinely mixed languages (as described by Thomason 2001 or Winford 2003). Mixed codes are frequently stigmatized by educational authorities but they nevertheless seem to be enjoying a high degree of covert prestige. One reason for this may be that language mixing implies cultural ambivalence, an attitude which is attractive in multicultural, ethnically complex societies in which unobtrusive power struggles are disguised as questions of language choice. It is not inconceivable that a truly mixed code like "Taglish" will be codified or accepted as a local norm; so the question is what the attitudinal consequence of code-mixing for English, coexisting with it, will be in the long run. Notably, Crystal (2004:30) observes language mixing with English to be "on the increase" and rates this process "the main linguistic trend of the twenty-first century."

3.2.5   Phase 4: Endonormative stabilization

3.2.5.1   Sociopolitical background This phase typically follows and presupposes political independence: for a local linguistic norm to be accepted also in formal contexts, it is necessary that a community is entitled to decide language matters as affairs of its own. But it appears that in some cases political independence, which may have been achieved considerably earlier, by phase 3, is not enough for phase 4 to be reached. What is ultimately decisive is not only political independence but also, and more importantly, cultural self-reliance, essentially the new identity construction that follows political separation. Take Australia and New Zealand as cases in point: for several decades after political independence both countries still perceived themselves as essentially British in their cultural orientations, and it was only after this conception was given up that the linguistic dynamism toward the birth of new varieties received an additional impetus.

While the transition between phases 3 and 4 may be smooth and gradual, it is also possible that it is caused (or at least strongly driven forward or symbolized) by some exceptional, quasi-catastrophic political event which ultimately causes the identity alignment of STL strand speakers to switch from a self-association with the former mother country, however distant, to a truly independent identity, a case of "identity revision" triggered by the insight that one's traditional identity turns out to be "manifestly untrue" or at least "consistently unrewarding" (Jenkins 1996:95). I call this "Event X" – typically it is an incident which makes it perfectly clear to the settlers that there is an inverse mis-relationship between the (high) importance which they used to place on the mother country and the (considerably lower) importance which the (former) colony is given by the homeland (as when Australia was left unsupported against attacks in World War II). Event X may frequently cause STL strand immigrants to feel a sense of isolation and being left alone at first, but it will then cause them to reconsider and redefine their position and future possibilities, to remember their own strength, and to reconstruct a radically new, locally based identity for themselves.

3.2.5.2 Identity constructions Members of the STL strand community now perceive themselves as members of a newly born nation, definitely distinct from their country of origin, and this regionally based identity construction includes the IDG strand community. It is noteworthy that the new identity construct will give greater prominence to a group's territory of residence, now understood to be permanent, than to historical background. As the emphasis on territory, and shared territory, by necessity encompasses indigenous ethnic groups, i.e. IDG strand speakers, the role of ethnicity, and ethnic boundaries themselves, will tend to be redefined and regarded as increasingly less important. After all, ethnicity is not a biological given but a social construct, a parameter of identity negotiation (Jenkins 1996; Kroskrity 2001). In a collective psychological sense, this is the moment of the birth of a new nation. We need to remember that "nations are mental constructs, 'imagined communities' " which are constructed discursively through emphasizing shared traits and ignoring internal differences (Wodak et al. 1999:4). Especially in multicultural and young nations a phase of "nation building" can be observed, often as an explicit political goal. Certainly this is also a matter of degree: in most cases ethnic boundaries are unlikely to collapse altogether.[14] Their respective prominence will depend to some extent upon the colonization type and the amount of persisting segregation in a society. But full integration becomes a goal for society at large and an option for individuals.

3.2.5.3 Sociolinguistic conditions By this point the newly achieved psychological independence and the acceptance of a new, indigenous identity result in the gradual adoption and acceptance of local forms of English as a means of expression of that new identity, a new, locally rooted linguistic self-confidence. This reversal is prototypically expressed by Gordon and Deverson (1998:108) in describing the New Zealand attitude as follows: "In language now we can and must go alone, creating our own standards." The existence of a new language form is recognized, and this form has lost its former stigma and is positively evaluated. Ultimately, the community reaches an understanding that the new local norm, distinct from the norms of the original colonizers, will also be accepted as adequate in formal usage (Newbrook 1997:236). This new norm may incorporate certain traits of IDG strand usage (certainly vocabulary, more hesitantly structural patterns). It needs to be remembered that a linguistic norm can be imposed only for formal written domains and as a target of language education; in oral usage and colloquial contexts all English-speaking communities tolerate some degree of deviance.

Given that not all strata and groups of a society adopt innovations and adjust to changes equally rapidly, traces of the previous stage will still be found, i.e. some insecurity remains (fostered by conservative members of a society who still long for old times and old norms). However, by this stage such an attitude, including residuals of the complaint tradition, is a minority position.

In terms of linguistic terminology, the difference between phases 3 and 4 is commonly given symbolic expression by substituting a label of the "English in X" type by a newly coined "X English." The former marks the dialect as just a variant without a discrete character of its own, while the latter credits it with the status of a distinct type, set apart from and essentially on equal terms with all others. This is exemplified by the discussion of whether there exists just an "English in Hong Kong" or whether by now a "Hong Kong English" in itself has evolved. The varying labels signal different conceptualizations of the status of the language.

The fact that by this stage a high degree of cultural as well as linguistic independence has been achieved in both developmental strands is also reflected in the emergence of a new and vigorous cultural phenomenon, viz. literary creativity in English,[15] rooted in the new culture and adopting elements of the new language variety. The emergence and role of "New Literatures in English" in the course of the last few decades has been one of the major developments in English-speaking literature (Ashcroft et al. 2002), and the linguistic ramifications of this process were highlighted and discussed in a recent monograph (Talib 2002). Many of these authors have been extremely successful, and quite a number of them have been awarded prestigious prizes, including the Booker Prize and the Nobel Prize for Literature. Many of them address both their cultural hybridity and their use of the English language or some variety of it in their writing, as Talib (2002), like many others, has shown. It is noteworthy that the leading representatives of postcolonial literatures in English comprise descendants of both the STL and the IDG strands, for example, South Africa's Nadine Gordimer, Nigeria's Chinua Achebe, and India's Salman Rushdie.

3.2.5.4 Linguistic effects **By** this time processes of linguistic change and nativization have produced a new language variety which is recognizably distinct in certain respects from the language form that was transported originally, and which has stabilized linguistically to a considerable extent.

It is characteristic of this phase that the new indigenous language variety is perceived as remarkably homogeneous,[16] and that this homogeneity is in fact emphasized. To some extent this homogeneity is a result of the stage of koinéization in earlier STL strand development, where some internally differentiating details were rubbed off and which typically ends in a crystallization stage also known as "focusing" (Trudgill et al. 2000); in addition, it is a product of the convergence tendency in nativization accounted for earlier. But the emphasis on the homogeneity of newly emerged varieties is a Janus-faced matter: certainly to some extent it builds upon actual usage, but not infrequently it is strongly an identity-driven discourse construct and convention, motivated by a young nation's desire to imagine "national singularity and homogeneity" (Wodak et al. 1999:4). Whatever linguistic heterogeneity remains (and there certainly is some, usually along ethnic and social class lines) will tend to be downplayed or ignored. Putting an emphasis on the unity and homogeneity of one's own still relatively new and shaky identity is a natural sociopolitical move with the function of strengthening internal group coherence. In times of uncertainty, with as yet shallow roots and an unpredictable future, it is always advisable for a group to stick closely together.

Of course, that is not to say that PCEs are really free of variation – the discourse tradition and the linguistic facts operate in the same direction but the two should not be mixed up. Differences between STL strand and IDG strand developments may still persist (depending on the degree of integration between the population groups), but they will be less conspicuous than in earlier phases, and they will be downplayed in the interest of national unity. By this time some, perhaps many, sometimes all members of indigenous ethnic groups have undergone a process of language shift, and in many, in fact too many cases the original indigenous languages are endangered, sometimes extinct. Typically, some of these people, especially members of an indigenous elite, have accommodated their speech to STL strand usage (whose forms were influenced and modified by the IDG strand in earlier phases) completely. Others have not and retain some linguistic distinctiveness which, however, tends to be ignored in the public discourse about language usage. Compare, for example, the integration of Europeans of non-English origin in the US, where there are hardly any traces of language shift to be detected today, with the same process in Australia, where perceptions of "wogspeak" are under discussion.

As was stated earlier, questions of linguistic norm acceptance are frequently social group struggles in disguise, so for a newly emerged language variety to be accepted as a local linguistic norm implies a need for it to be codified. In westernized societies, for a language to gain official recognition requires the existence of accepted reference books, i.e. dictionaries, grammars, and usage guides. Grammar books come later, because the number of grammatically divergent patterns is smaller than the number of local words, and in the light of the assumption of an internationally homogeneous "common core" of English grammar they are more difficult to accept as correct, it appears. But dictionaries are an obvious case in point, and it is a characteristic trait of this phase that dictionaries of the respective PCEs are produced, with recent examples including the Caribbean (Allsopp 1996), Malaysia, Singapore, and the Philippines (see chapter 5 below; see also Görlach 1995a, 1998).

Codification in these contexts may also be regarded as an interaction between spoken behavior and written norms in a society (or also between the lower and upper social strata, for that matter). It paves the way for and implies the acceptance of earlier spoken realities as appropriate to formal and written contexts. This is a mutually reinforcing process: new national identities cause an awareness of the existence of new language varieties, which in turn causes the production of dictionaries of these new varieties; once such a dictionary is out it strengthens the distinct national and linguistic identity, and also the forms used to signal it. The process works both bottom-up (with vernacular usage being recorded and thus awarded some dignity in formal contexts) and top-down (with the existence of the written record, or book, reinforcing the usage of local forms). The fact that working-class people are less likely to consult a dictionary may be taken as a counterargument to the top-down effect, albeit a weak one: in a modern media society the very existence of a new "national dictionary" is likely to be communicated to many and to increase their linguistic pride nevertheless. The most convincing example of this process is the publication of the *Macquarie Dictionary* in Australia (Delbridge et al. 1981), by now a hallmark of Australia's national identity. Similar effects will be documented for Canada (5.16.4).

3.2.6   Phase 5: Differentiation

3.2.6.1   Sociopolitical background By this time, the still somewhat shaky, slightly questioned independence of the previous stage has given way to the secure existence and life of a stable young country. Politically and culturally, and as a consequence also linguistically, a new nation has reached not only independence, having freed herself from some external dominant source of power and orientation, but even self-dependence, an attitude of relying on one's own strengths, with no need to be compared to anybody else's. The emergence of a new variety of English as a part and consequence of this process trails off, and is almost a thing of the past, recorded and remembered in recent history but largely completed, no longer a prominent, disputed issue. As a consequence of external stability, there is now room for internal differentiation: in the absence of an external challenge or need to demarcate a community as against some outside entity, differences within a society and between individuals with respect to their economic status, social categories, and personal predilections come to light and can be given greater prominence.

3.2.6.2 Identity constructions Consequently, the focus of an individual's identity construction narrows down, from the national to the immediate community scale. The citizens of a young nation no longer define themselves primarily as a single social entity in relation to the former colonial power but rather as a composite of subgroups, each being marked by an identity of its own. Within the overarching national identity, individuals therefore align and define themselves as members of smaller, sociolinguistically determined groups: as people of a certain gender, age, or ethnicity; through living in a certain area or locality; as members of a certain social group or stratum, and they derive primary as well as hybrid identities from these group membership patterns. In a sociological light Jenkins (1996:111) emphasizes the internal heterogeneity masked by umbrella-like "collective identities" under which diversity, almost always symbolized by language, flourishes. The expression of "group identification and social categorization" (111) becomes more important than the "collective identity" of the previous stage – which, in turn, need not have been "homogeneous or consensual" either, but the emphasis has definitely shifted (see Jenkins 1996:111; Wodak et al. 1999:16–18).

3.2.6.3 Sociolinguistic conditions One's identity construction determines one's patterns of socialization: "birds of a feather flock together." Hence, at this stage an individual's contacts are strongly determined by the individual's social networks, within which the density of communicative interactions is highest (Milroy 2002). And again, these patterns of dense interaction and mutual identification result in group-internal linguistic accommodation, like the selection of specific language forms as markers of group membership.

3.2.6.4 Linguistic effects Thus, when as a reflection of the birth of a new nation and the development of a new national identity a new national language variety has emerged, this is not the end point of linguistic evolution but rather a turning point from which something new springs: the stage of dialect birth. New varieties of the formerly new variety emerge, as carriers of new group identities within the overall community: regional and social dialects, linguistic markers (accents, lexical expressions, and structural patterns) which carry a diagnostic function only within the new country emerge.[17] In a strictly linguistic sense it is likely that what Trudgill (1986:152–3) called "reallocation" plays a major role in this, i.e. the case that select variant forms, irrespective of their dialectal origin, are assigned a new, sociolinguistically meaningful interpretation in the new community.

This differentiation has to be compared to the putative homogeneity of the previous stage, and, given that this homogeneity was found to be valid not in an absolute sense, the same applies here. It would be futile to assume that there would have been no conditioned variation at all before this stage. Colonial and postcolonial societies certainly were characterized by "internal fractions and divisions" (Loomba 1998:10). Irrespective of whatever variation may have existed before, however, phase 5 marks the onset of a vigorous phase of new or increased, internal sociolinguistic diversification. To some extent, this may simply be regarded as a function of the time that has elapsed: Trudgill has also observed that in colonial varieties "degree of uniformity [is] in inverse proportion to historical depth" (1986:145), and it is known that regional differences tend to increase as time goes by. It is likely that differentiation in this sense primarily concerns regional rather than social variation, given that in most societies some social variation is likely to have persisted but in a newly settled area there was no basis there for regional speech distinctions to emerge up to that point. Of course, this is hard to tell precisely: in practically all cases we simply do not have the evidence to tell when regional diversification may have started, so it may have been around earlier than we suspect (an assumption for which Bauer and Bauer 2002, in their case study of New Zealand, found some evidence). But it certainly is remarkable that, as the case studies will show, in those countries which have reached this stage a strong interest in new regional differences of speech is a characteristic phenomenon.

Differences between STL strand and IDG strand varieties are likely to resurface as ethnic dialect markers at this stage (as is happening most obviously in present-day South Africa; see de Klerk 1996 and the respective articles in Schneider et al. 2004). Depending on the relationships between people of different ethnicities in a nation and, consequently, the identity constructions of communities along ethnic grounds, such dialect differences may be reinforced or may actually develop afresh as markers of ethnic pride, or they may be relatively inconspicuous and be hardly perceived. To some extent, this depends upon the amount of bi- or multi-lingualism that has survived phase 4 developments. It is worth noting explicitly that phase 5 does not entail monolingualism in English at all; it is possible for varieties of English to coexist with other, mostly indigenous languages, with all of these fulfilling identity-marking functions. South Africa, with its eleven official languages and its ethnic, social, and regional varieties of English, is the most obvious example of this. In largely mono-lingually English-speaking countries, like Australia or New Zealand, some former IDG strand usage results in ethnic dialects of English. In multi-lingual countries, like Canada, Singapore, or South Africa, the IDG strand appears as either ethnic dialects or L2 varieties of English. But the difference between the two types of situation is less significant than traditional models suggest, and the latter may actually turn into the former in the course of time. Cases in point are Chicano English or Cajun English in the USA: L2 varieties for some speakers but an ethnic L1 dialect for others, with little linguistic difference between these two types perceivable.[18] These are "new ethnic identities" (Gumperz and Cook-Gumperz 1982:6), sym-bolically expressed through speech, frequently sources of pride.

3.2.7   *Summary*

Table 3.1 summarizes the main parameters of this model schematically.

3.3   Variations on the basic pattern

3.3.1   *On the nature of a model*

The above description of a developmental scenario is a model, meant to provide a uniform description of a set of processes that have occurred independently of each other in reality. As such, it represents a general-ization which abstracts from many complexities and details and which captures and highlights certain aspects of reality which are believed to be essential and insightful. It should not be confused with reality itself, which is always bound to a specific place and time and which tends to be infinitely more complex. It does not claim to account for each and every aspect of complex realities. A model is established for its usefulness: it accounts for a wide array of observations, points out similarities which would otherwise go unnoticed, and provides insights that are helpful or explanatory. Of course, it can be improved, modified and developed further as needed, to provide an even closer match with reality.

Obviously, this general proviso applies to my model as well. Individual PCEs have evolved over the course of several centuries, on all continents,

Table 3.1: *The evolutionary cycle of New Englishes: parameters of the developmental phases*

Phase	History and politics	Identity construction	Sociolinguistics of contact/ use/attitudes	Linguistic developments/ structural effects
1: Foundation	STL: colonial expansion: trade, military outposts, missionary activities, emigration/ settlement IDG: occupation, loss/ sharing of territory, trade	STL: part of original nation IDG: indigenous	STL: cross-dialectal contact, limited exposure to local languages IDG: minority bilingualism (acquisition of English)	STL: koinéization; toponymic borrowing; incipient pidginization (in trade colonies)
2: Exonormative stabilization	stable colonial status; English established as language of administration, law, (higher) education, …	STL: outpost of original nation, "British-plus-local" IDG: individually "local-plus-British"	STL: acceptance of original norm; expanding contact IDG: spreading (elite) bilingualism	lexical borrowing (esp. fauna and flora, cultural terms); "-isms"; pidginization/ creolization (in trade/ plantation colonies)
3: Nativization	weakening ties; often political independence but remaining cultural association	STL: permanent resident of British origin IDG: permanent resident of indigenous origin	widespread and regular contacts, accommodation IDG: common bilingualism, toward language shift, L1 speakers of local English STL: sociolinguistic cleavage between innovative speakers (adopting IDG forms) and conservative speakers (upholding external norm; "complaint tradition")	heavy lexical borrowing; IDG: phonological innovations ("accent," possibly due to transfer); structural nativization, spreading from IDG to STL: innovations at lexis – grammar interface (verb complementation, preposi- tional usage, constructions with certain words/word classes), lexical productivity (compounds, derivation, phrases, semantic shifts); code- mixing (as identity carrier)
4: Endonormative stabilization	post-independence, self-dependence (possibly after "Event X")	(member of) new nation, territory-based, increasingly pan-ethnic	acceptance of local norm (as identity carrier); positive attitude to it; (residual conservatism); literary creativity in new variety	stabilization of new variety, emphasis on homogeneity, codification: dictionary writing, grammatical description
5: Differentiation	stable young nation, internal sociopolitical differentiation	group-specific (as part of overarching new national identity)	network construction (increasingly dense group-internal interactions)	dialect birth: group-specific (ethnic, regional, social) varieties emerge (as L1 or L2)

for varying historical reasons, and in contact with a great many indigenous cultures and languages, so quite some degree of variability is to be expected and needs to be accounted for. However, such diversity does not invalidate the model itself as long as its central aspects remain applicable and convincing. In that vein, I hold that the Dynamic Model, even if it delineates a somewhat idealized process, is real and robust.

One form of variability that is definitely to be expected concerns its chronology, the existence of unequal duration times and overlapping characteristics of individual phases. In every developmental process the boundaries and succession of stages may be realized fuzzily. There are both dynamic periods when certain phenomena change very rapidly and periods of inertia when things stay rather stable for a long while. Similarly, not all characteristics of a given phase occur exactly simultaneously: it is normal for individual characteristics of a certain stage to appear earlier than others, or to be delayed, as well as for elements of subsequent but distinct stages to overlap and co-occur in time. To some extent the linearity of the model is also an abstraction from what in reality is a multidimensional interplay of dynamic processes.

Another obvious proviso is the fact that the model operates under the assumption of a quasi-linear progression of the social history of a community through time, assuming there are no unforeseen and sudden, "catastrophic" changes of direction in history and policy. This results from the priority of social changes over linguistic developments and the fact that these are ultimately unpredictable because people's attitudes and behavior are unpredictable (Thomason 2001:61). It is difficult to conceive of what might happen – wars, the outbreak of social hostilities, a military coup by some radical group, a major cultural reorientation – who knows. But certainly such events would affect the attitude toward and hence the fate of English in a given community, and might change, redirect or lift the drift implied in the Dynamic Model.

These are extreme, relatively unlikely examples, of course, but what may happen and has happened, on a lower scale – not as dramatic, not to be evaluated negatively, but still changing the directionality of English – is that a country deliberately decides to promote a national language and to do away with English. The consequence is that English is no longer taught in the education system to the same extent as before (typically it is reduced in status from a medium to a subject of education), and the domains of its use in a society are restricted; as a consequence, proficiency will decline. Adopting the notion of "fossilization" (halted development somewhere along a learner's process of progressively acquiring L2 rules) in second-language acquisition, I used this term to describe the situation that the development of English along the developmental cycle simply stops somewhere along the road (Schneider 2003c; cf. Winford 2003:245). The process will be discussed when looking at countries that have opted for this direction – Tanzania, Malaysia, and the Philippines.

Life comes in many shapes and sizes, a bewildering myriad of variants, in fact, and this holds true of the ecologies of Englishes as well, of course. Hence, the following sections briefly discuss four major causes and forms of variation within the basic pattern outlined above. These are "adstrates," creolization, elitism associated with English, and colonization types.

3.3.2   Adstrates

In many colonization settings, English-speaking settlers and the indigenous population were not the only agents in the history of a nation and of its linguistic setup. With the notable exceptions of the Boers in South Africa and the Acadiens in Canada, we can largely disregard non-indigenous groups who arrived earlier than the British, like the Portuguese in West Africa and Malaysia: typically they were ousted by the English immigrants, and had few lasting effects linguistically speaking, except for occasional loans and place names. What needs to be accounted for, however, is the case of large population groups migrating to a country where the English-speaking population had already established itself, usually alongside the IDG strand. If such groups were bound to stay in the territory as well, then the prerequisites of the Dynamic Model, language contact effects as shaped by identity rewritings by groups who reside together for good, apply to them as well, and they contributed in substantial ways to the linguistic equilibrium. In other words, they constitute another distinct "thread" in my model of interacting and increasingly intertwining linguistic communities. If we draw on and adopt the technical notions of "superstrate" and "substrate," which correspond to the linguistic contributions of STL strand and IDG strand people respectively, from creole studies, and modify them accordingly, then such a later group of immigrants can be called an "*adstrate*," a linguistic input that enriches and expands an existing contact scenario not from "above" or "below" but rather "from the side." I therefore refer to the linguistic adjustment of such a group as the "adstrate (ADS) strand."

In ADS strand situations, the "Founder Effect" posited by Mufwene (2001b) becomes particularly visible and influential. ADS speakers meet with a linguistic situation that is the product of an earlier contact history; they come to a country where communicative conventions already exist. Hence, typically they face the task of having to adjust to an existing linguistic norm and situation rather than being prime agents in a vibrant developmental scenario themselves. They contribute individual items from their own linguistic performance to the existing "feature pool" in the community, but their impact can be expected to be less profound due to the impact of the founder principle. Obviously, time depth plays a major role: the earlier in the history of an emerging linguistic community an ADS group comes to play, the more the situation is still flexible and ready to be fashioned, so the stronger their impact will be. Other factors that determine their linguistic influence are, as usual, their group sizes (and the demographic proportions in general), and the reason for their coming, which usually contributes to some extent to their social status in the target community.

I distinguish two basic types of ADS strands: immigrants and contract laborers. A third group, slaves, are similar to ADS strands in some respects but also to the IDG strand in others. I discuss their status in section 3.3.3.

Non-English speaking immigrant groups (e.g. Poles to North America, Greeks to Australia, or nowadays Polynesians to New Zealand) tend(ed) to come to English-dominated colonies and countries for a variety of reasons (economic, political, or religious ones) but usually out of their own will, and in small to medium numbers, so the typical pattern is for them to adjust linguistically within about three generations. They may maintain some cultural and also linguistic distinctiveness (i.e. develop a recognizable social variety), but they may also largely merge with the STL and/or IDG groups in the long run.

In the history of colonization large groups of non-English contract laborers are a relatively late phenomenon, usually one of the nineteenth century, when they replaced slave labor after the legal end of slavery and slave importation.[19] They came to their new territories under the terms of an indenture contract that obliged them to work for a certain period of time (e.g. five or seven years), after which an option of returning to their homelands was usually available. Many of them stayed, however, and became a new, quantitatively important, and ethnolinguistically distinct population group of their new lands – though in terms of social status and economic opportunities they ranked quite similarly to former slaves. Cases in point are Chinese and Japanese in Hawai'i (see Mufwene 2005a:155–62) or, most importantly, Indians in Guyana, Trinidad, or Fiji. The presence of such groups typically changes the bipolar relationship of STL and IDG strands into a triangular (or even multilateral) constellation, with the ADS strand to be added and considered in its own right. Even if many of them maintained their ancestral tongues (e.g. Bhojpuri), sometimes also in a koinéized form (Siegel 1987), they had to accommodate linguistically to communicate with earlier residents and get gradually integrated.

The basic parameter of the Dynamic Model holds for these groups like it does for the others: once it is clear that they are staying for good, once former contract laborers or their offspring generations realize that what at first used to be a foreign temporary destination has now become their new homeland which they need to share with the other groups, socially and linguistically integrative forces start to work. Depending on group sizes and their cultural distinctness and cohesiveness, such ADS strand groups may maintain a considerable degree of ethnic and linguistic distinctiveness for a long while, sometimes for many generations. In the long run, however, no human group has ever been able to keep itself isolated from its next-door neighbors, so they are bound to take their share in the process of adopting and nativizing their target language, local English. Take the Indian community of Trinidad as a case in point: even if in many aspects of culture (like religion, values, or family ties) they still live as and like Indians, without any doubt they are and feel also as, and increasingly first and foremost so, Trinidadians, and they speak like Trinidadians and can be recognized as such linguistically.

3.3.3   Creolization

Plantation settlement scenarios typically lead to very strong contact-induced restructuring and possibly to *creolization*. The precise role of the native-language input of slaves, the staple topic of decades of creole genesis theory debates, is still under dispute. This is not the place to review these theories (for summaries see Thomason 2001:174–89; Winford 2003:309–52; Mufwene 1993, 2001b). Suffice it to say that widespread agreement seems to have been reached on two issues. First, neither substrate nor universalist theories can account for creolization in themselves; rather, the two effects interact in that both substrates and superstrates provide input to the "feature pool" from which an emerging contact language selects its structural properties. General (cognitive, typological, ecological, and other) considerations play a role in deciding which of these is more likely to be successful, i.e. to be chosen as an element of the newly forming language (Mufwene 1986, 2001b, 2005b; Muysken and Smith 1986). Second, there is no single road to creole genesis. While "radical" or "abrupt" creolization theses are still being upheld, support is growing for "gradual" concepts of creole development (Arends 1993; Chaudenson 2001; Mufwene 2001b): Depending on a variety of demographic and sociopsychological factors, creoles result from different degrees of restructuring (Neumann-Holzschuh and Schneider 2000), which may result both in "deep" creoles and in "lighter," less heavily restructured varieties, sometimes referred to as "semi-creoles," which have only a certain, limited number of creole properties and features (Schneider 1990; Holm 2004).

Certainly in the present framework creolization represents a very special instantiation of the Dynamic Model, but, following Mufwene (2000a,

2001b, 2004b, 2005a) and DeGraff (2003), who reject a distinction in principle between creole and non-creole languages, I claim that the model, with required modifications, covers the case of creolization as well.[20] Creole formation is also a product of the agency and linguistic creativity of speakers who use linguistic means to express their identities (Siegel 2005; see also Baker 2000). It also constitutes a case of identity-driven, contact-induced mutual linguistic realignment. Once it is assumed and accepted that PCEs, including creoles, result from processes involving second-language acquisition and language shift as well as mutual linguistic accommodation, the precise amount of input from either side is a secondary question. In creole emergence, the amount of substrate input, in particular with respect to grammar, is extremely strong, while it is very weak in other contexts (like non-plantation settlement colonies). However, both processes represent points on a cline, albeit approximating different ends, and not a categorical difference.

This may be difficult to accept for creolists who have insisted on the status of creoles as separate languages as a matter of principle. Yet every linguist knows that with related varieties there is no way in principle of distinguishing a "language" from a "dialect of a language," as there are always varying degrees of structural overlap and mutual intelligibility – and in principle this situation applies to creoles as well, irrespective of the fact that for political reasons it may be advantageous to some creole speakers to have their codes recognized as distinct languages (Devonish 2003).[21] Mühleisen (2002:10–12) rightly also opposes "essentialist" views, insisting on the discursive rather than factual nature of criteria for the definition of creoles. The similarity between the emergence of intermediate Caribbean varieties and other products of language shift like Singaporean English is explicitly recognized by Winford (2000:215, 242; 2003:22).

In creolization scenarios, for instance on most Caribbean islands, there was frequently no IDG group, with the native population having been exterminated or marginalized. Naturally, this fact affects the applicability of the Dynamic Model, which builds upon the dynamic contact and interplay between the STL and IDG strands. Nevertheless, there are strong parallels. In the Caribbean, for example, societies were also composed of two major population groups, the European settlers and the Africans imported as slaves. How is the population group of Africans to be integrated into the constellation of agents in plantation societies in the perspective of the Dynamic Model?

Slaves are neither STL nor IDG strand members, and they typically arrived later than the earliest STL strand members (though in some cases not much). These facts would suggest categorizing them as ADS strands – but this assumption would not be convincing, neither on social nor on linguistic grounds. Socially speaking, the fate and also status of slaves was radically different from that of ADS groups. They came forcedly, under conditions of extreme cruelty, violence, and deprivation of the most essential human rights; they came to work and stay on plantations without any prospect of their fate ever improving during their lifetimes. Linguistically speaking, ADS groups needed to adjust to linguistic conventions which on account of the founder effect had evolved by then. African slaves, however, were the primary creators of such new linguistic conventions themselves, in the creolization process.

In many respects they took the role of an IDG group. Socially, they were the one important, erstwhile "other" group the STL strand speakers were faced with. Linguistically, like many IDG groups they were burdened with the task of adjusting linguistically to a target language established by the STL community. Unlike many IDG groups, however, they had no access to schooling and other support (and, indeed, they were denied improved language acquisition and formal education of sorts). They even lacked the minor benefits that resulted from the native, autochthonous status elsewhere, like, in the early phases, the advantage of familiarity with natural conditions and resources in the relevant territory and, in later stages, the moral dignity, and sometimes even the right to some degree of compensation, that comes from having been the original owners of the land. Nevertheless, like IDG groups slaves approached and acquired the target language, English, and accommodated and restructured it to their own purposes, which in this case happened to turn out an English-based creole.

Africans were brought together from different linguistic backgrounds and thus lacked a common vernacular. The plantation ecology was such that with very few exceptions for the slaves transported to the Caribbean their ancestral vernaculars had lost their value for everyday communication. To fulfill their communicative needs as human beings, they were therefore forced to adjust to the new linguistic environment as rapidly and as effectively as possible under the circumstances. This has important consequences for the timing of structural nativization: in the forms of partial language acquisition in language shift as well as creolization, it occurred much earlier than in other types of colonization, beginning in phase 1 and certainly in phase 2. Given the speed of this process and the lack of an IDG strand (and hence overt bilingualism), the linguistic differences between phases 2 and 3 become practically blurred.

Creolization, in that sense, is thus a special case of structural nativization typical of plantation settlement colonies, a process in which the amount of substrate input (in addition to universal principles of language evolution) is considerably higher than in other colonization types and the contribution of the European settlers' language surfaces most conspicuously in the vocabulary. The degree of restructuring is typically higher than in other cases of emerging PCEs. A higher proportion of substratal features is selected, or certain options provided by the superstrates and consonant with substrate properties may be favored. Basically, however, creolization represents the same, nativizing, phase of the overall development. Slaves constitute a group in their own right which, given the primary nature of their linguistic input, can be called the "substrate strand."

Most importantly, again, the central item of my thesis applies, the territory-based process of identity definition which results in the emergence of a regional language variety. Historically, in plantation colonies phase 2 corresponds to the period of slavery and its aftermath, and the correlation between linguistic and social developments is somewhat different from other scenarios, with structural nativization (as defined in the Dynamic Model) / creolization going on during that early phase already due to restricted access to the target variety. Typically, creolization starts out with a homestead phase in which relatively restricted numbers of slaves are integrated in small family units, a context which facilitates language shift and some degree of second-language acquisition. In a second stage, with the expansion to large plantations, on account of the founder principle the variety developed by these early slaves serves as a target for the language shift of later slave generations, i.e. the creolization process *per se* (Chaudenson 2001; Mufwene 2004b, 2005a).

Some time after the end of slavery, however, descendants of former slaves and descendants of former slave owners are faced with the same basic decision and insight: notwithstanding differences in background and wealth, they are tied together as residents of the same territory, they need to get along together as one nation (take the Bajan motto "All O' We Is One" as a case in point). Reaching that decision may take longer than in other cases, and it may be more painful for some, but it appears unavoidable in the long run. The stigma that is socially tied to the slaves' language, the creole, tends to be stronger and more persistent than that associated with "plain" PCEs, and this cleavage detains further development and hinders the acceptance of an endonormative standard – but only for a while, it seems. Take the case of Jamaica, for example: in recent years Jamaican Creole has made tremendous inroads into domains formerly reserved to the standard, like the media (Shields-Brodber 1997; Mair 2002), and attempts are being made at promoting its full acceptability, e.g. in an initiative to guarantee language rights to speakers of Patwa in the Jamaican Constitution (Devonish 2003:168–75), e.g. the right to use the language in Parliament. Similarly, both black and white Barbadians have reached the stage where they are first and foremost Bajans, with ethnic and social differences, though persisting, being secondary, and this state of affairs has found its linguistic mode of expression in the Bajan language (Blake 2002). In other Anglophone islands of the Caribbean the situation is quite similar.

Pidginization or a pidgin precursor stage in creolization are fundamentally similar in nature, but they typically occur prior to creolization and structural nativization, in earlier contact phases. "Genuine" pidgins, i.e. simple contact varieties and jargons in trade situations, may emerge already in phase 1 and get conventionalized and stabilized in phase 2. They are structurally reduced and do not function as identity carriers (although their usefulness for interethnic contacts and trade may give pidgin speakers a special role in their communities, comparable to elite bilingualism in more formalized settings). Both of these properties are likely to get modified in phase 3: in structural nativization pidgins develop new structures and adopt new functions, a process which leads to "expanded pidgins" (Mühlhäusler 1986). As the examples of West Africa and Papua New Guinea indicate, the label "pidgin" may stick to such varieties despite ongoing creolization.

3.3.4   English as a symbol of elitism

The Dynamic Model rests upon the assumption that English is being accepted and appropriated by IDG strand populations, and that in its indigenized forms it becomes an identity carrier. What may prohibit such a process in some countries is when English is perceived as an *elitist* language, i.e. restricted socially to the upper strata of a society and consequently rejected as a class symbol by the majority. As long as the language seems within reach for everybody and promises a chance of economic improvement, attitudes will remain positive, and its attractiveness will be unbroken. However, once the common people start believing that only members of the elite profit from the benefits associated with knowing English, and the use of English is perceived as a means of the upper classes setting themselves off from the population at large (as may have happened in the Philippines, according to Thompson 2003:260–5), the future of the language is in danger. This is found primarily in former exploitation colonies.

This possible tension is comparable to the distinction between overt and covert prestige in a society: there exists "a vernacular market in opposition to the standard language market," "a pull in opposite linguistic directions" (Eckert 2000:25). In a modern society, promoting democratic ideals, covert prestige is likely to be extremely strong and powerful! Striving toward English for economic improvement on the one hand and using vernacular local forms of English for solidarity on the other are two different, potentially conflicting goals in many countries. Obviously, this issue is closely related to broader issues of language use in a given society: questions of literacy and of the respective functions of written vs. spoken forms of language; sociolinguistic language attitudes; and the situational appropriateness of styles and register choices (and language choice, for that matter).

3.3.5   Variation by colonization type

Different colonization types (as categorized in section 3.1.1), resulting from specific, historically grounded goals and motives of the colonizing nation and her individual agents, characteristically bring about specific demographic proportions, behavioral patterns, and, correspondingly, linguistic and cultural attitudes. Hence, this is another parameter which, within the confines of the Dynamic Model, provides for some systematic variation.

In *settlement* colonies (or, in Gupta's terms, monolingual ancestral English countries) the continuous influx of immigrants and, hence, the demographic proportion of STL strand descendants are very high, a pattern which results in a strong STL majority before too long. Several corollaries stem from this fact. Koinéization in stage 1 is a strong and effective process, and, correspondingly, provides a solid basis for the emphasis on homogeneity in stage 4, a pronounced characteristic of such communities. Settlers demand land, and the continuous expansion of their territorial claims tends to result in hostilities between them and the IDG population – persistent in North America, insidiously in Australia, temporarily limited in New Zealand. As a consequence, the structural influence of the IDG strand on the emerging variety is more restricted than elsewhere. There is some, however, and it is a possible characteristic trait of this subtype that for political reasons it gains in importance in phase 5. At a late stage of a country's linguistic and cultural evolution, almost when it is too late, the cultural heritage, including the linguistic contribution, of the IDG strand is attributed a high symbolic value and begins to be cherished (as is the case in present-day New Zealand, where the Maori language, even if in practice it is seriously endangered, enjoys strong official support). By now the big settlement colonies have proceeded all along the cycle into phase 5.

In *exploitation* colonies (in Mufwene's sense), the STL community tends to be relatively smaller in numerical terms but politically and economically powerful. The primary goal of the (typically British) settlers is to make money and to secure Britain's political and military interests in a region, not to spread the English language or Britain's cultural influence. Thus, phases 1 and 2, consonant with these interests, may prevail for an extended period of time. In fact, not infrequently English is deliberately withheld from the majority of the local population, because access to knowledge is

considered a powerful, potentially dangerous tool in the hands of indigenous masses. The spread of English to select members of the indigenous
population originally comes "from above," i.e. through formal education,
thus affecting primarily an elitist stratum of the society which the colonizers intend to serve their interests as leading administrators.[22] In the
course of time, a wider range of functional intermediaries gains access to
the language, as described by the model. Frequently after a colony's
independence the STL community vanishes almost completely, having
left the country and returned "home" – but via the education system and
the needs of international and also intranational communication the
English language remains and retains a vital presence in the language
contact setup. Such a development has led to "multilingual scholastic
English" in Gupta's terms. Interestingly enough, some of these communities have experienced a grassroots growth of English, a dynamic internal
development, after independence, so that they have moved into and even
beyond the phase of nativization relatively recently.

In *plantation* colonies the indigenous population was mostly either
eradicated (as for example in Barbados) or soon becomes demographically
insignificant and powerless (as in Hawai'i). Instead, slaves and, typically in
the nineteenth and twentieth centuries, contract laborers are imported to
these colonies. It was pointed out above (in 3.3.3) that this results in a
scenario which is fundamentally similar to other processes of PCE-emergence
but different in some important respects. One similarity, for instance, is the
fact that like IDG strand members in exploitation colonies slaves usually
constitute the quantitative majority of the population, while the political
power rests with the STL group. On the other hand, the IDG population
in exploitation colonies is treated with some respect, and their leaders
retain formal authority, while in plantation colonies physical oppression
reigns. The ecologies of plantation societies thus typically result in
creolization.

Finally, *trade* colonization is similar to exploitation colonization in that
settlements are established for strictly utilitarian purposes (in this case,
securing trading activities and naval routes), and the size of the STL strand
is limited; in fact, trade colonies frequently develop into exploitation
colonies at a later stage. In trade colonies interethnic contacts are so
reduced that the kind of English acquired by members of the IDG population typically is a pidginized one. Because of restricted interethnic contacts for a long time, the development tends to stay halted in phase 2 for an
extended period of time, marked by the coexistence of English (in the STL
stream), limited in use and usefulness, and pidgin (in parts of the IDG
stream). Whether and when (Pidgin) English proceeds further along the
cycle depends upon two decisive developments.

First, English is frequently adopted as an interethnic lingua franca, competing with other inter-tribal and regional languages in that function; in this function, it obviously expands its range of uses, functions and also structural properties quite considerably. Secondly, it seems that in recent years in many such countries (e.g. in West Africa) Pidgin English has gained covert prestige, similar to other PCEs in exploitation colony contexts: though it is stigmatized and evaluated negatively by authorities, in fact it is widely used and cherished by substantial portions of population, most importantly but increasingly by the young, even the better educated ones, like university students. Again, similar to the exploitation colonies, the most vibrant developments have occurred after independence, since the middle of the twentieth century. In countries like Cameroon and Ghana the expansion of the use of and the covert prestige attributed to Pidgin English goes hand in hand with a strengthening of English, which is sometimes adopted as a family language (largely in urban and socially elitist contexts). Similarly to what can be observed in the plantation colony type, a gradual approximation of these two poles and developments can be observed: English is influencing certain forms of Pidgin and spreading to less well-educated classes while at the same time pidginized forms of English have gained entrance into the media and other relatively more formal domains, e.g. in Nigeria (Deuber 2002, 2005).

Against all these differences between linguistic evolution patterns by colonization types I emphasize again the underlying similarities, the common core which unites all these contexts. The decisive criterion for what will happen in detail in a given region in colonization is the set of extra-linguistic conditions which obtain, the sociology of the emergent society. Most importantly, the relative difference in the quantitative proportions between members of the STL and the IDG (and ADS) strands correlates strongly with the types of colonization scenarios. Also, power relationships and political distribution of power in a community play a role: it makes a difference (and also varies by colonization type) whether the authority of local leaders (e.g. sultans or chiefs) is accepted and upheld (and an attempt is made to integrate them as a branch of the English-based power structure) or whether no power or authority is granted to the dominated group at all. Nevertheless, the very basic pattern of identity adjustments and linguistic correlates still prevails in the long run, even in settlement and plantation colonies, where the social cleavage is greatest in the initial stages. Take Australia and New Zealand as examples: for the descendants of the European immigrants, accepting the importance of the heritage stemming from the IDG strand may have taken a long time, perhaps too long, but it is bound to happen and to have an effect in society (even if this remains controversial; after all, attitudes toward these developments are a political issue, and hence conflicting opinions will exist). In a similar, though perhaps also delayed, fashion we can now observe ongoing discussions on the acceptability of local forms of English and creole in the Caribbean, in Africa, and in Asia.

3.4   Wider applicability

Whether the Dynamic Model proposed here has wider applicability beyond contacts with English (and mostly British English) as the colonizers' language is a matter of speculation, and probably difficult to test given the rarity of comparable cases of long-term and far-reaching, quasi-global, language expansions. Three situations that appear to be possibly related, or at least comparable, come to my mind: the fragmentation of vulgar Latin into the Romance languages in late antiquity; postcolonial varieties of Romance languages; and the emergence of new Slavic "languages" in post-1990 Eastern Europe.

Somewhat similarly to English in the colonial period and today, during the Roman Empire Latin was spread throughout almost the entire known world (from a Eurocentric perspective). It came into contact with indigenous languages, many of which we may assume to have had substrate effects upon the spoken varieties employed in daily interactions.[23] It is noteworthy (and a parallel to the diffusion of English) that it is not the elegantly structured classical written language preserved by the Christian learning tradition but rather the spoken, so-called "Vulgar" vernacular that was the form of the language that ultimately became decisive as the input to long-standing linguistic transformation processes. In the course of a few centuries, Vulgar Latin in contact with earlier indigenous languages was transformed and broke apart into the Romance languages in late classical antiquity. The current diffusion of global English has been compared to this historical metamorphosis of Latin, arguing that we may be witnessing a similar linguistic fragmentation process that ultimately might result in a number of mutually unintelligible new languages, "post-Englishes."[24] While some parallels are obvious and worth considering, we should not stretch the analogy beyond credibility. A major difference certainly is today's ease and speed of supra-regional, even global communication through technology, media, internet, and travel – certainly a force strongly counterbalancing fragmentation tendencies, although no one can tell its exact impact and long-term effects. In the light of the Dynamic Model, it would be difficult to posit and document comparable socio-cultural conditions of identity constructions, an inalienable component of my proposal, across millennia. From what we know about the early Middle Ages, the phase of endonormative stabilization in particular seems difficult to posit, given that there is no evidence available to support the idea of a local, territorial identity associated with indigenous forms of speaking (the notion of vernaculars as expressing national identities originates much later, at the end of the Middle Ages).[25] Throughout Europe during the Middle Ages the "intellectual" elites were united by the medium of classical Latin, and essentially ignored the "bastardized" forms of "vulgar" speech – perhaps not all that dissimilar to the role of "international English" and the attitudes expressed by the complaint tradition today, as against vernacular dialects. Thus, to some extent similar conditions may have obtained, but in the absence of more detailed evidence from late antiquity and the very early Middle Ages this seems likely to remain inaccessible and obscure.[26]

A more promising test case for the generalizability of the model seems to be the colonial expansion of the Romance languages (notably, Portuguese, Spanish, and French) from the fifteenth century to the present. In many respects (historical and sociological setting, chronology, population relations, and so on) these processes are similar to the colonial diffusion of English, and the outcomes are also strongly reminiscent of what we find in the English situation. Varieties like Québecois French, Mexican Spanish, or Popular Brazilian Portuguese are linguistically distinct in terms of a number of their features on all language levels; most likely many of these new features are products of contact with indigenous languages; and these varieties are also being appropriated as local identity carriers.

A rather recent and interesting, broadly comparable situation may also obtain, or have obtained, with respect to some Slavic languages at the end of the twentieth century. Linguistic forms which used to be considered as varieties of one language came to be recognized as separate languages, so two former dialects spoken in Czechoslovakia became the Czech and the Slovak language, and what was considered as Serbo-Croatian before has been breaking up into Serbian and Croatian (Marti 1993). In both cases, the division processes were originally motivated by political separation processes which affected the identities of the populations in these regions in a most direct way. Macedonian is following this lead today, and similar parameters obtain with respect to the distinction between Ukrainian and Russian. In a strictly linguistic perspective, these are clearly further manifestations of the old problem of how to distinguish languages from dialects, largely accepted to be a political rather than a genuinely structural division: newly established states deliberately posit, and their speech varieties are now conceptualized as, new languages. The sudden change of status from dialect to language has not been matched by the amount of linguistic distinctiveness, and in the Serbian – Croatian and Czech – Slovak cases the two varieties count as still mutually intelligible. But the important observation, in line with the Dynamic Model, is that the linguistic gaps are deliberately being widened to reflect earlier decisions on sociological and political divisions. As soon as the new political entities and national identities of the smaller nations were established, the respective dialects started to drift apart, with speakers choosing to emphasize features distinguishing them from the other group, respectively.

While in the case of the Slavic languages nationalistic attitude and awareness preceded linguistic fragmentation (with structural differences being still rather small but widening), in the case of the PCEs the opposite conceptualization, that of a homogeneous "common core" or "international standard" English, is still widely upheld despite rapidly growing sets of linguistic idiosyncracies. By world regions and states, chapter 5 will show how the evolution and fragmentation of English has been proceeding, and how the Dynamic Model can be applied and its constituent components unfold and can be identified in different regions.

4   Linguistic aspects of nativization

From a strictly linguistic perspective, the core component and the most interesting parameter of the Dynamic Model is certainly the process of structural nativization, the emergence of locally distinctive linguistic forms and structures. This is a phenomenon which calls for explanation, and so the present chapter will look specifically into the structural, linguistic properties of PCEs and the issue of where they may come from. Questions that will be raised include the following:

> Are there any features which tend to occur in many PCEs, despite widely varying first-language backgrounds, historical evolution processes, and language contact situations?
>
> Are there similarities between the ways in which these varieties are conceptualized?
>
> Are there any fundamental principles of language evolution which account for their emergence?
>
> More specifically, which linguistic processes are responsible for the individual structural properties observed in PCEs?
>
> How does "structural nativization" proceed in detail?

While some twenty years ago knowledge of features of PCEs was still anecdotal, by now many investigations from a wide range of countries have been published, and a few helpful surveys of linguistic features shared by PCEs are available. Amongst the earliest were Wells (1982), for pronunciation only; Platt, Weber, and Ho (1984), with useful summaries of overall tendencies; and Kachru (1986, 1992). Textbooks with a strong emphasis on linguistic features include Trudgill and Hannah (2002, in its fourth edition); Bauer (2002), focusing upon native-language varieties, i.e. settlement colonies, only; and Melchers and Shaw (2003). Hickey (2004) includes not only descriptive statements on individual varieties but also a "checklist of non-standard features," which for many recurrent features provides a short linguistic description and assessments of their possible origin or spread. The best documented and most authoritative source to date, however, is Mouton's monumental *Handbook of Varieties of English*, which in 132 articles and on 2,394 pages provides painstakingly detailed descriptions of almost 70 varieties worldwide (Schneider et al. 2004 for phonology, Kortmann et al. 2004 for morphosyntax). I will draw on all of these and other sources, supplemented by data and investigations of my own.

In section 4.1 I survey and systematize structural traits found in a wider range of PCEs, on the levels of pronunciation, vocabulary, and grammar. Subsequently, I will turn to the issues of methodology (How do we, as the scholarly community interested in this subject, find out about these phenomena and their distribution?) and conceptualization (Do the speakers know about the distinctiveness of their speech behavior, and how do they react to that?). Thirdly, an attempt will be made to systematically outline the linguistic processes which shape these features: which processes of a more general nature have resulted in these features and similarities, as far as we can tell?

4.1   Structural nativization: characteristic features

4.1.1   Phonology

It usually takes only a few utterances by a speaker for listeners to make educated guesses about his or her regional, and to some extent also social, origins – our accents betray where we are from. Of course, the accuracy of a listener's judgment depends on his or her exposure to and previous experience with different varieties of English, but apart from this restriction the basic principle operates reliably for practically all global forms of the language. The pyramid structure described by Trudgill (1987:42) applies, i.e. there is a lot of dialectal variability with a wide range of pronunciation variants in lower-class and informal environments, while this variability diminishes with higher strata of society and in more formal contexts. However, the basic principle is not invalidated by this limitation: even "standard Englishes" from anywhere are phonetically marked.

A set of very insightful and useful generalizations of pronunciation phenomena in what they call "New Englishes" is provided in one of the earliest systematic discussions of these varieties by Platt, Weber, and Ho (1984). They observe the following tendencies, amongst others (illustrated by examples of my own from Schneider et al. 2004):

- shortening of vowels, e.g. pronunciation of the THOUGHT vowel[1] with [ɔ] or [o] in many African Englishes;
- obliteration of the distinction between long and short vowels, often producing homophony, as between KIT and FLEECE in South-East Asian Englishes;
- replacement of central vowels by front or back ones, e.g. NURSE with [ɛ] in West African Pidgins or [ɔ] in Cameroonian English;

- shortening or full ungliding of diphthongs, e.g. the FACE vowel with [e] throughout most of the Caribbean, West Africa, and South-East Asia;
- replacement of the dental fricatives, spelled with <th>, by the dental or alveolar stops /t/ and /d/, e.g. *this* as *dis* in Indian and Black South African Englishes (and many other varieties), and *thing* as *ting* in Jamaica;
- reduction of aspiration word-initially, e.g. in the word *time* in Indian English;
- shift of the main stress in complex words, compared to British English, e.g. *exer'cise* in Malaysian English;
- employment of a syllable-timed rather than stress-timed speech rhythm, e.g. in Maori and Aboriginal Englishes, most Asian, and many African and Caribbean varieties.

Schneider (2004a) systematically surveys the phonetic variability of global accents of English, based on the data collected for the Mouton *Handbook*. For many individual sounds and phonetic processes it is possible to characterize their main realizations as distributed in specific regions. However, there are no pronunciation variants which are exclusive to any given form of English: a fundamental, almost trivial observation which emerges is the fact that all accents of English are characterized by their respective combinations of phonetic features. Some features are diagnostically more useful than others, typically because they are less widespread, but it is not possible to recognize a speaker's origin on the basis of a single phenomenon only.

This comparison yielded a few very general results, including the following (Schneider 2004a:1127–8):

- The extent of pronunciation variability observed in any given region tends to correlate with the historical depth of the English dialect in that region. There is a great deal of dialectal variability in the British Isles. The range of dialectal forms is less pronounced in North America, although there are still strong regional and local accent differences, and in Australia and New Zealand, where pronunciation variants tend to be socially rather than regionally diagnostic. There is least of it in Asia and Africa (where the relatively more elitist status of English and its transmission through the education system may have prevented or eroded a greater amount of accent variability – though there definitely is some there as well).
- Two strong tendencies can be observed in PCEs which emerged as L2 varieties: diphthongs tend to get weakened or to lose their offglides altogether, and the number of short vowel contrasts is reduced (to a five-vowel system in West Africa, for instance, compared in RP to six stressed and two unstressed ones, following Upton 2004).

- Length differences between vowels are waning, becoming less important or not distinctive at all in many PCEs.

Based on a database derived from the *Handbook* data which documents which features are found in which varieties, Schneider (2005a) carries out a frequency-based analysis to determine which features are particularly diagnostic for specific kinds of varieties. A methodology is devised to select features which are highly frequent in at least one specific region or language type and relatively infrequent in at least one other. Thus, tables 4.1 and 4.2 are restricted to features which are relatively strongly diagnostic on a quantitative basis. Of course, entries should not be misinterpreted to imply exclusive existence of any phenomenon in a given category: the tables identify trends, not distinctive distributions. Two types of analysis are carried out, one by world region (defined as continents, basically) and the other by contact type.

Table 4.1 displays patterns of regional distribution. It identifies a wide range of pronunciation features which are widely found in major world regions, and thus it deserves closer attention, though there is no point in paraphrasing the distributions. Note that there are a few features whose distributions tend to be rather clear-cut and hence highly diagnostic, e.g. the phonetic realizations of TRAP, LOT, BATH or GOAT, peripheral realizations of KIT and FOOT, GOOSE fronting, open unstressed vowels in lettER or horsES, lack of aspiration in initial stops, /t/-flapping and glottalization, yod-dropping, and a few more.

Table 4.2 provides the same type of documentation, this time categorized by first-language, second-language, and pidgin/creole-varieties. This is an equally interesting tabulation, because it allows us to identify features which apparently are products of language contact more than anything else. This seems to apply to several types of vowel homophony, including KIT/FLEECE and FOOT/GOOSE, to raised and peripheral realizations of FOOT and, less so, KIT, to the lowering of TRAP and BATH, the shortening of FLEECE, the monophthongization of FACE and GOAT, the opening of the offglides in NEAR and CURE, open rather than central unstressed vowels, the lack of aspiration in initial stops, TH-stopping, consonant cluster reduction in all environments considered, and prosodic phenomena like syllable-timing and the maintenance of tonal distinctions.

Of these processes, some can be identified as *simplification* (like the reduction of vocalic contrasts), while others appear to be *transfers* (like the two prosodic phenomena mentioned at the end of the list). Obviously, in such a general breakdown the line of distinction between these two phenomena is not easy to draw. To identify it more precisely, it is necessary to go more into details. Two examples should suffice to make the point.

Table 4.1: *Features which are highly characteristic of specific regions*

(...) = feature less strongly characteristic; "/" = alternative realizations; "✓" = homophony

	Britain	America	Caribbean	Pacific	Africa	Asia
KIT	[ɪ]	[ɪ]	[ɪ]	[ɪ]	[ɪ]	[ɪ]
DRESS				[e]		
TRAP		[æ]	[a]			
LOT	[ɒ]	[ɑ]	[ɔ]	[ɒ]	[ɒ]	[ɒ]
STRUT				[ɒ/ɐ]		
FOOT					[u]	[u]
BATH		[æ]		[a]		[a]
NURSE		[ɜː/ɚ]	[o/ɔ]	[ɛ/e(r)]	[ɛ/e(r)]	[o/ɔ], ([ɛ/e(r)])
FLEECE						[i/ɪ]
PALM	([ɑ(ː)])	[ɑ(ː)], [aː/ɑː]		[a(ː)]		([a(ː)])
THOUGHT						
GOAT		[ou/ou]	([o(ː)])		([o(ː)])	[o(ː)]
GOOSE	[ʉ(ː)]					
MOUTH			[ʌu/ou]			
NEAR	([ɪə(r)]), ([ɪ(ː)ə])	[ɪə(r)], [i(ː)ə]		[ia]	[ia]	([ɪə(r)])
SQUARE	([ɛə], [ɛ(ː)/r]), ([ɛ(ː)/r])	[ɛə], ([ɛ(ː)/r])	[e(ː)/r]	[eə/ea]	([ɛ(ː)/r])	([ɛ(ː)/r])
START	([ɑ(ː)/r]), ([ɑ(ː)/r])	([ɑ(ː)/r]), ([ɑ(ː)/r])	[a(ː)/r]	([a(ː/r)])	([a(ː)/r])	[a(ː)/r]
NORTH		[ɒ]		([ɒ])		
CURE		[ʊə/ʊr]				
letter	([ɪ])	[ɪ]	([a/ʌ])	[a/ʌ]	[a/ʌ]	([a/ʌ])
horsES	([ə])	[ə]		[a/ʌ]	[a/ʌ]	([a/ʌ])
commA				✓	(✓)	✓
KIT = FLEECE		✓				
TRAP = BATH		✓		✓		
Mary = merry		✓		✓		

Table 4.1: (cont.)

	Britain	America	Caribbean	Pacific	Africa	Asia
TRAP = DRESS before /l/				✓		✓
FOOT = GOOSE				✓	(✓)	
NEAR = SQUARE			✓			✓
nasalized vowels		✓	✓	✓		
initial p/t/k unaspirated			✓	✓		
t-flapping		✓		(✓)		
/t/ as glottal stop	✓			✓		
initial h-deletion	✓					
clear /l/ onset		(✓)	(✓)			✓
yod-dropping		✓	✓			
intervocalic /v/ > [b]			✓			
consonant cluster reduction		(✓)	✓	✓		
rhoticity	Ø, (r)	r	(Ø)	(Ø)	Ø	(✓)
/r/ flapped	(✓)		✓	✓		(r)
initial syllable deletion		(✓)	(✓)	✓	(✓)	
syllable timing			✓	✓		✓

Table 4.2: *Pronunciation tendencies by language types*

	L1	L2	Pidgins and Creoles
KIT	[ɪ],[ə]	[i]	[ɪ],[i]
TRAP	[æ]		[a]
LOT		[ɒ]	[a],[ɒ]
FOOT	[ʊ]	[u]	[u]
BATH	[æ]		[a]
NURSE	[ɜː/ɚ]	[ɛ/e(r)]	[o/ɔ], [ɛ/e(r)]
FLEECE	[iː]	[i/ɪ]	[i/ɪ]
FACE		([eː])	[eː]
PALM	[ɑ(ː)]		[a(ː)]
GOAT		[o(ː)]	[o(ː)]
GOOSE	[ʉ(ː)],[ʊu/ɪu/ə(ː)ʉ]	[uː]	[uː]
PRICE	[əɪ/ɜɪ]		
MOUTH		[aʊ/ɑʊ]	
NEAR	[ɪə(r)], [i(ː)ə]	[i(ː)ə]	[ia]
START	[ɑ(ː/r)]		[a(ː/r)]
CURE	[ʊə/ʊr]	([ua/oa(r)])	[ua/oa(r)]
letteR		[a/ʌ]	[a/ʌ]
horsEs	[ə],[ɪ]		
commA	[ə]	[a/ʌ]	[a/ʌ]
KIT = FLEECE		✓	✓
DRESS = FACE		✓	✓
FOOT = GOOSE		✓	✓
LOT = THOUGHT		✓	(✓)
initial P/T/K unaspir.		✓	✓
T-flapping	✓		
voiced TH > d (*dis*)		(✓)	✓
voiceless TH > t (*ting*)		(✓)	✓
initial h-deletion			✓
clear /l/ in onset			✓
yod-dropping	✓		
CCR monomorphemic		(✓)	✓
CCR bimorphemic		(✓)	✓
CCR initial		(✓)	✓
rhotic	✓		
/-ŋ/ in *down* (etc.)			✓
syllable timing		✓	✓
tone distinctions		(✓)	✓

Investigating consonant cluster reduction (CCR) in a wide range of varieties which represent different degrees of contact histories, Schreier (2005) shows convincingly that the frequency of CCR in any given variety correlates strongly with the amount of language contact it has experienced in its evolution. There are even some qualitative differences between varieties with and without a contact history. In hetero-voiced clusters (i.e. in words like *jump*, *milk*, or *help*, where one consonant is voiced and the other voiceless) CCR is permitted only in contact-induced varieties. The effect of a following pause is also different: in varieties with contact histories, but not in others, a pause has an effect similar to that of a following consonant, i.e. favoring CCR. The process contributes to a simpler, more natural phonotactic structure of consonant – vowel sequences (CVCV), and can thus be regarded as an instance of a universal simplification strategy.

On the other hand, the role of *substrate transfer* in shaping the phonology of a new variety of English is amply illustrated by Wiltshire (2005). She investigates the second-language English pronunciation of Indians of Tibeto-Burman origin, and contrasts her findings with the phonologies of their mother tongues. The results are indicative of how innovations originate and diffuse. The areal, Tibeto-Burman accent of Indian English is characterized, amongst other things, by the maintenance of the distinction between /v/ and /w/, which corresponds to the phonology of Angami, one of the local languages, while the others, Ao and Mizo, do not have this feature. Similarly, /r/ is realized in a highly distinctive fashion, as a voiced apical post-alveolar central approximant, which corresponds to the phonetic shape of this sound precisely in one of the L1s, Ao, though the others have different /r/ variants. In both cases, however, all speakers from the region, irrespective of their mother tongues, display the respective features in their English accents. The explanation is that these pronunciation peculiarities originated as L1 transfers by some speakers but spread to the accents of others as areal markers later on. Other features, like coda consonant devoicing or cluster reduction, also correspond to some but not all substrate phonologies but seem supported by their character as simpler and less marked. Thus, substrate transfer is ultimately responsible for the origin of certain pronunciation features in the English of this region, but this isn't the full story; L1 transfer interacts in a complex fashion with universal constraints to result in the further dissemination of these innovations.

4.1.2   Lexis

The vocabularies of PCEs are characterized by lexical expansion, based on a small number of source processes. These include borrowing from the IDG strand, coining new words using strategies of word formation, and adjusting the meaning of existing words to novel environmental conditions.

Most importantly, words are borrowed from indigenous languages and integrated into the lexical stock of the newly emerging variety. The labels of *borrowing* or "loan words" are actually misnomers, not only because these items are never "given back" (as the notion of borrowing should imply). More importantly, perhaps, these notions imply a hierarchical relationship between languages (a donor language offers words, the recipient language accepts them), and the recipient language is viewed as being transmitted in a stable and largely undisturbed fashion – two assumptions which fail to describe the process of the emergence of a new variety adequately. Therefore, "word selection" from the IDG strand would be a more appropriate designation, although I will also keep using the traditional terms, simply because they are so well established.

As was pointed out in chapter 3, typically lexical items selected from indigenous languages stem from a small number of specific semantic domains and are taken over at characteristic evolutionary phases, namely, in turn, toponyms, terms for fauna and flora, and words for culturally distinctive items and customs. It is interesting to see that in observing this chronological order subsequent layers of new words are moving from the periphery to the center of the lexical stock, as it were, i.e. they gain in semantic weight and denotational load.

Place names, it is frequently argued, are not really "words" in the narrow sense of "lexical stock of meaningful items" in the language, as they do not really have a semantic denotation: they refer to individual locations, but they do not really "mean" anything, and even their reference potential (their extension, in the sense of philosophers of language) is typically restricted to precisely one item only (a city, a river, a mountain, or whatever). Underlying this borrowing process is presumably a rather naive folk-linguistic concept of places simply "having" a name, not being assigned one by convention. It was pointed out in the Dynamic Model (and many examples are provided in chapters 3, 5 and 6) that place names are amongst the earliest and most persistent loans in a process of colonial expansion, consonant with phase 1.

Soon, in phase 2, place names are followed by words for animals and plants. Again, in the eyes of the early settlers these may have been viewed as pre-existing in direct association with their referent objects, so the colonists may have chosen to use their "natural" names rather than allocating arbitrary labels to fauna and flora themselves. Unlike place names, however, these words do not have a unique reference potential: loans for animals and plants denote classes of objects, not individuals, so these words are more explicitly "meaningful" rather than purely referential.

This line of thinking can be continued to encompass the third type of borrowings, words for elements of the indigenous culture. Again, in the eyes of colonists these customs and objects may have been taken to exist in themselves, outside of their own sphere of activity, and "have names" as such (though these clearly entail a lot of semantic value, i.e. meaning); but with increasing involvement, cultural exposure, and mixture these items increasingly become parts of their own world in one way or another. Uses of such terms abound in indigenous texts; here are just a few examples from the International Corpus of English (ICE; italics mine):

(4.1) I went to my grandmother yesterday and we ate *adobo* and *kare-kare* (ICE-Philippines; S1A-037)

(4.2) President Moi held the spirit of *harambee* which he noted that had helped raise funds for needy cases in the country (ICE-East Africa; br-newsk)

(4.3) Maori cultural survival has been seen as of equal importance to children's needs within the *te kohanga reo* movement. (ICE-NZ; w2b018)

Lexical expansion is achieved also by means of *word formation*. While word-formation products found in specific PCEs have been pointed out in a number of cases (e.g. Kachru 1983:36–9, 153–62 on Indian English, Baumgardner 1998 on Pakistani English, Dako 2001 on Ghanaian English, or Tent 2001a:232–6 on Fiji English), so far only two systematic comparisons across varieties have been carried out, namely Görlach (1995b) and Biermeier (2007), whose work is based upon ICE corpora. According to these sources, the word-formation potential of PCEs is not fundamentally different from that of native Englishes; all major word-formation processes can be used to coin new items in PCEs as well. However, in terms of their productivity some processes are less widely employed (and these are primarily the reductive types, i.e. blends, clippings, and also acronyms), while others seem to generate new words with exceptional frequency. The latter include, above all, compounding, in particular the creation of hybrid compounds which combine English and indigenous elements. Conversion and certain kinds of derivation are also highly productive – although this also varies from one variety to another.

Biermeier (2007) shows, for instance, that Philippine English is extremely liberal and effective in generating many new words, while East African Englishes display a reduced range of new types which, on the other hand, are then employed with exceptionally high token frequency. For example, Kenyan English uses the item *master* quite commonly as a determinatum, yielding *sportsmaster*, *careers master*, or *drug masters* in addition to both British and Kenyan *housemaster* and *paymaster*. Agent noun formations tend to yield a fairly high output of new types and frequent tokens, e.g. in Singapore *food maker*, *batikmaker*, *tomb maker*, *film goer*; in the Philippines *repeaters* "contract workers who are rehired," *healthchecker*, *chairholder*, *gunholder*, *foregrounder*, *homewrecker*. Generic terms, like *wallah* 'person (connected with a particular thing or activity)' in India and Pakistan, enter compounds very liberally (*autowallahs, paperwallah, auto rickshaw wallah, plastic wallah, juice wallah, fruitwalas*). Certain formatives are particularly productive in certain regions, e.g. *–holder* in the Philippines (*flower holders, needlepoint holder, agreement holder, chalk holder*) and *–monger* and *–master* in Kenya (*rumour-monger, catastrophe-monger; careers master, paymaster, drug masters*). Gender-marking morphology is also productive but regionally variable: *lady* tends to function as a determinant in Singapore (*lady divers, lady colleague*) and India (*lady participants, lady fans, lady friend*) but as a determinatum in Kenya (*business lady, chairlady*); the suffix *–(r)ess* is used widely (Singapore: *instructress*; India: *female temptress*) except for Kenya, where the analytic form *–woman* is preferred. In compounding, different lexicalization strategies are employed in different regions for the same concept: a British *petrol station* is a *petrol kiosk* in Singapore, a *gas(oline) station* in the Philippines, and a *petrol pump* in India; fishermen carry *fishing tackle* in Britain and New Zealand, *fishing equipment* or *fishing gear* in Tanzania, and a *fishing kit* in New Zealand. (All examples in this paragraph are from Biermeier 2007.)

Note that all these formative types and examples stand between grammar in the generic sense, i.e. those properties of language which are regular and predictable, and lexis, i.e. the idiosyncratic properties of individual words: they occur in paradigms but with restricted productivity. According to the Dynamic Model this is the domain of language organization where variety-specific innovations are most likely to occur. The frequent occurrence of compounds, hybrids, and other neologisms in PCEs thus confirms the assignment of this type of creativity to the expansionist tendencies of phase 3, nativization.

Moving one step further from structural options to idiosyncratic coinages, we get to the realm of *collocational preferences* and idiomatic *phraseology*. Both of these are also extremely characteristic of PCEs. In collocations, certain words co-occur preferably, and increasingly frequently, with certain other words. Individual speech communities are free to develop habits as to which words tend to co-occur, and so this is an element of language organization which readily permits the emergence of inconspicuous regional features. When such co-occurrence tendencies become lexicalized and restricted to firm combinations only of specific words, new phraseological units or idioms evolve. Again, these are often highly specific to any particular variety. For example, the phrase *This is it* to assert one's commitment to the truth of a proposition could be coined and used anywhere, but based on my anecdotal observations it occurs frequently in and is thus highly characteristic of Cameroonian English only. It is also noteworthy that the phrase is fixed: it does not occur in any other tense; it cannot be embedded; and so on.

The last type of lexical expansion to be mentioned here concerns *semantic shift*, the fact that the formal shape of words remains unaltered but their meaning gets adjusted to new referential needs. Similar to traditional categorizations of semantic change, word meanings can get narrowed down (e.g. *corn* 'maize' in American English, or *outdoor* 'bring out a new-born baby to recognize it, celebrate its birth and give it a name' in Ghanaian English) or widened (e.g. *bush* 'wilderness' in Australian English or *auntie/uncle* 'any respected elder,' in India, Malaysia, South Africa, and Fiji).

4.1.3   Grammar

4.1.3.1   Pattern distributions Some of the very fundamental observations made above with respect to pronunciation apply to the grammatical level as well:

1) When comparing the grammatical structures and properties of many different PCEs, a wide range of variability can be observed: many PCEs have distinctive rules and patterns which are unique to them or characteristic of their region but not shared by others. Given that to a certain extent at least some structures of PCEs can be attributed to transfer from indigenous languages, this is not surprising: with many typologically distinct substrate languages involved in different world regions, the results of contact processes are also bound to vary considerably.

2) Nevertheless, and perhaps surprisingly so, it is possible to sketch a number of grammatical phenomena which appear in a fairly large number of PCEs from different world regions. Some of these, but certainly not all, can be explained as strategies of "simplification." I hypothesize that in the absence of convincing sociohistorical explanations for such similarities the reason for their existence may be assumed to lie somewhere in the psycholinguistic domain, in principles underlying L2 acquisition.

3) The pyramid-shape relationship between linguistic variability on the one hand and social class and style stratification on the other applies as well. At the bottom of the pyramid, in the domain of lower-class speech and informal orality, many different usage patterns and structures can be observed, many of which are overtly stigmatized as "nonstandard." The higher one moves on the sociostylistic continuum, the fewer such forms occur; and on top, in formal speech production, and most characteristically in writing, a "standard" form of language can be observed which is largely devoid of localisms. Nevertheless, there are usually some: even standard forms of PCEs have their characteristic

patterns and grammatical features. However, these tend to be less conspicuous and not overtly branded, so in many cases speakers are not aware of what in a comparative perspective is special about their own way of constructing phrases and sentences.

In addition, the Dynamic Model makes a strong claim that ties in with isolated earlier observations but has not been projected as a general principle earlier, and which thus needs to be substantiated:

4) Innovations and distinctive structural properties of PCEs are frequently positioned at the interface between lexis and grammar, i.e. certain words but not others of the same word class prefer certain grammatical rules or patterns. The patterns as such are not new, nor are the words, but what is novel is the habitual association between them in specific varieties.

In the following paragraphs I illustrate and substantiate these points, extrapolating a little further from them.

Let us begin by listing just a few apparent idiosyncracies of select varieties as examples. Singaporean English has a passive construction with *kena*, e.g. *The thief kena catch by the police* (Fong in Lim 2004: 98–9), which is subject to very specific syntactic and semantic constraints: it is followed by an infinitive or past participle form of the verb; it may combine with an optional *by*-phrase; it does not occur with stative verbs; and it suggests that the subject is adversely affected by the action. Kenyan English has a "reduplicated modal" *can be able*, as in *you cannot be able to succeed* (Buregeya 2006). New Zealand English uses the verb *farewell* transitively. Xhosa English in South Africa uses *very much* and *too much* as premodifiers of adverbs and adjectives, e.g. *very much badly* and *too much dark* (de Klerk 2005:93). African-American English has a peculiar negative inversion construction, e.g. *Didn't nobody tell me*. And so on – the list of possible structural idiosyncracies is long.

However, and perhaps more interestingly so, there is also a long list of features shared across countries and contexts. An early but still very useful survey was provided by Platt, Weber, and Ho (1984). Amongst others, they list the following tendencies (65, 85–6):

- omission of the nominal plural marker (e.g. *In both area*, Sri Lanka) but pluralization of mass nouns (e.g. *furnitures*; Nigeria);
- marking of a specific/non-specific distinction rather than definiteness in noun phrases (e.g. *I'm staying in one house* but *Everyone has car*; India);
- unusual constituent sequences within a noun phrase (e.g. *this our common problem*, apparently with two determiners, in Nigeria);
- omission of the third-person singular marker on verbs and use of present tense forms for the past tense (e.g. *She drink milk*; *then I go to Public School*; Philippines);

- delimitation of verbs with aspect rather than tense markers (e.g. *she done eat*; Caribbean); and
- use of the progressive *-ing* with stative verbs (e.g. *I was doubting it*; India).

Kortmann and Szmrecsanyi (2004) systematically analyze the distribution of 76 morphosyntactic features in 46 nonstandard dialects and PCEs in a global perspective, and some of their results are worth reporting here. They find 11 features to be extremely widespread, i.e. to occur in about three quarters or more of all the varieties under investigation. These are (1154; examples are mine, from Kortmann et al. 2004):

- lack of inversion in main-clause *yes/no*-questions, e.g. *The children are studying?* (Cameroon);
- *me* instead of *I* in coordinate subjects, e.g. *Me and Elizabeth speaks English* (Cape Flats, South Africa);
- *never* as a preverbal past tense negator, e.g. *I never knew* 'I didn't know' (Ghana);
- adverbs that are homomorphic with adjectives, e.g. *an awful ill teacher* (Appalachia);
- absence of plural marking after measure nouns, e.g. *two spoon coffee* (Butler English, India);
- lack of inversion or of auxiliaries in *wh*-questions, e.g. *You buy what?* (Singapore);
- multiple negation (also called "negative concord"), e.g. *I couldn't see no snake* (Tasmania);
- special forms or phrases for the second-person plural pronoun, e.g. *y'all* (Southern US), *yous* (West Coast New Zealand), *oonah/yinnah* (Bahamas);
- leveling of the functional distinction between present perfect and past tense, e.g. *Then he's hit her* (Australia); and
- double comparatives and superlatives with adjectives, e.g. *more brighter* (New Zealand).

Hence, these phenomena come close to what Chambers (2004b) calls "vernacular universals" (though he lists different ones), i.e. nonstandard patterns which can be found in a majority of nonstandard dialects around the world. Many of these forms can be accounted for by historical diffusion from British dialects. To what extent independent developmental tendencies, yielding identical results at different locations, have played a role is difficult to tell at this stage (Chambers 2003:266–70); presumably both sources have interacted, and either one may have been reinforced by substrate similarities as well.

A closer look at the precise distributions of these patterns across world regions reveals, however, that Africa and the Pacific and, most strongly,

Asia, display a relatively smaller proportion of these nonstandard uses than America, the Caribbean, Australia, and the British Isles. This conforms to the fact that in these regions exploitation colonies (rather than settlement colonies with transported nonstandard forms) and the transmission of English through the education system predominated. Features which are particularly widespread in Asia and Africa (in addition to some of the above-mentioned ones) include

- idiosyncratic use/omission of articles, e.g. *Depreciating value of naira and increase in cost of wheat ... have been identified* (Nigeria);
- weakening of the count/mass distinction in nouns, e.g. *slangs* (Fiji), *furnitures* (India);
- an inverted word order in indirect questions, e.g. *I asked him where is he?* (Pakistan)
- the use of progressive forms with stative verbs, e.g. *She is owning two luxury apartments* (Malaysia); and
- invariant non-concord tags, e.g. *You have taken my book, isn't it?* (vernacular Indian English).

In second-language varieties in general, Kortmann and Szmrecsanyi (2004:1188–9) find uninverted main clause questions, irregular article uses, and the lack of a perfect vs. past distinction to be especially common.

4.1.3.2 Origins and diffusion All of these structural options constitute elements of the feature pool from which emerging PCEs select their distinctive grammatical patterns, so each of them is successful at some locations but not so at others. As was pointed out earlier, it is difficult to say whether these structures are inherited or coined afresh, though with grammatical phenomena which are so widespread historical diffusion seems more likely – it is difficult to imagine that identical rules of grammar should evolve independently of each other at different points in space and time. From the perspective of structural nativization, innovations are more interesting, as they represent the immediate outcomes of contact situations and dynamic processes of language emergence.

Research into language change has shown that linguistic innovations in most cases are not absolutely novel in the strict sense; typically, what happens is that forms and uses which existed somewhere, in structurally or socially restricted contexts, begin to be used in slightly different environments (linguistic or social), and spread from there into the speech community. That is, such patterns begin as occasional uses, perhaps preferred uses, in the speech of some individuals,[2] and then get picked up by others who for some reason find these uses worthy of copying. Through increased frequency of usage such patterns then become continuously more deeply "entrenched" and get established in the minds of an increasingly large number of speakers – like the ruts of a wagon trail, every subsequent use deepens and intensifies the path for future uses along the same track, of the same kind. Thus, occasional preferences turn into firmly established habits and, in the long run, through regular usage into newly established grammatical patterns.

4.1.3.3 At the crossroads of grammar and lexis While the vocabulary of a language is typically regarded as consisting of a large number of idiosyncratic items (words) which exist independently of each other, grammar counts as the realm of the regular. Consequently, while words fluctuate relatively easily, the grammar of a language tends to be much more stable and resistant to change. It should not come as a surprise, therefore, that grammatical innovations, also in the process of structural nativization, typically start out where the regular meets the chaotic, i.e. at the intersection of grammar and lexis. Therefore, many of the characteristic innovations of PCEs can be located at this boundary; they concern the co-occurrence potential of certain words with other words or specific structures. A classic example is the complementation patterns which verbs and also adjectives typically enter: in new varieties, in the process of structural nativization, verbs begin to allow and later prefer new structures to complement them and build a complete sentence. Well-known examples include the New Zealand use of *to farewell somebody*, mentioned above, the variability of the prepositions introducing complements of the adjective *different* (known to vary regionally between *from*, *than*, and *to*), or similar patterns such as *to resemble to somebody*, *to pick somebody* (East Africa) or *to protest something*.

Of course, it takes a long while for such innovations to spread and get established, to proceed through the stages of individual preference to habit formation and cognitive entrenchment in the speech community. During the transition phase we therefore find variability, the coexistence of old and new forms, with the latter typically spreading in the S-curve fashion which sociolinguists have described. So, to take up one of the above examples, in East Africa today (and not only there) we come across both the innovative *to pick somebody* and the traditional *to pick up somebody*, as the following two examples illustrate:

(4.4) you could not go out unless you were *picked* by a car (ICE-East Africa; conver-2)

(4.5) We can *pick* them *up* later (ICE-East Africa; br-talkt)

A recent comparative study (Schneider 2004b:241) shows, however, that in East Africa, unlike all other varieties considered, the form without the particle is much more common than the one with it; in spoken Kenyan English in particular it occurs about four times as frequently.

Lexicogrammatical examples like these, especially if high-frequency words are involved, have a certain degree of salience, so at some point a speech community becomes aware of the existence of the innovative usage (and then it may become a subject of debate, with conservatives and liberals arguing about whether such usage is admissible). In other cases, however, tendencies are purely quantitative (but nevertheless real and firm) and typically below the level of anybody's awareness. To illustrate this point, let us have a brief look at two recent investigations of Indian English syntax. Olavarria de Errson and Shaw (2003) looked into the complementation potential of two semantically similar groups of verbs, namely *provide, furnish, supply, entrust,* and *present,* and *pelt, shower, pepper,* and *bombard.* In both cases they find systematic quantitative differences between Indian and British English. With "provide"-type verbs, the construction types *someone provided them something* and *someone provided something to them* were found to be more likely in Indian than in British English, while *someone provided them with something* was considerably more common in British English. With "pelt"-type verbs, British English prefers constructions with *with* (*to pelt someone with something*), while in Indian English the pattern *to pelt something at/on someone* prevails. In a similar vein, Mukherjee and Hoffmann (2006) investigate ditransitive verb uses in both varieties, and also find "clear and identifiable differences" (147). *Give* is found to be a less prototypically ditransitive verb in Indian English, being used more frequently in the construction types *give something* (without expressing the recipient) and also (though less so) *give something to someone,* as against the more typically British *give someone something.* Furthermore, Indian English has developed "new ditransitives," e.g. *presented each donor a travel bag, supplying us the foodgrain, inform the appointing authority the amount, gift him a dream, notify us the date.* These are stable and noteworthy results, and it is worth pointing out that they operate way below the level of linguistic awareness: without quantitative methodology no observer would have suspected such differences to exist. Mukherjee and Hoffman rightly conclude: "Further research into the endonormative stabilization of New Englishes will thus have to delve much more deeply into the verb-complementational profiles of varieties of English" (2006:167).

A related phenomenon which is one step further from the regular toward the idiosyncratic but also still located at this interface of words and their patterns which is so productive in structural nativization is lexical co-occurrence, leading to the establishment of collocational tendencies and, ultimately, idiom formation. An intermediate stage toward such innovations may be what Mesthrie (2002b:352–3) calls "near-misses": structures which, presumably in a second-language-learning process, are altered but slightly, as in South African Indian English *catch up* for 'catch on,' *can't stick the heat* for 'can't stand the heat,' or *play fools* for 'play the fool.' Subsequently, if more elements are modified or freshly combined, the result are completely novel collocations and phrases. In PCEs we find localized set phrases such as *no worries* (originally an Australianism), *spot on, double mind* 'doubtful' (Nigerian English; Igboanusi 2002:96), *make no bones about* 'do not hesitate' (Indian English; Yadurajan 2001:98), or others. I do not want to explore the issue of the theoretical interpretation of such innovations, but let me just point out that here we are moving in a direction which has received some attention in recent linguistics, toward emphasis on lexical bundles and constructions. It is one of the innovative features of the grammar by Biber et al. (1999) that an entire chapter is devoted to what they call "lexical bundles," loosely defined as recurrent word combinations (992). These, in turn, can be viewed as closely related to the notion of "constructions," multi-word combinations of form and meaning (Goldberg 1995). PCEs are characterized by the emergence of new constructions, new habits of word combinations which are meaningful (only) in a given speech community.

4.1.3.4   Possible causes – ? For the obvious question of why this is so there is no simple and obvious answer available. Actually, the question can be broken down to its many different facets: why did any innovation occur at all; why has it been successful and adopted in the speech community while other, competing patterns have vanished; why these particular types of novel patterns rather than any others; and so on? These are highly complex issues. Many of them relate to general problems of understanding language change and language variation; others, however, are specific to PCEs. Any shortcut explanation would simply be insufficient in a situation which is characterized by multicausality. So this puzzle, while standing behind much of what follows, must be left unsolved. However, I would like to draw attention to three ideas, suggestions, and observations which in this context I find particularly interesting and noteworthy.

First, it is obvious that language is closely related to culture, and in many ways it is a mirror of the culture which is expressed by it. While this applies without any doubt to the lexis of a variety, the question of whether any grammatical properties can possibly be accounted for as manifestations of a particular culture is a challenging but unresolved issue. Olavarria de Errson and Shaw (2003:159) venture to propose a possible cultural explanation for their syntactic findings on verb complementation outlined above. They suspect that a "Northern European" culture of subjectivism can be juxtaposed to an Asian culture which sees the individual as a part of a larger whole, and that accordingly British English may prefer constructions which "profile" the individual, and vice versa. In contrast, for example with *provide*-type verbs, Indian English syntactically emphasizes not the recipient but what is provided. Certainly, as the authors concede, this is a speculative thesis, but it is also an intriguing one, worth being pursued further.

Second, it seems likely that a number of the phenomena found in PCEs can be explained to some extent by universal laws of ontogenetic second-language acquisition and phylogenetic language shift – which are the contexts which have given rise to them. Williams (1987) elaborated on this idea and pointed out that many of the features of PCEs can be viewed as instances of simplification (like the tendencies to omit inflectional endings, pronouns, copulas, or articles) or overgeneralization (i.e. a rule extension to new contexts, for instance the extension of plural endings to mass nouns or of the progressive to stative verbs). In general, she argues that all of these tendencies represent speakers' shortcuts to increase the economy of speech production, observing a principle of "avoid exceptions" (170), as is the case, for example, with the use of invariant tags, morphological regularizations, the overuse of a canonical SVO (subject–verb–object) word order, and so on. It is true that all of these modifications eliminate some complexities of the target language and thus make a learner's task easier, but there are at least two factors which impose a limit to possible simplifications. One is the communicative need to secure encoding, a central function of language: when too much loss of morphology, for instance, eradicates meaningful distinctions in a paradigm then some relevant, and possibly necessary, information is lost – and this cannot be tolerated beyond a certain point, because otherwise language would no longer fulfill its core function of carrying complex information from the speaker to the hearer. The other one is the fact that a great deal of structural complexity comes in through the contact situation, because the learner's L1 competence offers new grammatical parameters and options to the pool of available features which through transfer and replication (see section 4.3.2.3) have the potential to influence, enrich, and complexify the emerging new variety. Hence, while some individual properties of PCEs may be explained as cases of simplifications, the overall language systems as such are anything but simple.

Third, is there a possibility of a language developing a distinct new character of its own by consistently selecting forms and patterns that conform to an overarching language type, with many innovations being typologically similar in nature and strengthening one specific parameter? This would be broadly comparable to Edward Sapir's famous notion of a language having a "drift," a direction of change toward a coherent language type (though not necessarily just a reductive and analytic type, characterized by the loss of endings, as in Sapir's original and well-known example of the long-term change of English), and it would also be in accordance with Keller's (1994) theory of an "invisible hand" guiding language change. So far I know of only one study which implicitly makes such a claim (and which therefore in my opinion is an important one): Mesthrie (2006) shows that a wide range of characteristic properties of Black South African English consistently operate in the same direction. Mesthrie calls it "antideletion," a tendency to avoid the omission of constituents which can be left out in many other varieties of English. This may take three different shapes: retention or insertion of constituents that are conventionally left out (e.g. the infinitive marker in structures like *I let him to speak Zulu* or the dummy *it* in *As it is the case elsewhere ...*); the retention of elements that can be deleted in some related varieties (e.g. the copula in *We are five* or the avoidance of gapping as in *I can read them and write them*); and insertions of redundant grammatical morphemes (e.g. the two conjunctions in *Although I'm not that shy but it's hard ...* or the explicit presence of "underlying," semantically implied prepositions, as in *mention about something*). Any single one of these patterns may be unspectacular, but the fact that these and many similar ones all occur in one and the same variety is impressive and most likely to be grammatically meaningful. Of course, it would be possible to interpret this character of Black South African English in the light of the psycholinguistic principle discussed in the previous paragraph, as all these features can be viewed as contributing to the explicit marking of grammatical categories and relationships. It would be interesting to see whether such movements toward a consistent language type could be documented for other PCEs as well.

4.2   Tracing structural nativization: methodological and conceptual issues

Taken together, the above-mentioned distinctive features of PCEs give each of them a unique character, and set them apart from other varieties of English. Do they result in the creation of an explicitly new linguistic entity, however, or do they just sprinkle the language as such with a few features of local interest only? This section inquires into the holistic conceptualization of PCEs on account of their structural properties. Specifically, three questions will be asked. How different from each other and from their one-time ancestor, British English, are PCEs? How do we, the community of observers and scholars interested in these issues, know about the amount and nature of these differences? And how do the speakers of these varieties perceive and think about their own linguistic usage?

4.2.1 Degrees of difference

What makes a specific PCE distinctive; what, if anything, is it that tells a listener where a given speaker, or text, comes from? With a speaker the primary means of identification is of course a person's accent, the distinctive regional way of pronouncing sounds and words. With written samples, this is clearly much more difficult. Of course, practically every text betrays its regional origin by the place names and personal names in it, and perhaps by some cultural or distinctly local terms. But if you strip it of those, what remains? Not very much, but something inconspicuous but nevertheless powerful and consistent: preferences – tendencies to use specific words in combination with specific other words consistently more frequently than elsewhere, to prefer certain structural patterns over others, perhaps to use certain words with exceptional frequency (in the eyes of an outsider), or to pursue a certain style with its "soft" characteristics.

To illustrate the point, let us have a look at the number and nature of the differences between British and American English, assuming that the number and character of differences between (other) PCEs and British English will ultimately be similar in nature. The point I am trying to make is that the familiar lists of alternative choices like *petrol/gas*, *got/gotten* or *do you have/have you got* (Strevens 1972) are insufficient to grasp the relationship between national varieties of English, scratching only the tip of the iceberg – differences are much more complex and also subtle. Algeo (1989) provides a nice example which documents very neatly how the British and the Americans say the same thing differently. When living in England as an American, he happened to come across a sign at an office where gas bills can be paid:

Avoid queuing – Customers not requiring a receipt should pin their cheque to the payment counterfoil and post here

This, he says, struck him as odd and "labyrinthly British," so he started to experiment with Americans, asking them to rephrase the message in their own words. He found that apart from the obvious issue of replacing regional lexical choices (like *queue*, *pin*, or *payment counterfoil*) they also wished to simply avoid certain constructions, like the use of the third person in *customers should . . .* or the construction *not requiring*, for which they preferred a finite relative clause *who do not . . .* In the end, he came up with a suggested "translation" by American respondents:

Don't wait in line – If you don't need a receipt, attach your check to the bill and put it in the slot here

And then, a few weeks later in Athens, Georgia, he came across a real sign conveying exactly the same message:

For check payment only
Insert bills and payments here if you do not want receipt

Algeo concludes that the style of instructions in British English is more "ornate," formal, complicated, and like a command, while American English is laconic, even telegraphic, more direct, and less formal. Certainly he is right in that, but the most important point is more general, and I am convinced it applies to the relationship between all PCEs: individual varieties differ from each other first and foremost in their combinatory preferences, in their constructions, in the frequencies of their lexicogrammatical choices, collocations, word uses, and so on. It is not only, and perhaps not even primarily, the occasional occurrences of well-known "distinctive features" that attribute its uniqueness to a variety; it is the subconscious set of conventions regulating the norm level of speech habits, of what is normally done and uttered, the "way things are said" in a community.[3]

For the British – American distinction, Mittmann (2004) is an impressive study which confirms the importance of idiomaticity and the phraseological level. Based on a comprehensive quantitative study of computer corpora, the author points out hundreds of conventionalized preferences in either variety and shows how prefabricated, ready-made word chunks, presumably stored in speakers' memories as holistic entities, subtly characterize the major national varieties of English. For other PCEs, more comprehensive analysis of this issue is required, yet it is possible to cite a few studies which confirm the importance of this line of thinking. In section 4.1 two such attempts were outlined, namely the articles by Olavarria de Errson and Shaw (2003) and Mukherjee and Hoffmann (2006). These two papers prove that in Indian English certain structures and verbal complementation patterns are strongly preferred over others which prevail in British English – so Indian English is going its own way in terms of quantitative structural preferences, slowly but consistently. Some work has been done on varying preferences of functionally equivalent constructions and uses in different PCEs, e.g. on modal verbs by Collins (2005). Schneider (2004b) finds that there are variety-specific preferences with respect to uses of phrasal verbs: in Singapore, phrasal verbs are extremely common and colloquial, displaying both a wide range of types and a high frequency of tokens, while in East Africa, and in Tanzania in particular, they are used rather rarely and in comparatively formal contexts. An example of a specific preference is the fact that East African English tends to avoid *help out* but uses the word *assist* and its derivatives with exceptional frequency. Such distributional relations are precisely what we would expect on the basis of the above considerations and observations.

4.2.2   Sources of knowledge How do we know, then, which properties characterize individual PCEs? Typically, the earliest evidence at any location is rather anecdotal, based on personal observations. Obviously, this approach is prone to lead to the mistaken classification of indigenous uses as "deviance" from a putatively correct norm of reference. An interesting case in point is reported and analyzed by Gordon (1998), who systematically collected early written commentaries, primarily by school inspectors, on features of contemporary New Zealand English speech (and found them to be fairly inaccurate when compared to recordings from the same period). For instance, she quotes a school inspector complaining in 1908 about the fact that some New Zealanders say " 'paintud' for *painted*" (76), thus providing early evidence for the centralization of /ɪ/. This is certainly interesting and useful but too strongly dependent on chance findings of such remarks, so later investigations have built on more systematic data compilations.

Serious scholarship requires and has led to the strategic collection of representative data, i.e. recordings and text collections, which are now available for many PCEs. Nowadays, it is customary to analyze large electronic collections of texts, spoken and written. The most widely used source for comparative investigations of PCEs is the "International Corpus of English" (ICE) project with its individual subcorpora (see Greenbaum 1996 and the project's homepage at http://www.ucl.ac.uk/english-usage/ice/), used, for instance, in the above-mentioned studies by Collins (2005) and Schneider (2004b). However, for certain queries, notably research into low-frequency phenomena, it turns out that the ICE corpus size of about one million words per variety is not enough, so some researchers have compiled considerably larger corpora, usually based on online versions of local newspapers, for their own purposes (such as Olavarria de Errson and Shaw 2003, and Mukherjee and Hoffmann 2006). Typically, standard corpus-linguistic software allows easy access to such text collections, providing, as it does, automatically generated word lists, frequency counts, keyword-in-context concordances, etc. Again, however, for certain types of problems it is necessary to go beyond what is conventionally available. For instance, Mittmann (2004) had some computer programs specially written to extract recurrent word sequences from her corpora.

4.2.3   Perception, attitudes, reactions Let us turn to the speakers' perspective now: to what extent are they aware of the properties of local varieties of English, and what do they think about them? The first question is difficult to answer, and of course assessments would also vary from one region to another. Basically, speakers can be assumed to consider their own speech habits as unmarked unless this assumption is questioned somehow, e.g. by deriding them (Mufwene, p.c. 2005). In many cases speakers will be aware of features that distinguish their speech from that of their neighbors or from that of other social groups in the vicinity. In other cases, a persistent exonormative tradition of comparing PCEs with a British standard may have made them conscious of salient forms and patterns as well as of the special status of local words. For instance, every Singaporean knows about "Singlish," the subject of a lot of public debate; and most Indians and Australians would probably be aware of the distinctiveness of their accents. On the other hand, whether white South Africans would consider their speech as special is difficult to judge (Raj Mesthrie agrees they do not consider it as "marked" in world terms; p.c. 2006); and West Africans uphold the ideal of a British pronunciation although the vast majority of speakers from the region speak with a distinctive accent.

The situation is different, however, when we turn to those properties of a variety which seems specifically distinctive: quantitative tendencies of word co-occurrences, recurrent patterns, speech habits, prefabricated phraseology – most of this operates subconsciously, below the level of speakers' awareness.

Knowledge about the existence of locally distinct speechways is of course a prerequisite for norm discussions, which tend to focus upon a few salient linguistic features. In the early phases of a contact situation, the goal is successful communication, with no attention paid to issues of linguistic correctness. Once a local variety has emerged, however, we find the typical cleavage between those who use it without caring too much, and the conservative critics who are the prime agents of the "complaint tradition" (take, for example, the school inspectors whose observations were analyzed in the work by Gordon 1998, just mentioned). For South Asia, for example, Kachru (1986:50–1) reports on the "traditional conflict between linguistic behavior and linguistic norm[:] the hypothetical norm continues to be British English, especially RP, although this norm is seldom available and even more seldom attained." The strive toward an endonormative orientation characterizes the transition to phase 4 in the Dynamic Model; typically this is a matter of public debate, with its pedagogical and political dimensions considered (see Kachru 1986:96–7). It usually takes a while, and in some cases fierce debates and conflicts, for the balance to tip toward the acceptance of an endonormative orientation.

The wider context of all of this, of course, is the issue of language attitudes. For Inner Circle varieties, this has been a traditional topic of sociolinguistic research, beginning with Labov's classic study of the speech of New York City (1966). In the newly vibrant PCEs, there is less interest in attitudes toward indigenous varieties and their features, though there is of course discussion on the suitability of standard English versus locally colored usage for formal purposes like business contexts (see Gill 2002a, 2002b for Malaysian English as an example). What is more commonly debated is the role of English in general, both in a given society and as an international language. English has been portrayed as a means of both liberation and oppression, and the history of the language is full of strange paradoxes. For instance, the traditional policy of British administrators in "exploitation colonies" of trying to withhold English language competence from the masses, with access to learning of the language only granted to an elite of prospective co-administrators, stands in direct juxtaposition with the strive toward English which is visible in so many countries in Asia and Africa today (Brutt-Griffler 2002). This works down to the family level, where many parents wish to pass English on to their children to provide them with better opportunities in life. So while English is a despicable "killer language" for some, it is "associated with universalism, liberalism, secularism and internationalization" (Kachru 1992:11) for others.

Let us now get back to the micro-level of the relationship between attitudes and the evolution (i.e. selection or avoidance) of individual linguistic forms. It is undisputed that a speaker's attitude toward languages and language varieties will be a major factor in his or her linguistic choices. The Dynamic Model, supported by accommodation and identity theory, predicts that via language attitudes a speaker's social identity alignment will determine his or her language behavior in detail. Note that there is no implication made here that these developments have anything to do with language consciousness: accommodation works irrespective of whether the feature selected and strengthened to signal one's alignments is a salient marker of which a speaker is explicitly aware or an indicator which operates indirectly and subconsciously.

Documentations of an immediate connection between a speaker's language attitude and social alignment on the one hand and his or her linguistic accommodation, e.g. accent choices, on the other are rare, and hardly available at all from L2 contexts. I would like to show how this happens in everyday contexts, at the down-to-earth speaker level, by quoting two suggestive examples from North America. The first one shows how tiny accent differences are strongly meaningful (and thus deliberately chosen or avoided) by individuals; the second one illustrates how speech communities adopt a new pronunciation to position themselves quite delicately in a complex sociolinguistic setting.

To get an impression of how speakers consciously manipulate their accent choices, consider Bernstein (2006). The author documents the varying social significance of a single vocalic feature, the monophthongization of /aɪ/, in different regions and environments in the Southern US. In Texas, using [aː] for /aɪ/ in all environments, including before voiceless consonants, is a marker of regionality, also regional pride. However, in Alabama it is only pre-voiced and open-syllable environments in which [aː] is positively evaluated and associated with a traditional Southern identity. In contrast, before voiceless consonants speakers find ungliding indicative of a "country" or "hick" person. For instance, a young female respondent from Alabama comments on people who pronounce *light* as [laːt]: "That sounds really hick. In a job interview, you can't say that, or people will think you're ignorant – that you go barefoot and wear overalls" (227). Thus, speakers deliberately select or avoid pronunciation variants to project the social images and alignments which they desire.

Similar processes can be observed on the level of the speech community. For illustration, I have chosen an example from the Great Lakes region in the US. For a few decades sociolinguists have shown the "Northern Cities Shift," a rotating change of the short vowels, to be spreading in a cascade-like fashion across the big cities in the northeastern US, including Detroit. Based upon acoustic analyses of a single change, the raising of /æ/, Evans et al. (2006) investigate how the accommodation to this innovative urban norm is adopted at different speeds, to different degrees and for different motives by three social groups in the countryside surrounding Detroit. Long-standing rural Michiganders adopt the innovation fairly rapidly but a little hesitantly, which reflects their split attitude to the city: for females, the urban area is perceived as fashionable but also crime-ridden and thus problematic for raising families; for males, city people have better opportunities but as practitioners of a rural hunting culture they deride the urban weekend hunters. The so-called "Ypsituckians," descendants of in-migrants from the Appalachian mountains, adjust to what they perceive as the local norm, with females, the young, and the middle class in the lead, thus loosening their home network density and ultimately paving the way for the abolishment of their post-Appalachian identity. African-Americans who live in the area gradually adopt the changes as well but do so for instrumental, not integrative purposes, due to racial discrimination; i.e. their continuing identity primarily as African-Americans, linguistically and culturally, remains intact. Evans et al. conclude: "we have found here ... that local identities are important in the delimitation of dialects and the progress of dialect change" (2006:196).

4.3 The road to nativization: linguistic processes

4.3.1 Background: parameters of language change

The linguistic processes which are involved in the genesis of PCEs are manifold and difficult to distinguish, given the complexity of issues and the constant interaction between various factors. In specific situations, individual components in this multi-layered setup of influences may be dominant or recessive, as determined by the context, and to a certain extent also by chance effects. Ultimately, understanding the factors which shape the emergence of PCEs is rooted in the broader linguistic domain of understanding the principles of language change (e.g. Aitchison 1991; McMahon 1994; Croft 2000; Labov 1994, 2001). When we compare the evolution of PCEs with processes of change in general, we do come across a few specifics and differences, like the importance of contact effects in the genesis of PCEs; but basically there are many similarities between descriptions of both processes – the former can be regarded as a subtype of the latter.

Factors which keep the ball of language change rolling have generally been divided into language-internal and language-external ones (e.g. Gerritsen and Stein 1992; Labov 1994, 2001); I will consider these in turn.

All languages are always changing – that seems a trivial observation, and it seems to be the delicate and unstable balance between certain language-*internal* properties (excluding language use and social settings) which is responsible to some extent for this continuous process. It is more difficult to account for why this is so. After all, wouldn't a stable system be preferable for a variety of reasons? It may be hypothesized that constant fluctuation reflects the biological foundations of human language as one facet of human behavior: a complex system in which chaotic components alternate with phases and components characterized by relative equilibrium (and it is true that some subsystems of language organization are stable for a certain period of time) seems advantageous in the need to continuously adjust to changing environmental conditions. The complexity and instability of language presumably derives from both internal system imbalances and the interaction between subsystems. Internal imbalances may have to do with articulatory conditions, for instance: a greater flexibility of the front articulators in the oral cavity (as against the back ones) may conflict with a desire to equally divide the space available amongst vowel and consonant phonemes; consonant inventories show a trend toward systematic relationships (of pairs of voiced and voiceless consonants, for instance, or series produced at specific places of articulation), and so on.[4] On the basis of such factors sounds may be redistributed (phonemes shift, merge, split, or get lost). Universally "marked" sounds, which are rare in languages of the world, are likely to be replaced by others. This explains, for example, why both in many dialects of English (e.g. in Shetland and Ireland) and in many PCEs (e.g. in Newfoundland, Maori English, and Fiji English) the interdental fricatives /ð/ and /θ/ tend to be replaced by the homorganic stops /d/ and /t/, respectively (Blevins 2006: 11; using Schneider et al. 2004 as evidence, Blevins documents many more "natural" tendencies of evolutionary phonology in PCEs.)

However, phonological change (especially erosion, the loss of certain sounds in specific positions) may affect the morphological marking system of grammatical categories. This, in turn, has consequences for syntactic arrangement principles.[5] Furthermore, discourse markers and other lexical items can become grammaticalized; syntactically relevant words may be cliticized and thus become factors in the morphological subsystem, and so on – the potential for continuous internal innovation seems infinite.

In addition, there are possible effects of the relationship between language and cognition. In recent years linguists have come to increasingly accept that language is not a self-sufficient "system," hanging out there somewhere "in thin air," as it were, but it is determined strongly by human cognition and its conditions. Hence, cognitive principles (of whatever kind), e.g. trends supporting simplicity, iconicity, paradigmatic regularity, a one-to-one relationship between form and meaning, or the explicit marking of semantically salient categories, clearly play a role in language evolution. They are best viewed as related to the language-internal causes of change, perhaps as one strong determining branch in addition to physiological factors in the narrow sense. Note, however, that conflicting tendencies typically interact with each other, so it is not implied that cognitive factors lead to anything that could be called "optimization."

Ongoing internal changes, this proneness to introduce linguistic innovations without any noticeable external trigger, characterize PCEs like any other language, of course, and may account for some of the structural features of these language varieties. In addition, PCEs may simply be viewed as branches of the English language, sharing its inherent tendencies for long-term change. Trudgill (2004:133–6), for instance, argues that New Zealand English inherited and continued some sound changes which had been initiated but not carried out further in its British donor dialects.

Major *external* factors of change have to do either with contact, when different linguistic systems interact with each other and one system adopts elements from the other, or with social criteria (like prestige, status orientation, or the signaling of group alignments), which may cause certain linguistic elements to be preferred over others.

Contact results in the "remolding of features, often from diverse dialects or languages, into a new system" (Mufwene 2001a:318–9). In many situations of language contact, including those which lead to PCEs, the relationship between the speaker groups and language varieties involved is not equal in terms of power and persistence, so based upon a model drawn from pidgin and creole studies it is customary to distinguish superstrate and substrate components, the input of the socially superior and dominant "high" status group as against the "low," dominated group's contributions, respectively. In PCE-forming situations, this dichotomy tends to correspond to the contributions of the STL and the IDG (or also ADS) strands, respectively, and, given that PCEs are varieties of English after all, it is customary to view their superstrate-derived components as manifestations of continuous transmission from the superstrate, while conspicuous substrate contributions are typically filed as contact effects. A special subtype of inter-variety contact within the STL strand, however, is dialect contact.

Social factors derive either from the varying prestige attributed to specific groups in a society (and, correspondingly, their speech characteristics) or from purely demographic conditions. These factors regulate the uses of linguistic forms in communication. Status differences may influence people's linguistic choices because they determine who wishes to copy whom (with accommodation and identity marking being variants of this mechanism). Demographic relations, in purely quantitative terms, are responsible for the frequencies of use of individual forms by speakers and, conversely, the regularity of listeners' exposure to them, and hence they determine their amount of perceptive and cognitive entrenchment. Forms used by the majority group of speakers will be uttered as well as perceived more frequently than minority uses, and are thus likely to be copied and spread even further.

The distinction between internal and external factors of change intersects with processes grounded in the idiolect and mechanisms that cause innovations to spread to the communal level and to be adopted by a community. It may be hypothesized that innovations occur in the speech of individuals because of internal conditions but they spread to the community for external reasons.

4.3.2   Filling the feature pool: linguistic processes

When looking into the sources and processes which have ultimately produced the elements of PCEs, again we find a set of complex, interacting phenomena. On a top level, we can distinguish continuity, i.e. the transmission of English forms and elements; innovation, i.e. the emergence of

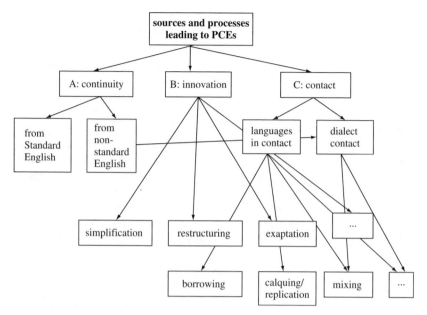

Figure 4.1: Sources and processes leading to PCEs

new elements for internal reasons; and contact, i.e. the selection and adoption of elements from different, competing systems. Each of these phenomena can then be broken down into constituent components. Some processes and components cannot be uniquely assigned to just one of these top-level domains, which adds to the complexity of relations. Dialect contact, for instance, is obviously related to language contact. The difference between these two is that in dialect contact the subsystems which get in touch with each other and influence each other mutually are historically related and more or less similar; on the other hand, many of the processes to be observed in contact between different languages can be identified in contact situations between dialects as well. Dialect contact could thus be viewed as either a type of contact or simply as a subtype of continuity from nonstandard English input of different kinds.

Figure 4.1 brings some order to these phenomena by pointing out important sources and processes which have contributed substantially to the emergence of PCEs and their mutual relationships. These components will then be discussed in turn. Note that by containing empty cells the diagram suggests that the listings are not exhaustive, and the arrangement is definitely not the only possible one; the figure just suggests one way of systematizing a set of complex interrelationships. Furthermore, it should be clear that most of these factors are closely related to each other and interwoven with each other (contact triggers internal innovation; restructuring modifies transmitted, inherited forms, and so on). Like all model-building, singling them apart is a useful conceptual and heuristic exercise but obscures the complexity of processes and fuzzy boundaries in reality.

4.3.2.1 Continuity The backbone of the grammar of PCEs remains the grammar of English through a process of direct historical transmission across generations, originally in the STL community during the process of colonial migration, later via all speakers who have adopted English and speak it regularly. This concerns the retention of both standard and non-standard English features, albeit to varying degrees. In exploitation colonies, with primarily scholastic transmission of English through the education system, as for instance in India or Malaysia, mostly standard patterns have been preserved, so that in these countries even nonstandard uses which are otherwise extremely common and widespread, such as multiple negation, are exceptional. Style assignments may shift as well, of course. Written Indian English, for example, has the reputation of being relatively stiff and conservative, of using constructions and expressions which in British English are stylistically marked as highly formal in a wider range of contexts.

In settlement colonies and also trade colonies, on the other hand, many nonstandard forms have been passed on and constituted the basic input for the formation of new varieties. In historical and theoretical linguistics there has long been a tendency to neglect the impact of nonstandard diffusion, because especially in language pedagogy the emphasis lay on the educated standard. It is clear, however, that the majority of settlers and emigrants – merchants, sailors and soldiers in addition to administrators to Asia; convicts to Australia; farmers to New Zealand; and so on – came from the lower walks of life and brought their dialectal speech with them. Hickey (2004b) explicitly set out to examine the "legacies" of English dialect transportation to the colonies, and this book also contains a comprehensive and very useful listing of dialectal features which have been spread around the globe, looking into their origins and diffusion. Simo Bobda (2003:18–30) argues that nonstandard dialect diffusion may have played a larger part than is traditionally assumed in Africa as well, suggesting that a wide range of African pronunciation features may well have been derived from colonial dialect input rather than mother-tongue interference, as has mostly been assumed. Examples include eastern Nigerian /ɛ/ in NURSE (possibly transported by Scottish and Irish missionaries), West African /u/ and /ʊ/ in STRUT (possibly from northern

England), and /l/ vocalization in parts of West Africa (which is common in London and some southern English counties as well).

4.3.2.2 Innovation and exaptation The second major parameter to explain features of PCEs is innovation. In contrast with contact-induced phenomena to be dealt with in section 4.3.2.3, like calques or borrowings, by innovation I mean the results of internal change and linguistic creativity, something that, as was stated earlier, characterizes all languages at all times. I will discuss three major, broadly defined types which highlight specific properties of processes but need not be considered as mutually exclusive: simplification (and regularization), restructuring (together with analogical formation and grammaticalization), and exaptation (which is closely related to the notion of reallocation).

To say that *simplification* makes language simpler is not as simple a statement as it may seem. The notion of simplicity is largely a pre-theoretical, intuitive one, lacking a precise definition. Certainly it has something to do with the number of units in a system: The system of five short vowels without length distinctions in East African English (/i, e, a, o, u/ after Schmied 2004b:928) is clearly "simpler" than the RP system with six short and six long stressed and two unstressed vowels (after Upton 2004:220). However, there is also a down side to this: while articulatory movements are allowed more freedom because fewer vocalic contrasts need to be distinguished (and are thus "simpler" to perform), on the lexical level the reduced set of vowel phonemes leads to a much higher probability of word homophony, which may result in misunderstandings and thus make communication, and the language as a whole, less efficient. A second, important form of simplicity is regularity: when a single rule applies throughout a paradigm and there are no exceptions this is clearly a processing advantage, and also easier from a learner's perspective. For example, when Malaysian English extends the rule "append an *–s* to express plural" to all kinds of nouns, yielding forms like *staffs* or *accommodations* (Baskaran 2004a:1076), this seems intuitively simpler than the standard English rule of pluralizing some words but not these (and many others) because they are "mass nouns." On the other hand, Malaysian English is thereby giving up a distinction which is meaningful and may thus be of value in some contexts. So, whenever we talk about simplicity we have to take this with a pinch of salt – there is a natural limitation to oversimplification in language (see below toward the end of this section).

Mechanisms which can be subsumed under the umbrella notion of simplification include the following:

Loss: when units fall into disuse, this reduces the number of items in opposition with each other, and hence makes the resulting set of options simpler. For example, African-Bahamian English speakers regularly omit the possessive -*s* (Reaser and Torbert 2004:399); Australian Aboriginal English lacks past-tense marking (Malcolm 2004a:658); and Tok Pisin makes no gender distinctions in third-person singular pronouns (which is always *em*; Smith 2004:723). Loss of forms also occurs in the process of koinéization, in an early phase which Trudgill (2004) labels "rudimentary levelling": "any very localised features which diminished mutual intelligibility would have been particularly susceptible to loss" (89).

Regularization: this is a term which is usually applied in morphological paradigms when for the expression of a consistent grammatical category the same formative (e.g. morpheme) is appended to all possible units (stems), while in a reference or source variety it is not used with certain words (which are then typically categorized as irregular). Classic cases, which are fairly common in several nonstandard dialects of English, include the adoption of regular past tense endings by verbs which in standard English do not allow them (e.g. *knowed* for *knew*) or (less commonly) the use of the noun plural suffix with irregular nouns (e.g. *mouses* for *mice*).

Analogy: analogy typically denotes the transfer of a pattern or relationship from one domain to another one which shows some similarities but is not identically structured before the application of an analogical change. Regularization, as just described, can thus be regarded as a form of analogy; but there are other forms of "generalization" as well. For example, Cameroonian English has extended the use of the tag *isn't it* to practically all tagged clauses, irrespective of the matrix verb and polarity in the main clause, as in *Ngwana didn't do the work, isn't it?* – "a clear case of simplification," according to Mbangwana (2004:905). What has happened here is that in analogy to one set of main clauses with *be* and positive polarity, where *isn't* would be used in many other varieties as well (as in *This is easy, isn't it?*), the form of the tag has been generalized to be used with any other main clause predicates, too. Hence, the number of alternatives from which to select in the paradigm has been reduced. My second example introduces an additional level of complexity, however. Following Chambers (1999), the form *snuck* for *sneaked* has been spreading vigorously in Canadian English over the last few decades, and Chambers hypothesizes that it "originated analogously" (124) to other verbs which have /ʌ/ as a highly salient past tense and past participle marker (e.g. *dug, spun, stuck; begun, drunk, sung*). So in one way this represents a case of analogical formation and introduces a quasi-paradigmatic regularity in some respect: when compared to *dig–dug, spin–spun*, etc., the paradigm *sneak-snuck* is analogously formed and transparent and may seem logical and simple. However, it actually runs counter to the principle of regularization and thus introduces new complexity and irregularity: in comparison with *reach–reached* etc. the form *snuck* is abnormal and requires separate storage in the mind and additional effort on the side of a learner.

Reduction of markedness (see Trudgill 2004:84 on "unmarking"): This is another concept which is intuitively appealing in principle but which becomes problematic when we start looking more closely, essentially because it is ill-defined and difficult to grasp. In pairs of unmarked and marked forms or choices, the unmarked ones are those which come naturally, occur regularly and frequently, and fit neatly in an overall system, e.g. regular forms. Marked forms, on the other hand, are unexpected and unnatural, frequently irregular and in opposition to some sort of paradigmatic principle. Hence, deleting a marked form and replacing it by an unmarked one clearly simplifies the system as such. However, this is also not without problems. One difficulty is that the concept of markedness builds upon different factors which can also operate independently of each other and may even conflict with each other: frequency of occurrence, regularity in a system or paradigm, and a psycholinguistic assessment as something being "natural" need not always coincide. Secondly, there is the tension between system-internal and cross-linguistic markedness: a phenomenon which is unusual in the world's languages in a comparative, typological perspective (i.e. cross-linguistically marked) may be perfectly normal and common within the structure of any given language which happens to employ this particular device on a regular basis. Actually, it is unclear whether such typological considerations should be taken into account, because individuals may not even have access to the putatively less marked options (Mufwene 2001b and p.c. 2005). Finally, marked forms are not necessarily disfavored, as the above considerations might seem to imply; they may in fact be highly useful because they are so salient and can thus holistically encode and evoke an entity instantaneously, while a compositional segmentation and analysis might be more demanding in terms of the cognitive energy spent in the perception and analysis of an utterance. Hence, it is not a chance coincidence that irregular forms in languages at the same time tend to be high-frequency ones (while less frequent units succumb to regularization more easily). It is economical to encode a frequently recurring, complex concept holistically rather than to go through a compositional analysis at every instance of its occurrence. The classic example of this in English is the paradigm of *to be*, which, with its highly suppletive forms *be, am, is, are*, etc., has departed widely from the former regular option (*beom, bist, bið*, etc.) which it once had (in addition to alternative options derived from other paradigms).

Restructuring involves the systematic rearrangement and reinterpretation of constituents and constituent sequences in language evolution, including "loss of some units or rules, addition of new ones, and certainly modifications in the direction of simplification, generalization, or complexification by the addition of conditions to the application of a rule" (Mufwene 2001b:13). In that sense, it can actually be regarded as a superordinate term of grammatical change which subsumes simplification, exaptation, and so on – though for reasons of clarity it seems advisable to keep these special types apart. Restructuring may operate via reanalysis, i.e. subsequent speaker generations analyze and understand the same constituent sequences differently in their mental grammars, and this repositioning in a grammatical system may lead to further modifications and realignments, the emergence of new patterns and relationships.

A rather simple example of restructuring can be drawn from observing the interrogative system of Pakistani English as described by Mahboob (2004:1051). In this variety, *wh*-questions may lack inversion (as in *What this is made of?*) but inversion is observed in indirect questions (e.g. *I asked him where is he?*). The relationship and similarity with standard English (and other dialects with similar innovations, for that matter) remains obvious, but some constituent sequence conventions have been modified, thus yielding a slightly different system of arrangements and uses of certain structures.

Another case in point is the "associative plural," the use of *and them* in some varieties. The constituent sequence is transparent as such, meaning 'including a set of contextually defined people.' In some varieties (e.g. Appalachian English in the US, Montgomery 2004:261; or Fiji English, Mugler and Tent 2004:775) the meaning of this form gets pragmatically narrowed down to not any people but only those conventionally associated with the previous referent, so *John and them* is 'John and his relatives (and possibly close friends)' – restructuring imposes a new semantic constraint. The pattern may be further reduced to the form *them* only, for example in Gullah (*Sara dem* 'Sarah and her family/friends/associates,' Mufwene 2004b:359), Liberian Settler English (Singler 2004:888), or South African Indian English (Mesthrie 2004b:985–6). Finally, the last stage most explicitly illustrates grammaticalization (which can be regarded as a very special subtype of restructuring): *dem*, placed immediately after a noun, turns into a plural morpheme (e.g. in Jamaican Creole, Patrick 2004:434–6), so *di member dem* means 'members.'

A system is also restructured in a special way in cases of *split* (or bifurcation), when one unit splits up into two. Deterding (2005) documents an interesting case of an ongoing phonological split in Singaporean English. He shows that independently of any British input the mid-front vowels of Singaporean English are realized in clearly two phonetically distinct ways: some words, including *egg, bed, dead* and also *vague, made* have a relatively close /e/ vowel, while others like *peg, bed, fed* or *bread* have an open /ɛ/ quality.

Grammaticalization, the transition of a lexical item to a grammatical marker, is a process which has been widely discussed in linguistics (e.g. Hopper and Traugott 1993), and is commonly viewed as a special case of reanalysis. It involves constituent processes such as formal reduction, semantic bleaching, and functional specialization. Wee (2003) provides an example from Singaporean English which can be viewed in this perspective, with part of a lexical phrase turning into a discourse particle. Wee observes that *know* behaves like the well-documented discourse markers of Singaporean English (*lah, meh,* etc.), e.g. in utterances like *The coffee very hot, know* (7). Investigating the track of nativization of this form, he argues that it derives from the English discourse marker *you know* but adjusts it to structural conditions of colloquial Singaporean English. The Singaporean discourse particles are all monosyllabic, occur clause-finally, and serve discourse–pragmatic functions. English *you know* possesses two of these three properties, and Singaporean English as a pro-drop language allows the third one to emerge, so ultimately *you know* becomes *know*, and this form joins the class constituted by *lah, lor,* and so on, and becomes a new discourse particle itself. In this process it not only changes its formal make-up and restricts its functional range but it also gives up some of its distributional potential: unlike *you know, know* no longer occurs clause-initially or clause-medially.

Some contact varieties, notably pidgins and creoles, of course provide many further examples of grammaticalization, typically with an English lexical item turning into a new grammatical marker. An interesting example is provided by new and distinct third-person singular pronouns in Fiji English, categorized by human and non-human referents and derived from *fellow* and *thing*, respectively: *Fella wake up* 'she woke up'; *the thing take time* 'it took ...' (Mugler and Tent 2004:774). Interestingly enough, the word *fellow* was also grammaticalized in Tok Pisin, but in a totally different direction: in the form *–pela*, it became a noun classifier and a formative in the pronoun paradigm (Smith 2004:722–3), as illustrated by *nupela* 'new' or *mipela* 'exclusive first-person plural pronoun.'

Another interesting type of structural innovation involves what Lass (1990) very pointedly called "doing things with junk," conventionally known as *exaptation*, "the opportunistic co-optation of a feature whose origin is unrelated or only marginally related to its later use" (80): at any given time, useful items and structures which arose without any particular reason and just happened to be available, as it were, started to adopt a function. Related labels and notions, also emphasizing the assignment of a new function though not necessarily the lack of one before, are "recycling" or, conventionally used in the context of dialect contact (Trudgill 2004), "reallocation." Mufwene rightly observes: "there is little in the structures of the new vernaculars that has not been 'recycled' ... features have been modified, 'exapted', to fit the new systems" (2001b:5). Actually, there are two different kinds of reassigning a function to an existing form: its new role may be either functional (i.e. a form adopts a structural function) or sociostylistic (in the sense of Trudgill's definition of reallocation: forms "will in the new dialect become social class variants, stylistic variants or, in the case of phonology, allophonic variants"; 2004:88).

Interesting examples of exaptation in the structural sense are provided by some of the preverbal markers of Caribbean or West African pidgins and creoles. For example, in the creoles of Jamaica and Tobago or in Ghanaian Pidgin the word *been* has been "recycled" to become a marker of a remote past. In Cameroonian Pidgin the word *fit* is assigned a new use as a marker of polite request (*We fit go sinima dis nait?*; Ayafor 2004:919). And so on – further examples are not difficult to find.

Sociostylistic reallocation can be illustrated by both grammatical forms (e.g. the use of *ain't* in North America) and pronunciation features (like the low-back diphthong onset of North Carolina's *hoi toiders*). Both are commonly employed and identified as group and class indicators – an option which, of course, derives immediately from the role of individual linguistic forms to serve as identity markers through accommodation.

4.3.2.3 Contact Language contact can interfere with most of the afore-mentioned mechanisms, triggering or accelerating various types of innovation, and it contributes some phenomena of its own. Typically, contact results in the transition of some kind of linguistic material from a source language to a recipient language. The easiest and most obvious case is lexical *borrowing* – discussed and illustrated in section 4.1.2 and elsewhere in this book, also with respect to the developmental phases in which typical kinds of loans occur. Grammatical morphemes and items can also be borrowed, though this occurs much less readily and typically goes hand in hand with some sort of restructuring. Heavy borrowing of extended stretches of linguistic forms leads to code-switching or, trans-cending a simple notion of one language taking something in from another, language mixing and blending. It was mentioned in 3.2.4.4 and will be illustrated in chapter 5 that in some respects mixed codes are closely related to PCEs.

With respect to the grammatical make-up of contact varieties, perhaps the most interesting product of contact is the process known as "calquing" or, more broadly, "grammatical *replication*." A recent book (Heine and Kuteva 2005) has surveyed such processes systematically, looking into the relationship between contact-induced changes and grammaticalization in particular. Grammatical or conceptual material is transferred from a "model language" to a "replica language." In this process speakers seek equivalence relations between both languages and thus transfer both patterns (recurrent discourse pieces) and functional categories. What happens in most cases, according to the authors, is that a minor pattern of the replica language gets re-functionalized under the impact of some element or pattern of the model language. This process frequently follows the principles of grammaticalization and results in a new grammatical system in the replica language.

My observation that structural nativization in PCEs typically affects the lexicogrammatical borderline is indirectly confirmed by Heine and Kuteva (2005:43), who state that "speech formulas" and "syntactic categories with variable lexical filling" are primarily affected. They find that in contact varieties "incipient categories" emerge which have a characteristic set of properties: they are optionally used, morphosyntactically and phonetically similar to source categories, functionally ambiguous between earlier and innovative meanings, and not generally recognized by speakers (as is characteristic of the "complaint tradition" in the emergence of PCEs): "'purist' grammarians and language planning organizations are likely to deny their existence, and their use is discouraged in formal education" (71). In contact-induced grammaticalization, speakers use the resources available in the replica language to create an equivalent of a model language category (81); the process as described by Heine and Kuteva (2005) clearly also captures what happens in the emergence of PCEs:

> In order to develop a structure that is equivalent to the one in the model language, speakers choose among the use patterns that are available in the replica language the one that corresponds most closely to the model, frequently one that until then was more peripheral and of low frequency of use, and they activate it – with the effect that a peripheral pattern gradually turns into the regular equivalent of the model, acquires a high frequency of use, and eventually emerges as a full-fledged grammatical category. (121)

They also agree that grammatical replication in pidgins and creoles "does not differ essentially from what can be observed in other languages" (243).

Dialect contact represents a special context, similar to language contact in many respects but involving exchange between closely related and normally mutually intelligible varieties of a language rather than two different languages. In the present context it is relevant primarily for what happens in intra-settler communication in phase 1 and thereafter, the process of koinéization. Trudgill (1986) and more recently Trudgill (2004) – building upon his earlier study but incorporating new insights from the "Origins of New Zealand English" project – provide comprehensive surveys of the processes to be observed and the problems involved (but see also the classic study by Siegel 1987 and the eight principles outlined by Kerswill and Williams 2000). Trudgill's (2004) thesis seems provocative in that he proposes dialect contact to operate deterministically, i.e. he believes that if the input ingredients of a mixture are known the broad outline of results can be predicted. Looking more closely, however, a reader will find that he introduced a number of sensible caveats which drastically reduce the predictive power of this claim (like restricting it to "tabula rasa" situations of previously uninhabited territories, in which an early generation of children finds no peer group to adjust to). Trudgill lists and illustrates six different mechanisms involved in new-dialect formation:

- *mixing*, "the coming together in a particular location of speakers of different dialects of the same language, or of readily mutually intelligible languages" (84);
- *leveling*, "the loss of demographically minority variants" (84);
- *unmarking*, the tendency for unmarked forms to survive "even if they are not majority forms" (85);
- *interdialect development*, the emergence of "forms which were not actually present in any of the dialects contributing to the mixture, but which arise out of the interaction between them" (86);
- *reallocations*; and
- *focusing*, "the process by means of which the new variety acquires norms and stability" (88).

Furthermore, he posits "three different chronological stages in the new-dialect formation process which also roughly correspond to three successive generations of speakers" (89), namely first, rudimentary leveling and interdialect formation; then, variability and apparent leveling; and finally, determinism (i.e. the survival of majority forms) (see Trudgill, Maclagan and Lewis 2003; Schreier 2003b:16–21).

4.3.3   *Choosing a path: factors in diffusion and selection*

How all of this happens, i.e. how innovations in PCE-speaking societies get coined and rooted, has been mentioned before (and corresponds in principle to the classic model of language change as proposed by Weinreich, Labov and Herzog 1968), so a very brief summary should suffice here. Innovations are rarely radically new in the sense of being *ab ovo* creations that simply had not existed before; rather, they tend to be forms which were rare or restricted to certain environments, individuals or small user groups before which begin to be spreading. From individual choices such forms expand to becoming group habits, and through further cognitive entrenchment they ultimately become regular choices (rules and constructions) in a speech community.

Early on in this chapter the crucial "why" question was asked: why all these complex interactions and changes, why not stability and order? Why structural nativization, after all, which introduces new linguistic complexity and, possibly, social fragmentation? The answer, if there is a single one at all, lies in the nature and complexity of human language as "complex adaptive systems" (Mufwene 2001b:157), in the constant re-creation of language by individuals and its transmission across generations in what unavoidably remains "imperfect replication" (193). I do not think that there is an answer which is peculiar to PCEs – they are shaped by the same conditions of language change and evolution as any other language. Their individual adaptive strategies are caught by the same, characteristic tensions that shape human language, for instance between efficiency and clarity, between a tendency toward economy, striving to save (articulatory and cognitive) energy, and a tendency toward explicitness of marking, redundancy, and maximizing transparency, trying to secure communication.

Finally, given that "[n]atural selection (out of competing alternatives) plays an important role in language evolution, at the mercy of ecology" (Mufwene 2001b:147), which are the road signs or selectors which determine which forms or constructions survive while others vanish (see Mufwene 2005b)? Again, a set of factors interact, and it may be hypothesized that in this case the external ones are more powerful than internal constraints. The following factors play a role (and no claim is made that this list is exhaustive or mutually exclusive):

• *demography*: Forms used by a majority of speakers have a greater chance of survival than minority uses.[6]

• *frequency*: Forms which occur frequently in communication, thus being more deeply cognitively entrenched, stand a greater chance of survival than rare ones. (Note that this criterion is related to demography, which also feeds into the intensity of production and perception, and thus entrenchment, of a form.)

• *historical depth*: According to Mufwene's "*founder principle*," newcomers adjust to norms established by earlier generations, so the earliest settlers, the founders of a new community, will establish a strong convention which is bound to persist. Note that this is related to the frequency and demography considerations – established forms of long historical standing are simply bound to be in use more frequently than those used by newcomers who at any given time are a minority; they "have acquired more and more carriers, hence more transmitters" (Mufwene 2001b:29).

- *markedness* (structural embedding) of forms: Unmarked forms, i.e. those which come naturally and those which are embedded in a systematic relationship with other, related forms, are more likely to be selected.
- *salience* of forms: Forms which are particularly salient, i.e. perceptually more conspicuous, have a greater chance of survival. (Note that this principle may conflict with the previous one, as there may be a certain correspondence between salience and marking.)
- *transparency* and *regularity*: According to Siegel (1987), regular patterns and transparent ones (whose constituent morphemes are isomorphic with specific meanings) are preferred. (Obviously, both criteria contribute to markedness.)
- *status* of speakers: Forms used by high-status speakers will tend to be copied and are thus likely to spread and survive, unlike those typical of low-status speakers. Note that "status" in this sense need not conform to official status in a society. It is not uncommon for the average person to more or less privately resent persons with an "official" high status in society, including their habits, and to feel sympathy with and copy people and uses with "*covert prestige*" instead. It may also be specific to different settings: An educated Nigerian may hold a higher status regarding western-style life but a lower one regarding ancestral culture (Mufwene, p.c. 2005). All of this is related to the complex and not easily transparent topic of people's attitudes to different speaker groups and their distinctive speech forms.
- *identity*-marking functions of linguistic forms: This is obviously related to the previous topic, though not quite the same. Speakers will copy and adopt forms used by those they wish to accommodate to, and so forms used by popular groups will tend to spread. This alignment operates both subconsciously and, less commonly, consciously.
- *similarity* or difference between L1 and L2 forms and patterns: On the one hand, similar or identical forms and patterns will tend to reinforce each other; on the other, partial similarity only may introduce misunderstandings and reanalysis. A case in point are so-called "camouflaged" forms, which seem to match familiar target language forms but obscure significant functional differences employed by a shifting group. Typological dissimilarity can be an obstacle (Heine and Kuteva 2005:234).

Going more into detail, Schreier (2003:267) lists as factors which support the retention and stabilization of nativized structures "extensive contact with non-Anglophone settlers and substantial input from non-native varieties of English, restricted formal education and absence of norm-enforcing language authority, limited out-migration and interaction with other communities."

Taken together, all of these factors are subsumed by what Mufwene (2001b) aptly called the "ecology" of a language, and the above observations elaborate on his dictum that "ecology rolls the dice" (145).

5   Countries along the cycle: case studies

In this chapter the evolutionary model developed in chapter 3 and its ensuing claims are applied to specific countries and language varieties. For obvious reasons a selection of case studies to focus on was necessary. This includes the most important PCEs and those which are particularly typical of their respective regions.

The order of presentation is basically geographical and, in the case of neighboring countries, also historical. Starting from the Pacific, we move in a broadly westerly direction. Along the Pacific Rim, the countries to be discussed are Fiji and the important settler communities of Australia and New Zealand. The former crown colony of Hong Kong represents the major stronghold of English in East Asia.[1] In South-East Asia and South Asia, the Philippines, Malaysia, Singapore, and India will be covered. Africa, with a number of countries where English holds a special status, requires a selection of regionally important and typical countries: South Africa; Kenya and Tanzania in East Africa; and Nigeria and Cameroon in West Africa. In the Caribbean, Barbados and Jamaica will be looked at more closely. Finally, in North America, Canada will deserve closer attention. The case studies discussed here serve as examples; in principle, it should be possible to apply the model to most, ideally all of the PCEs around the globe.

In each case I will identify the elements of the Dynamic Model characteristic of the phases a country has gone through so far. Typically, the presentation will primarily be structured by the phases of the Dynamic Model. Within each of these, to the extent that information is available, observations concerning the four main constituent components (history; identity constructions; sociolinguistic situation; structural consequences), as listed in Table 3.1, will be discussed in turn. In a number of cases I am suggesting cut-off dates between phases in section titles. This is for convenience and orientation – it goes without saying, as was pointed out in chapter 3, that phases always overlap in their constitutive properties and transitions take time, so in most cases such dates are symbolic icons of enduring processes and should therefore be taken with a pinch of salt.

5.1   Fiji

Phase 1, regular use of English in Fiji (see Map 5.1), by whalers, traders, and beachcombers, started early in the nineteenth century, and was reinforced by the presence of missionaries after 1835 and by the opening of a missionary school in 1894 which introduced the formal teaching of English (Siegel 1987: 29–38; Tent and Mugler 1996; Tent 2000a, 2000b, 2001a, 2001b). Early contacts with English were also enabled by a small number of European and Australian settlers as well as by visits of American ships. In 1874 Fiji was ceded by the leading local chiefs and became a British colony. Beginning in 1879 and lasting for about four decades, some 60,000 Indians (from Uttar Pradesh, Bihar, and Madya Pradesh) came to the islands of Fiji as contract laborers to work on its sugar-cane plantations (Siegel 1987), and most of them stayed after their contracts expired in 1920, laboring on small-scale leases or businesses (Tent and Mugler 2004). In addition, about 27,000 Pacific Islanders came during that period, mostly also as plantation laborers (Siegel 1987:51).

It is clear that the native Fijians have considered themselves the rightful residents of the islands, while the identity of the Indian workers and their descendants has been strongly shaped by their origin and the persistence of their culture and religion. The two main ethnic groups socialized primarily

Map 5.1: SW Pacific (Fiji, Australia, New Zealand)

amongst themselves, as Fijians worked on the plantations only in exceptional cases (Siegel 1987:39–40). Fijian, including a reduced, pidginized
form of it, also served as a lingua franca on many plantations, particularly
those where Pacific islanders were involved (69–77). Acquisition of some
Fijian by white planters was not uncommon. Its acquisition by British
administrators was officially encouraged, and the missionaries had always
used it for evangelization. Melanesian Pidgin English was in use in the
nineteenth century, but it remained restricted mainly to interactions
between Pacific Islanders and Europeans. Knowledge of English was
largely associated with formal education and restricted to elite minorities
with close contact with whites, mostly sons of chiefs. The number of
European residents has never been large. Today, according to the 1996
census, the proportion of Europeans is less than 0.5 percent (Tent 2001a:
210), and the proportion of native speakers of English is estimated to be
at about 2 percent (Tent 2001b:241). Thus, in quantitative terms a STL
strand development has been of marginal importance (though there is a
variety labeled "part-European English" by Tent 2001a:213 and 2001c,
spoken by people of mixed ethnic descent). On the other hand, English has
been shaped by the IDG strand spoken by native Fijians and by a strong
ADS strand spoken by Fiji Indians. In addition, significant minorities of
Chinese, Rotumans, and other Pacific Islanders live on the islands and
speak different forms of English.

   In line with the linguistic characteristics of phase 1, place names are local
in origin almost throughout, except for English-derived determinatum
constituents in compound toponyms. Examples include *Viti Levu, Vanua
Levu, Nabavatu, Nabukaluka, Ovalau, Suva; Suva Point, Namosi Peaks,
Kandavu Island, Yasawa Group*, and *Nanuku Reef*. The early contacts to
some extent employed an incipient pidgin, frequently labeled "South Seas
Jargon." Among Fijians of Indian descent a koiné of their Indian native
tongues called Fiji Hindi has evolved (Siegel 1987).

   Phase 2 started in the 1930s, when a policy to use English as the medium
of instruction in the education system after the first three years of elementary education was instituted, and the colonial administration handed the
authority over the education system to New Zealand institutions. This
practice resulted in large numbers of New Zealanders coming to Fiji as
teachers. Indians set up schools of their own, with English as an important
element of the curriculum; by this time it was clear that many Indians
were there to stay. English was now taught widely and promoted heavily
as a lingua franca to form a bond between the two major population
groups, and bilingualism with English started to spread rapidly. From
about the 1930s the Indians and their descendants constituted the majority
of the population, outnumbering the native Fijians, yet they gained in

political influence only slowly. Early in the twenty-first century the demographic proportions turned again, with native Fijians constituting slightly more than half of the population. In 1970 Fiji became independent. Two military coups, in 1987 and 2000, were meant to perpetuate the continuous dominance of ethnic Fijians, though in both cases democracy was successfully restored, and there have been Indian-led governments. In 2005 a "Reconciliation and Unity Commission" was proposed to overcome the nation's "coup culture." So far, both ethnic affiliations and ethnic tensions have remained strong.

Today English is used as "a de facto official language" in the country (Tent and Mugler 1996:251), the language of government, jurisdiction, the media, commerce, and, to a large extent, education, and a second language for the majority of the population. The contexts of language use as well as the semantics of loan words in Fiji English (Tent 2001a) place Fiji in phase 2, although it has reached political independence (which is normally associated with phase 3). The orientation is clearly exonormative (Tent and Mugler 2004:751). Bilingualism is fairly widespread but associated with education and, especially, urbanity. So, as is characteristic of phase 2, it is still group-specific and sociolinguistically conditioned (see Tent 2001b). Establishing English as a lingua franca between the two major population groups may have been successful for communicative purposes (although even for that function other languages, including simplified versions of Fijian or Fiji Hindi, may also be chosen), but it does not appear to have affected identity constructions, which, given persistent ethnic tensions, are still predominantly ethnicity- rather than nation-based. "The motivation to learn and use English is almost purely instrumental, not integrative" (Tent 2001a:212).

Consequently, at this point several ethnic varieties can be observed which correlate with education and are predominantly marked by lexical interferences from the respective ethnic mother tongues. Tent (2001a:213–4) lists not only Fiji English and Indo-Fijian English, but also Chinese Fiji English and Rotuman English, with a continuum between acrolectal and basilectal forms occurring in each of these cases (see Siegel 1991; Tent and Mugler 2004:752–3).

Mugler and Tent (1998) provide some interesting survey data on uses of English in specific domains and document its slow expansion, especially among Indo-Fijians, but they make it perfectly clear that whatever shift may be occurring is no more than a shift toward an increase in bilingualism, not involving loss of the ethnic native language. On the other hand, Moag observes that "the present generation of Chinese have already switched to English" (1992:247). Even if this relates to a minority group in Fiji it constitutes an interesting model case, in line with my (rather than Moag's) cycle. What may play a role in the future is the fact that English seems to be encroaching into the home environment, into parent–child interactions, and into intra-ethnic communication. This concerns especially the written mode, given difficulties associated with written Fijian and Hindi (Tent and Mugler 1996:254–5). The inclination to shift to English may be somewhat higher among Fiji Indians because of the low prestige associated with Fiji Hindi.

Linguistically speaking, the lexical characteristics of phase 2 are strongly visible in Fiji English (see Tent 2001a; Tent and Mugler 1996; Siegel 1991). Words for flora and fauna (e.g. *baka* 'banyan tree,' *yaqona* 'kava,' *tanoa* 'bowl for making kava,' *tiri* 'mangrove tree'; *dri loli* 'sea cucumber,' *walu* 'kingfish,' *kaikoso* 'kind of shell fish,' *qari* 'mud crab') and cultural objects and customs, both from Fiji and Hindi (e.g. *bure* 'Fijian-style hut,' *sulu* 'Fijian-style sarong,' *meke* 'kind of dance,' *reguregu* 'condolence gathering,' *sawai* 'kind of dessert,' *puja* 'Hindu religious rite'), abound. Some of these have ousted English synonyms: *kana* 'food, to eat,' *leqa* 'a problem,' *yaya* 'things, belongings,' *paidar* 'on/by foot,' *paisa* 'money,' *acha* 'okay.' Conversely, English words were also adopted and phonetically adjusted in the indigenous codes; for instance, *girmitiya* 'indentured laborer' stems from *agreement* (Siegel 1987:130).

There are weak indications of further progress along the cycle, although these should not be overestimated. Features typically associated with nativization, assigned to phase 3, include semantic shifts (e.g. *beans* 'salted peas,' *fibre* 'open fiberglass boat,' *playground* 'sports field,' *plastic* 'supermarket bag'), lexically complex formations like indigenous compounds made of English constituents (e.g. *big father* 'father's elder brother,' *grass-cutter* 'man who mows lawns for a living,' *carryboy* 'young man who brings customers to handicraft vendors,' *showglass* 'shop window'), as well as hybrid compounds, consisting of both English and Fiji or Hindi constituents (e.g. *bula man* 'tout,' *full kasou* 'completely drunk,' *no ghar* 'homeless,' *talanoa session* 'chat'). On the pronunciation level, Tent (2001c) examines the possibility of a pronunciation feature emerging as a local shibboleth across ethnic groupings, and Tent and Mugler (2004) provide a detailed phonetic description of the main varieties of Fiji English. Furthermore, innovations at the boundary between lexis and grammar, typical of phase 3, and some local grammatical features of uncertain spread and stability have been observed (Siegel 1987:235–7, 1991; Tent and Mugler 1996:256–7; Mugler and Tent 2004). For example:

- count uses of mass nouns like *slangs, furnitures, a legislation, show a disrespect*;
- *fella* as a third-person pronoun for "he/she";
- two innovative 1st person pronouns, viz. *us-two* as a dual exclusive and *us-gang* elsewhere; *one* as an indefinite article;

- new phrasal verbs (*cope up*, *discuss about*, *request for*) but also loss of particles in phrasal verbs (*pick* 'pick up,' *lock* 'lock up,' *throw* 'throw out');
- *been* used as a preverbal past marker (*I been study all week*) – a feature shared with other contact varieties;
- ongoing grammaticalization of *always*, *all the time* and *sometimes* as aspect markers; and
- a set of invariant tags: *èh, na, isn't it, or what, like that*.

Clearly the potential for progress toward phase 3 is visible, but all of this is not enough to diagnose the beginning of structural nativization on a broader scale, and there are no signs of codification.[2]

In the long run, the future of English will depend upon political developments: if the two major population groups succeed in getting along with each other peacefully and in constructing a joint national identity, some form of English might well be its expression; otherwise, it is unlikely to expand its present form and status substantially.

5.2   Australia

Australia (see Map 5.1) constitutes a classic case of an "ENL" or "Inner Circle" country in which the STL strand has prevailed, at least quantitatively, with the indigenous populations having been subjugated and having experienced an extreme form of an IDG-strand-type language adjustment, almost a complete shift away from their indigenous languages. By now, the country has reached phase 5, although the progression from the previous phase is an event of recent history, still in living memory.

5.2.1   Phase 1 (1788–ca. 1830s)

After earlier sightings and short landfalls by Dutch and British navigators, including James Cook, phase 1 began when the "First Fleet" landed at Botany Bay in 1788 to establish a penal colony, thus creating the colony of New South Wales. The transportation of convicts to Australia continued into the middle of the nineteenth century, though they were followed by an increasing number of free settlers. Based on this distinction, class boundaries were sharp throughout this phase (Turner 1994:278; Pawley 2004:614). Many convicts stayed after having served their sentence (in most cases for seven years) and were assigned land by the government, and the number of children born in the colony grew quickly (Kiesling 2004:419). Gradually, the area of white settlement and Britain's claims were expanded to include south-eastern and later also western and northern Australia, where new colonies were established.[3]

Clearly, the identity of the early generation of settlers and convicts was purely British. They encountered an indigenous population who practiced a totally different culture and religion. Early contacts tended to be peaceful but relatively restricted: "the local people preferred to keep with their own kind and entered communication with the English speakers only on an intermittent basis" (Malcolm 2004b:657; see also Leitner 2004b:43–4, quoting contemporary accounts). With increasing numbers of incoming Europeans, however, contact grew, and the effects upon the Aboriginal population proved devastating. They had little to resist the white men's desire for expansion, in addition to being threatened by germs against which they had no resistance. Thus, they were driven off their traditional lands and substantially decimated, also by violence, including some massacres, but primarily by epidemic diseases and the consequences of expulsion from fertile lands. The abuse of alcohol, introduced by the Europeans, has also had a devastating effect on them.

In a sociolinguistic perspective, within the white community convicts and settlers were brought together from all over the British Isles – though with a predominant fraction from south-eastern England, especially London, and also many Irish. Thus, dialect contact was the norm (Kiesling 2004:418–25; Gordon and Sudbury 2002:69). Cross-ethnically, some Aboriginals acquired some knowledge of English and assumed an active role in trade and negotiations, serving as interpreters. The most familiar case in point is the tragic story of Bennelong, the Aboriginal man perpetually commemorated by Bennelong Point in Sydney. He was captured by the British, acquired the English language, adjusted to the European culture, and was brought to England for a few years, yet when he returned he was alienated from his own people, ending up with alcohol problems and essentially without cultural roots. His story is better known and documented than many others, and perhaps it represents an extreme case, but it is probably not untypical of what happened to many of his people in the face of European settlement and expansion. There were also marginal attempts by Europeans to learn Aboriginal languages, but this remained an exception.

The linguistic characteristics of phase 1 can all be identified. The STL community provided for a classic example of dialect mixture and koinéization, documented to have occurred in the 1820s and 1830s (see Collins and Blair 2001:1–2 or Turner 1994, and the evidence cited there) and described in some detail on the phonological level by Trudgill (1986:129–46) and in Trudgill et al. (2000).[4] Presumably, this happened on two socio-stylistic levels, thus laying the foundations for the social varieties later identified by Delbridge. In addition to a middle-class, educated form an "emergent Australian working-class vernacular had probably stabilized by the mid-19th century" (Pawley 2004:614). Secondly, despite the limited impact of the indigenous population on their conquerors Australia's toponymy is strongly indigenous in character: a very large number of place names were taken over from the Aboriginals, e.g. *Wagga Wagga, Wodonga, Mundabullangana, Mungallala, Youangarra* (see Guy 1991:216; Turner 1994:305). Baker (1978:276) confirms that Australians "have used Aboriginal names fairly freely" and estimates that one third of all Australian place names derive from Aboriginal names. A jargon which later stabilized to become a pidgin developed amongst the Aboriginal people (Malcolm 2004b:657).

5.2.2   Phase 2 (ca. 1830s–1901)

There is no clear cut-off date between phases 1 and 2, an observation which, in a sense, appropriately reflects the fact that English continued to expand regionally, and thus to be rooted in new parts of Australia. The transition can reasonably be assumed to have occurred with the number of free immigrants beginning to exceed that of prisoners (ca. 1830–50) and the associated population growth and regional expansion, reflected by the establishment of new colonies (from Van Diemen's Land – now Tasmania – in 1825, via South Australia in 1836, and others, to Queensland in 1859). The expansion and transition to a stable colonial period may be taken to have been concluded by the mid-nineteenth century, with the granting of regional autonomy in 1850 and the gold rush soon thereafter. Phase 2 itself continued throughout the nineteenth century.

  No doubt the identity construction of the British settlers conformed fully to that stated for phase 2, as British (including Irish) people living on foreign soil, and so did their exonormative orientation (Leitner 2004a:94) and contact experience. There are early signs of distancing as well, however: the "Eureka Stockade," a miner's rebellion in Victoria in 1854, may be interpreted as an upheaval against a British exertion of authority experienced as unjustified. Little is known about attitudes in the IDG strand during this period. Some exchange continued, but a positive attitude amongst Aboriginals toward the Europeans was certainly prevented by the cruel treatment and indifference which they had to face. Nevertheless, English spread gradually among the Aboriginals. With their traditional patterns of life and sources of livelihood disrupted, Aboriginal people became increasingly dependent upon the settlers' communities, and some of them began to labor for the white men in exchange for food and basic commodities. Christian missions and schools were established, and brought further exposure to the European language (see Leitner 2004b:45–53). Thus, the earlier lingua franca developed into ethnolectal forms of English (Malcolm 2004a:657–8).

We find the lexical processes characteristic of this phase: the borrowing and coinage of words for fauna and flora (e.g. *kurrajong* 'kind of tree,' *waratah* 'kind of tree,' *lowan* 'kind of bird,' *bobiala* 'kind of shrub,' *coolibah, kangaroo, dingo, koala, wallaby, woylie* 'small rat-kangaroo,' *boobook* 'kind of owl,' *wobegong* 'kind of fish,' *kookaburra* 'species of kingfishers,' *currawong* 'kind of bird'; *gum-tree, grass-tree, bottlebrush, whipbird, redbill, laughing jackass*) as well as elements of the indigenous culture (e.g. *nullanulla* 'Aboriginal club,' *wurley* 'Aboriginal hut,' *kylie* 'boomerang,' *coolamon* 'hollowed out knot of wood') and, generally, objects characteristic of the new environment (*bush, outback, station, backblock*; see Ramson 1966; Turner 1966, 1994; Leitner 2004a). Similarly, Ramson (1966:114) lists "names for fauna and flora and for features of Aboriginal life" as the most important categories of early borrowings (Guy 1991:216). Leitner quantifies nineteenth-century Aboriginal loans by onomasiological categories and finds that 35.8 percent refer to flora, 27.9 percent to fauna, and 25.6 percent to social organization (2004a:154).

5.2.3   Phase 3 (1901–1942)

The onset of phase 3, nativization, and politically the time when Australia became practically independent, can be dated to 1901, when the former colonies were federated to form the Commonwealth of Australia. This was preceded by a period of early "republicanism" and, interestingly enough, early interest in Australian English (Moore 2001b:48–50). However, during the first half of the twentieth century the country remained closely associated with Britain politically (as a dominion and later Commonwealth member and through remaining constitutional ties), economically,' and culturally, as the source of the history-based identity of the STL strands. It is frequently stated that the World War I experience of the Australia and New Zealand Army Corps (ANZAC), involving heavy losses but bringing Australia to the world scene, caused a feeling of nationhood in the antipodes, and this is reflected by the intensity with which these events are still commemorated today on ANZAC Day. By that time the identity of Australians had turned to be primarily grounded in their territory of residence rather than their country of origin. In the IDG strand, marginalization continued, though population shrinkage, after heavy decimation, gradually came to a halt in that period. Indigenous men served in the military, and in turn some became accepted as citizens.

Regular contacts between whites and Aboriginals had thus become normal, and so was bilingualism amongst the indigenous population. In fact, many of them in the long run succumbed to the pressure to adjust and underwent large-scale language shift toward English (with many

Aboriginal languages having become extinct or strongly endangered; see Leitner 2004b:55–68). In the STL strand, while nativization and indigenization were going on, in formal contexts the external British language norm remained largely unchallenged.

On the strictly linguistic level, local forms and patterns on the levels of pronunciation (Horvath 2004, Bradley 2004), vocabulary (Turner 1994) and (less conspicuously) grammar (Collins and Peters 2004) developed; these have been described frequently (see Turner 1966, 1994; Leitner 2004a). In line with a general observation made in phase 3 of many PCEs, Collins and Peters (2004) explicitly note that distinctive elements of the grammar of Australian English concern "the interface between grammar and lexis" (593). Examples include a preference for *different to*, the use of *less* rather than *fewer* with plural count nouns, and a dispreference for *shall*. Pawley (2004) surveys some characteristics of colloquial, nonstandard Australian English.

Aboriginal English, partly based upon the earlier New South Wales pidgin, but then approximating nonstandard English, developed as a new ethnolect (Malcolm 2004b:657; see Leitner 2004b:110–144).[5] In a sense, this is an umbrella term for a range of IDG strand varieties, with internal regional differentiation: Malcolm (1995) gives examples of features which are "particular to specific areas" (25), and Malcolm and Koscielecki (1997:57–73) compare some differences between dialects from Western Australia and New South Wales. In general, Aboriginal English displays characteristic phenomena in its phonology (Malcolm 1995:22–6, 2004b; Malcolm and Koscielecki 1997:20–5, 57–9, 65–7), grammar (Malcolm 1995:24, 2004a; Malcolm and Koscielecki 1997:25–39, 60–4, 67–73) and lexical semantics (Malcolm 1995:25, 2001; Malcolm and Koscielecki 1997:39–41) but also, and perhaps most importantly, in its rules for the cognitive organization and pragmatic uses of texts, representing different discourse conventions (Malcolm and Koscielecki 1997:54–9), textual schemata and a different worldview (Malcolm and Rochecouste 2000; Malcolm 2001). Aboriginal English now functions as "a focus for Aboriginal identity," partly replacing lost ancestral languages of which it has preserved cognitive organizational principles referring to kinship, spirituality, environment, hunting patterns, etc. (Malcolm 2001:233).

5.2.4   Phase 4 (1942–ca. 1980s)

Phase 4, an endonormative orientation after having severed connections with the former "mother country," can be tied to a specific incident in Australian history, an "Event X" in the framework of the Dynamic Model. In 1942, during World War II, Australia was left unprotected against the threat of a Japanese attack after the fall of Singapore. To the population this event made it clear that there was a markedly disproportional relationship between themselves and the "mother country" with respect to their mutual importance for each other; it "dispelled the myth that the mother country would defend her son or daughter at whatever cost to herself" (Moore 2001c:50). Thus, in the long run the incident resulted in political self-dependence (replacing the earlier state of what could be called "dependent independence") and, ultimately, the emergence of a new, regionally founded national identity.

In the long run, the territorial foundation of this new identity brought about two sociopolitical reconsiderations with important consequences for the nation's self-definition. One, derived from the geographical location of the continent, was an orientation away from the settlers' European roots and toward the neighboring Asia-Pacific region. The "white Australia policy" which had practically restricted immigration to Europeans was gradually abolished by the 1970s, and Australia accepted a large number of new immigrants predominantly from Asian countries (Leitner 2004b:155–216). Secondly, the renewed local, territorial focus forced the dominant group of European Australians (some of them, at least) to rethink their attitude toward the indigenous populations and their assessment of their ancestors' behavior toward these groups. It is not a chance effect, therefore, that Aboriginal rights (including land titles) have become a major issue in Australian politics (Moore 2001a). Beginning in the 1970s, Aboriginal peoples fought back against their oppression with the white men's weapons, i.e. within the legal and judicial system. Notable consequences, symbolic of the increasing attention paid to the wrong that has been done to the Aboriginals, include the Aboriginal Land Rights Act of 1976, the institution of a "National Sorry Day" in 1998 (see Moore 2001c:56; Leitner 2004a: 164–5), and, in general, the initiation of a process of "healing." A High Court decision of the 1990s lifted a 1970s decision which declared Australia prior to European settlement an unoccupied *terra nullius*, thus gradually opening the road for Aboriginals to successfully reclaim some of their traditional lands. Language preservation and revitalization projects have flourished. It is impossible to undo the past, however. Not surprisingly, all of these moves have remained highly controversial. In recent years, a new conservative government has brought a backlash to these reconciliation and liberalization policies. The marginalization of Aboriginals and their deplorable fate still continue, albeit on a weaker scale than before and, perhaps, with better prospects for improvement.

Nevertheless, there is no doubt that the second half of the twentieth century saw an identity construction fully in line with phase 4: Australia was viewed as a young, self-dependent nation, rooted in her territory, connected with her

Asia-Pacific environment, increasingly accepting a multicultural and multi-ethnic population setup including the contribution of immigrants and, at least theoretically and to some extent, the indigenous population.

This entailed the acceptance of the Australian way of speaking English as a source of regional pride. Moore (2001c) dates this change: "The cultural nationalism of the 1970s went hand in hand with the acceptance of Australian English" (53; see Leitner 2004a:100–6). Today's orientation is endonormative, also in the media. Leitner (2004a:267–70) tracks the ABC's changing conventions toward endonormativity, a process which he dates between the 1940s and the 1980s. Furthermore, Australian English has been accepted internationally as one of the major reference varieties on a global scale. In Asian countries in particular, which send substantial numbers of students to Australian universities, it constitutes a possible norm of orientation (see Leitner 2004a:341–3).

Australian self-confidence, associated with Australian language, is also backed by a growing body of Australian literature, including primarily poetry and novels (some of which try to capture vernacular language). Australia has produced one Nobel Prize winner, Patrick White, Booker Prize winner Peter Carey, and other notable writers like David Malouf or Nevil Shute. Malcolm (2001) mentions the fact that "the growth of literature using Aboriginal English for non-Aboriginal (as well as Aboriginal) readers and audiences" constitutes a source of pride (2001:233).

There is strong evidence of the linguistic characteristics of phase 4, the claim to homogeneity and the beginnings of codification. Notwithstanding social-class differences, a remarkable regional homogeneity despite the size of the continent counts as standard wisdom: statements on the "much-reported extreme uniformity of Australian English" (Trudgill 1986:143) have been stereotypically repeated and can be found in most writings on the subject (e.g. Guy 1991:218–9; Gordon and Sudbury 2002:68). As Pawley points out, this observation is also valid, relatively speaking, for nonstandard speech: the high mobility of working-class Australians in the second half of the nineteenth century "ensured that regional differences ... remained small" (2004:614). Another factor which may have contributed to this homogeneity may be the deeply entrenched egalitarianism in Australian culture, also known as the "tall poppy syndrome," an inclination to "cut down the tall poppies," i.e. to stigmatize over-achievers and overly ambitious people (Peeters 2004). In a sense, this is also embodied in the distinctively Australian meaning of the word *mate* and the notion of *mateship*, which explicitly occurred in a proposed preamble to the Constitution (Moore 2001c:54).

The process of linguistic codification has also proceeded substantially in Australian English, with new national dictionaries providing the authority needed to underline the autonomy of a new national variety of English

(Moore 2001c:52). The *Macquarie Dictionary* (Delbridge et al. 1981) can practically be regarded as an explicit declaration of linguistic independence, a cornerstone in the process of the codification of a distinctly Australian variety of English and "evidence of the autonomy" of Australian English "in the public mind" (Guy 1991:215; see also Delbridge 2001; Leitner 2004a:282–9). It was soon followed by another dictionary which carries the word *National* in its title (Ramson et al. 1988). Other sources and bodies, like the *Style Manual* (Australian Government Publishing Service 1988), the *Australian English Style Guide* (Peters 1995) or the Australian Broadcasting Corporation, have also promoted endonormative orientations (Collins and Peters 2004:593). This reflects the fact that an indigenous linguistic norm is widely accepted in the country by now: based upon a longitudinal study, Bradley and Bradley (2001) report an increasingly positive attitude among Australians to Australian English.

With respect to the level of grammar, there are some structurally distinctive patterns which have been investigated and documented (see Newbrook 2001; Collins and Peters 2004; and, for the nonstandard level, Pawley 2004; and references cited there), though a distinct grammar of Australian English is unlikely to appear in the near future, given that its rules largely conform to the norms of a "common core" of standard English.[6]

5.2.5   Phase 5 (ca. 1980s–)

In the present context, perhaps the most interesting observation concerning Australian English is the ongoing birth of new dialects, the sign of having reached the end of the cycle, phase 5. In contrast with the earlier standard statements about the variety's homogeneity, in recent years the fact that internal differentiation has been developing has been receiving public awareness and scholarly attention. Among the first to observe this was Trudgill (1986), who stated: "It is interesting to note, however, that the relatively new, mixed, uniform Australian variety is now showing definite signs of beginning to develop regional differentiation" (145; see also Collins and Blair 2001:9–10) With respect to pronunciation, Australians increasingly claim that they can identify a fellow Australian's regional origin by their accent. Trudgill (1986:145), Bradley (1989) and Horvath and Horvath (1997, 2001) documented emerging regional differences on the sound level; a systematic survey is offered by Bradley (2004), who concedes that such differences are subtle but "growing" (654). For vocabulary, Bryant's work (e.g. 1989, 1997) documented regional diversity within Australian English, producing a range of word maps. Another recent source of regional words is Jauncey (2004). It is significant that in 2001 the Macquarie Dictionary Company, upon the initiative of Sue Butler and in collaboration with the

ABC, launched a large-scale project based upon a public invitation to help collect and catalogue regionalisms for the dictionary's next edition. Public reactions have been lively, and the project has yielded a broad documentation of regional words (Sue Butler, p.c. 2006) as well as some specific outcomes: the 2003 *Macquarie ABC Dictionary* and Richards (2005), which focus on Australian regionalisms, and the inclusion of many regionalisms in the fourth edition of the *Macquarie Dictionary*, published in 2005.[7]

Variation by social class, represented by the cline between "Broad," "General," and "Cultivated" varieties (Mitchell and Delbridge 1965), has always persisted in Australia, and continues to be associated with levels of formality and education. Social variation also encompasses Aboriginal English, the ethnic variety that has emerged under IDG strand conditions, discussed earlier.

Ongoing diversification within Australian English has not only meant the emergence of regional differences and an indigenous variety, however, but also the development of new ethnic dialects (Horvath 1985; Clyne 2003:152–7; Kiesling 2005). These are associated with ADS strands, i.e. immigrant groups of different origins who in their way of speaking English retain traces of their heritage languages. In Australian English awareness of this process has found its widespread tag in the term *wog*, originally – roughly since the 1950s, corresponding to a more polite "New Australian" – used derogatorily but now increasingly reclaimed as an affectionate self-designation by Australians of non-Anglo, primarily southern European, descent. For the distinctive accent of these people the term *wogspeak* has been coined and used. Such new "ethnolects" are increasingly becoming symbols of group membership, positively evaluated as such. Horvath (1985) investigated differences between Greek, Italian, and Anglo speech in Sydney. Clyne, Eisikovits, and Tollfree (2000) looked into Greek, Jewish, and German ethnolects in Melbourne. Kiesling (2005) shows how in Sydney backed and lengthened word-final *-er* has become "indexical of being Greek for some" (2), with Lebanese speakers also adopting this change. Clyne (2003) provides a thorough documentation of multilingualism and language shift in Australia, covering a range of different immigrant groups, and argues that ethnolects in some cases have taken over the socially indexical functions of the heritage languages:

The ethnolect may be identified by the younger family members, typically third-generation, as the community language. Many third-generation Italians regard the ethnolect as their Italian though it may only embed a small number of items of food and family relationships (155).

Thus, a fragmentation of Australian English along ethnic lines seems to be evolving.

Collins and Blair (2001) have captured the binary perspective that characterizes phase 5 in Australia (and, correspondingly, elsewhere):

The role of language as a badge of social identity means that English in Australia serves a double social function. Within Australia, the range of varieties (or Englishes) provides a set of cultural and social indicators of ethnicity, social class, gender and age. From an external viewpoint ... the language provides a marker of "Australian-ness" (11).

5.3   New Zealand

The development of English in New Zealand (see Map 5.1) is similar to the Australian case in many respects – although New Zealanders would strongly resent being mistaken for Australians.[8] New Zealand is also a settlers' colony, founded by migrants with socially and regionally similar origins (though not convicts) and at about the same period (postdating comparable Australian experiences by just a few decades). The IDG strand, the Maoris, were similarly subdued and endangered, though overall their language and culture have been preserved a little better than those of the Aboriginals in Australia. Some of the general assessments of section 5.2, in particular those relating to identity constructions and socio-linguistic relations, can therefore be applied here as well. Interestingly enough, however, while a European perspective of a fairly uniform "anti-podean" language prevailed for a long time, the last few decades have experienced a conscious drifting away of New Zealand accents from those of Australia, emphasizing their own, distinct identity.

5.3.1   Phase 1 (ca. 1790s–1840)

The history of English in New Zealand began with whaling ships and traders touching upon the islands' shores late in the eighteenth century and with uncontrolled settlement early in the nineteenth. Of course, this entailed early contacts with the Maoris.

The discussion on the local origin of Australian English mentioned above is valid for New Zealand English as well; in addition, the issue is how closely related and similar to each other they were in the early phase (see Bauer 1994:420–8, Gordon and Deverson 1998:25–9). According to the evidence available, the similarities between these two countries can be explained by the fact that the input to their respective linguistic mixtures (the founder populations at certain periods) was quite similar (Trudgill 2004), in addition to regular migration between them (Kiesling 2004:429–30; Bauer and Warren 2004:580–1).

Dialect mixture and koinéization shaped early New Zealand English as well, although the evidence available suggests that this process set in fully a little later, in phase 2 (see below).

Indigenous place names, another one of the characteristics of phase 1, predominate in New Zealand as well, e.g. *Aotearoa, Rotorua, Whangarei, Timaru, Oamaru, Omarama, Waitangi, Takapuna*. Baker (1978:276) gives a figure of 57 percent of all New Zealand place names as being Maori in origin. Gordon and Deverson (1998:9) refer to the fact that James Cook adopted Maori names for the North and South Islands, which, however, due to their complexity were replaced among the Europeans later, and they explicitly identify "proper names, especially place names" (65) as having been amongst the earliest borrowings from Maori.

5.3.2   Phase 2 (1840–1907)

Phase 2, a stable colonial status, begins with a clear demarcation date. The Treaty of Waitangi of 1840, in which Maori chiefs yielded sovereignty to the Crown in return for promises of protection, prototypically fulfills the function, important in the identity construction of a nation, of a "myth of origin," a "nameable beginning" (Wodak et al. 1999:22, 24). Whether the terms of the contract and its consequences were fully clear to the chiefs, who were assured the retention and respect of their authority, remains disputed. In any case, it set a massive influx of British settlers rolling, who came in large-scale migration patterns organized by the New Zealand Company. Massive immigration, in several waves, continued, mainly from England, also Ireland, and, with a strong concentration in the Otago region of the South Island, Scotland (see Gordon and Sudbury 2002:77–8; Gordon et al. 2004:39–53; Bauer and Warren 2004:580–1; Gordon and Trudgill 2004:441–5). The colony thrived on livestock, producing wool, meat, and dairy products. The Maori population was recessive for a while, affected by diseases and military losses (in the so-called "New Zealand Wars" of the 1860s), but it recovered before too long and, with the permanent presence of and dominance by the British unavoidable, gradually adjusted. This entailed the ongoing spread and acquisition of the English language, through interaction, missionary activity, and – primarily for an indigenous elite – schooling.

We may assume that the identity of the British people operated on a basis similar to what present-day New Zealanders would call "OE" (overseas experience), with an emphasis on the maintenance of one's roots but enriched by the experience abroad. Gordon et al. (2004), based on contemporary records, describe the original settlers' motivations as "to make a new Britain in the South Pacific," stating that they "took great comfort in the fact that they were living in a British colony and tried to make New Zealand as British as possible" (63). For example, they quote an 1873 account of a settler's wife who enjoys "everything about me so English and homelike" (63). Later generations, however, the locally born Pakeha, no longer wished to simply replicate Britain but felt superior to the stream of newcomers (63), even if "attachment to Britain remained strong" (64). The self-image of the Maoris must have been shaky, as far as can be deduced from their activities: on the one hand, they ceded their homeland more or less voluntarily and welcomed the white men, on the other their culture and freedom were threatened, and there was overt resistance.

Due to the efforts of the Origins of New Zealand English (ONZE) project based in Christchurch the process of new dialect formation is exceptionally well documented (Trudgill et al. 2000; Gordon et al. 2004; Trudgill 2004). The project has shown that the earliest speakers of English born in New Zealand, in the 1850s and 1860s, still displayed a wide range of variability in their speech, while the process of linguistic focusing, i.e. the emergence of a recognizable New Zealand accent, set in with speakers born in the 1870s.[9] Thus, essentially the second locally born generation set the standards for a "founder effect" to determine the essentials of the colony's accent for times to come (Gordon and Trudgill 2004; Trudgill 2004:esp. 158–60).

Lexical transfer follows the characteristic pattern of phase 2, concentrating upon certain semantic fields. These include words for fauna and flora (e.g. *kiwi, kauri, pohutukawa* 'kind of tree,' *kahikatea* 'white pine,' *matai* 'kind of tree,' *toetoe* 'pampas grass,' *tuatara* 'kind of reptile,' *tarakihi* 'kind of fish,' *kea, moa, kotuku* 'white heron'; *white pine*) and native cultural terms (e.g. *waka* 'canoe,' *whare* 'house,' *marae* 'courtyard of a meeting house,' *hei tiki* 'good luck carving,' *hui* 'meeting,' *hangi* 'earth oven,' *whanau* 'extended family,' *mana* 'prestige, standing'; Bauer 1994). Gordon and Deverson (1998:65) confirm that words for native fauna and flora and for "Maori society itself" predominate amongst the early loans (66–74; see Macalister 2006:2, who, following Morris, dates these words to the 19th century). Leitner (2004a:154), referring to an analysis of the *Dictionary of New Zealand English* by Kennedy and Yamazaki, adds quantitative backing: "69 percent of all Maori loans come from fauna and flora," and 17.6 percent refer to "distinctively Maori concepts" (cf. Macalister 2006:5, 15–7).

5.3.3 Phase 3 (1907–1973)

Loosening ties with Britain introduced phase 3 early in the twentieth century, formalized in the Dominion status in 1907 and full independence in 1947. However, New Zealand's loyalty to and association with the British Empire remained strong throughout much of the century, symbolized by the country's participation in the Boer Wars in South Africa and in ANZAC, mentioned in section 5.2.3. To a large extent, the economy rested on preferential access to the British market for agricultural export products, made possible by refrigerated shipping. Linguistically speaking, nativization and indigenization were going on, and a New Zealand accent stabilized. At the same time, the external British language norm remained valid. Of the Maori population, a vast majority succumbed to the pressure to adjust and underwent large-scale language shift toward English.

While many New Zealanders developed and used speechways of their own, this process was scorned by conservative members of society. The "complaint tradition" is exceptionally well documented for New Zealand. Fittingly, Bauer (1994:393–4) and Gordon and Deverson (1998:23–5) date the onset of the complaints about the deteriorating New Zealand pronunciation in the early 1900s. Here is a selection of contemporary and also more recent statements indicative of this persistent attitude (from Gordon and Abell 1990, Gordon 1998:65–6; and Hundt 1998:159–75):

- a dialect, and . . . not a defensible one, is becoming fixed in the Dominion [1910]
- faulty methods of production . . . have uglified the young colonial's voice [1910]
- this objectionable colonial dialect [1912]
- "We are always waging war against the colonial accent." "Do you think things are becoming worse?" "Yes I think so." [1912]
- Well educated New Zealanders speak of hospiddles, . . . and I repeat that this is just slovenly and without excuse [1945]
- New Zealand speech, characterised by its sloppiness due to inattention to the appropriate value of both vowels and consonants [1994]
- lumpen-proletarianisation of English [1994]

The effects of the nativization process are most strongly visible on the levels of pronunciation and vocabulary (see Bauer 1994; Gordon and Deverson 1998). Bauer and Warren (2004) is a recent, authoritative survey of the variety's pronunciation (see also Gordon and Maclagan 2004; Warren and Bauer 2004; Gordon and Sudbury 2002:79–83). New Zealand's distinctive lexis includes both further loans from Maori and the subtle creative processes that are typical of this phase: semantic shifts (e.g. *dairy* 'corner shop,' *field* 'paddock,' *stream* 'creek'), new compounds (e.g.*walkway, sharemilker*), and hybrid compounds (*whare boy, blind pakihi, manuka blight, akekake money*; Macalister 2006). Distinctive grammatical characteristics of New Zealand English are comprehensively summarized, in comparison with other PCEs, in Hundt, Hay and Gordon (2004) and analyzed in some detail in Hundt (1998; see also references cited there, especially earlier work by Laurie Bauer, Quinn 2000). In several respects New Zealand usage is found to be variable, but the overall frequency of specific choices is idiosyncratic. A number of distinctive innovations are located at the lexicogrammatical interface, as is typical of nativizing PCEs. Cases in point include the transitive use of *farewell*, *protest*, and *appeal*; intransitive (mediopassive) use of *screen* 'to appear on a movie/TV screen'; a ditransitive complementation with *provide* (e.g. *provide students facilities*); *look* followed by a *to*-infinitive; the noun *chance* collocating with the preposition *for*; and so on.

5.3.4   Phase 4 (1973–ca. 1990s)

Phase 4, an endonormative reorientation, followed an "Event X" experience which caused New Zealand to cut herself loose from the former mother country mentally. In 1973 Britain joined the European Union, without softening provisions for New Zealand, for whom this step meant the abrupt loss of her protected, up to then almost exclusive export market (Gordon and Deverson 1998:108). This required a painful restructuring of the economy and ultimately, similarly to Australia, caused a reorientation toward the neighboring Asia-Pacific region, and, of course, a new sense of complete self-dependence, a regionally rooted identity construction. As in Australia, one consequence of this was an increased attention given to (and demanded by) the Maori population, whose culture and language have come to be recognized as part of the country's distinctive national heritage – although this seems "too late to reverse a century of neglect and opposition which has brought it to the edge of extinction" (Bell and Holmes 1991:153). The country is now officially bilingual – a status which is manifested most explicitly, however, at locations fraught with symbolic importance like the *Te Papa* national museum in Wellington. In practice, this policy does not really reflect the linguistic reality any longer, with the Maori language being regularly spoken only by a very small fraction of the population. However, the Maori renaissance of this period has caused a wave of new loans adopted into English late in the twentieth century (Macalister 2006).

New Zealand English in the last quarter of the twentieth century betrays the same indicators of phase 4 as Australia: literary creativity, homogeneity, and codification. With the exception of the Otago region, marked by its Scottish heritage, the lack of regional differences has also been commented on, e.g. "geographical dialects are not obvious" in New Zealand (Kuiper and Bell 2000:12) or "regional phonological variation in New Zealand (apart from Southland) has so far not been demonstrated" (Gordon and Maclagan 2004:605). Perhaps less nationalistic in tone and impact but equally effective descriptively, New Zealand has also had a series of national dictionaries of various shapes and sizes by now (e.g. Orsman and Orsman 1994; Orsman 1997). A separate grammar of New Zealand English is also unlikely to appear in the near future, but a set of syntactic peculiarities (as listed above) have clearly been generally accepted and are employed in "formal" contexts as well (as is indicated, for example, by the road sign *Moerewa farewells you*, seen on the North Island in 2001). There is no doubt that the linguistic orientation is endonormative nowadays (Gordon and Deverson 1998:171), although there is also a residual appreciation for RP amongst some speakers (Bell and Holmes 1991:161).

Gordon and Deverson (1998) conclude their book by explicitly emphasizing the connection between "New Zealand English and New Zealand identity":

There is now a shift apparent in the way some New Zealanders at least are viewing their own form of English speech. Perhaps the chief factor in this is New Zealand's new, or heightened, sense of independent nationhood. ... New Zealanders have come to see themselves as carving out their own destiny in a distinctively Pacific setting. The word "antipodean" has come to seem rather outdated ... We are where we are, rather than at the other end of the world from somewhere else. We are now evolving our own ways, our own standards, looking less over the shoulder at the example of Mother England ... Language is an integral part of any country's cultural make-up. A growth in national maturity and self-respect inevitably brings greater prestige to the national language or variety. New Zealand English, then, is slowly acquiring more "respectability" (among New Zealanders themselves, most importantly) as the country's individual choice, one of our national assets (175).

5.3.5   Phase 5 (ca. 1990s–)

Like Australia, New Zealand shows signs of beginning dialectal fragmentation, both regional and social, which suggests that in the framework of the Dynamic Model the country can also be positioned early into phase 5. It is also most interesting to observe that in terms of the emergence of regional diversification New Zealand seems to be lagging precisely the few decades behind Australia that its identity-changing "Event X" occurred later. During the 1990s and after, a vibrant sociolinguistic scene in New Zealand has analyzed several ongoing sound changes, which are being functionalized to mark social and ethnic identities (see Gordon and Maclagan 2004:610–2, Bell and Kuiper 2000, and references listed there) and which have increased its distinctiveness, mainly setting it apart more explicitly from Australian English. These include the centralization of /ɪ/, the merger of /ɪə/ and /ɛə/, the raising of /e/ and /æ/, and the vocalization of /l/.

Except for a customary concession to regional speech found in Otago/ Southland due to its Scottish background (see Bauer 1997; Trudgill,

Maclagan and Lewis 2003), and occasional notes concerning minor lexical localisms (see Bauer 1997; Gordon and Deverson 1998:126–34), however, in general the statement about the regional homogeneity of New Zealand English is still accepted. This is likely to change in the near future, however: in a large-scale research project, Bauer and Bauer (2002) observed the emergence of regional dialects in New Zealand English among school-children. Gordon and Trudgill agree that "there are today perhaps some signs of regional variations beginning to appear in phonetic detail" (2004:448).

Social variation is also well documented and, of course, not new as such (see Bell and Holmes 1990, Bell and Kuiper 2000).

Emerging ethnic varieties of English are analyzed amongst Maoris and relatively recent immigrants, who have mainly come from Pacific Islands like Samoa, Niue, the Cook Islands, Tonga, and Tokelau since the 1950s (Bell and Holmes 1991:153, 157), a new ADS strand. Maori English has been claimed to exist perceptually, though linguists found it to be relatively "elusive" (Bell 2000:221). Bell (2000) documents some of its features, and Warren and Bauer (2004) describe its phonology (see also Bauer 1994:413–7). Stubbe and Holmes (2000) explicitly identify it as a marker of Maori identity, with discourse characteristics of its own. Starks (2000) discusses how an innovative "fronted" realization of /s/ is being adopted as an emerging feature of Pacific Islanders' speech.

5.4   Hong Kong

Hong Kong (see Map 5.2) is similar to Fiji in the historical depth of its contact with English and in its very small percentage of native speakers and residents of British descent. However, a considerably tighter colonial grip by the British for a long time has resulted in a more advanced stage: it can be regarded as having reached phase 3, with some traces of phase 2 still observable.

5.4.1   Phase 1 (ca. 1841–1898) and phase 2 (1898–1960s)

Since the seventeenth century activities by the British East India Company had brought English to the region and had resulted in the emergence of Chinese Pidgin English, now believed to be extinct. The beginnings of the developmental cycle in Hong Kong can be dated to 1841–2, when Hong Kong Island was occupied and became a colony in the wake of the first Opium War, and to missions' activities, which brought English education soon thereafter (Bolton 2000a:267). Britain's power base was then expanded through a lease of Kowloon peninsula in 1860. Phase 1, still a rather

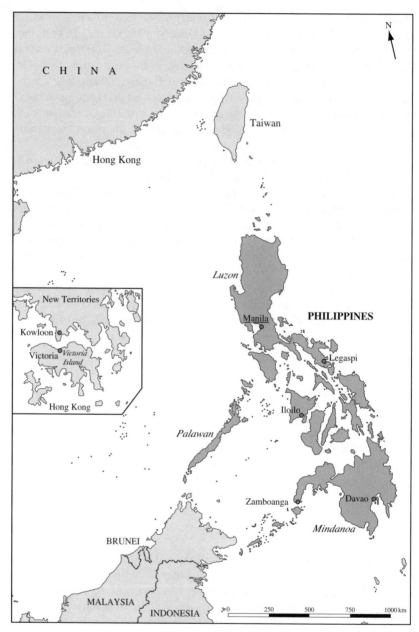

Map 5.2: Hong Kong and the Philippines

incipient stage with very limited immigration and bilingualism, then lasted throughout the nineteenth century. As elsewhere, missionary schools contributed to the gradual spreading of English (Bolton 2003:192–4, 229–31).

Given the small number of Europeans resident there, dialect mixture was probably not an issue. Place names within Hong Kong (in addition to a few English-imposed ones) are of course indigenous (e.g. *Kowloon, Wan Chai, Cheung Chau, Lam Ma, Ngong Ping, Shau Kei Wan, Chek Keng*). Chinese Pidgin English is likely to have played an important role in interethnic communication during that period (Bolton 2003:156–8).

A distinctive transition to phase 2 can be identified with the Treaty of 1898, in which to secure Britain's hold and the economic basis for the island itself the New Territories were leased for ninety-nine years. This step guaranteed stability to the entire territory for the next century, and Hong Kong became a major center of the trade between Britain and southern China. Throughout the twentieth century the colony's population continued to multiply, mainly through Cantonese immigration. Continuous development and expansion was only temporarily interrupted by the war years of Japanese occupation and influenced to some extent by post-war changes, including the communist takeover in mainland China.

The characteristics of phase 2 can be identified during this period, beginning with the politically stable status as a British crown colony in Asia. Certainly the identity constructions of expatriates as representatives of Britain in an Asian outpost, positively evaluated, or, conversely, of their local contacts as Hong Kong people with British cultural contacts and experience, corresponded to the Dynamic Model. Bilingualism kept spreading, though it had a decidedly elitist quality because education in English was only accessible to a small segment of the indigenous population. An unchallenged exonormative orientation in language teaching and usage prevailed. The vocabulary of Hong Kong English includes its share of terms for local plants and animals (e.g. *choy sum* 'green leafy vegetable,' *bamboo snake, dragon's eye* 'kind of fruit'), cultural terms (*bo lei* 'kind of strong tea,' *dim sum* 'kind of Cantonese dish,' *wantan* 'kind of Cantonese dish') and other localisms (e.g. *Canto-pop queen*) (from Butler 1997, *Grolier International Dictionary* 2000).

5.4.2   Phase 3 (1960s–)

The beginnings of phase 3 can best be dated in what Bolton (2000a:268) calls "late British colonialism" since the 1960s, "the economic transformation of Hong Kong from a relatively poor refugee community to a wealthy commercial and entrepreneurial powerhouse." Concomitant political developments, with the end of the lease in sight, also had the effect of transforming the internal definition and external orientation of the crown colony. Since the 1970s negotiations were conducted about the future status of the territory, and they ultimately led to the Joint Sino-British Declaration of 1984 with an agreement on the handover of 1997, imposing conditions on the future status of Hong Kong as a part of the People's Republic of China, at least for a fifty-year transition period. Thus, as Joseph (2004:150) points out, the situation of Hong Kong is not a typical postcolonial one in that it did not gain independence but was turned over to another power. Taken together, these processes have also substantially transformed the make-up of Hong Kong's population structure and social organization. A development from roughly the 1970s which probably had important consequences for the role of English as well was the emergence of a "new middle class" (Bolton 2003:62; see 50–98). Further important social changes included a new cosmopolitan orientation, the growth of a service economy, the fact that for the first time the majority of the population was locally born, the spread of education, also the expansion of the role of English. Taken together, all of these factors contributed to the fact "that the period from the 1980s to 1997 was one of rapid and dramatic change in the economic structure of the territory" (Bolton 2003:64).

The agreement on the future changes resulted in the gradual weakening of the political and psychological ties between the colony and the (political) metropole, and of course it affected the identity constructions of the Hong Kong people. British expatriate residents needed to consider and decide whether to stay or not, and those who stayed needed to rewrite their identity from "outpost/representative of Britain in Hong Kong" to "permanent Hong Kong resident of British origin." In a similar vein, it is stated that the identity construction of Cantonese Hongkongers changed during that period: "The 'them vs. us' mindset directed toward the British and 'their' language gradually vanished even before the departure of the last governor" (Li 1999:103). Hyland's (1997) language attitude investigations documented the emergence of "a distinctive and healthy Hong Kong identity" (207). This new self-image combined Chinese traditions, like family orientation, with western values, like pragmatism and materialism; it found a popular cultural expression in Cantonese films and music that became popular since the 1970s, and it was epitomized in the newly emerging notion of "Hong Kong people" (Bolton 2003:66).

Hong Kong's economic change and self-projection as a "global city," associated with internationalization and thus closely connected with the use of English, also boosted positive attitudes toward, and hence the spread of, English. Associated with this, and equally important, was a new educational policy of introducing "Anglo-Chinese" secondary schools since the 1970s, which did away with "elitist bilingualism" and introduced "mass bilingualism" instead (Bolton 2000a:269, 2000b:95, 2003:84–7). Bilingualism has been spreading steadily, with 33.7 percent of the population claiming to speak English "quite well," "well" or "very well" in 1993, with only 17.4 percent admitting to not speaking it "at all" (Bolton 2000a:275). Bolton (2000b:96) documents the rise of knowledge of English from 6.3 percent in 1931 to 38.1 percent in 1996; for 2001 Bolton (2003:87) quotes a figure of 43 percent of the population knowing English.[10] Li (1999) suggests the epithet "value-added" to appropriately describe the current status of English, also doubtless an indication of the positive attitude toward the language that prevails and shapes identities associated with its command. By now a knowledge of English has become "the marker of a general middle-class (new middle-class) identity for Hong Kong Chinese" (Bolton 2003:115). English is commonly used in writing, in particular in e-mails and chats, in businesses, and also at times as a lingua franca between speakers of Cantonese and Putonghua (201–3).

Another factor which confirms Hong Kong's progress into phase 3 is the fact that "[f]or at least thirty years, Hong Kong has had its own localized complaint tradition about 'falling standards' of both English and Chinese" (Bolton and Lim 2000:431; see also Bolton 2003:108–11; Joseph 2004:134–8). The timing of this process also corresponds with the expansion of English: this "ideology seems to have emerged among academics in the early seventies, and then gathered steam in the eighties" (Bolton and Lim 2000:431), "reached a peak in the late eighties" and "has continued ... to the late nineties and to the present" (432). The following quotations provide examples:

• "the university today has become a symbol of the decline in local English standards in Hong Kong" (W. McGurn in *Far Eastern Economic Review*, 21 March 1996; quoted in Bolton and Lim 2000:433);
• "the problem of poor English standards has spilled over from schools and the tertiary institutions and is directly affecting the performance of business" (Hong Kong Bank representative, quoted in Evans 2000:193, where further examples are available).

Thus, the constituent features of phase 3 fit together remarkably well in the case of the Hong Kong of the last third of the twentieth century.

Accordingly, the status of the variety itself has been disputed, though decreasingly so in recent years, and now it is being redefined. Some twenty years ago Luke and Richards (1982:55) observed a clearly exonormative orientation of "English in Hong Kong" and denied the existence of a distinct "Hong Kong English." Among teachers in Hong Kong this attitude still prevails, as Tsui and Bunton (2000) show, and Li (1999:95) essentially also still upholds this categorization. Now, however, Bolton (2000a) suggests that the time has come to accept a revaluation of the role and status of

English. In an article of 1987, the *South China Morning Post* used the label "Hongkong English," called the variety an "incipient patois," and indirectly, from a layman observer's perspective, confirmed the existence of transfer features, noting that it "cannot avoid absorbing the characteristics of the vernacular, especially one as vibrant as Cantonese" (quoted from Bolton 2003:50). The genesis of a new variety is closely associated with both the emergence of syntactic interlanguage features and the perception of "declining standards" (Joseph 2004:139). Joseph suggests that structurally Hong Kong English is "well along the path of emergence," but as it still lacks recognition it "will be a future development" (149).

No doubt Hong Kong English has developed a distinct vocabulary segment of its own, largely to be explained as loans or interference phenomena from Cantonese in particular and Chinese in general (Benson 2000; Bolton 2000b:108–10, 2003:106, 209–14). Examples include *tai tai* 'supreme wife,' *kwailo* 'foreign residents,' *char siew* 'Chinese-style roast pork,' or *yum cha* 'tiny servings of food eaten while drinking tea,' or loan translations like *lucky money, blue lantern,* or *Double Tenth*. Internal lexical creativity has produced new compounds (e.g. *typhoon shelter, field chicken* 'kind of dish,' *dragonhead* 'top leader of a triad,' *black society* 'triad,' *black hand* 'mastermind of criminal activities,' *almond cream* 'sweet desert of crushed almonds'), hybrid compounds (e.g. *chim sticks* 'bamboo sticks used in telling someone's fortune,' *hoisin sauce, Tin Hau Festival*), or semantic shifts (*astronaut* 'person commuting between a family abroad and a job in Hong Kong,' *cage* 'partitioned bedspace,' *harsh* 'demanding'). On the phonological level, it cannot be disputed any longer that there exists a Hong Kong English accent which can be described phonologically (Hung 2000; Bolton 2003:206–9), which is developing distinct rules and other features of its own (Peng and Setter 2000), and which for Hong Kong students is beginning to be regarded as a positively valued source of identification (Bolton 2000a:277–8; but cf. Li 1999:101). With respect to syntax, Gisborne (2000) documents putatively unique features in the relative clause system, thus documenting the variety as being on the path to structural nativization. Joseph (2004:144–7) accounts for the lack of a count – mass distinction in Hong Kong English noun phrases, as in *a bowl of noodle*, by pointing out partial structural transfer from Chinese. Lexicogrammatical peculiarities include redundancies in predication (e.g. *discuss about, return back, seek for*), the widespread pluralization of non-count nouns (*underwears, equipments, aircrafts*), or the invariant tag *isn't it* (Bolton 2003:106, 213).

An interesting parallel to phase 3 in other PCEs is the emergence and positive attitude toward code-switching and mixing. Among university students a code called *mix* or *u-gay-wa* has come to be highly popular, combining "the status associated with English" with neutrality, thus projecting an image that is neither fully westernized nor "uncompromisingly Chinese" (Bolton 2003:103–4, 114). Joseph (2004:134) states that for young people educated at Hong Kong universities "the hallmark of their identity is their ability to code-switch, relentlessly and seemlessly, between Chinese and English."

Of course, as always, the future is impossible to predict, and perhaps even more so given the uncertainties associated with Hong Kong's, and even China's, future economic, sociological, and political developments and choices. Hong Kong may become an interesting test case for the predictive implications of the Dynamic Model and the inherent power of the developmental dynamism which it describes; and a first assessment a few years after what might have been a major turning point suggests that the drive toward English seems to be stronger than might have been anticipated. With the handover of mid-1997, the political status of the city and its hinterland, now a Special Administrative Region of the Republic of China, changed fundamentally. This change of sovereignty could have resulted in strong and adverse consequences for the status of English, after one and a half centuries of permanent and intense presence, but actually that does not seem to be the case. Politically, English remains a co-official language, together with Chinese, with this status enshrined in Hong Kong's Basic Law. However, at first it seemed that access to the language would be severely restricted in the future: a new educational policy (decided on shortly before the handover) sought to drastically reduce the proportion of English-medium schools from about 90 percent to about a quarter of all secondary schools (Li 1999:78–9; Bolton 2003:96–7, 2000b:99–101; Evans 2000), a development which would have interrupted and redirected the evolution of English in the country. On the other hand, the implementation of this policy has met with considerable resistance among Hong Kong people (see Bolton 2000b:99–101), and it is no longer seriously pursued in its original form. Parental demand for English remains strong. With government support, English is also spreading beyond the middle class: since about 2002 in an effort called "Workplace English Campaign," a high proportion of the tuition costs of voluntary English courses for workers are refunded. (David Li, p.c. 2004; see http:// www.english.gov.hk/, accessed in April 2006). English is clearly regarded as indispensable and inalienable in Hong Kong. Joseph (2004:159–61) hypothesizes that Hong Kong English might become "a locus of cultural identity and expression" especially if the Beijing government should decide to suppress the Cantonese or southern Chinese identity that prevails today to force a more mainstream northern Chinese, Putonghua orientation upon Hong Kong people unwilling to pursue such a direction.

5.5   The Philippines

Unlike all of the other varieties discussed in this book, Filipino English is not a product of British but of American colonial expansion. Its history has been fairly short, basically restricted to the twentieth century, but unusually intense, with the language having spread very rapidly. Similarly to Malaysia and Tanzania, to be discussed later, due to the explicit promotion of an indigenous language as a new national language in the Philippines English seems to be losing ground, reverting from an ESL status to a more marginal role.

Phases 1 and 2, with only a small STL strand but a broad IDG strand development, seem to have practically merged and progressed very rapidly. After more than three centuries of Spanish colonization, as a consequence of the Spanish-American War, the United States were given authority over the Philippines (Map 5.2) in 1898. Building upon a voluminous commission report, imbued by a desire to supplant the Spanish heritage, and filled with "the sort of arrogance to be expected of a conquering power" (Brutt-Griffler 2002:34), the Americans were quick and radical in their decisions on the future course of the country, judging their own culture and language superior to the indigenous ones. English was declared her official language, accompanied by its "formal introduction as the main and only language of instruction in public schools in September 1901" (Sibayan and Gonzalez 1996:139). To impose this rule, the US sent a first load of 523 teachers on board the USS Thomas in 1901, so the name "Thomasites" became "lovingly applied to all American teachers" by the Filipinos (Thompson 2003:21; Gonzalez 2004:8).[11] The teachers were extremely successful: the English language spread rapidly, at a speed "unprecedented in colonial history" (Gonzalez 1997:28), supposedly because of the role of English as "a socioeconomic equalizer" which gave access to poor children from the towns and barrios to desirable civil service jobs (Sibayan and Gonzalez 1996:140). People were eager for education, though conditions were difficult, to say the least, and dropout rates were high. Nevertheless, speaker percentages rose from 26.6 percent in 1939 to 36 percent in 1948, 45 percent in 1970 and 64.5 percent in 1980 (Bolton 2000b:97; Gonzalez 2004:9).

Unsurprisingly, place names in the Philippines mostly derive from indigenous languages, and many of the early loans, found also in writings by the Thomasites, denote plants (*camote* 'sweet potato,' *ilang-ilang* 'type of tree,' *nipa* 'kind of palm'), animals (*carabao* 'water buffalo') or cultural objects (*bolo* 'heavy long knife') (Bolton and Butler 2004:95, 97).

Phase 3 can be assumed to have begun a decade before independence, in 1946, eleven years after the Philippines were granted limited sovereignty under a "commonwealth" status. Language choice was an issue from the outset, and in 1937 the new government decided to develop Tagalog, the lingua franca of southern Luzon, into a national language. The war years actually strengthened English even more, however: it was "becoming indigenized" as "a sign of resistance" against Japanese occupation, and in many families it became increasingly one of the languages "learned at home" (Thompson 2003:30). After the war, a bilingual education scheme, renewed and revised in the 1970s, promoted both English and Tagalog, which in the 1973 Constitution was officially renamed Filipino. However, with limited resources available, need for language development, and some resistance against the choice of a national language, the implementation of the national language policy proved difficult, and room was left for the further development of English in local contexts. Thus, remarkably, in the post-war years and after independence the use of English continued to spread vigorously. Thompson (2003:34–5) called the 1970s, the Marcos era, the "Golden Age" for English, which was deeply entrenched in the national self-projection, continued to move into home environments, and developed audibly indigenous forms that prompted Gonzales to call for "the Filipinization of English standards in the schools" in 1976 (2003:34). It was only later that English became associated with colonialism and an undemocratic elitism.

The bilingual education policy and the fact that English has been deeply rooted and widely used in society, especially but not exclusively in urban domains and formal and public contexts, are two factors that explain its continuously strong role in the country and the fact that it has proceeded well into the stage of nativization. Nowadays, English is very much the language of formal domains: business, politics, higher education, and parts of the media; and consequently Philippine English tends to be monostylistic and close to written norms (Gonzalez 2004:12). For intimacy, local vernaculars, Tagalog or the mixed variety are preferred (Gonzales 1982:223). But the speaker numbers are still impressive. According to a national survey of 1993, "73 percent read in English, 59 percent write English, 74 percent understand spoken English, 56 percent speak English, and 42 percent think in English. Only 7 percent claimed no ability in the language" (Thompson 2003:73).

For the last few decades the quality of English has been reported to be deteriorating – an indicator of phase 3. The "falling language proficiency in the upcoming generation was of concern to all classes of Filipinos" in the 1990s (Thompson 2003:41). English is still seen as the passport to well-paid jobs, and also to overseas employment, although with the growing number of jobs that are locally oriented this attitude is losing ground (54–5).

Philippine English has been screened copiously for linguistic characteristics. Its vocabulary encompasses loans from the preceding colonial language Spanish (*merienda* 'mid-morning or mid-afternoon snack,' *querida* 'mistress,' *despedida* 'farewell party,' *encargado* 'person in charge of a property'), from local languages (*barangay* 'community,' *kundol* 'winter melon,' *sayang* 'exclamation expressing sympathy') as well as new coinages like idioms (*open the radio*), compounds (*comfort room* 'toilet,' *hold-upper* 'someone engaged in armed robbery,' *bed-spacer* 'one who rents a bed in a dormitory'), derivatives (*jeepney* 'large jeep for public transportation,' *presidentiable* 'candidate for president,' *academician*) and semantic shifts (*bold* 'movie talk for semi-nude,' *jingle* 'urinate') (Bautista 1997; Thompson 2003:53–4; Bolton and Butler 2004). On the level of phonology, unlike other PCEs, its target is American English (Tayao 2004; Llamzon 1997). A number of grammatically distinctive features have been identified (Bautista 2000a; Thompson 2003:53), including the lexicogrammatical innovations which are characteristic of PCEs: intransitive uses of verbs which in metropolitan varieties are transitive (*I cannot afford. I don't like.*), count/mass-noun confusion (*hairs, a research*), and varying prepositions (*This results to ...., The solution cannot consist in ...., interested on*). Based on analyses of the ICE corpus from the Philippines, Schneider (2005b) and Nelson (2005) work out distinctive patterns of subjunctive and future time marking, respectively.

Given the ambivalent attitudes toward English in the Philippines because of its associations with the political elite, it is interesting to observe that as the language of regular informal communication it has been strongly challenged, even replaced by a mixed code of English and Tagalog elements commonly called *Taglish*. This new variety combines the status-related appreciation associated with English with the sociable qualities of Tagalog and reflects the historically grown hybrid identity of the country. Bolton observed that "in Manila ... the use of 'Taglish' tends to be the unmarked code of choice" (2003:201; see also Thompson 2003:40–1). Platt, Weber, and Ho (1984:147–8) were amongst the earliest to observe the widespread use and special status of this variety, which, they say, is also referred to as "mix-mix," in informal conversations. As a statement by an educated Filipino which they quote indicates, the use of this variety carries subtle social implications, negotiating the formality of the situation and the distance between the interlocutors: "If I go into an office in Manila and try to get a clerk to do something ... if I speak to the clerk in English, the situation becomes over formal; if I mix-mix the situation is easier to handle" (148). Analyzing newspaper styles, Gonzales (1982) also identifies "mix-mix" (also called *halo-halo*), which he prefers to refer to as "the code-switching variety" (214), as the central means of expressing familiarity. Thompson's comprehensive documentation (2003) presents the use of Taglish as the most characteristic and vigorous trait of current trends of language use in the Philippines. Thompson gives lively illustrations of the intertwining of English, Tagalog, and Taglish in everyday situations (1–2), in the media (127–54, 191–230), advertising (155–90) and in many other spheres of life. He quotes Sibayan's interesting suggestion that "Taglish will eventually become the Filipino version of English" (57).

Signs foreshadowing codification in phase 4 can be detected, though they remain highly restricted. There is "a body of Philippine literature in English" (Tayao 2004:1047; see Gonzalez 2005 and pertinent articles in Bautista and Bolton 2004). Standardization, codification, and an endo-normative orientation of language education have been proposed (Llamzon 2000; Bolton 2000b:104–6; Bolton and Butler 2004). The recent publication of *Anvil-Macquarie Dictionary* (2000) might be taken as such an indicator, but this is just an inclusive dictionary of English seasoned with an assortment of Philippine English words. In addition, an awareness of the pressing issues of norm selection and codification for teaching purposes as shown, for instance, in Gonzalez (1983) also indicates the fact that the dynamic presence and development of English require decisions on the future course of action.

The Philippines appears to be an example of a country where the in-built developmental trends of the Dynamic Model get overruled by changing external conditions, thus coming to a halt. A backlash to English occurred in 1986, when the Marcos dictatorship was replaced by Aquino's presidency. Since then "there has been a concerted cultural revolution to promote a new mass culture based on local rather than Western traditions" (Thompson 2003:211), which has to do with the failure of unrealistic promises and expectations associated with knowledge of English. In fact, Thompson presents recent political upheavals in the country – President Estrada's election in 1998 as the anti-establishment candidate of the masses and the impeachment and revolution staged against him in 2001 – very much as a language struggle, with the people opposing an elitist leading stratum in society whose symbol is English (260–4). The situation is "quite stable at present" (Sibayan and Gonzalez 1996:160), with Filipino established as a national language and English being strong in certain functional domains but showing no signs of proceeding any further. Currently, a "resentment" against the use of English has been observed in the lower classes, where speaking it would be considered "a sign of affectation" (144; similarly Thompson 2003:55). On the other hand, it continues to be in use in higher classes, in the professions, and in discussions of technical subjects, and even as a home language in some families especially among the "economic elite" (Sibayan and Gonzalez 1996:150). In general, however, Sibayan and Gonzalez see "little possibility ... that it will dominate Philippine life" (1996:165). It is indicative that in adopting Moag's (1992) scheme (in its original 1982 version) Llamzon (1986) focused upon the "restriction phase."

5.6   Malaysia

5.6.1   Phases 1 and 2 (1786–1957)

The British came to South-East Asia (Map 5.3) late in the eighteenth century to secure trading outposts and, at the same time, to challenge the economic and political power of other European nations in the region, most notably the Dutch.[12] The colony of Penang was established in 1786, as a safe harbor for the East India Company. After some struggle, in 1824 Melaka was ultimately taken over from the Dutch, and soon thereafter the "Straits Settlement," comprising the core British possessions of Penang, Melaka, and Singapore, were united. Throughout much of the nineteenth century, until it gained the status of a crown colony in 1889, the colony was governed from India, which accounts for quite some impact of Indian English (which had been established earlier) in the early shaping of its variety through the immigration and employment of many Indians, for instance as teachers in English-medium schools (Platt, Weber and Ho

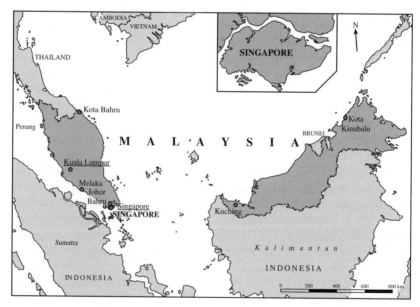

Map 5.3: Malaysia and Singapore

1983:8). Throughout the second half of the nineteenth as well as the early phase of the twentieth century the British influence expanded politically and geographically, if only rather slowly. In the Treaty of Pangkor of 1874 a British advisor was assigned to the Sultan of Perak, and 1896 saw the foundation of the Federation of Malaya, subject to the jurisdiction of a British Resident General. Malaya was originally a trade colony in Mufwene's (2001b) terms, i.e. British immigrants performed functions in the interest of the Empire and their trade company but did not perceive themselves as settlers in the strict sense. Therefore, the breadth and impact of the STL strand, like the number of expatriate residents, were relatively limited.

The transition from phase 1 to phase 2 cannot be dated precisely, having been marked by a gradual extension of the colonial grip and impact. In that respect the region is not a unity, because British influence and power spread slowly and gradually from a small number of coastal enclaves along the coastal regions and into the interior as well as, even later, to the states of Sarawak and Sabah. The implication is that the onset of phase 2, a stable, endonormative colonial orientation, can be dated perhaps a century earlier in Penang and Melaka than, for instance, in the non-Federated States.

Large-scale population movements caused by the British during that period are the basis of Malaysia's present-day multicultural make-up. Notwithstanding migrations of smaller groups and the presence of indigenous "Bumiputra" (Malays and Aboriginal groups), two major ADS groups were attracted: Mostly throughout the second half of the nineteenth century Chinese people came to work in the tin mines; and predominantly the early twentieth century saw the immigration of Indian (primarily Tamil) workers to labor in the rubber plantations.[13] In addition, the British colonial government provided incentives for smaller groups to migrate as well and to bring into effect their own special skills – like the Punjabi Sikhs, who originally constituted a large portion of the police force.

To a large extent the identity writings of the parties involved, European settlers and the Asian indigenous population, were in line with the model's predictions. Agents and representatives of the Empire perceived themselves as British outposts in the tropics – an identity construction which renowned authors like Somerset Maugham, Joseph Conrad, and Anthony Burgess have represented in English literature and which we see symbolized in the "Hill Stations" which the British established, preserving a reminiscence of a home environment in a foreign climate. Conversely, it is clear that the indigenous rulers accepted an English education for their sons and also daughters as an enriching contribution to their enduring local roots and status. Consequently, in the IDG strand bilingualism spread continuously, although locally it remained largely associated with elitism and reserved to a minority.

With the stable colonial status of the nineteenth and twentieth centuries came an ever-increasing demand for English. English-medium schools, run both by Christian missions and the government, were established, beginning early in the nineteenth century in the Straits Settlement but gradually spreading to the Malay states as well. The goal of these institutions was strictly utilitarian, serving the interests of the British: to train a local elite for administrative and service functions. Essentially, formal access to English was a privilege to those of higher status amongst the indigenous population. This attitude is epitomized by the establishment of the Malay College of Kuala Kangsar (known as MCKK) in the 1920s, a boarding school reserved for the sons of the Malay rulers and those of noble birth which nurtured civil servants and top administrators (Asmah 2000:13). In a similar vein, the foundation of a corresponding girls' school, the MGC in Kuala Lumpur as late as in 1947, was originally meant to educate suitable partners as matches for the local elite. Education at these institutions implied complete immersion into English. Thus, "when the British began to withdraw from the area in the late 1950s, English had become the dominant language of the non-European élites, both as a language of power and prestige and as an inter-ethnic link language" (Lowenberg 1991:365). This educational policy had long-lasting effects that went beyond what the British had had in mind: English-medium education in these institutions created interethnic bonds and established a value system that soon thereafter paved the way to a desire for independence. Certainly through many daily interactions and also some less upwardly orientated institutions, also through stipends for the gifted but less affluent, English in that period also spread beyond these social confines into the vernacular domain, but only hesitantly so: "English prior to Independence in 1957 had an exclusionist-cum-divisive function" (Asmah 1996:515).

Sociolinguistically, the two adstrate groups can be compared to the ethnic Malays but adopted distinct accommodation strategies of their own. In a global British perspective the Chinese and Indians, together with the original Malays, constituted the Asian, indigenous population. An additional cross-ethnically unifying force was the fact that the upper echelons of the Chinese and Indian population segments shared the orientation toward British education and culture. Consequently, a shared Malaysian (versus British) leaders' identity, transcending ethnic boundaries, was gradually forged. At the same time, ethnolinguistic boundaries have been preserved. (They appear to have been reinforced in the recent past by the government's categorization of the population and distribution of certain privileges by "Bumiputra" vs. "non-Bumi" status after independence.) Also, the Asian immigrant groups have settled successfully and distinctively within Malaysia's society, especially in the urban settings, while most of the Malays remain rural. This residential division of labor seems to be correlated with professional orientations, especially as many Chinese have prospered in small-scale businesses and trade while more than an average number of Indians work as doctors, lawyers, or higher administrators. To date, both groups have typically adopted English as their vernacular more readily than the Malays have.

The structural effects typically associated with phases 1 and 2 also apply. The earliest and most persistent foreign elements that entered English (some actually predating the colonial period itself) were mainly toponyms: while a few localities important to the British were given English names (like *Georgetown, Cameron Highlands, Port Dickson*, or *Fraser's Hill*), place names are overwhelmingly indigenous in origin (like *Penang, Selangor, Perak, Seremban, Kuala Terengganu, Kota Bahru*, and many others). Soon thereafter these were followed by indigenous borrowings for fauna and flora (*orang-utan*, for which the OED gives an earliest citation date of 1631, *rusa* 'kind of deer' 1783, *kanchil* 'species of chevrotain' 1829, *tupaia* 'Malaysian squirrel' 1820, *seladang* 'gaur' 1821, *mengkulang* 'timber tree' 1940) and culturally significant terms (*temenggong* 'high-ranking official' 1783, *adat* 1783, *tuak* 'palm wine' 1850, *mee goreng, merdeka* 1954, etc.).

5.6.2 Arrested development? The impact of Malaysia's nationalist language policy

With the constitution of 1957, the role of English began being curtailed. English was retained as a co-official language in addition to Malay, but the pronounced intention was to develop Malay into a national language and to remove this special status of English after a ten-year transition period. Due to regional differences caused by the union with part of Borneo this period was somewhat extended: the official status of English ceased in peninsular Malaysia in 1967, in Sabah in 1973, and in Sarawak in 1985 (Asmah 2000:15). Formally, the "National Language Act of 1976 … disestablished English as the joint official language, giving sole status to Malay" (Gill 2002a:25).

The policy of replacing English by Bahasa Malaysia was also an element in the power struggle between the Malays and the successful and increasingly influential Chinese and South Asians (Lowenberg 1991:365). Depriving English of its formerly privileged status was a logical and in a sense an unavoidable step on the side of the government, as Gill (2002a)

points out – otherwise, no room would have been left for the full development of Bahasa Malaysia. In practice the most important step in the
implementation of the new policy was the Ministry of Education's decision
to turn all English-medium schools into Malay-medium, beginning in
1969, a process which was completed, reaching university entrance level,
by 1983. Today, it is widely accepted that Bahasa Malaysia has securely
established its position as a truly national language (Jernudd 2003:59). On
the one hand, in many regions of rural Malaysia, English is of little use; on
the other, it is true that young Malaysians of all ethnicities are fully
conversant in and comfortable with the Malay language.

It is perhaps this security that has resulted from the practical success of
the national language policy, the fact that Bahasa Malaysia is deeply and
widely entrenched in the nation now without serious challenges, that has
allowed a partial redirection of the nation's language policy that started in
the early 1990s. This newly pragmatic orientation was presumably triggered, certainly fostered by the former Prime Minister Dr Mahathir's
policy of "Vision 2020," the goal of turning Malaysia into a fully developed
country by that year. The implied emphasis on globalization and technological advancement requires full fluency in English on the side of
Malaysian engineers and businesspeople, amongst others. Consequently,
the Education Act of 1996 approved of the reintroduction of English as a
medium of instruction in technical subjects. On the other hand, there is a
Malay intelligentsia in the country, represented by the Malay Intellectual
Congress, who resisted the early proposals in 1993 to reintroduce English
as a medium of instruction in the sciences (for documentation see Gill
2002a:110–2; also Nair-Venugopal 2000:49), arguing that it would weaken
the further development of the Malay language. Hence, it was only in 2003
that the new English-medium policy for teaching Maths and the Sciences
was put into effect. In sum, Malaysia's recent language policy has been
marked by non-linear developments and opposing tensions and tendencies,[14] and it is too early to predict its long-term effects.

5.6.3   Phase 3 (1957–)

Despite the opposing forces just discussed, however, Malaysian English
has proceeded substantially into phase 3: nativization.

Politically, although Malaysia gained her independence decades ago, it
retains loose ties with Britain, for instance through membership in the
Commonwealth. This ambivalence characterizes the identity constructions of the various population groups as well. The number of expatriate
Malaysians of exclusively European ancestry is very small, but their heritage is also accepted by the minority group of so-called Eurasians, people

of mixed European and Asian descent. Their identity is clearly genuinely Malaysian but at the same time includes part-European roots. Similarly, the Malays and also the other major population groups – at least those who had an English-medium education – see themselves both as Malaysians and as members of their respective ethnic groups in addition to the experience of the colonial British heritage which has influenced their worldview.

In terms of its sociolinguistic status and domains of usage, English is still widespread and deeply rooted in the country, most notably in urban environments. Bilingualism in English and Malay, and multilingualism in these two plus further ethnic languages, are extremely common. In interethnic communication, English still holds a very strong position: "The mesolect is the variety that is used for intranational communication, between Malaysians of varying ethnicity, as a medium of local communication" (Gill 2002a:52). In addition, English is being acquired as a mother tongue by some Malaysians, especially in Kuala Lumpur and other urban areas (David 2000:65). While this is of course a most significant development in the present context, it should not be overestimated either: the proportion of native speakers of English of local origin in present-day Malaysia – mostly Eurasians but also some urban Indian and Chinese families – is relatively low (Asmah estimates it to be about one percent of the population). Perhaps more importantly for an assessment of their potential future impact, they "do not form a community that can be culturally or geographically defined" (Asmah 2000:13). Still, David (2000) documents its vitality by citing slang terms which these young Malaysians coin and use to express their group identity.

Beyond the issue of its native-speaker status, however, English is widely available for daily exposure and easy acquisition, at the very least with respect to passive language skills. It is readily accessible in the mass media, through radio, TV, and newspapers (Nair-Venugopal 2000:48). It is noteworthy that 31.6 percent of all radio listeners listen to English radio stations (Gill 2002a:85). Asmah (2000:19) argues that English is also acquired quite naturally, even if only passively, by small children in the *kampungs* (villages in rural areas) through watching popular TV blockbusters: according to her findings, they tend to understand the English TV programs remarkably well even if they cannot formulate a fluent sentence in English. Some early, informal acquisition of English also operates through the influence of elder siblings even in non-English speaking families (Platt, Weber, and Ho 1983:9). And finally, the fact that basilectal English is also used by blue-collar workers, as shown by Morais (2000) and others, testifies to the range of informal domains into which Malaysian English has diffused.

All of this evidence suggests that at least in some circles the outreach and attraction of English in Malaysia goes significantly beyond the confines of formal, international, and business uses attributed to it in the light of the national language policy. Nair-Venugopal (2000) shows that in some business training sessions informal, mesolectal Malaysian English is the natural language of choice, called for by social needs to strengthen solidarity and decrease social distance. In other words, in many social contexts an informal register of Malaysian English has clearly become an unmarked language of everyday informal communication. English has lost much of its former elitist character (see also Gill 2002a:91).

Moreover, it seems quite clear that mesolectal Malaysian English serves as a carrier of a distinctly Malaysian identity (a role which should be reserved for Bahasa Malaysia). Here are a few pertinent statements:

- nativised English ... is perfectly acceptable for communicating socially and informally and gives one a strong sense of identity (Gill 2002a:47).

- We have developed a generation of Malaysians who very comfortably communicate in informal English – English which is Malaysian in identity – and this is reflected by the distinct phonology influenced by their ethnic tongues, lexical items which are socioculturally grounded and syntactic structures which are distinctly Malaysian in form. This is the English that is used by Malaysians to create rapport and establish our sense of identity (Gill 2002a:91).

- ME [is] the sociolect of pan-Malaysian identity (Nair-Venugopal 2000:224).

- there is a growing sense of pride and affinity associated with this localised variety of English ... there is often a tendency among speakers of ME to exaggerate the Malaysian accent in casual interactions, so as to assert their identity and project a sense of shared membership in a local speech community. ... especially among young people localised English is highly valued as an expression of cultural identity ... colloquial ME is often the preferred choice, as a sign of solidarity and camaraderie, even for speakers who are highly proficient in standard English (Rajadurai 2004:54).

Actually, trying to adopt a "native-speaker," foreign (e.g. British or American) accent is usually rejected as "put on" (Salleh 2000:57–8). Quite obviously, colloquial Malaysian English in its natural settings enjoys covert prestige. This is also confirmed by a group of Malaysian students with whom I conducted an interview (Schneider 2003a:60–2), although they also see a "good accent," i.e. British or American, as a goal worth striving for and display a deeply entrenched exonormative orientation. Most importantly, however, they rejected the binarism implied in a statement like "Malay and English are both essential in nation-building" (Asmah 2000:20), and also the exclusive focus of Malaysia's language policy upon these two languages. Conversely, particularly students of non-Malay descent said that they would like to see their own ethnic native languages recognized more generally as important elements of the country's heritage and reality.

Malaysian English has also reached the stage of being subject to its own complaint tradition. This attitude can be observed at times in Malaysia's public discourse, in laments on "falling standards of English" (Asmah 1996:520; see also Nair-Venugopal 2000:17; Lowenberg 1991; Gill 2002b), commonly voiced in English-language newspapers.

Malaysian English has undergone structural nativization on all levels of language organization. Some of these features are shared with other varieties, more so with those in close geographical proximity (most notably, of course, Singapore). Some others may be unique to Malaysian usage, but essentially it is the mix of features in their respective sociostylistic contexts that gives the variety its distinctive character. Phonological features include vowel mergers, accent shifts (e.g. ([ə'kædemɪk] "academic," [kɔm'pɪtens] "competence," [rɪ'sentlɪ] "recently"), suprasegmental features like intonation and a syllable-timed rhythm, the omission of single coda consonants (e.g. *spea'(k)*, *abou'(t)*, *loo'(k)*), and final consonant cluster reduction (*earlies'(t)*, *wen'(t)*, *affor'(d)*; see Baskaran 2004b, 2005; Zuraidah 2000; Schneider 2003b:56–7). Many of the grammatical innovations are attested at the interface of lexis and syntax: "Many of these features ... involve the selection of complement structures (*to*-infinitive, *-ing*-participle, etc.) following particular verbs, adjectives, etc. ... [or] the use of phrases where clauses would be usual in other varieties" (Newbrook 1997:244). Further examples (see Platt, Weber and Ho 1983; Newbrook 1997; Morais 2000, 2001; Nair-Venugopal 2000; Gill 2002a; Schneider 2003b:57–9; Baskaran 2004a, 2005) include:

- variant complementation patterns (*instead of merely present detached information, a view to take ...*, *interested to join, ready in accepting*);
- pluralization of mass nouns (*staffs, stationeries, accommodations*); missing arguments (*Ø Is very difficul'; why they don' have Ø ready; By restricting Ø to 300 minutes*);
- missing concord in noun phrases (e.g. *much ... resources; much more of these qualities; this two languages*);
- missing articles (e.g. *I was educated at Ø University of Malaya; Ø Study by NN suggested that ...; English is used at Ø tertiary level; ... perception of Ø falling object*);
- progressive uses of stative verbs (*is containing, I am smelling, She is owning*).

Baskaran (2005) shows that some aspects of the grammar of Malaysian English can be accounted for by substratal influence from Bahasa Malaysia. The local vocabulary has incorporated borrowings from indigenous languages (Baskaran 2004b, 2005). This includes many spheres of life, predominantly culturally distinctive terms (e.g. *tudung, kampong, sawi* 'spinach,' *bomoh* 'medicine man,' *penghulu* 'village chief'), including words for different kinds of ethnic food (e.g. *sambal* 'hot chili paste,' *kacang* 'nuts,' *mee* 'noodles'). There are also hybrid local compounds (*meranti wood, syariah court, nobat drums*) and coinages (e.g. *Datukship* 'lordship'), semantic shifts (*cut* 'overtake, beat'), and local collocations (e.g. *open light / socks / tap / hooks*). Lowenberg (1991:367–9) shows that Malaysian policy thrives upon what he calls "banner words", terms loaded with political and cultural significance in public discourse; he cites *gotong-royong, adat, bumiputra*, or *rakyat* as examples. David (2000) probes into another segment of vocabulary which is both regionally and socially restricted, namely newly emerged adolescent in-group slang; she lists the following examples (amongst many others): *dungu* 'stupid,' *wasted sperm* 'useless individual,' *chun* 'nice,' *lepak blues, bang* 'criticise,' *slambar* 'relax,' or *Like reallah!*

Another feature closely associated with phase 3 in many PCEs is very strong in Malaysia as well, namely the emergence of code-shifting and code-mixing as an unmarked communicative device. It is not surprising that in a multilingual country like Malaysia, and especially among the young who have expressly been raised multilingually, this occurs on a fairly regular basis. There are signs that this "mixed code" is assuming the role of a positive identity carrier, either in addition to or replacing Malay and/or mesolectal English in that social function (Lowenberg 1991:372; Nair-Venugopal 2000:55; David 2000:71). In the interview mentioned above, the Malaysian students expressed a strongly positive emotional attachment to the practice of continuously mixing the languages which they command, mainly but not exclusively Malay and English. They stated that code-mixing for them seems the most natural way of using and choosing between languages and felt it to be a most direct expression of their personalities (Schneider 2003a:61–2).

5.6.4   ... and beyond??

Certainly, at this time it would be futile to claim that Malaysia has moved or is moving beyond phase 3 of the Dynamic Model, but traces of even later phases are discernible.

While Malaysian English, even in its acrolectal form, is not yet accepted as adequate in formal contexts, and the linguistic orientation is still exonormative, an endonormative orientation and its future codification are occasionally envisaged in statements like this: "There is as yet no grammar of Malaysian English and this will need to be written before this variety can be accepted by the local and international community of users of English" (Morais 2000:104). A few of the papers in Halimah and Ng (2000) tentatively address the issue and possibility of accepting certain elements of Malaysian English usage as correct in the educational system. Gill (1999) advocates the development of endonormative standards, and Gill (2002a) presents a strong case for a future codification of Malaysian English, talking of the need to develop "our own standards, for example, Standard Malaysian English" (28). While for the time being she argues for educated non-native English as a pedagogical model (58–61), she also explicitly posits the existence of a "pragmatic post-independence/endonormative phase" of Malaysian English (69–71).

Literary creativity, another indicator of the acceptance of a local variety, in Malaysian English is documented and surveyed, for instance, by Merican (2000).

Codification entails the production of dictionaries. As yet no exclusive dictionary of Malaysian English is in the making, but a distinct lexicographic coverage of Malaysian English, together with Singaporean English, has begun with the publication of the second edition of the *Times-Chambers Essential English Dictionary* (1997) and with the inclusion of Malaysian words in the *Macquarie Junior Dictionary* (1999) and the *Grolier International Dictionary* (2000).

5.7   Singapore

The evolution of English in Singapore (Map 5.3), especially in the second half of the twentieth century, is largely a product of a unique language policy toward "English-based bilingualism" (Tickoo 1996:438). It is far advanced, having reached many characteristics of phase 4, and appears likely to go all the way along the cycle, given the linguistic dynamics that can be observed.[15]

5.7.1   Phases 1 (1819–ca. 1867) and 2 (ca. 1867–1942)

Phase 1 began in 1819, when Sir Stamford Raffles obtained the rights from the Sultan of Johor to establish a trading outpost for the British East India Company on what was then little more than a jungle island with potential. The fact that he established it as a free port soon attracted Chinese, Malay, and Arab traders, travelers, and others, and the population grew rapidly. In 1826, Singapore formally became a part of the Straits Settlement, together with Penang and Melaka. By that time, the population exceeded ten thousand people, the majority of whom were of Chinese extraction (including the Peranakans, Straits Chinese; on this group see Mufwene

2005a:57–8). The strategically ideal location resulted in a continuing massive influx of more traders, colonial agents, and contract laborers of predominantly Chinese and Indian origin but also others from a variety of Asian, European, and mixed backgrounds (Gupta 1999). The segregation of society into ethnically distinct streams, reflected by ethnic quarters in settlement and, still, in present-day educational policy, goes back to that early phase and the "capitan" system established then (Lim 2004; Wee 2004b).

While in a process of ongoing expansion and prosperity there is no single significant turning point, the transition to phase 2 can conveniently be associated with the year of 1867, when Singapore, as a part of the Straits Settlement, became a crown colony. In the following decade further political and economic incidents boosted its growth: the opening of the Suez Canal, the advent of steam ships, and the growing importance of the rubber trade kept increasing the importance of Singapore's port as an international trading center. By the late nineteenth century the island had experienced massive population growth and was home to a small European ruling class (of under 10 percent of the population), many Asians who managed to get by, and also a growing Asian elite. Leading members of the Chinese, Malay, and Indian communities constituted a stratum of professionals who were subjects to the British crown and adopted aspects of a British lifestyle, thus resulting in a cultural blend of Europe and Asia. This stable situation lasted until World War II.

In terms of the identities and mutual relationships between the parties involved, early Singapore may be assumed to have been similar to Malaysia and largely in line with the general assessments of the Dynamic Model. Group alignments were ethnicity-based but broadly collaborative, and certainly seasoned by the sense of place. Nothing hindered a fundamentally exonormative orientation, and the English established institutions reminiscent of home, like a cricket club, a race course, and a cathedral. Bilingualism was spreading but had an elitist touch. During the second half of the nineteenth century government-run schools were expanding. As an 1891 school advertisement announced: "To English lads is offered a home, and to Chinese lads an opportunity to learn a correct accent and facility in expressing themselves in the English language" (quoted from Gupta 1999:112). Early in the twentieth century the number of Chinese children in English-medium schools increased drastically, a fact which may have triggered the emergence of colloquial Singaporean English (Gupta 1999:114–6; see also Wee 2004b:1017–8; Low and Brown 2005:14–25).

English speakers represented a variety of regional and social backgrounds, including Scots, Irish, and American Methodists, so some dialect contact must have been going on (Gupta 1999), although we have no first-hand documentation of this. Many place names were adopted from indigenous languages; newly coined ones reflect the contributions of the polity's major ethnic groups (e.g. *Jurong, Katong, Tekong Kechil, Serangoon Harbour, Selat Pandan, Bukit Timah Road*; but also *Victoria Street, Fort Canning Road*). The local lexicon, largely shared with Malaysian English, contains a strong component of Singaporeanisms, including fauna and flora words (e.g. *brinjal* 'aubergine,' *taugeh* 'beansprout,' *rambutan* 'kind of fruit,' *lalang* 'kind of tall tropical grass') as well as cultural terms (*kelong* 'fish trap,' *baju kurong* 'Malay dress for women,' *sinkeh* 'newcomers,' *hawker stall, red packet*). Via a "founder effect," contact forms of Malay had a disproportionally strong impact on emerging Singaporean English at that time (Mufwene, p.c. 2005; Gupta 1999:125); even Chinese-origin elements apparently were transmitted via Malay (Gupta 1999:112–3).

5.7.2   Phases 3 (ca. 1945–ca. 1970s) and 4 (ca. 1970s–)

Singapore's continuous development was interrupted by three years of Japanese occupation during World War II (1942–5), and when the British assumed authority again, things had changed – and these changes of attitude can be assumed to have introduced phase 3 in terms of politics and, consequently, identity constructions. The colonial tradition was broken, and a resistance movement emphasized the island's Asian roots, so upon their return in 1945 the British were faced with a desire for *merdeka* ('independence'), promoted by a newly founded political party, the PAP (People's Action Party). After self-government and a Constitution in 1959, as well as a brief period of unification with Malaysia, these movements led to independence in 1965. At that time, Singapore still seemed a tiny island nation with an uncertain future, full of socioeconomic problems, marked by ethnic fragmentation, and lacking natural resources.

However, the young nation soon experienced a stunning development. Modernization, economic growth, and nation building are the processes that in the post-independence period, mostly in the 1970s, transformed the country quite radically and introduced the transition to phase 4. Both the unprecedented economic success of the young state and its language policy played a major role in this process. Politically, the country has been ruled by the same party since independence, with the state gently but persistently guiding its citizens toward common goals and ideals but also prescribing a great many aspects of daily life. Economic growth and prosperity turned the country into a highly modern and highly industrialized nation with a unique and novel identity which has combined European and Asian components. It is characterized by a blend of a western orientation in business and lifestyle with an emphasis on fundamentally Asian values. Multilingualism and a special status assigned to English, as a language transcending ethnic boundaries, have been important pillars in this process. Today the vast majority of inhabitants consider themselves primarily Singaporeans rather than Chinese, Malay, Tamils, or whatever. Language has been an important aspect in this process: 'English educated Singaporeans are seen as being potentially less ethnocentric and demonstrating greater loyalty to Singapore," states Rubdy (2001:344; see also LePage and Tabouret-Keller 1985:176). Singaporean English has come to be the means of expression of this newly emerging Asian-cum-western culture.

Several factors have contributed to the present-day exceptional status of English in Singapore. One is certainly its ethnic neutrality. Mufwene works out another one, the fact that the lack of intelligibility between Chinese varieties and the immediate proximity to Malay-speaking states all around have made an "exogenous contact setting more likely to thrive with a colonial language" (2004b:216). The strongest immediate cause, however, was the nation's strictly imposed educational policy of ethnicity-based bilingualism. Every child is educated in English as a "First Language" and his/her ethnic language out of the other three official languages (Mandarin, Tamil, Malay) as a "mother-tongue Second Language" (Foley 1998:130–1). Two important facets of this policy have had decisive consequences. First, English is the only common bond shared by everybody (at least in the younger generation raised under this policy) in a highly multilingual and multicultural community. Secondly, the language education policy has had the indirect, and probably unintended, effect of alienating children from the varieties spoken by their parent and grandparent generations: there is no choice for one's ethnic language taught in the school system, which practically bars the Asian languages from developing into a lingua franca. Furthermore, the Asian languages promoted at school are the standard varieties of these languages, frequently distinct from and thus not supported by the dialectal home varieties spoken by ancestral generations. Chinese children, for instance, descend from speakers of many dialects, especially from southern China, but Mandarin has been promoted by the government in a "Speak Mandarin Campaign," run since 1979. The campaign has been successful: Mandarin has been spreading at the expense of other Chinese varieties (see Rubdy 2001:342–3), but this is an intra-ethnic, not a pan-Singaporean, development, and at the national level another bond has been needed. Similarly, Tamil is officially projected as the mother tongue of Indian children, which in many cases fails to reflect reality (Pakir 1991:168). Whether intended or not, this policy has effectively weakened the position and usefulness of the indigenous languages and, conversely, strengthened that of English.[16]

Consequently, striking increases in speaker numbers, also and especially in the home environment and as a first language, have been recorded. In a study reported by Platt and Weber (1980:103; regrettably based upon an unspecified sample) 11.7 percent of all respondents in the 18–35 age bracket claimed to use English when talking to their mother, 29.3 percent to their father, and an impressive 75.4 percent (of the same group of respondents!) in conversations with their siblings – clearly English is the language of and for the younger generation. In 1980, 11.6 percent of all families chose English as a household language (Foley 1998:130). According to the 2000 census (Singapore Census of Population 2000: Advance Data Release No. 3), this figure has risen persistently, and it is going up even more drastically among the young:

Compared with 1990 English had become more popular as a home language for all ethnic groups. The proportion speaking most frequently in English at home increased from 19 percent to 24 percent among the Chinese, from 6.1 percent to 7.9 percent among the Malays and from 32 percent to 36 percent among the Indians [4] ...

English appears to be emerging as the language of the young among the Chinese resident population. Proportionally more children used English most frequently at home than youths and adults. In 2000, 36 percent of the children aged 5–14 years spoke in English compared with 22 percent of youths aged 15–24 years and 25 percent of those aged 25–54 years [5].

Similar age distributions, with 9.4 percent of all Malay children and 43.6 percent of all Indian children using English at home, are reported for the other groups as well, so the process of language shift is gradually progressing in all ethnic communities.[17] The 2000 census also reports 71 percent literacy in English (2). According to Gupta (1999:119), a "Singaporean born in the 1970s is almost certain to be able to communicate in and to read English," while this was not at all the case half a century earlier.

These processes have produced a unique language situation and a range of local language forms, spanning from an informal, basilectal variety to formal uses. Singaporeans are "English-knowing bilinguals," with proficiency and formality determining distinctive sub-varieties (Pakir 1991). English in Singapore is nowadays used in a wide variety of domains and contexts, both formal and informal, though the situation is highly complex. Despite the remarkable spread of English as a first or dominant language, mastery of it still is closely correlated with social class. Figures on its spread as a L1 may mask its role as a co-L1 for many speakers. In any given situation, language choice (and also dialect choice, given the relationship between standard and colloquial forms of English) may depend on sophisticated assessments of domain, situational parameters, and one's interlocutor's age, status, and background (Gupta 1999).

Singaporean English has gone through a vibrant process of structural nativization, more visibly on the basilectal level but also in formal styles. The situation is generally described as diglossic, but there is also a "high degree of variability between the informal and formal registers," and the diglossia cannot easily be reduced to register variation (Bao and Hong 2006:113). On the informal level, a distinctive local variant commonly called Singlish (or Colloquial Singaporean English), strongly marked by a Chinese substrate[18] and regarded as a "creoloid" by some, has evolved. Low and Brown (2005) confirm the above dating of nativization: "Singlish has only come into existence in the last 20 years or so (since the late 1970s). The reason for its birth can be linked to the second generation of English speakers in Singapore, born in the post-independence years" (30).[19] Singlish definitely qualifies as a dialect to express emotionality and proximity or to play with, a language of one's heart, an identity carrier. This is exemplified most vividly by public debates triggered by the success of the 1999 TV sitcom *Phua Chu Kang Pte Ltd.* and the 2002 movie *Talking Cock* and its restrictive rating by the government, in line with its "Speak Good English Movement": the public reaction was vigorously in defense of its right to use the local vernacular form of English, expressing strongly positive attitudes toward it (Tan 2002). Local TV comedies with Singlish-speaking characters are highly popular, and Singlish is "increasingly being foregrounded in the consciousness of English speakers" (Rubdy 2001:345). Of course, the public discussion about Singlish also reflects Singapore's version of the complaint tradition, fuelled by "a fear of falling standards" (345).

Discussing the case of Singapore, Joseph (2004:161) points out that "recognition of the linguistic distinctiveness is the necessary precondition for the development of a sense of local identity," and he dates such a step to "some decades after the end of colonial rule." Singaporean English has characteristic features on all levels of language organization – features which are increasingly noted, analyzed, and also accepted.

Singapore's phonology is quite distinctive, including features like reduced consonant clusters word-finally and word-medially, a tendency to use glottal stops for /t/ word-finally and dental plosives for word-initial fricatives, monophthongs for mid-high diphthongs, no length contrasts, unique stress modifications in many words, and a tendency toward syllable-timing (Tay 1982; Platt, Weber and Ho 1983; Bao 1998; Wee 2004a; Lim 2004:19–56; Low and Brown 2005:115–75). While many of these properties can ultimately be accounted for as linguistic transfer from source languages, Deterding (2005) shows that certain vowel distinctions are emerging in Singaporean English which cannot be explained by referring to outside varieties and thus represent genuine indigenous innovations. For instance, many speakers now make a systematic distinction between a close /e/ vowel in *egg, bed, dead* but an open /ɛ/ vowel in *beg, fed, peg*, and *bread* – and this seems to have emerged over the last twenty years, as a comparison with work by Tay (1982) suggests. Similar distinctions are emerging in other word groups as well: use of /ʌ/ in *want* but /ɒ/ in *won*, /ʊə/ in *tour, poor* and *sure* but /ɔː/ in *cure* and *pure*, and a schwa in unstressed vowels of initial syllables in some words but full vowels in others. As Deterding himself points out, this is strong evidence of Singaporean English moving substantially toward endonormative stabilisation.

The local vocabulary kept expanding, integrating words from a wide range of domains of everyday life (e.g. *kiasuism* 'strongly competitive attitude,' *jalan* 'stroll,' *sayang* 'love, beloved person,' *chin chai* 'lazy and careless,' *cheem* 'difficult to understand').[20] Indigenous lexical productivity builds upon the same types found elsewhere: compounding (*airflown* 'freshly imported (food),' *shophouse*) including hybrid compounds (*botak head* 'bald head,' *cheeko peg* 'dirty old man,' *karang guni man* 'rag and bone man'), derivation (*heaty, irregardless*), phraseology (*catch no ball* 'fail to understand'), semantic shift (*knock* 'remove a dent from a car,' *bluff* 'joke,' *stay* 'live,' *fellow* 'person, incl. females'), and so on (Wee 1998; Chng 2003; Low and Brown 2005).

Finally, the syntax of Singapore English, especially on the level of Singlish, is also marked by many distinctive rules and patterns, e.g. the use of *Can* as a complete utterance, without a subject or complement, or count uses of noncount nouns, like *a fruit* or *staffs* (see Alsagoff and Ho 1998a, Lim 2004 and Wee 2004a for competent surveys of phenomena). Some of these have been analyzed in greater detail in recent years (see Low and Brown 2005:88–114), and in general there has been a tendency in research to work out potential substrate influences, particularly from Chinese. For example, Bao and Wee (1999) trace the *kena*-passive back to Malay, and the *give*-passive to Chinese; Bao and Wee (1998) point out that *until* has adopted properties of the Chinese particle *dao*; Alsagoff and Ho (1998b) document the blending of superstrate and (Chinese) substrate influences in forming typical relative clause constructions; and so on (e.g. Alsagoff, Bao and Wee 1998; Alsagoff 2001; Lim and Wee 2001). Singapore's distinctive and well-known discourse-pragmatic particles like *lah, meh*, or *lor* (see Wee 2004a:1068–70; Lim 2004:117–26) also serve to illustrate both substrate transfer and the importance of the boundary between syntax and lexis, as do characteristic patterns of reduplication (Lim 2004). Less conspicuously, there are also distinctive patterns in formal English of the kind mentioned for phase 3. For instance, Ooi (2001:xii) illustrates the tendency to complement the verb *clarify* by a *that*-clause (rather than by a noun phrase or a *wh*-clause). Pakir (2001:8–10) documents distinctive uses of the verbs *send, bring,* and *fetch.*

By now Singapore has clearly reached phase 4 of the cycle. The country's unique, territory-based, and multicultural identity construction has paved the way for a general acceptance of the local way of speaking English as a symbolic expression of the pride of Singaporeans in their nation. It encodes both sides of the national identity: its world language character expresses the country's global outreach and striving after economic prosperity, and its distinctively local shape on some linguistic levels ties up with the country's location and traditions. The title of Ooi's book on Singaporean English, *Evolving Identities* (2001), is indicative of what is going on. Furthermore, this process is effective all across the stylistic range.

At the formal end of the cline, professional Singaporeans nowadays state that they are able to identify compatriots abroad by their accent, and that they are proud of this.[21] Singaporean English has also been in use in creative literature (Talib 1998; see also Low and Brown 2005:181–93).

At the informal end, the willingness of the population to defend and stick to Singlish is remarkable, especially so in the light of the government's stern rejection of this speech variety, which receives its official expression in an ongoing campaign known as the "Speak Good English Movement" (SGEM), officially launched in 2000 (see Low and Brown 2005:33–4, 198–200, 205–6; Chng 2003). Rubdy (2001) discusses this public debate in some detail, and comments on how in the 1999 discussion a majority "vociferously defended the use of Singlish," now "an icon of national identity" which has come to assume "a symbolic function as a language of solidarity, identity and pride" (347). Chng (2003) discusses the resistance to SGEM as a political conflict which reflects variant conceptions of Singapore's society. She argues that in a multilingual society there is clearly room for "Singlish" – "the quintessential mark of Singaporean-ness" (46) – as a variety appropriate in certain informal situations, not to be confused with contexts which call for the use of Standard English.

The issue of norm selection is still under discussion (see Pakir 1993, 1994). Ooi (2001:x) believes that "exonormative standards continue to define the study of English in the classrooms," but the development of an internal, Singaporean standard is also called for (Tay and Gupta 1983:177). In any case, a local linguistic norm, positively evaluated by many, is simply a piece of reality, and its formal recognition is called for (Ooi 2001:xi) and envisaged (Foley 1988:xiii–xiv; 2001:32). Gupta (1988) goes a long way toward defining elements of an endonormative standard on the level of syntax. Pakir (2001) argues that Singaporean English is moving into Kachru's "Inner Circle." Literary writing in Singaporean English is flourishing. Linguistic homogenization is observable as well, for instance when Platt and Weber (1980:46) note the "increasing similarity of Singaporean English as spoken by those of different ethnic backgrounds." Ansaldo (2004) also comments on the variety's increasing homogeneity, indicated by the observation that "local politicians tend to converge more and more toward a mesolectal variety" (144); he regards this development as a consequence of a local identification and progression into phase 4. Lim (2001), anticipating phase 5, already documents and discusses ethnic varieties within Singaporean English. No doubt the new variety has stabilized, and codification is under way: The *Times Chambers Dictionary* of 1997 was the first dictionary to systematically record Singaporeanisms and to advertise precisely this feature (see Schneider 1999:201–3). Lim (2004), a comprehensive scholarly analysis and description of distinctive features on the levels of phonology, grammar, and pragmatics, constitutes an important step forward in the process of codifying Singapore English. The recent book by Low and Brown (2005), targeted at a general audience of interested Singaporeans but not language specialists, may contribute to the dissemination of the idea of Singaporean English being a respectable variety in its own right to the broader public.

5.8   India

English in India (Map 5.4) is a topic marked by never-ending paradoxes (see Kachru 1983, 1994; Mehrotra 1998; Krishnaswamy and Burde 1998). The language was rooted there without the British really intending to leave this heritage. Controversies between "Anglicists" and "Orientalists" led to the victory of the former yet it turned out to be but a pyrrhic victory: English became not only an instrumental tool for "brown sahibs," serving the British interests, but a vibrant Asian language in itself. Post-independence India struggled with how to get rid of the colonial language as fast as possible, only to be caught ever tighter into its grip. And so today in terms of speaker numbers Indian English is one of the most important varieties on the globe. Locally it nevertheless constitutes a minority lect, largely restricted to utilitarian functions and certain domains and strata of society. Thus, we should not forget that the application of the Dynamic Model to Indian English accounts for only that segment of society that has been infiltrated by English, even if this is a strongly visible and powerful cohort. The majority of realities and lives of people on the subcontinent are untouched by the presence of English.

Map 5.4: India

5.8.1   Phase 1 (1600–1757)

There were earlier individual visits of Englishmen to India, but the onset of phase 1 can be dated precisely and conveniently. On December 31, 1600, Queen Elizabeth I granted a charter, guaranteeing a lucrative trade mono-poly, to the East India Company, a group of courageous London-based merchants. So sailors and traders brought the language to India's shores, and in the course of the seventeenth century they established the first permanent bases for their own activities, which triggered the linguistic and cultural infiltration of English in South Asia. So-called factories, trad-ing posts, were set up – 1612 at Surat, 1639–40 in Madras, 1674 in Bombay, 1690 in Calcutta. The other, perhaps even more important agents of the introduction of English to India were the missionaries, who throughout the seventeenth and eighteenth centuries proselytized some of the indigenous populations. Although they often used indigenous languages in this endeavor, the schools which they established at various localities through-out the country typically were run in English and thus spread the language. In 1659 they were permitted to share the ships of the East India Company, which simplified and strengthened their efforts. Some of the missionaries presumably had some education, but basically the early English input to India was far from elitist: "those who came to India were mostly uneducated merchants, sailors, and soldiers" (Krishnaswamy and Burde 1998:80).

So for almost two centuries, in a rather prolonged phase 1, English gradually gained more, but still limited, influence in India. The spread of English gained momentum rather late, during the second half of the eighteenth century, when the motivation shifted from purely economic inter-ests to a strive for political authority, with the British Crown getting involved and assuming joint responsibility with the Company in the India Act of 1784 (Kachru 1994:502). Thus, the Anglicization of India began with trade and turned into exploitation colonization only later, in the transition to phase 2.

Within the constraints of these subtypes we may assume the parameters of the Dynamic Model to apply. Certainly the identities of the parties involved were not yet affected: the merchants, sailors, and missionaries were Englishmen, and the people they encountered were the indigenous population. In numerical terms the size of the STL stream was rather small. Bilingualism with English spread slowly in the local populations, and some missionaries acquired some knowledge in indigenous languages. There is no evidence of koinéization, which is not surprising, given the absence of a sizeable settler community, though some dialect contact must have occurred: Mehrotra (1998:5) asserts that in the formative period "Northern British dialects and Cockney" constituted the major English language influences in India. Of course, place names are indigenous, and are used in English texts as well (see Yule and Burnell 1886:xvii).

5.8.2   Phase 2 (ca. 1757–ca. 1905)

The transition from phase 1 to phase 2, a stable colonial status with exonormative orientation, is difficult to date precisely. Basically, this is a process which progressed throughout the second half of the eighteenth century. In 1757, in the Battle of Plassey (north of Calcutta), the East India Company defeated the last independent Nawab (provincial viceroy) of Bengal, thus changing from an economic organization to a political power. During the next few decades the Company, supported by the British Crown, expanded and secured its authority throughout most of the subcontinent through political maneuvering (bribery is frequently mentioned), various treaties and charters, land grants, and minor military action. It was only in 1858, after the "Indian Mutiny," that the Crown assumed direct-rule authority and dissolved the East India Company.

The growing political grasp of the British in India was reflected by the rapid spread of English language teaching and bilingualism with English as a second language. "The period from 1780 to 1830 is characterized by the mushroom growth of a large number of English teaching schools in and around metropolitan towns such as Calcutta, Bombay and Madras" (Mehrotra 1998:3). In my view, the most fitting event and date to symbolize this transition and the onset of phase 2 is Raja Rammohan Roy's letter to Lord Amherst of 1823 (reprinted in Krishnaswamy and Burde 1998:164–5). Raja Roy, "a liberal and enlightened intellectual" (Krishnaswamy and Burde 1998:15) and a representative of modernist Indian leaders with similar thoughts and intentions, discarded the support of Sanskrit schools and thus indirectly asked for English to be taught systematically to the Indian leadership, viewing it as a window to western learning and the sciences. In our context this statement is interesting because it can be read as a direct expression of a characteristic identity construction of a member of the indigenous population (or at least its leadership), combining local roots with the putative advantages that the English language and through it access to western culture have to offer. In contrast, it is clear that the British in India saw themselves as representatives of their country and agents in her interest.

Raja Roy's letter is assumed to have boosted a debate between "Orientalists," who wanted Indians to be educated in their own languages and traditions, and "Anglicists," who favored the introduction of an English-based education system. The argument was decided in favor of the latter by the adoption of Macaulay's famous "Minute" of 1835, in which he vehemently fought for an English education to be established in India. It is clear, however, that Macaulay's goal was quite different from Raja Roy's, though leading to the same result. He was interested in the benefit not of the locals but in that of the British Empire, namely in forming "a class who may be interpreters between us and the millions whom we govern – a class of persons, Indians in blood and colour, but English in taste, in opinion, in morals and in intellect" (quoted from Kachru 1983:22).[22] Whatever one may think of this attitude, Macaulay's policy was officially endorsed, a step which marks the beginning of systematic and widespread bilingual education in India throughout the nineteenth century, the basis of the firm roots of English in the country. In the late nineteenth century English was the medium of instruction in over 60 percent of all elementary schools in India (Krishnamurti 1990:17). Around the turn of the twentieth century, under Viceroy Curzon, more emphasis was placed again on "vernacular" elementary education, and

English became gradually reduced in many schools to the status of a subject taught from grades 5 or 6 onwards (see Brutt-Griffler 2002:46, 53). Another major step in the institutionalization of English in India was certainly the foundation of three universities in 1857 at Bombay, Calcutta and Madras, followed by smaller colleges as well.

Hence, throughout most of the nineteenth century a sociolinguistic situation typical of phase 2 can be observed in India. Language contact between English and indigenous languages was widespread and regular, and bilingualism spread rapidly within the indigenous population. The linguistic orientation was clearly exonormative, with British English being the target. Knowledge of English was related to social class, characteristic of an elite, but this notion should not be defined too narrowly, because a functional communicative ability in English was also required in a wide range of middle-ranking functions (clerks, railway agents, military personnel, servants, etc.). According to Kachru (1983:23), English was also spreading "among the middle and lower classes of Indian society" by the early twentieth century.

Linguistically speaking, this is the period of heavy lexical borrowing from Indian languages into English (Kachru 1983; Mehrotra 1998). There is the usual share of fauna and flora words (though it seems that exposure to the wilderness and hence adoption of pertinent vocabulary was less direct than elsewhere): *bamboo, mango, betel, poon* 'timber tree,' *banyan-tree, doob* 'creeping grass,' *chiretta* 'Himalayan plant'; *bandicoot* 'kind of rat.' And there is a wide range of "Indianisms," words which denote elements of the indigenous culture and life styles: *calico, cheroot* 'kind of cigar,' *chitty/chit* 'letter, note,' *dhoti* 'loin-cloth worn by men,' *curry, loot, nabob, sahib, thug* 'swindler, robber,' *ghaut/ghat, veranda*; etc. Many of these were taken over into international English, while many more remained in local use. Yule and Burnell (1886) represents a remarkable early collection of such items.

5.8.3   Phase 3 (ca. 1905–)

During the twentieth century Indian English progressed into the process of nativization. This may seem surprising, as the country's intention clearly was to get rid of English as a piece of colonial heritage after independence, but, interestingly enough, quite the contrary happened: "Since 1947, English has grown and spread in India" (Gupta 2001:148); the language "has flowered in India to an extent it had never done in British times" (R. Bond, quoted in Mehrotra 1998:13). Let us look into the causes and the evidence for this assessment.

Again, it is difficult to posit a clear cut-off date for the onset of phase 3. Ferguson (1996) suggests independence as the third of a series of major, though "symbolic and arbitrary," dates in the coming of English to India. From a linguistic perspective this seems too late, however: both the fundamental rooting of the language in the country (a prerequisite for its later persistence) and the emergence of its structural peculiarities must have predated the year 1947. Krishnaswamy and Burde assume that it was after 1900 when English became "gradually detached from the British rule" and turned from a foreign to a second language (1998:110; see Kachru 1983:23). Political incidents to which the beginning of the linguistic phase may be tied also point to the early twentieth century. The "Swadeshi Movement" after the partition of Bengal in 1905, essentially an attempt at boycotting the British, is a good candidate: twenty years after the foundation of the Indian National Congress resistance against the British raj and the strive for independence became visible and seriously entered the political arena.[23] Gandhi's return from his South African exile in 1916 marks another important step which gave momentum to the process which culminated in independence in 1947. It is noteworthy that the language of the independence movement, in public but also beyond, was English (though Gandhi himself did not support English but campaigned for Hindustani as the language of unity).

In the social domain, more and more Indians used English for communication among themselves; formal and informal correspondence took place in English. Members of the Indian National Congress, lawyers, political activists, and other prominent Indians started using English in their social communication (Krishnaswamy and Burde 1998:112).

The post-1947 struggle about the future political status of English in India, reflected in various changes to the Constitution, is well documented (e.g. Kachru 1983). The language which formerly had been viewed as superimposed by the colonial power now became officially recognized in the Indian Constitution, if only for a transition period, until 1965. However, the idea to replace English by Hindi, which was to be developed into a national language, proved impracticable, and in the Official Languages Act of 1967 the Indian Lok Sabha (the lower house of Parliament) accepted the co-official status of English for an indeterminate period of time. The "three-language formula," adopted subsequently, called for education in Hindi, a major regional language, and English. The policy has not been successful, however, because of resistance against Hindi dominance in the South and the lack of interest of Hindi speakers in learning a Dravidian language in the northern parts of the country (Kachru 1994:552; Krishnaswamy and Burde 1998:16). Obviously, this constellation leaves English, at least in the official domain, with a very special status – unintended like this, but factually uncontested. So, contrary to expectations, nativization was actually accelerated after independence: "The process of Indianization of the English language got a fresh boost after the departure of native speakers from the Indian scene in 1947" (Mehrotra 1998:17).

The identity constructions of English speakers in India during the twentieth century were presumably as compartmentalized and versatile as the uses of the language were. Certainly in the STL strand, while it lasted, the basic identity remained British, though a strong admixture of a positive association with India may be assumed on the side of long-time residents. Especially among the lower ranks we have evidence of so-called "white Babus" who were culturally Indianized to a certain extent. This terminated with independence, however – in present-day India the STL stream has practically vanished, although it has left strong cultural and linguistic traces. The heritage that comes closest to this strand is the group of "Anglo-Indians," descendants of relationships between Europeans and Indians, and they are normally native speakers of English. Numerically speaking, this is a relatively small proportion of the population, however. In the IDG strand, the identity of Indians is also straightforward, as expected. Following Krishnaswamy and Burde (1998), it is marked by a "desire to accommodate the advantages of English within the indigenous orthodox sociocultural framework ... they will use English for certain purposes but their identity remains rooted in their cultural heritage" (110).

One aspect that distinguishes India from many other PCE-speaking countries, however, is the fact that a local form of English has not adopted the function of an identity-carrier. English is a marker of education, and it is useful for many purposes. In a country where there exists a tension between different language groups, notably Hindi speakers on the one hand and speakers of Dravidian languages on the other, it serves its classic role in an ESL country, that of an interethnically neutral link language which is qualified as a public and semiofficial language precisely because it is nobody else's (or at least not the competing group's) mother tongue. But despite this status it does not signal a pan-Indian identity.[24] It is conceivable that a distinctively Indian form of English could grow into the role of a national symbol, though at present, given the strong position of Hindi and the small fraction of English speakers, this seems highly unlikely.

In any case, on the sociolinguistic plane in the twentieth century we do find a number of the traces that characterize the phase of nativization. English is deeply rooted in the country, and bilingualism involving English is widespread, and practically universal among the educated. The shape of English is a strongly localized one, a characteristic which is due to some extent to the fact that learners have approximated not inaccessible external models but rather local ones: the teachers and linguistic models of learners of English in India have usually been other Indians, not native speakers (Gupta 2001:154; Bhatt 2004:1017–8; Gargesh 2004:994). While the STL strand seems largely negligible in the present-day Indian context, it is illustrative of the dynamics of the variety. In the period before independence some lower-class whites also started to approximate the Indian way of speaking English and adopted some of these features into their own speech. Kachru (1983:228) observes:

On the analogy of *brown Sahibs* ('brown Englishmen,' used for Westernized Indians) we have the term *White Babus* used for 'English officers who have become de-Europeanized from long residence among undomesticated natives' ... In due course the *White Babus* developed certain features in their English which separated them from those Englishmen who had not "gone native."

While the "White Babus" represent the sociolinguistically innovative speakers who approximated IDG strand ways of speaking, it is clear that the norm remained external, and we actually do have occasional traces of a "complaint tradition." Krishnamurti writes: "the standard of English has been declining at an alarming rate because the demand is outstripped by supply of qualified teachers (sic)" (1990:21). Mehrotra (1998) maintains that the national movement before independence resulted in "estrangement with English and lowering of its standard" (5). Mathai, in his Preface to Nihalani et al. (2004), warns Indians to "note the peculiarities in their English and avoid those which may damage communication" (viii). Bailey (1996) quotes complaints by Indian scholars about the "steady decline of English" in the late twentieth century (though many others disagree with this assessment).

Present-day Indian English is a language variety which is primarily, though not exclusively, associated with certain domains: it is the language of government and politics, higher education, the judiciary except for the local level, business and the media (again, with the exception of activities in a local or regional context). It comes in a range of varieties, both regional and social. Regionality shows in speakers' accents, which frequently display interference from regional L1s and thus warrant labels like "Marathi English,' "Hindustani English," "Kannada English," etc. (e.g. Wiltshire 2005; see also Kachru 1994:508). Socially, lower-class speakers who operate in certain kinds of jobs (as servants, in tourism or trade, etc.) typically have a sufficient functional command of English down to pidginized forms, a situation which is reflected in labels like "Boxwallah English," "Butler English," "Babu English," "Kitchen English," and so on (Kachru 1983:70). Whether the language is spreading beyond these fairly narrow sociofunctional confines is difficult to say and to generalize. In urban contexts there is a strong demand for English, motivated by purely utilitarian considerations, on the side of lower-class Indians, and something like a grassroots spread of the language seems to be observable in some places.

For example, Viniti Vaish observes on the urban poor of New Delhi: "this community does not speak English though members of it can listen, read and write. It is not the class that speaks Indian English. But this community uses English to improve their job prospects just as one might learn to drive a car, so as to get a job as a driver" (p.c. 2003). What, if anything, will result from such developments in the long run seems impossible to judge.

Indian English shows strong signs of structural nativization, involving all levels of language organization. On the phonetic level, in addition to pronunciation details which can be regarded as transfer from different L1s and which therefore are regionally restricted, there are a number of features which characterize Indian English as such, including the following (Kachru 1983, 1994; Gargesh 2004):

- syllable-initial voiceless stops are unaspirated;
- /t/ and /d/ tend to be retroflexed;
- dental fricatives tend to be replaced by dental or alveolar stops;
- in many words the placement of accent is different from other varieties;
- the speech rhythm is marked by syllable-timing.

Lexical borrowing continues. In addition to loans from indigenous languages, some English words have changed their meaning and acquired distinctive denotations in India, for example *alphabet* 'letter,' *boy* 'male servant,' *mother* 'term of respect.' The creative potential of word formation is also fully employed (Kachru 1983), including both words which combine English constituents in a fresh way (e.g. *inside water, upliftment, maid-runner* 'procurer,' *cow-eater, flower-bed, sister-sleeper, sacred-ash*) and hybrid compounds (e.g. *burning-ghat, dhobi-washed, city-kotwali*) and derivatives (e.g. *Brahminhood, cooliedom, goondaism*). A tendency to reduce phrases to premodifying noun sequences has been observed, e.g. *key bunch* 'bunch of keys,' *God-love* 'love of God.'

Indian English outside the formal and written domain is also characterized by a large number of morphosyntactic innovations and other distinctive features. These include general patterns, some shared with other PCEs, like the following (Verma 1982; Kachru 1983, 1994; Sridhar 1996; Bhatt 2004; Schneider 2000a):

- invariant tags like *isn't it?* or *no*;
- pluralization of certain mass nouns, like *alphabets, furnitures, apparels*;
- omission or insertion of articles;
- use of the progressive with stative verbs;
- *wh*-interrogative clauses without inversion, e.g. *Where you are going?*;
- reduplication of adjectives and verbs;
- a wider range of uses of the past perfect structure, including present perfect and past meanings and a new function of pragmatic viewpoint marking (distancing from a narrative focus) (Sharma 2001).

In addition to these, a lot of the lexicosyntactic creativity that characterizes structural nativization can be observed here as well. This includes innovative collocational tendencies and phraseologisms (Kachru 1983; Sridhar 1996), e.g.:

- *Where does your wealth reside?* 'Where do you live?'
- *I bow my forehead*; *touch your feet*;
- *the touched man*; *fear of touch*; *untouchable*; *touched me and defiled me*; etc.
- *under the hands of men* 'subservient to'; *in her small age* 'young,' *outside man* 'stranger.'

Most notably, there is a wide range of innovative verb complementation patterns. Of the following list, the first two were mentioned in chapter 3 because they were disclosed and thoroughly documented in two recent studies of large-scale electronic corpora; the next two have been listed as observations and await further in-depth investigation (see Kachru 1983, 1994); and the last one documents Indian English structural uses which Shastri (1996) found in a corpus-based study:

- Verbs like *provide*, *furnish* or *supply* prefer the pattern types *someone provided them something* and *someone provided something to them* over a construction with *with*, and with verbs like *pelt*, *shower*, and *bombard* Indian English speakers prefer *to pelt something at/on someone* over *to pelt someone with something* (Olavarria de Errson and Shaw 2003).
- In ditransitive constructions, Indian English tends to either omit the recipient (so that *give something* is acceptable without another constituent) or to express the recipient as a complement of *to* rather than place him/her as an indirect object immediately after the verb. Ditransitive uses are possible with a wider range of verbs than in British English (Mukherjee and Hoffmann 2006).
- idiosyncratic transitive or intransitive uses of verbs, e.g. *reach*, *waive* used intransitively but *preside*, *dissent* transitively;
- particles added to verbs: *rear off*, *eat off*;
- further verb-complementation patterns. Of these, some are relatively common in Indian English in comparison with a British corpus: *interested to leave*; *prevent it doing something*; *like talking*; *hesitate at spending*; *suggested asking*. Others are also attested but found less frequently: *fail in making contact*; *failure in marriages*; *forbidden from speaking*; *want + that*-clause (also observed by Verma 1982:183); *want him eating*; *announced regarding . . .*; *informed that . . .*; *told to somebody*.

Finally, it is interesting to observe that in India, as in the Philippines or Malaysia, language mixing is going strong. This is a form of linguistic expression which both exploits a bilingual's creativity and opens inroads to communication in something like English, the prestige language, to speakers without much formal education. Kachru (1983:193–205) and Mehrotra

(1998:14) observed this a while ago, and if Baldauf (2004) is right this trend has skyrocketed since then: a mix of English and Hindi labeled Hinglish is the "fastest-growing language in the country," "the language of the street and the college campus," "a bridge between two cultures that has become an island of its own," a "jumble" which is "hip" and used by all multinational corporations in their ads. Examples include McDonald's *What your bahana is?* ('What is your excuse?') and Coca Cola's *Life ho to aisi* ('Life should be like this'). The explosion of Hinglish is dated back to the mid-1990s, especially to the introduction of cable television with its youth channels. It remains to be seen whether "Hinglish" or any other mixed code can fill the vacuum of a non-existing pan-ethnic informal identity carrier and can be viewed as the penetration of an English-derived variety into the lower echelons of society.

5.8.4 Early symptoms of phase 4?

Is Indian English moving further along the cycle? More than half a century after independence and with the process of nation-building far advanced (though, as we saw earlier, still disputed by some), this would not be surprising – if English were a carrier of such a national identity and a language which is accessible to a major portion of society. Neither of these conditions is true, however. A few factors are foreshadowing endonormative stabilization, but they are disputable or weak; they should therefore not be overestimated.

An endonormative attitude as such is definitely gaining ground, but it is also far from being generally accepted. A necessary first step is to get rid of negative sentiments, and even that is a recent development. According to Kachru (1994:526), "attitudinally it is a post-1960s phenomenon that identificational models such as 'Indian,' 'Sri Lankan,' and 'Pakistani' are used with a localised variety without necessarily implying a derogatory connotation." There is a change going on toward the "increasing acceptance of the endocentric educated varieties" (526). In a survey of Indian faculty and graduate students, Kachru found that the majority preferred British English as a model, but about a quarter of all respondents indicated a preference for Indian English. In a similar vein, Sahgal (1991) writes "while initially these innovations were rejected by purists, they are now becoming increasingly accepted, since English is treated not as a foreign language but as part of the cultural identity of India" (303), and he finds an even higher acceptance rate, of 47 percent, for "ordinary Indian English" (304). Gupta believes that "an acceptable SIE [Standard Indian English] has developed and has come to be recognized" (2001:155). These are minority views, however; in theory, what Kachru (1994:426) calls the "idealised linguistic norm" of British English is still upheld in educational institutions.

An advanced factor, indicative of the strong acceptance of Indian English as a language of the educated, is literary creativity. It is well known that for a number of decades India has produced great and internationally successful writers who write in English but at the same time emphasize the Indian-ness of their texts and their cultural affiliation (see Kachru 1983:42, 85–9, 1994:528–33; Paul 2003).

Stabilization, homogenization, and codification are lagging far behind, however. Given the wide range of different Indian Englishes that can be observed the notion of a "General Indian English," an intersection of some non-regional features of educated pronunciation, perhaps represents an approximation to a uniform national standard (see Kachru 1994:515). Gargesh (2004) states that "many ... features converge into what can be considered a 'general' phonology of IndE" (992). Codification is called for occasionally (Kachru 1983:165–89). Works like Yule and Burnell (1886), for lexis, and Nihalani et al. (2004), for general usage issues, may be regarded as forerunners, but they are clearly a far cry from an adequate descriptive account of Indian English. In fact, these two works are motivated by intercultural curiosity and an exonormative attitude, respectively. However, Macmillan Australia, in collaboration with the Macquarie Dictionary company, is branching out into Asia. Together with Macmillan India it is producing a series of learners' dictionaries of various sizes for the Indian market, and the production of a bigger Indian dictionary is on the agenda (Susan Butler, p.c. 2006).

So Indian English remains a complex, elusive, and problematic entity, "janus-like" (Mehrotra 1998:6) and "a unique case of linguistic schizophrenia" (Kachru 1983:179). On the one hand, we find assessments which assign positive emotional qualities to Indian English: for educated Indians the variety is "very much a part of themselves and their daily lives," "inseparable from everyday concerns," "not merely a means of learning marketable subjects," and its speakers express "feelings, ideas, and knowledge ... all as much in the English language as in their mother tongue" (Paul 2003:360). On the other hand, we get quite the opposite attitudes as well:

English and English education have been with a section of the urban population so long that it has uprooted quite a few, and the result is that they are neither here nor there; this section of the population has no mother tongue and no cultural roots in the conventional sense. (Krishnaswamy and Burde 1998:127)

Given the current situation, Indian English is likely to stay and to defend the compartmentalized domains which it controls, and probably to keep growing further in terms of speaker numbers and competence levels. At present it seems unlikely, however, that the language is going to cross the line and acquire new, emotionally more laden functions in Indian society. There are indicators pointing in that direction: Sahgal's study shows "that educated Indians are beginning to use English in the more intimate domains of family and friendship," though more strongly in Bengali and Tamil communities than in Hindi ones (1991:303). Such indicators are few and rare, however. For the majority of Indians the assessment of English as a tool for social advancement and functional purposes is still valid. As long as the *raison d'être* of Indian English is still essentially utilitarian and it is not a medium for community solidarity, the language is not likely to change its character and status in the near future.

5.9   South Africa

The complexity of the sociolinguistic constellations in South Africa (Map 5.5) probably exceeds that of any other country treated in this

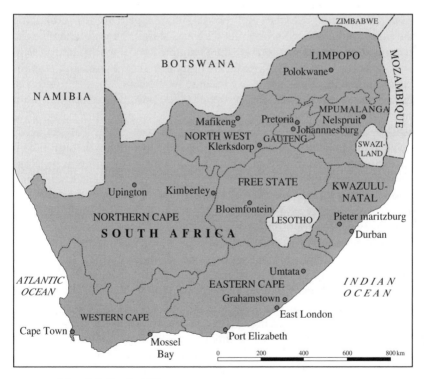

Map 5.5: South Africa

book. It is no coincidence that the country typically fails to show up in ENL – ESL or Inner – Outer Circle listings: South Africa would qualify for both of these categories at the same time, and also for neither of them, depending on which aspect of its language situation is emphasized. This complexity arises not primarily from the country's multilingualism but rather from the fact that a comparatively high number of distinct, compartmentalized speech communities have entered the arena at different points in time and have interacted with each other under varying social circumstances. Various forms of English have had different histories and social meanings for each of these groups at different periods. Furthermore, South Africa has experienced an unusually large number of radical changes of direction in its linguistic and cultural history – certainly so with the beginning and the end of Apartheid. The present-day democratic but also demanding language policy, adopted after the peaceful "rainbow revolution," presents another challenge to the country's linguistic evolution and to the speech communities and speakers affected.

Thus, on a nationwide basis converging tendencies have been weaker than elsewhere, though basically all of the population groups involved have shared the colonial and postcolonial experience of occupying the same land and need to interact with each other. Therefore, unlike the classifications mentioned earlier, the Dynamic Model works here as well, although it is more difficult to identify its different phases and components. Different ethnic groups (Africans, Afrikaners, whites, Coloureds, Indians) have proceeded along the cycle at their own pace, depending upon group-specific circumstances which have determined their respective attitudes and identities. So the chronology of constituent features needs to be handled a little more flexibly: at the same point in time but in different groups we find concurrent manifestations of different developmental stages. South Africa accommodates several PCEs, as it were, and some authors have argued for the status of each of the major varieties as one of the "New Englishes" and treated them accordingly (e.g. Watermeyer 1996:109–10 for Afrikaans English). However, the overarching political conditions like statehood and language policy, with their ramifications for educational settings and norm definitions, tie them all together under the cover term of South African English (SAfE). And it is interesting to observe that in the recent past, in the new democratic, socially unified South Africa many of the old categorizations of the pre-apartheid days are losing importance, a fact which has linguistic consequences. Of course, ethnic compartmentalization has not vanished overnight, but it is definitely less important and less prominent than it was, and consequently, as we will see, ethnolinguistic differences are beginning to get blurred.

As before in the case of India, the Dynamic Model applies only to the segment of society which is in touch with and affected by English. In this case, however, this definition includes a substantial majority of the population. By today, South Africans without any contact with English, largely rural, uneducated and poor people, are relatively few. Multilingualism plays a role, however, because for many speakers there are a variety of language options, in addition to varieties of English, as identity markers.

5.9.1   Phase 1 (1806–1822/1870s)

English got to South Africa around the turn of the nineteenth century, when the Cape region was a minor holding disputed among European powers in the wake of the Napoleonic wars.[25] The area had been a Dutch possession since 1652. Both a first occupation of the Cape in 1795 and its seizure in 1806 were directed against French expansionist claims (after French occupation of the Netherlands), and in 1815 the Congress of Vienna formally established British sovereignty over the Cape. A few years of transient relocation of administrators and military personnel were followed by a systematic settlement move by the so-called 1820 settlers, mostly lower-class people from southern England, who occupied primarily the eastern Cape (the area around Grahamstown and Port Elizabeth). Under harsh conditions they formed a frontier society and came to dominate the earlier residents, the Dutch (with whom initial relations were relatively egalitarian, as they possessed valuable expertise) and the black Africans.

A few decades after the establishment of the Cape colony another branch of the STL stream brought a new phase 1 to a different region, Natal. In another organized settlement, between 1848 and 1862 about the same number of settlers but quite a different group of people, more strongly from the middle and upper classes and from the Midlands and the North, came to create "a corner of Victorian England on alien soil" (Lanham 1982:325).

For a long period of time both English settler groups remained rather distinct, and both have produced different varieties of South African English, so it makes sense to distinguish two different streams of the STL strand. What began as two settlement waves and a regional difference came out later, by the twentieth century, as a sociolinguistic distinction. The speech of the 1820 settlers, who were predominantly rural and unsophisticated, resulted in the lower-class white South African dialect, variously called "Extreme" (Lanham 1982) or "Broad" (Bowerman 2004b) SAfE. The Natal settlers, on the other hand, who were higher in status, more urban and laid more emphasis on education, developed a speech form labeled "Respectable" or "General" SAfE. In both cases a recognizable founder effect is worth noticing: despite their relatively small numbers (in comparison, for instance, with the hundreds of thousands of settlers who followed them after 1870) these two groups laid the foundations for the main accents of present-day SAfE.

Unlike in many other comparable situations, the British settlers on South African soil encountered not one but two resident groups – not only Africans but also Afrikaners (then known as the Boers). Actually, for the Africans (including the Khoisan populations) conditions under British rule did not change substantially in comparison with those under Boer dominance. The nineteenth century saw significant warfare between the British and the Xhosa and other tribes, but to some extent they had been used to the presence of, and the dominance by, Europeans and their descendants, and most of them continued to live in their traditional lifestyles. But British control made a real difference to the Boers, the descendants of Dutch immigrants, who had lived in the area for centuries and had established a slave society. In the light of the Dynamic Model, it makes best sense to regard them as another indigenous group, despite their European ancestry: they had resided on the Cape for generations, maintained few contacts with and enjoyed no support from the Netherlands, and had been thoroughly Africanized culturally and linguistically, including the transformation of their original Dutch language to the strongly contact-induced Afrikaans. This assessment conforms to more recent judgments in the country: "it is becoming quite common to hear claims that Afrikaans is an African language and an indigenous one at that ... [It is a] unique creation within Africa, ... not spoken outside southern Africa" (Mesthrie 2002c:6) Thus, even the initial setting explains some of the complexities of South Africa's linguistic contact landscape: two distinct branches of the STL strand met with two independent IDG strands.

The relationship between the English and the "Dutch" after the 1820 settlement was reasonably good, including some intermarriages, and many of the Dutch soon acquired English as a second language. Fundamentally, however, it was a dominance relationship: the "Dutch yielded to English in all domains of public life ... except on the remote dorps and farms" (Lanham 1982:324). Thus, in the "Great Trek" of 1836 and later many Dutch colonists evaded English rule and founded Boer republics to the north and east of the Cape (including Natal, where they would soon be under British dominance again). Having been anglicized to some extent before and recognizing the value of English, many of these so-called *Voortrekkers* brought English, in addition to their native Afrikaans, with them and thus initiated phase 1 in the hinterlands of South Africa.

It is clear that at this stage the identities of the parties involved were largely unbroken. Due to their status and orientation, the Natal settlers maintained considerably stronger ties with England than the 1820 settlers. As to the English and the Dutch, it may be presumed that their shared European ancestry and complexion offered them the option of a certain degree of an "us" reading as against the Africans. Though the anglicization of many Afrikaners and the acquisition of Afrikaans by many descendants of the English indicate some cultural and linguistic assimilation, the Great Trek makes it clear that it was the Afrikaners' desire to maintain their distinctiveness and independence.

So, sociolinguistically speaking, contacts between the English settlers and the Dutch were rather extensive (more so than is customary for a STL – IDG strand relationship at this stage), though the burden of linguistic adjustment was distributed according to the power relationship: Many more Afrikaners became bilingual in English than the other way round (Branford 1996:39). Contacts with the African IDG group were much more restricted, though of course some did occur. As in India and elsewhere, bilingualism in English spread to blacks primarily through missionary schools, which reached a relatively small and somewhat elitist proportion of the black population. In line with the Dynamic Model, some language influence occurred also in the other direction: missionaries struggled with Zulu and other African languages, and even "many British children born in Natal learnt Zulu" (Mesthrie 2002d:17).

The contact situation between Europeans and Africans has actually produced a distinct community in South Africa's ethnic setup, the "Coloured" population group, predominantly of mixed ancestry. With people of part-Dutch parentage the community antedated the arrival of the British and was traditionally close to (but not merged with) the Afrikaners, and strongly Afrikaans-speaking. Given this background, membership in the community was somewhat fuzzily defined; it was a "catch-all" category with a restricted identity of its own (Finn 2004). However, up to the days of Apartheid when the label was functionalized for ethnic segregation, and continuing since then the Coloured have been considered a distinct group. The group soon participated in Afrikaans–English bilingualism and also multilingualism involving Bantu languages, and was actually even more prone to adopt English for the socioeconomic advancement that came with such a shift.

As is to be expected, the language structure of the British settlers showed marked koinéization. It occurred twice, actually, once in each of the two temporally and regionally separated settler streams. Concerning the Eastern Cape province, Lanham states: "Social leveling produced a homogeneous form of speech within a generation or two" (1982:325), a dialect largely based upon input from the Home Counties. As was stated earlier, due to the low social status and rural character of these speakers, this dialect later resurfaced as the lower class, "Extreme" form of white SAfE, while the koiné which resulted from the dialect contact situation in Natal became a middle-class norm, the "Respectable" accent.

The tendency of PCEs to accept and integrate toponyms from the IDG strand applies, but it is much stronger with respect to one of the IDG streams, the Afrikaans-based one, than the other. There are African place names as well (e.g. *Mdantsane, Thabazimbi, Nobokwe, Mkambati,* etc.), but the vast majority are Dutch-derived (e.g. *Kruidfontein, Roggeveldberge, Kroonstad, Klerksdorp, Stompneuspunt, Grootrivier,* etc.). Interestingly enough, SAfE borrowed not only place names in the proper sense from Dutch but also a surprisingly large number of "topographical words" to denote landscape features: *berg* 'mountain,' *dorp* 'small town,' *drift* 'ford,' *land* 'cultivated field,' *poort* 'narrow pass,' *rand* 'ridge,' and *veld* 'open country' were all borrowed between 1795 and 1838 (Branford 1994:446), and many more of that kind could be listed (e.g. *kloof* 'deep valley,' *kopje* 'hillock,' *krantz* 'overhanging cliff-face,' *vlei* 'lake, swamp,' and, from Zulu, *donga* 'eroded watercourse'; Silva 1997:164, 2001:86; Branford and Branford 1991).

5.9.2   Phase 2 (1822/1870s–1910)

After the initial settlements, the English influence was strongest in the Cape region and in Natal, which were colonies, but it was increasingly felt outside these core regions as well. A convenient early cut-off date to symbolize the onset of phase 2 in the Cape is the year 1822, when Lord Charles Somerset, the governor of the colony, proclaimed English to be the only official language of the Cape. In subsequent years this policy was deliberately implemented by importing teachers. So the Anglicization of the Cape and, later, Natal was the product of explicit political moves. Outside this region, the language also spread, due to its practical importance in the vicinity of English colonies and the bilingualism of many Afrikaners, but only slowly. This changed drastically in the 1870s, however, when the discovery of, first, diamonds near Kimberley and, then, gold in the Witwatersrand boosted the influx of English speakers into former Boer territory. In a short period of time cities mushroomed, and a new urban, socially stratified society based on a mining economy and growing wealth emerged. Politically speaking, growing tensions between the English and the Dutch led to two Anglo-Boer Wars around the turn of the century, and their outcome ultimately produced the unification of the British colonies and the Boer republics as the "Union of South Africa" in 1910.

Clues to the identities of the ethnic and social parties in that period can be derived from their moves and actions. Although the Boers accepted some degree of Anglicization and in general had reasonably good relationships with the British, the Great Trek and the foundation of their own republics, and later the readiness to go to war, shows that their primary goal was the independent maintenance of their own cultural identity, based upon their Dutch-African background and symbolized by the Afrikaans language. Blacks got pulled into the sphere of English in increasingly large numbers; in the lives of many of them English was "a necessary evil" (de Klerk 1999:312). On the one hand, this happened through education in mission schools, with conditions and results varying from an elitist character and a high standard of English proficiency in some institutions (Lanham 1982:326) to rather mediocre language training and acquisition. Problems included, for instance, the fact that many of the missionaries (and early teachers) were broad dialect speakers or not even the British (Mesthrie 2002a:111). Throughout the history of black education most teachers were L2 speakers themselves. On the other hand, an increasing number of Africans acquired a smattering of English or more through direct language contact, for example in urban labor contexts. In the STL communities a fundamentally English identity, though mixed with the African experience, was upheld, more so in the more cultivated contexts of Natal than in the harsh rural conditions of the Cape.

In Natal in the 1860s a new, large, and important group entered the scene and contributed to South Africa's ethnolinguistic kaleidoscope. To meet the labor shortage on sugar plantations after the abolition of slavery, large numbers of contract laborers from India were brought in, and most of them stayed after their five- or ten-year contracts had expired. Between 1860 and 1911, more than 152,000 Indians immigrated. While they strongly upheld their Indian identity and cultural heritage, they recognized the utilitarian value of English, and so bi- and multilingualism involving English spread gradually, and certainly more rapidly than among the Africans. Mesthrie observes that "Ghandi mentions the use of English by some urban youths amongst themselves, in a newspaper article of 1909 – i.e. before the end of the period of indenture" (2004a:954), and by the early twentieth century the proportion of Indians who knew English had already reached 40 percent (see Mesthrie 1992, 1996, 2002a, 2004b, 2004c).

While the sociolinguistic conditions in the old settlement regions evolved only slowly (with the exception of the arrival of the Indians, who were, however, not strongly integrated), the new mining economy with its population influx and explosion on the diamond and gold fields brought South Africa into the industrial age and caused a radically new, urban rather than rural, society structure. The cities attracted people from all across the country and were thus the sites of both social struggle and radically new sociolinguistic alignment processes. The newly emerging urban societies were strongly stratified socially. Johannesburg in those days is reported to have been "very British"; the "reference figures were the home-born, upper-class men and women" (Lanham 1996:22). Natalians were better prepared for this new orientation and competition. They usually succeeded in establishing themselves as an urban middle class, while the rural Cape settlers and the Afrikaners typically occupied the lower social positions. Many Africans worked in the mines, along with low-status whites and new immigrants from Europe. A relatively larger group of newcomers were Jews, who had left eastern Europe after pogroms. Their background and their emphasis on education enabled them to be upwardly mobile and to integrate successfully, which usually implied the adoption of English with a middle-class, Natal-based accent.

Hierarchy differences in this newly stratified society were symbolized, amongst other things, by linguistic means. At the top end, the exonormative orientation was a matter of status and faith: "British upper-class speech symbolically conveyed the attributes of the power group: social sophistication, British nationalism, leadership and authority, good education, correctness, and knowledge of proprieties"; "elocution teachers" provided access to these non-material status symbols to newcomers (Lanham 1982:328). In comparison, local accents were disregarded, and among these former regional dialect differences were reallocated as social status indicators, as was mentioned earlier: while the rural Cape and Afrikaner accents were stigmatized, Natalian speech came to occupy an intermediate position. In the upper class it was denigrated as non-British, but for many South Africans who lacked access to British models and sophisticated discriminations it served as a reasonably accessible model (328). Many features of Natal English thus established themselves as an informal standard of spoken SAfE, the "Respectable" accent (Lanham 1982, 1996; Gordon and Sudbury 2002). Natal English was also the variety to which the Indians were primarily exposed and accommodated. This pattern of a stratified industrial society, with accent discrimination by social class and an exonormative orientation at the top end, lasted well into the twentieth century (Lanham 1996:21).

The IDG strands participated in these developments, but only to a certain extent. Among the blacks, a growing number of schools and an extended range of opportunities for interaction in urban contexts caused bilingualism with English to keep spreading slowly but gradually. The Afrikaners, typically rural in orientation, tended not to profit from urbanization and industrialization, and their accent was stigmatized. Consequently, during that period the gulf between the English and the

Afrikaners grew, Afrikaans grew in importance within the group, and their standards of English are reported to have declined (Lanham 1982:329).

The linguistic effects resulting from these extended contacts primarily include a wide range of loan words from both IDG strands, documented in two big dictionaries (Branford and Branford 1991; Silva et al. 1996; see also Branford 1994; Silva 1997, 2001; Bowerman 2004a:958–60). The relatedness and relative similarity between Dutch and English facilitated loan translations rather than direct loans: "Many animal and plant names are translations from South African Dutch: *bamboo fish, bushbuck, puff-adder, night-adder, redbuck, reedbuck, sea-cow, springbuck*; and *bitter apple, blackwood, ironwood, milkwood, monkey-rope, stinkwood, sugarbush,* and *yellowwood*" (Silva 1997:165). Some Afrikaans fauna and flora words are direct borrowings: *vygie* 'little fig,' *fynbos* 'bush vegetation'; *meercat, boomslang* 'tree snake,' *wildebeest* 'wild ox.' Fauna and flora words from African languages include the following: *buchu* 'kind of plant,' *dagga* 'kind of hemp,' *morogo* 'wild spinach,' *marula* 'kind of tree,' *madumbi* 'kind of plant'; *tsessebe* 'antelope,' *mahem* 'crane,' *nunu* 'insect,' *tegwaan* 'kind of bird.' And there is a wide range of cultural terms, for local objects, habits, etc.: *bakkie* 'very light delivery van,' *boerewors* 'spicy sausage,' *braai* 'barbecue,' *koeksister* 'plaited doughnut, dipped in syrup,' *rondavel* 'circular, single-roomed building,' *veldskoen* 'shoe or ankle-boot of rough leather'; *abakwetha* 'Xhosa initiate to manhood,' *bonsella* 'small gift,' *indaba* 'tribal discussion,' *tagathi* 'witchcraft,' *induna* 'leader,' *diretlo* 'ritual murder,' *kaross* 'traditional clothing,' *kgotla* 'tribal (now political) meeting-place,' *imbongi* 'praise singer,' *muti* 'objects used in (traditional) medicine,' *sangoma* 'witch doctor,' and so on. According to Branford (1994:442), 10 percent of the loans in SAfE denote plants, 15 percent animals, 37 percent material culture, and 12 percent features of nature; about half of all loans are from Afrikaans, 11 percent from Bantu languages, and 12 percent from other languages (444).

5.9.3   Phase 3 (1910–1994)

The political status of the region changed decisively in 1910. In the Boer Wars, Britain gained sovereignty over the two Boer republics, Transvaal and the Orange Free State. The Cape and Natal colonies and these two now jointly formed the Union of South Africa. Although this new polity remained formally under British dominance, this was a decisive step toward a self-contained state, able to handle her affairs largely on her own. In the years up to World War II, ongoing urbanization, industrialization, and interethnic contacts brought the country closer to modernity, though the basically British cultural orientation remained unchallenged.

The cleavage between the English and the Afrikaners grew, however, and a definitive change occurred when a national election (with the blacks disenfranchised) brought the National Party, comprised mainly of Afrikaners, to power in 1948. They steered the country into the infamous system of Apartheid, and thus into international isolation, until early in the 1990s the leaders were wise enough to recognize that change was unavoidable and set the course toward real democratization and a new constitution. In between, in 1961, South Africa became a republic and thus formally independent, but in practice this date did not critically change the course of the country's history.

So in the light of the Dynamic Model the conditions for phase 3, nativization, to set in vibrantly were given after 1910: the country was practically free to decide on her own fate, and the role of Britain as a distant point of cultural orientation, valid as such for only a fraction of the population anyhow, diminished. Both the identity writings of the major ethnic groups and the sociolinguistic conditions and attitudes reflected this state of affairs.

Rising Afrikaner nationalism resulted in a growing promotion of Afrikaans, fostered by the political conditions after 1948. However, despite an ongoing urbanization of the Afrikaners, in the cities the economic power, associated with cultural status, strongly rested with English-speakers. Among them, exonormative attitudes persisted with some but kept diminishing for most in the course of time: "For many older anglophiles 'English' is still 'British', but younger ones feel less strongly" (Lanham 1982:345).

By mid-century, in the ADS strand, within the Indian community, the balance tipped toward English, which gradually became the home language and even the language which some parents and grandparents learned from their children and grandchildren. The segregation of the Apartheid years certainly contributed to the crystallization of a separate variety of English as used by Indians (Mesthrie 2002a:115). By the late twentieth century South African Indians, while not having given up their Indian-descendant identity, were mostly English-speaking, with a distinctive accent having some similarities to Indian English.

Similarly, though not as vibrantly, English kept encroaching among the IDG-strand community of black Africans. In addition to the general range of contacts, two political events strongly increased the prestige and attractiveness of English in this group in the second half of the twentieth century, even before the end of Apartheid. One was the struggle for a proper language of instruction, especially in elementary education. The Bantu Education Act of 1953 provided for elementary education in the mother tongue, a policy also recommended by UNESCO. However, its South

African implementation under the Apartheid regime lacked the essentially humanitarian motivation behind this recommendation. It was intended to keep blacks in the status of a semi-educated labor force (Mesthrie 2002d:22). The fact that access to English was discouraged seems to have made it even more attractive, however. Consequently the government's attempt to replace its status as a medium of instruction in secondary education by Afrikaans led to the Soweto riots of 1976, initiated by schoolchildren. Secondly, English was the language of the African National Congress and its largely exiled leadership; so in the black community it also enjoyed political support and attractiveness "from above," as it were. Thus, by the end of Apartheid, the attitude of blacks toward English, the language of struggle and liberation, was in general thoroughly positive. Estimates about speaker proportions vary between about one third and two thirds of the black population (de Klerk 1999:314).[26]

So, in South Africa's sociolinguistic arena of the twentieth century English was ubiquitous, despite Apartheid and Afrikaner political dominance after mid-century. The major ethnic groups largely maintained their distinct languages. In addition, they developed specific varieties of English in a rich array of contact situations, marked by bilingualism and multilingualism. Accents of English became loaded with sociolinguistic meaning. We also find the resistance to these new developments which is typical of this stage. As early as in 1953 the Public Service Commission deplored "a grave decline in standards of English" in entrance examinations (Lanham 1982:329), and occasional outcries of this complaint tradition by conservative speakers have continued to the present day. However, the formerly loud complaints have now "quietened down to a muted whimper [even if] die-hard prescriptivists will undoubtedly continue to rage against the 'damage' which English is suffering at the hands of BSAE" (de Klerk 1999:318).

Structural nativization has been going strong on the phonological, lexical, and grammatical levels, and has produced a set of social and ethnic varieties with many shared features and some features of their own. White dialects of English are most obviously socially stratified, but it is clear that conservative, British-oriented upper-class forms are marginalized, and the common, general norm of English derives from Natal speech and the "Respectable" accent. Afrikaner English still has a few peculiarities (Watermeyer 1996), but it has largely merged with lower-class white speech from the Cape and to some extent with Coloured English. Indian English expresses an ethnic identity, though its educated form closely approximates general SAfE except for accent. Black South African English has of course been projected to a special place of prominence by the end of Apartheid and the rise to power of African leaders. Lanham assumes that it has been moving away from its former high standards and been influenced by African languages (i.e. nativizing strongly) especially since the mid-twentieth century (1982:326, 333).

For all of these varieties, excellent documentations of their manifold phonetic and grammatical properties are available.[27] Suffice it therefore, in the present context, to state that we also find the types of phenomena that have been identified as specifically characteristic of newly emerging PCEs, although my impression is that perhaps due to the complexity of the conditions of their evolution these features are less prominent than in other PCEs. There are of course distinctive accent features, some of which can be accounted for as transfer from erstwhile native languages. Innovations on the lexical level include:

- new word formation products (*blueground* 'diamond-bearing ground,' *bossboy* 'black team leader,' *national road* 'inter-city highway,' *monkey's wedding* 'rain and sunshine simultaneously'),
- hybrid formations (*bundu-bashing* 'traveling over rough terrain,' *bushveld*),
- semantic changes (*drift* 'ford'), and
- phraseologisms (*have a cadenza* 'react hysterically,' *hold thumbs* 'cross fingers,' *go well* 'goodbye' (said to the one leaving), *stay well* (said to the one left behind), *is late* 'has died,' *cope up with*; black SAfE: *you are scarce* 'haven't seen you for a while,' *pass my regards*; Indian SAfE: *can't stick the heat* 'stand ...,' *take out one's clothes*).

Some of the formations of the Apartheid days were politically loaded, like *exit permit* (which did not entail the right to return), *reference book* (ID required by Africans), or *homeland*. There are also lexicogrammatical innovations, e.g.:

- special complementation structures (white SAfE: *reply me, explain me, lecture sth.*, intransitive *bring, capable to do sth.*; Cape Flats English: *throw someone with something, promise for someone*; Afrikaans English: *importance to do sth.*, black SAfE: *try + that*-clause, *in order that + clause*), or
- distinctive preposition uses (*by the house* 'near', *anxious over*; Cape Flats: *be scared for, on school, take photos from*).

A progressive structure with *busy* but an extended meaning range (*I was busy losing my house*) is supposed to be a transfer phenomenon from Afrikaans. Jeffery and van Rooy (2004) show how the adverb *now* has acquired two new functions in SAfE, one as an emphasizer (possibly a transfer product) and the other, when placed between *to* and a verb, to express an emotional stance, marking the action as a nuisance (most likely a structural innovation). The list could be continued easily.

Remarkably, language mixing, which we found to be a strong indicator of hybrid identities in many other multicultural societies, is going strong in

South Africa as well. De Klerk remarks: "This may in fact be where BSAE is heading, and the need to sprinkle one's English with one's mother-tongue may well become absolutely essential – playing that all-important role of marking identity" (1999:315). A similarly positive attitude to code-switching is expressed by Murray (2002), who indirectly attributes covert prestige to mixing, as it is used "by students to subvert the power of teachers" (440). The most substantial documentation of this phenomenon is provided by Slabbert and Finlayson (2000), who present mixing in townships as an expression of hybrid, western plus African identities. McCormick (1995) shows that in Cape Town's District Six a mixed code between Afrikaans and English has "become a marker of the community's sense of identity" (193).

5.9.4 Into phase 4 (1994–)

The non-violent "rainbow revolution," which culminated in the free election of 1994 and brought Nelson Mandela and his ANC-led government to power, radically transformed the course of South Africa's history. It gave full civil rights to all citizens, irrespective of ethnicity, and in a sense, for the first time, it gave the country the features of political independence: freedom to decide on her own fate, no longer under the sovereignty of Britain nor under the dominance of a single group oppressing the others. In the light of the Dynamic Model, this event clearly qualifies as an "Event X," a spectacular, quasi-catastrophic change of direction.

Most importantly, this transformation affected the identity of South Africans – it actually introduced a redirection of the emphasis of a collective identity from one's social or ethnic group to one's status as a member of a newly forging nation. Precisely as is implied by the identity features of phase 4 in the Dynamic Model, this new national identity builds upon the unity of the nation derived from sharing the soil to build a transethnic and multicultural society. All of this is epitomized in the beautiful image of the "Rainbow Nation," reportedly coined by Archbishop Desmond Tutu and picked up by President Mandela immediately after taking office: "Each of us is as intimately attached to this beautiful country as are the famous jacaranda trees of Pretoria and the mimosa trees of the bushveld – a rainbow nation at peace with itself and the world." More than a decade later, there are also voices to be heard that accuse "rainbowism" of "sugar-coating" the harsh realities that the country now has to face, but the nation-building process as such remains unchallenged.

No local variant of English is the carrier of this newly emerging national identity, however. The debate about language issues in the country tends to revolve around the radical language policy of the 1996 Constitution which, as is well known, grants official language status to as many as eleven languages – English, Afrikaans, and nine African tongues (see Mesthrie 2002d:23–4). Serious efforts are being made to turn this policy statement into reality by developing the African languages (e.g. by expanding their vocabularies), by introducing them into secondary and even tertiary education, and by promoting their use in as many spheres of life as is possible, but these efforts are constrained by economic difficulties and some doubt as to the feasibility and desirability of this process.

Sociolinguistic realities are, however, different from what some language planners want them to be. In practice, the attraction of English is immense, and it appears to be a much stronger force than well-meant policy measures. Only about 8.1 percent of the population speak it natively, according to the 2001 Census (about half of these are descendants of Europeans and the majority of the others are of Indian ancestry). Most of the others want to learn and use it, however, mostly for utilitarian purposes as the entry ticket to better jobs, internationalization, and so on, but also because of its rapidly growing importance in interethnic communication in the country. De Klerk (1997) provides a nice case study of three females who represent successive generations of a Xhosa family, looking into their exposure to, proficiency in, and attitudes to English. It is quite clear that the importance of English and the desire to master it grow strongly in each generation. In a similar vein, de Klerk and Barkhuizen (1998) show that in the military, English, having replaced Afrikaans in that role, is quite automatically the language of choice when interethnic understanding is at stake. "In reality, the decline of Afrikaans in public roles has been drastic, while the dominance of English is almost total, particularly in education . . . English is the language to aspire to in the New South Africa. . . . It is likely to retain this role for the foreseeable future" (Bowerman 2004b:934). Silva aptly summarizes the situation as follows:

English is scarcely neutral, but it is the only possible political choice as lingua franca. Afrikaans, probably understood by more rural people, is not an option because of its history. And how could one of the nine [other] official languages be chosen over the others? Politicians and position papers condemn the hegemony of English, and call for the development and modernisation of the African languages for higher education; yet, the reality is that practicality, cost, and public opinion all lead to English. (2001:91)

Of course there is also resistance to these developments: English is not only the language of access but also a barrier for those who do not command it (Silva 2001:85; Kamwangamalu 2002a, 2002b, 2003; Murray

2002:443). Attitudes vary, and some South Africans' attitude to English is certainly ambivalent. Slabbert and Finlayson (2000) show that a delicate balance holds in the township which they study: English is esteemed, but too much English is viewed negatively as "too white" (128). They believe that a "shift back to the African languages and cultures, indeed to an African renaissance, is therefore a distinct possibility" (134). Right now, however, indicators for such a development are very weak at best.

Despite occasional complaints and remnants of conservative prescriptivism (e.g. Silva 1997:174), South African English is slowly moving toward endonormativity, though not to homogeneity. Occasionally, mention is made of differences between ethnic varieties getting slowly blurred (Silva 2001:88), but if it is really true that a focusing process toward a pan-South African norm is being initiated the outcome of such a process certainly is still a few generations down the road. So far, group-specific norms have emerged, which are accepted by many as adequate in certain domains and contexts. Rajend Mesthrie (p.c. 2006) sees signs that the "Respectable" accent, with some additional influence from "American sitcom English," is becoming a non-racial norm among many middle-class teenagers and university students. He is carrying out a research project to study this accommodation process.

At the upper end of the social spectrum, an endonormative consensus may not yet have been reached, but it is clear that at least the days of an exonormative orientation, e.g. as mirrored by the requirement to use RP in the media, have ceased (Gordon and Sudbury 2002:76). White SAfE, derived primarily from Natal speech and "Respectable" SAfE, constitutes a de-facto norm of SAfE in education. Bowerman (2004b) suggests that "children from 'non-white' communities who attend [prestigious] schools which uphold WSAfE norms are increasingly adopting these norms into their own speech" (935). According to Branford, a "striking change of attitude" has occurred during the last few decades, caused by literary achievements and "the obvious delight of the popular press in the expressive potential of South African English." He therefore expects SAfE "to become more South African" in the future (1994:494). These remarks imply a clear move toward endonormativity. Indian SAfE has also crystallized to the point that an educated pronunciation norm with a few ethnic features exists (Mesthrie 1992, 2004c).

Of course, endonormative acceptance relates primarily to the pronunciation level. Nonstandard grammar is not accepted, and the acceptance of local structures which are not explicitly marked as nonstandard varies (and is not a topic that speakers tend to be aware of anyhow). De Klerk (1999:315) showed, for instance, that 80 percent of a sample of Xhosa-speaking teachers accepted the pattern *She was refusing with my book* as grammatical but 90 percent rejected *I tried that I might see her.*

In the context of discussing encroaching norms and standards in SAfE, Black SAfE, especially as spoken by educated speakers, occupies a very special position. This is due not only to the fact that the majority of the South African population consists of Native Africans but also to the continuous presence of the accent as used by black political leaders in the media. Some authors believe in an explicit "restandardization" of SAfE with the Black variety as a target, a "new standard" (Brutt-Griffler 2002:163; see de Klerk 2003; van der Walt and van Rooy 2002). Black SAfE is now gaining native speaker status: there is an increasing (though still rather small) number of children who grow up speaking it as their first language.[28] It is clear that the variety has for a long time enjoyed covert prestige among Africans. Consider the following, telling, statement: "Black children who attend private schools are sometimes embarrassed to be seen to speak standard SAE, and they therefore adopt a more typical African pronunciation in the townships" (Silva 2001:89). De Klerk and Gough see this prestige now becoming explicitly overt (2002:370), as is evidenced by observations like the following: "serious announcements and up-market advertisements are increasingly in BSAE accents, reflecting changing perceptions of its status" (371; see Coetzee-van Rooy and van Rooy 2005). So there seems to be potential for the variety to be not only an "established symbol of identity, solidarity and of aspirations of black South Africans" (Lanham 1996:27) but of becoming even "a powerful national unifier, bridging the gap between speakers of very different indigenous languages" (de Klerk 1999:318).

Two more indicators suggest that SAfE has been making progress into phase 4. One is a broadly based and generally recognized literary creativity, spearheaded by two recent Nobel laureates: Nadine Gordimer in 1991 and J. M. Coetzee in 2003. The other is a decisive step toward codification, though only on the lexical plane, with the production of two substantial scholarly dictionaries, Branford and Branford (1991) and, in the style and quality of the *Oxford English Dictionary*, Silva et al. (1996).

Thus, SAfE has made deep inroads into phase 4, although it is not justified to talk of a single, stabilized variety, and an endonormative orientation is highly disputed at best. Homogeneity seems a future possibility in the middle classes (Mesthrie, p.c. 2006), though it is unlikely ever to characterize the entire society, with ethnic and social identities and varieties persisting. At the present stage it is impossible to tell how much a growing national identity will contribute to further homogenization. Besides, SAfE operates in the context of strong multilingualism, and African languages (including Afrikaans) are likely to remain the primary ethnic markers. No doubt the strong role of English in the country will persist, and it will be interesting to see where the present momentum toward English will lead.

5.10   Kenya

English in East Africa (Map 5.6) is frequently treated as a coherent topic, because the region shared much of its early colonial history and some of its language features. Since independence, however, the three big states of the region have gone radically different ways. In Uganda, a cruel military dictatorship in the 1980s disrupted the country's evolution, and little documentation is available on the present state of English there (with the notable exception of Mazrui and Mazrui 1996); hence it will not be discussed here. Tanzania, to be discussed in section 5.11, deliberately followed a quasi-socialist path and pursued an African-centered language policy. Kenya, on the other hand, has opened itself to the world and has seen the English language thriving, within limitations.

5.10.1   Phase 1 (1860s–1920)

Although the first British ships reached the East African Coast in the late sixteenth century, a serious onset of phase 1 can be dated only into the 1860s, when (after a brief interlude which turned Mombasa into a protectorate 1824–6) the British became interested and involved in the coastal cities of East Africa, essentially as stepping stones to India.[29] At about the same time the first explorers and missionaries began to venture into the hinterland, mostly along established trading routes. After the so-called "scramble for Africa," the 1884–5 Berlin conference assigned formal authority in the region to the British. Their interest in the region remained small, however, until the construction of a railway in 1902, connecting the coast with Kisimu on Lake Victoria and later continuing into Uganda, called for more economic activity to make the investment profitable. Hence, early in the twentieth century a large number of settlers established a plantation system in the highlands north and west of Nairobi, forming one of Africa's few large-scale European settlements.[30]

    In the nineteenth century, contact with English in the interior grew but slowly. The impact of explorers was restricted and not lasting. Missionaries brought English with them, and started teaching and spreading it systematically. However, they also, and in many cases primarily, used indigenous languages, chiefly Kiswahili, already an established lingua franca, for evangelization. In some cases soldiers, like the King's African Rifles, also disseminated English (Mesthrie 2002a:111). Exposure with English on a larger scale, however, only came with the white settlers who were attracted in large numbers by fertile lands and economic opportunities. Still, for a long time education was left to the missions, as the State did not want to spend money on it and the settlers were primarily interested in their profits.

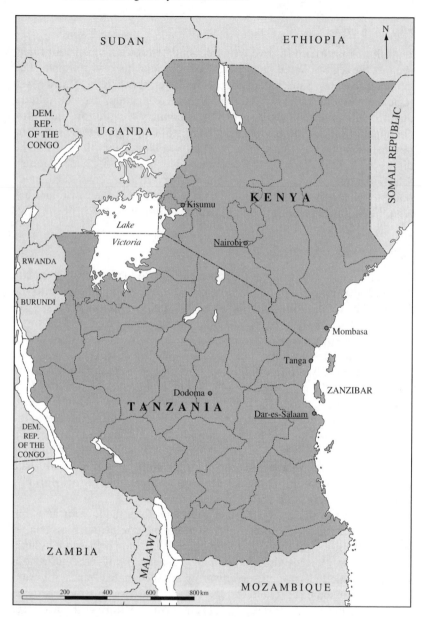

Map 5.6: East Africa (Kenya and Tanzania)

Thus, during this period initial, if highly restricted, bilingualism emerged in the IDG stream. Of the other linguistic features of phase 1 we have no explicit documentation, but also no counterevidence. Some accommodation must have occurred in the STL community, but the whites tended to live on scattered farms, not in larger urban communities, so if koinéization occurred it presumably took longer than elsewhere. As any map will show, the toponymy of the region remains indigenous, of course (e.g. *Kigumo, Kerugoya, Nyaru, Molo River, Menenga Crater,* ...).

5.10.2 Phase 2 (1920–late 1940s)

The formal establishment of the colony in 1920 provides a convenient cut-off date for phase 2 in Kenya. British settlers kept immigrating in substantial numbers,[31] and English became firmly established as the language of administration, business, law, and other higher domains in society. In education, of course the British standard was uncontested. The settlers definitely felt British on foreign soil, maintained strong ties with the homeland, and refrained from socializing with Africans (Abdulaziz 1991:394).

With respect to the language education of Africans, the British pursued their classic "divide-and-rule" policy, i.e. they trained a small indigenous elite as administrators but essentially were not interested in disseminating the English language. For instance, the Phelps-Stokes Report of 1925 on African education recommended using the vernacular in primary and an African lingua franca in middle education, reserving English for the upper strata, to which few Africans progressed. Colonial officers had to learn Kiswahili, and until independence their promotion depended upon demonstration of their African language skills. The settlers in particular are reported to have resisted the spread of English to Africans on a larger scale, deliberately using kiSettla, a reduced form of Kiswahili, instead. Many of them were well aware that knowledge of the dominant language means access to power, and that they did not want to share. Thus, interestingly enough, "the presence of a significant English-speaking white population in Kenya from the 1920s to the 1940s was often more a liability than an asset to the spread of the English language in the country" (Mazrui and Mazrui 1996:272).

Conversely, while we have no immediate identity statements of Africans from that period it is clear that they saw English as an asset. In the 1920s an "enormous demand for English" grew (Kembo Sure 2003:251), and in the 1930s the first African-run primary schools opened, teaching English earlier than was suggested by the authorities (Zuengler 1982:113). Hence, the colonial language distribution in Kenya is interesting in that bilingualism involving the indigenous language is more common in the STL strand than in many other colonies, but this was not intended as a step toward accommodation but rather as a strategy of restricting access to English from the IDG strand as much as possible, and thus of maintaining social distance between the colonized and the colonizers.

Kenyan English (which in its early phase is hardly to be distinguished from East African English in general) has its usual share of loanwords from the IDG strand, though we lack substantial historical documentation to discuss the timing of borrowings. According to the OED, the word *baobab* (also called *monkey-tree*) can be found in Livingstone's travel report of 1857 (though there is an even earlier record, relating it to Ethiopia). Encounters with indigenous fauna provide *simba* 'lion.' Words for indigenous objects and customs include *njohi* 'homemade beer,' *kuan* 'boiled cornmeal,' *ojuri* 'type of Luo food,' *jembe* 'hoe,' *shamba* 'cultivated plot of land,' *thahu* 'curse,' *safari* 'journey,' *ugali* 'maize dish,' *githeri* 'Kikuyu bean dish,' and *matatu* 'collective taxi' (Zuengler 1982:116; Schmied 2004a:939–40).

5.10.3   Phase 3 (late 1940s–)

The stable colonial status, with its clear separation of STL and IDG strands, was concluded by the aftermath of World War II. Africans returning from the war demanded political rights, including language education, with more self-confidence, and even India, the "jewel" of the Crown's possessions, was released into independence. The British were reasonable enough to understand that independence of their African colonies would come before too long. In a sharp turn of their policy, their goal now was to "modernize" these countries and prepare them for independence (amongst other things by teaching English on a broader scale), thus building the ties that would preserve privileged cultural, political, and economic relationships in the future, in the form of membership in the Commonwealth.

The Mau Mau rebellion (1952–9), soon followed by Kenya's independence in 1963, caused the identities of the country's two major population groups to crystallize and their relationship to polarize. In the STL strand, a decision was unavoidable, and the majority of settlers, who apparently felt more English than African or simply did not feel safe any longer, decided to leave the country. Since then, the STL strand has been insignificant in Kenya, though it still exists: there is a small resident population of African-born white people of English (or European) descent, estimated to be up to 40,000 (Skandera 2003:16), who definitely regard themselves as Kenyans and Africans. In the IDG strand, of course the African identity as rightful owners of the land predominated and gained political and also violent expression, but the Anglicization and the strive toward English had taken roots and had transformed the local culture. Ironically, the leaders of the independence movement, including President-to-be Jomo Kenyatta, were recruited from the English-trained, in many cases highly educated, elite of Africans that the British had wanted to serve the Empire as administrators. Clearly, their cultural background was hybrid, and their identity, and therefore that of most of their fellow countrymen, was strongly shaped by their exposure to English customs and language.

Thus, it was after the late 1940s that the English language became nativized in Kenya and spread rapidly, even "down the social hierarchy" (Schmied 2004b:921). Both parties contributed to this effect: the British with their modernization policy and attempt to now, unlike earlier, get the language rooted in East Africa for good, and the Africans with their broad desire to acquire it, motivated largely by utilitarian considerations. Ngugi wa Thiong'o, the famous Kenyan author, attests how in the 1950s English was forcefully imposed upon Kenyan school children, who were punished severely for speaking their mother tongue in the vicinity of the school (see Skandera 2003:13).

Kenya adopted a capitalist economic system and has always remained open to the western countries for business relationships, cultural exchange, and tourism, and this has helped to preserve the importance and special status of English in the country. It has not gone unchallenged: Kiswahili was proclaimed the "national language" in a constitutional amendment of 1974, and there was a period when Kiswahili was officially promoted against English, for instance as the sole language of parliamentary debate (a function which English regained, however, in another amendment just a few years after, in 1979). However, the status of English as a strong second language and a co-official language was never seriously threatened. The constitution of 1998 calls for English and Kiswahili as the languages of the Parliament and for legislation in English (Skandera 2003:15).

So today the presence of English in Kenya's sociolinguistic make-up is strong. Its importance has actually "increased after independence and it occupies as a second language a secure role as the language of education, administration, commerce and modernisation in general" (Abdulaziz 1991:393). Certainly it has an essentially elitist and utilitarian character, as a language that is an indicator of a good education and the entry gate to desirable professions and white-collar jobs. Its use or non-use in any given situation depends upon a complex array of factors: social setting of the situation, medium, topic of conversation, status, ethnicity and language skills of interactants, and location. Its use is tied with upper- or middle-class status and with urban rather than rural contexts, but no longer exclusively so: according to a recent survey, "English is the unrivalled language at the place of work, both in urban and in rural areas." Even in the rural sample (meant to be broadly representative) more than half of all respondents and even 35 percent of primary school graduates report using it (Kioko and Muthwii 2004:37). In the absence of reliable data (the latest survey dates back more than thirty years), speaker numbers are notoriously difficult to define and estimate.

Assumed speaker proportions of English vary between 5 percent (Kembo Sure 1991:246) and 80 percent (Michieka 2005:179), with Skandera (2003:19) and Schmied (2004a:922) reporting 15–20 percent. All observers agree that English is spreading, even beyond the middle and upper classes. In a 1987 study of urban poor "in the Nairobi slum of Kibera, 235 out of 485 respondents claimed some proficiency" in English, and of these 13 claimed extensive home usage (Mazrui and Mazrui 1996:284) – certainly a noteworthy phenomenon. At the other end of the social scale, there is a growing number of African native speakers, typically children who are raised in affluent urban families by educated parents of different ethnic backgrounds (Mazrui and Mazrui 1996:283).

The strong role of English is also reflected in its growing importance in education. In the mid-1960s the so-called "New Primary Approach" "kept spreading like wildfire," and reportedly half of all primary schools used English as a medium of instruction under this scheme (Mazrui and Mazrui 1996:279). Today English is the medium of instruction usually in the second half of primary education and in all of secondary education (Skandera 2003:20; Schmied 2004b:923; see also Kanyoro 1991:406).

Attitudes toward varieties of English are variable, and partly schizophrenic (Schmied 2004b:924). At least theoretically, British English and RP are still upheld as the target forms of language education, and the Kenyan National Examination Council accepts only the British standard, with the exception of a small number of loan words which are explicitly listed (Kembo Sure 2004:105). There is also a local form of a "complaint tradition" lamenting "falling standards" of English, primarily voiced in newspapers and government reports (Mazrui and Mazrui 1996:281; Kembo Sure 2003:255). This is unrealistic and undesirable, however, and in practice several surveys have yielded the result that Kenyans are willing to accept a non-ethnic accent of educated Kenyan English as their own standard (Kembo Sure 1991; Skandera 2003:24–5). There is even some evidence of covert prestige being assigned to Kenyan English: Skandera (2003:37–8) reports a statement by a speaker who has "full command of the standard forms" but uses them mockingly, clearly preferring a distinctively Kenyan, nonstandard variant.

To date progress toward acceptance of local forms as a norm or standard seems slow and painful, but it is being made. Occasional calls for an endonormative orientation can be heard, e.g. "The standards must be established from local varieties and not imported ones ... Serious work must start toward establishing a realistic standard" (Kembo Sure 2003:256). Kioko and Muthwii (2004:47–8) find that Kenyans appreciate a distinctly national, non-ethnic, and not foreign type of English, and they argue that "Kenyan 'stars' in the media and successful professionals" should be accepted as "norm setters, the models that speakers in Kenya approximate to," and their English should be "studied, documented and used for teaching in the school system" (see, with similar views, Abdulaziz 1991:394; Kembo Sure 2004:101). A study by Buregeya (2006), based on a questionnaire with students in Nairobi, can be regarded as a step in that direction. The author tested twenty six putative grammatical features of Kenyan (but not British or international) English and found that fourteen of these, slightly more than half, scored acceptability ratings of more than 60 percent, a rate considered "broadly acceptable" as features of Kenyan English, and three more had rates between 50 and 60 percent, considered "fairly characteristic." Features which were accepted by more than half of all respondents include *second-born*; *enable them improve* (without *to*); intransitive *revenge* (instead of *take revenge on*); genitive relative clauses without *whose*, e.g. *words which are easy to find the meanings*; intransitive *have* 'possess,' and the pattern *type for me this letter*. These relatively high acceptability ratings for a number of "deviant" syntactic structures seem indicative of a growing tolerance even for grammatical idiosyncracy.

Thus, structural nativization has been in full swing for many decades, and it is assumed to have gained even more momentum since the 1970s, when both teachers and textbooks were almost exclusively of local origin (Skandera 2003:13). And it has produced the outcome that is to be expected: distinctively Kenyan forms on the levels of vocabulary, pronunciation and grammar (Schmied 1991b; 2004a, 2004b; Skandera 1999), embedded in a wider framework of East African features (Hancock and Angogo 1982:312–8).

Loan words are numerous, and were illustrated earlier. There is creative and hybrid word formation (*joblessly, impressment* 'burden,' *pedestrate* 'walk,' *overlisten, young husband* 'son,' *dry coffee* 'coffee without milk or sugar,' *mitumba cars* 'second hand ... ,' *panya routes* 'unofficial routes (esp. across borders),' *clean heart* 'without guile,' *wife inheritance* 'widow inherited by brothers of the deceased husband,' *youth winger* 'young party member,' *members' day* 'social gathering'), semantic change (*township* 'small town,' *upcountry* 'away from the city,' *heavy* 'pregnant,' *cut* 'refuse'), and the coinage of indigenous phraseology, studied in an entire book (Skandera 2003; e.g. *slowly by slowly* 'take it easy,' *talk nicely* 'give a bribe,' *queue-voting* 'voting by lining up behind a symbol of the candidate chosen,' *lie low like an envelope* 'behave inconspicuously,' *we shall meet/ talk* 'farewell').

The phonology is partly to be accounted for by ethnic-language transfer. So Luos lack [ʃ], Kikuyus tend to insert nasals, and Bantu interference frequently causes a confusion of /r/ and /l/. Some of these peculiarities are national; others are shared with other East African countries.

On the level of grammar, except for non-acrolectal patterns which are considered deviant, most innovations can be found at the interface of lexis and structural behavior, as predicted by the Dynamic Model. For example, a tendency to omit or insert particles is well documented (*pick* 'pick up,' *crop* 'crop up,' *leave* 'leave out/in'; *cope up with*). Of course, verb complementation patterns are also creative: *stay/remain with sth.* 'keep,' *wouldn't mind to give, discuss about, mention about, request for, allow him go, made him to do it, mind to tell, stop to deliver*; *rest, protest,* and *attend* used transitively. According to Schmied (2004a:931) the choice between infinitives and gerunds "varies freely." Mwangi (2003), in a dissertation on the topic, and others have shown prepositional usage to vary: *attach with, concentrate with, congratulate for*; a tendency to substitute *in* for *on, at,* or *to*; a tendency to use some complex prepositions particularly frequently (e.g. *according to, due to, apart from, irrespective of*) and to coin new complex prepositions (e.g. *in reference to, in respect to, with a view of*).

Similarly to other, comparable countries, a high degree of multilingualism results in much language mixing in Kenya. In fact, in Nairobi a variety with a name of its own, *Sheng*, has developed, which is essentially a composite of English, Kiswahili, and ethnic vernaculars used as an in-group jargon by young people (Abdulaziz 1991:397). Unlike Kenyan English itself, Sheng is a symbol of group solidarity, an explicit "attempt by the youth to construct a new identity" (Kembo Sure 2003:257).

On the basis of the above observations it can be stated that the process of nativization is still going on in Kenya and the English language is spreading gradually, though its potential scope seems largely confined by its coexistence with ethnic languages as the primary tools for group solidarity and human proximity and with Kiswahili as a regional lingua franca, especially in less formal domains. The process of nation-building and "detribalization" is still going on, and English certainly plays a role in this process, but at this point it seems unlikely to emerge as a symbol of a national identity. Further progress along the cycle of the Dynamic Model seems possible but is difficult to predict. Expressions of a positive attitude toward a Kenyan accent and variety of English, discussed above, and observations of some inter-tribal leveling may foreshadow endonormativity and a higher degree of homogeneity. There is some literary creativity in English (see Zuengler 1982:114; Abdulaziz 1991:393), but there is also opposition, the pivotal case being Ngugi, who explicitly returned from writing in English to writing in his native Kikuyu (see Kembo Sure

2003:253–4; Michieka 2005:183). Descriptive work on properties of Kenyan English is increasingly done, but codification cannot really be envisaged at this point.

In hindsight, it is interesting to observe that contrary to general expectation but in line with the Dynamic Model Kenyan English has been shaped by "colonial disadvantages and post-colonial windfalls" (Mazrui and Mazrui 1996:299). Despite ongoing debates on an appropriate language policy, English continues to thrive.

5.11   Tanzania

Tanzania (Map 5.6) shares some aspects of its linguistic evolution with its northern neighbor Kenya: a similar time frame of European and English colonization, similarities in cultural background and linguistic substrates, coexistence with Kiswahili, and geographical proximity, which accounted for a common "East African" region and form of English. On the other hand, there are also far-reaching differences: Tanzania was never a settler colony, and the colonial grip of the British was much lighter and shorter, so the role of English has largely been limited to education, administration, and a small range of "high" domains. Most importantly, however, independent Tanzania steered a persistent endoglossic course, and so the country provides a model case for the assumption that the developments described in the Dynamic Model can in fact come to a halt and the course of things can be changed at any stage. Also, in line with the weaker status of English many of the constituent elements of the model can be identified only much more weakly. I adopt the phases proposed by Schmied (1985:325).[32]

Phase 1, initial contacts with English on a broader scale, also began in the mid-nineteenth century with coastal contacts, mainly in Zanzibar, which was a British protectorate from 1890 until its independence in 1963, followed by unification with Tanganyika in 1964. The contacts were made especially by explorers and missionaries, although they used primarily Kiswahili, the region's established lingua franca. However, they also taught some English. Things did not change much when Tanganyika became a German colony from 1885. The Germans utilized Kiswahili as an administrative language. The presence of English during this period was restricted, and except for missionaries there was no STL strand worth talking about.

After World War I, in 1919, the League of Nations mandated Tanganyika to the British, a date which may be taken as the onset of phase 2. The interest of the British in the country remained reluctant, as it was not economically attractive and their legal hold was less immediate than in a colony. So to some extent, at least initially, they continued to rely on the system left by the Germans, run by using Kiswahili, though in addition they introduced English systematically in education and administration. Schools expanded, and missionary activity increased, even in the northern region. So, the presence of English became a reality, in its characteristic form associated with elitism and education. Some bilingualism spread, and some lexical borrowing into a local form of English occurred (e.g. *foforu* 'fancy,' *pole* 'sorry,' *gagaa* 'small fish,' *ngoma* 'traditional dance,' *khanzu* 'male garment').

Similarly to the Kenyan situation, it was only the post-World-War-II situation that triggered a much more extensive exposure to English, and thus a short period of nativization. Tanganyika was reassigned to Britain as a United Nations trust territory, and the country needed to be "modernized" and prepared for independence – hopefully, in the eyes of the British, with an English inclination left. After independence, in 1961, both English and Kiswahili were admitted as parliamentary languages (and a triglossic situation pertained, including the ethnic languages as the primary tools of socialization). A radical change of direction came with the Arusha Declaration of 1967, however. Tanzania adopted an African version of socialism, called *ujamaa*, and steered toward *kujitegema* 'self-reliance.' Kiswahili was deliberately (and with significant success) promoted into a truly national language, a carrier and symbol of this new African state. In an environment which emphasized the building of socialism, English, hitherto associated with inequality, was no longer welcome.

These political goals and situations determined both the attitudes and identities of the agents of language policy and use and the sociolinguistic climate which shaped English in Tanzania, most directly in the education system. British administrators, teachers, and so on did not consider themselves permanent residents, and almost all left at the time of independence. The indigenous political elite was Anglicized to a certain extent (for example, Julius Nyerere, the country's founding President and *mwalimu* 'teacher,' had been an English teacher for a while and had studied in Edinburgh). However, despite the official Africanization, it seems that unofficially this state of affairs has not really changed: according to Mafu (2003:275–6), expensive English-medium kindergartens and primary schools have mushroomed in Tanzania, although they are affordable only to the administrative elite, who are "not serious about promoting swahilization," at least not for their own children, and "will not abandon their educational advantage" (see Schmied 2004b:224).

During the post-1940s British colonial days and also for the first few years of independence up to 1967 English was taught intensively, introduced as a medium of instruction "even in primary schools" (Yahya-Othman and Batibo 1996:374), and used widely in public domains and also as the medium of secondary schooling. In the 1950s a new "middle school" was opened, and, on parents' demand, general teaching of English already began in standard 3 (376). However, after the Arusha Declaration Kiswahili replaced it in all levels of administration, the armed forces, the civil service, and in primary and secondary education. With very few exceptions, this policy was implemented rapidly and successfully, as the extensive documentation by Schmied (1985:56–68) shows. In the mid-1980s the pendulum seemed to be swinging back a little: the general decline of the standards of and familiarity with English caused some concern, motivated by the fear of disadvantages in international economic relations, so a little more emphasis was paid again to the teaching of English. For instance, a ten-year "English Language Teaching Support Project," heavily subsidized by the British Council, was launched (Mafu 2003). Today English is used as a medium of instruction almost only in post-secondary teaching, and even some University teaching is done in Kiswahili. It is still strong as a language of some commercial domains, like banking and insurance, and of international travel. It is estimated that 5 percent of the population have some knowledge of English (Schmied 1985:89, 2004b:922). Attitudes toward it vary "between very warm acceptance by some Tanzanians and indifference from others" (Abdulaziz 1991:393).

English in Tanzania has developed some structurally distinctive properties, though due to its restricted status they are fewer than elsewhere. Some are shared with other East African countries, and the line between interference phenomena and learners' errors on the one hand and stable features on the other is difficult to draw. In educated Tanzanian English, e.g. in newspapers, one can find unusual preposition usage (*indulge on, an effect to, a cause to*), verb complementation (transitive use of *suffer* and *deputise, justified to think, enable the Prime Minister work better*), and idiomaticity (*mid in the week, added more butter on our slice of cultural revival*).

Compared to Kenya, West Africa, and other nations, however, all of this impact is clearly less intense, and it seems clear that the evolution of English in Tanzania has not moved far into phase 3, and there it got stuck. I concur with Schmied, who posits a "repression phase" (1985:325, 1991a:194–6) and classifies the language as having been reduced from an ESL to an "EIL" (English as an International Language) status (1991a:44).

5.12   Nigeria

5.12.1   Phase 1 (early 19th c–ca. 1900)

The earliest appearance of English in West Africa (Map 5.7) dates back to the sixteenth century, when British trading ships began to land on the coast

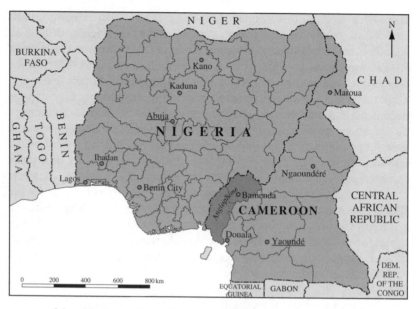

Map 5.7: West Africa (Nigeria and Cameroon)

and later, in the seventeenth century, trading posts and forts were established (Spencer 1971b). Contact was largely restricted to the needs of trade, including the infamous slave trade. Except for these local settings, however, phase 1 in the region which is now Nigeria began with growing political, economic, and religious concerns in the nineteenth century, which led to an expansion of trading activities and, specifically, to the advent of missionaries in the 1840s, near Lagos and in Calabar. Further missionary stations were founded by different societies, and throughout the late nineteenth century they gradually penetrated into the hinterlands, usually following established trading routes.[33] Lagos was occupied in 1851 and became a British colony in 1861 (Gut 2004). Commercial interests in the interior were pursued by the Royal Niger Company, founded in the 1880s, whose possessions were turned into a protectorate in 1900. Of course, both processes brought in soldiers, government officials, and other colonial personnel. Thus, English came to the region essentially during the second half of the nineteenth century.[34]

Little is known about the exact nature of the contacts between Africans and Europeans during the early phase, and hence we can only speculate about identity constructions of the parties involved. It is clear, however, that the association of English with prestige and success was grounded in those days. Spencer maintains that "servants in the European forts" succeeded in rising "to wealth and power" (1971a:10) because of their familiarity with the language.

Although many missionaries intended to spread the word of God using vernaculars, for practical reasons evangelization activities were strongly operated through the medium of English. Of course, missionary stations were early centers of education and cultural contact. In the 1880s they were explicitly ordered to teach English to meet the increasing demand for literate indigenous English speakers, and state schools followed for the same reason. Conversely, there are reports of a strong demand for English from the side of Africans as well. In Muslim regions, particularly in the north, where missionary education was not available, state schools were demanded (Gut 2004:814–5). Thus, early bilingualism spread, associated with elitism.

All along the West African coast, the coastal trading contacts produced an incipient pidgin, presumably in a rather rudimentary form but nevertheless as a variety setting off a "commercial ... elite" (Egbokhare 2003:32). It is disputed where exactly in Nigeria the Pidgin first originated: in the south-eastern Niger Delta region or in the south-west in and around Lagos. Furthermore, it has been suggested that Nigerian English in its formative period may have been influenced by Krio and ultimately West Indian forms of English (for details, see Deuber 2005:2–3 and Huber 1999). In any case, it is clear that by the 1860s it was well established in the British regions. With the missionaries, who found it useful, and the colonial expansion Pidgin English moved inland, but it became stigmatized when a new elitist class of English-speaking Nigerians was trained (Jowitt 1991:13). Nevertheless, it gradually expanded its functional range, mainly by becoming an interethnic lingua franca. According to Huber (1999:78), many phonological properties of Nigerian Pidgin were shaped in the early coastal contact phase, around 1800.

5.12.2   Phase 2 (ca. 1900–late 1940s)

A stable, British-dominated colonial period began earlier in the south than in the north, but it was ultimately achieved by the establishment of the inland protectorate in 1900 and formalized by the unification of the British possessions as the colony of Nigeria in 1914. This was where Lord Lugard, governor since 1913, developed his famous "indirect rule" policy (later adopted in other colonies as well) of administering the country through an indigenous power structure, whose members, of course, had to be educated beforehand (Brutt-Griffler 2002:56–7; Wolf 2001:67). English thus became firmly established as the language of administration, education, commerce, and the law. More government posts also meant an influx of native speakers in various functions. At the same time, the amalgamation of previously heterogeneous regions into one country increased interethnic contacts in cities and non-elite institutions like the police and the army. These strengthened the ethnographic position of Pidgin (Jowitt 1991:13).

The identity constructions of Europeans and Africans during that phase appear to be in accordance with the Dynamic Model. British colonial officers were representatives of their country in the first place, but they were faced with the realities of the tropics, and were personally molded by the colonial experience. Lugard, as a prototypical example, was born in India, educated in England, and served in Hong Kong between his two stints in Nigeria. Conversely, in the IDG strand African chiefs realized the importance of getting along with and communicating with the white rulers, and a "new breed of Nigerians emerged who sought to establish close relations with the white man" (Igboanusi 2002:9), if only as an elitist minority phenomenon. It is quite indicative that "the first crop of Nigerian District Officers behaved as though they were British. They spoke English even to those with whom they shared a Nigerian language and their speeches were translated into the appropriate Nigerian languages" (Bamgbose 1996:357).

The majority of British residents in Nigeria in the first half of the twentieth century were middle- and upper-class members and RP ("Received Pronunciation") speakers (Gut 2004:815), and earlier African models like the Krios had also "identified strongly with Britain" (Todd 1982b:296), so the prestige form and accent of English were Standard English and RP without any qualification. This exonormative orientation, the "myth" that Nigerian English is and should be identical to British English (Bamgbose 1992:149), was upheld for a long time after independence, and at least officially it has not been given up to the present day. In practice, English was mainly transmitted through formal education, and the emerging variety was colored by influences from the learners' mother tongues. Its role as the colonizers' language caused it to spread widely, though it remained associated with formal settings and was accessible only to a minority of the IDG population.

The expansion of English in formal domains had its counterpart in the spread of Nigerian Pidgin in everyday informal contexts. According to Mafeni (1971:98), the modern variety of Pidgin in Nigeria is essentially a product of urbanization, as the rapidly growing towns were melting pots of tribes and races, a context for which Pidgin had established itself.[35] Being used now mainly for communication between Africans of different ethnic origins, the language underwent what Huber (1999:124) and Deuber (2005:3) call "tertiary hybridization," an expansion of functional domains and structural properties. This happened with regional differences: most intensively in the multilingual southeast, less so in the Yoruba-dominated southwest, and least in the Hausa-dominated Muslim north. Pidgin was useful, and it was perceived by the uneducated as a variant of English, so despite its stigmatization in more educated circles it participated in the prestige which English enjoyed.

As corollaries of these developments, two distinct types of structural effects can be observed in phase 2.

The first one, in Nigerian English, is vocabulary transfer from indigenous languages, an obvious consequence of the widening range of contacts and the increasing exposure to indigenous cultures. Animal and plant words (like *gorilla, chimpanzee, okra,* and *yam*) are attested, but they mostly date back to earlier contact periods and cannot be assigned to a particular region of origin. A wide range of words reflect the impact of West African culture: *juju* 'charm, amulet, fetish,' *chi* 'personal god,' *oga* 'headman,' *akara* 'beancake,' *akwete* 'type of cloth,' *bolekajia* 'bus with tightly packed seats,' *sokoto* 'men's garment,' *buka* 'cheap eating place, hut,' *elubo* 'yam flour,' *agbada, buba* 'types of garment,' *oba* 'title of traditional ruler,' etc.

Secondly, in the Pidgin, its functional expansion went along with significant structural innovations. Huber (1999:78–86) details earliest attestation dates of a large number of diagnostic features in a number of West African countries and ethnicities, including Nigeria. Based on this set of data, quite a number of the characteristic properties of Nigerian Pidgin originated in the first half of the twentieth century prior to independence. These include the following:

- palatalization of word-initial velar consonants before *a* (*ka, ga* → *kja, gja*);
- *na* as an equating copula, in cleft sentences, and in focus constructions;
- *de(y)* as a locative copula;
- *de/di* as a progressive marker;
- *make* as a causative or imperative marker;
- *never* as a completive negative marker;
- *we(y)* as a relativizer;
- a "noun phrase 1 – pronoun – noun phrase 2" possessive construction;
- *(h)im* as a possessive form ("his, her");
- *una* as the second person plural pronoun "you, your (pl.)";
- and lexical and functional items like *broke* 'break,' *hungry* 'hunger,' and *small-small* 'a little, little by little.'

Hence, the nativization of Nigerian Pidgin, not constrained by policing school contexts, antedates that of Nigerian English, but of course it did not stop; Huber also documents a number of innovations from the later twentieth century.

5.12.3   Phase 3 (late 1940s–)

As elsewhere in Africa, phase 3 began after World War II and the independence of India, with a modernization program meant to prepare Nigeria for future independence, which then came in 1960.[36] In addition to measures toward agricultural and technological advancement, this implied a far-reaching expansion of education, including the teaching of English no longer to just an elite of functionaries but to the population at large. Widespread secondary education was introduced, and the University College of Ibadan was founded in 1948. English thus turned from an elitist language of administration, with constrained access, to a prestigious symbol of modernization (Igboanusi 2002:12) which was, at least theoretically, available to anybody.

With independence, this state of affairs, including the role of English in the country, did not change substantially. On the contrary, responsible posts formerly held by Europeans now became available to Nigerians, command of English was the condition for assuming them, and the new rulers kept conducting business in English. Furthermore, after independence and in the 1970s efforts to expand access to education and English, especially in rural areas, increased, far beyond Britain's late colonial efforts (Spencer 1971a:22; Bokamba 1991:496). Nigeria counts as the most strongly Anglicized country in sub-Saharan Africa and has fully embraced the English language as an ethnically neutral tool for everyday formal communication. On the informal level this is supplemented and mirrored by the role of Pidgin. English counts as the country's "official" language, a widespread assessment which goes back to a clause in the Constitution which stipulates that "The business of Parliament shall be conducted in English" (quoted from Bamgbose 1996:357). The 1979 Constitution also provided for the use of the three major Nigerian languages in the National Assembly, but in practice English is usually the language of choice. There has never been a serious attempt at pursuing an Africanization policy; bilingualism in a second one of the large Nigerian languages is encouraged but not enforced at all in the education system. All of this translates into an education policy which, except for the first three years of primary education, where the vernaculars are encouraged, calls for English as the medium of instruction throughout. Some private fee-paying schools in urban areas even provide for English instruction from kindergarten age, but the majority of Nigerians are exposed to English as the language of schooling normally from their fourth year (provided that they attend school regularly, which in rural areas is a limiting factor).

Independence brought with itself a large-scale removal of the STL strand, though not a complete one, because "the development of the

economy meant that after independence large numbers of Whites continued to find employment in Nigeria, in education, construction-work, the
oil business, etc." (Jowitt 1991:15). Whether living in Nigeria constituted
part of their identity is difficult to say and probably depends upon individual factors. Irrespective of that, a strong presence of English was
secured in the Nigerian environment, and, judging from the strongly and
generally positive attitudes toward English, it is safe to assume that a self-
image of English-driven modernity has been incorporated into national
identity concepts.

This is clearly reflected in the ubiquity of nativizing English and Pidgin
English and the attitudes to these varieties in the Nigerian sociolinguistic
setting. A convincing estimate puts the proportion of Nigerians who speak
English reasonably well and use it in some aspects of their daily lives at
20 percent (Bamgbose 1996:366; Gut 2004:813). For Pidgin, the corresponding figure is much higher, at well over half of the 140 million inhabitants
(Faraclas 2004:828). Whatever the precise figures may be, everybody
agrees that they are rising rapidly. For example, Faraclas estimates the
rate of Pidgin speaker to be 70–80 percent "by the time the present generation of children reaches adulthood" (2004:828). The number of secondary school students and also university graduates has increased
dramatically since about 1950 (Jowitt 1991:38), and with them the number
of Nigerians who have been educated in English. Apart from administration and education, English is the dominant language of the mass media,
business transactions, politics, advertising, the courts, science and technology, and so on, and simply the language of interethnic communication
amongst educated Nigerians. Despite the massive expansion of its domains
and accessibility, Bamgbose believes that "English still remains the property of an elite" (1996:367), though this statement disregards Pidgin, which
most Nigerians regard as a form – if a corrupted one – of English and
usually call "Broken." How far English has spread can be judged from
observations like the following: "an average person in the remotest village
in Nigeria who has never been to school can boast of a few English words
and sentences" (Udofot 2005:4; similarly Udofot 2003a); "non-literates
residing in urban centres are expected to learn street or non-educated
varieties of English that they in turn spread to other residents"
(Bokamba 1991:497).

In addition, the uses of Pidgin complement the spheres in which English
predominates in a fashion which has been called diglossic (Deuber
2005:52–3, 207). Originally mainly restricted to trade, Pidgin has spread
to become the language of market places, sports, the army and police force,
taxi drivers, playgrounds, university campuses, and generally of interethnic discourse in lower-class and informal contexts. In recent decades it has

therefore been utilized for mass communication – in advertising, political campaigning, government propaganda, announcements, and mass media, e.g. news broadcasts on the radio (Deuber 2002, 2005). It is labeled "the most widely spoken language in Nigeria, as well as the indigenous African language with the largest number of speakers" (Faraclas 2004:828).[37] Though the language still carries a strong stigma in the eyes of many educated Nigerians, many others have come to use it in informal conversations, also in banks, offices, and businesses, utilizing its ethnographic role as a code of friendliness and proximity.

In Nigerian English, the usual sociolinguistic parameters of variation play a major role, though a western concept of social class cannot be transferred literally to the West African context. Regionally, eastern, western, and northern forms are distinguished primarily, corresponding to the locations of the country's major indigenous languages, Igbo, Yoruba, and Hausa, respectively. Social lects are usually correlated with levels of education; a common system of classification builds upon Banjo's labels "Variety I/II/III" (see Bamgbose 1992:149–51), largely corresponding to Udofot's (2003b) "Nonstandard," "Standard," and "Sophisticated." Proficiency levels vary strongly on an individual basis, however, not necessarily correlating with schooling. Sociostylistic variation ranges from a Standard type, where little more than an accent and a few loans differ from metropolitan norms, via a widespread, non-stigmatized type with localisms which Jowitt (1991) calls "Popular," to rudimentary forms influenced by (but not identical with) Pidgin which serve limited and very basic communicative needs, as for example associated with *market mammies* (who tend to command utterances like "bring money"). Similarly, in Nigerian Pidgin there is a range from an acrolect, influenced by Nigerian English, via a mesolect, the most widespread form, to a basilect (Faraclas 1991), and there is some regional variation.

Attitudes to both English and Pidgin, indicative of the extent to which the identities of Nigerians have been influenced by contacts with Europe and modernization, also vary widely but tend to be predominantly positive in both cases. There are of course educated conservatives who would even deny the existence of a Nigerian type of English and who strongly condemn Pidgin as a bastardized language. Voiced concerns regarding the association of English with a colonial past and the threat of alienation from African roots deserve to be taken more seriously. For most Nigerians, however, English not only has the advantage of being ethnically neutral in a country marked by ethnic tensions (an advantage it shares with Pidgin) but is also the privileged language of modernization, social advancement, and access to material gains. "Nigerian English" as such is a problematic concept, because the prejudice that it is just a deformed and inferior realization of the real, "Queen's" English is still widespread and promoted in educational circles: "Some Nigerians – and foreigners – even today assume that Nigerian English means the same thing as Pidgin" (Jowitt 1991:28). But since the 1970s a discussion about the existence and nature of a Nigerian English has been going on among Nigerian linguists, and many speakers have a much more relaxed and realistic attitude.

As to Pidgin, it still suffers from the stigma of being nothing but "broken" English and from its association with socially inferior strata. However, there is no doubt that it also enjoys an enormous amount of covert prestige, as is indicated by its successful diffusion (see Egbokhare 2003:23–7). For a great many Nigerians today Pidgin is "a symbol of solidarity" (Agheyisi 1988:230) and also a sign of an informal, relaxed atmosphere, thus strongly imbued with a positive attitude. According to Adetugbo, "many Nigerians regard Pidgin English as *the* informal variety of the English language" (quoted from Jowitt 1991:14). Pidgin is a sign of intimacy and thus "bristles with potential symbolism" (14) – no wonder it is spreading rapidly. Some propose it even as "a viable candidate for a national status" (Simire 2004:139).

The intensity of the nativization of English in Nigeria is probably best illustrated by the reality of the literal sense of this word: both English and Pidgin have acquired first-language, native speakers. English is a family language, and thus becomes the mother tongue of children born to these families, predominantly with educated parents of different ethnicities in urban contexts. In addition, there are many cases in which even couples who share an African language give it up in order to give their children access to English from the earliest age possible; Bamgbose (1996:367–8) tells an instructive story of such behavior involving his own son and grandson. Udofot provides strong evidence along these lines: based on a questionnaire among members of the University of Uyo she finds that many "admitted making their children acquire English as their first language and actually enforcing the use of English by the children" and that many of her respondents use English also for intimate conversations and prayers (2005:5). She expects that "by the middle of the twenty-first century this nativised English may become the mother tongue of many Nigerians" (2003a:10). Similarly, Schäfer and Egbokhare (1999) provide a compelling documentation of "the European language, English, replacing an indigenous minority language" (389), Emai, in the south. They find that the multilingual language behavior of the parent generation is being replaced by a stratified bilingual strategy amongst adolescents (using indigenous vernaculars in home settings with parents but English at school and with peers) and a predominantly monolingual language profile, moving toward "vernacular abandonment" (389), among children.

With respect to Pidgin, the same process, without class restrictions and in even larger numbers, can be observed, predominately in the Warri-Sapele region in Delta State – so, in terms of traditional creolist theory, the Pidgin is "creolizing" (Mafeni 1971:95; Todd 1982b:291; Bokamba 1991:504; Egbokhare 2003:27; Elugbe 2004:831). A rapidly growing segment of the population acquire Pidgin English as their first language or simultaneously with an ethnic mother tongue from earliest childhood (Agheyisi 1988:229, 232; Faraclas 2004:828). Faraclas et al. (2006:64) quote an illustrative incident in a transcript of children playing: a ten-year old girl says, when another child starts talking Igbo, "Tokam fòr inglish nà, à no dè hyar di ting we yù dè tok" 'Say it in English now, I can't understand you,' repeated after more Igbo talk – she speaks Pidgin but does not command the regional vernacular any longer!

In the popular mind, Pidgin is usually perceived as a "corrupt" form of English (see, for example, the above quote from Adetugbo). It is clear that the grammar of Nigerian Pidgin is substantially different from that of English, but it is equally indisputable that through a shared, if phonologically modified, vocabulary and many other properties the two are somewhat similar to each other. Unless one wishes to exclude such relatedness as a matter of principle, they are definitely historically related, though they originated at slightly different periods and have served different purposes and different strata of society. In any case, the gap between Pidgin and English is closing and becoming "highly obscured" (Agheyisi 1988:231), at least in some contexts. Under English influence, acrolectal forms of Pidgin, primarily as spoken by educated people, are "decreolizing" (Faraclas 2004:828). The situation can widely be characterized as bidialectal, with many educated speakers of English also commanding Pidgin but not vice versa (Bokamba 1991:505). The precise linguistic nature of a possible "depidginization" process is disputed. Jibril (1982) believes that a "continuum ranging from pidgin to something that is unmarked and cosmopolitan" (78) is emerging, whereas Deuber (2005:201) remains reluctant to accept the existence of an intermediate range. Deuber (2002) is an interesting study of the problems arising from translating English news into Pidgin for radio broadcasts, including issues of intelligibility and the amount of tolerable Anglicization.

Whether, or to what extent, English or Pidgin can challenge indigenous languages as identity carriers is difficult to say, and will be interesting to observe in the future. Certainly African vernaculars remain the primary signals of intimacy, and in many situations using English would imply "an impression of distance and unfriendliness" (Bamgbose 1996:368). On the other hand, except for Hausa in the north the major Nigerian languages have not really been accepted as lingua francas, mainly because ethnic rivalry remains a touchy subject. Thus, a resident of Lagos interviewed by Deuber, discussing the question of which language he would use to address an unknown interlocutor, asserts that "speaking Yoruba would mean using a symbol of ethnicity that would not be tolerated in public" (2005:55); so Pidgin English is likely to be chosen. Given such a situation, attempts at promoting indigenous languages to achieve "enlightenment" (Adegbite 2004, Simire 2004) appear rather academic. On the other hand, it is probably true that English "falls short of the country's quest for the African 'soul' or identity" (Simire 2004:139), although some uses of "Popular Nigerian English" may be "indexical" (Jowitt 1991:47).

That leaves Nigerian Pidgin as the candidate for national language, at least on the affective level, if it ever can overcome the stigma and lack of recognition that it started out with. Simire muses that Pidgin "should be considered a viable candidate for a national status" (2004:139), and attitudes like the following, from an interview, support such a possibility: "Pidgin is that language that you have taken from the colonizer and you have made it your own" (quoted from Deuber 2005:51). Egbokhare (2003) explicitly asserts that for young people Nigerian Pidgin has become "a symbol of their identity and consciousness" (36). The dynamics of this variety seem so strong that its ultimate future status is impossible to predict at this stage.

With an eye on the components of the Dynamic Model and evolutionary patterns in comparable nations, two more aspects of language use in Nigeria deserve to be noted. One is the fact that like in many other countries code-switching and code-mixing are widely employed and positively evaluated in informal contexts (Jowitt 1991:20; Bokamba 1991:499; Bamgbose 1996:368; Udofot 2005). Secondly, Nigeria also has its own version of a complaint tradition, lamenting the poor performance of students and the decline of the standards of English in the public domain in recent decades (see Jowitt 1991:25–6; Bamgbose 1996:362; Egbe 1996:115).

The structural nativization of Nigerian English embraces all the phenomena observed with other PCEs at this stage, including some innovations at the lexis – grammar interface. A few categories and examples must suffice here:[38]

- verb complementation: *enable him do it*; *make her to do her work*; *to*-infinitive after *instead* (*Instead of him to travel ...*), no gerund after *be used to*, *look forward to*, *object to*; *refuse Ving* but *avoid, resist to V*; *disappoint, enjoy* and *reach* used intransitively; *dispose, operate, reply* used transitively;
- prepositional usage (according to Jibril, quoted from Mwangi 2003:3, "the point of greatest divergence in Nigerian English from World

English"): *at my old age, at the middle, at my arrival, on my expense, on the long run, interest on, with the belief, with the hope that* ...;

- phrasal verbs/verb-preposition combinations: *cope up with, plan up, voice out, discuss about, congratulate for, advocate for, demand for, emphasize on, lack of, culminate to*;
- word formation: *chewing stick* 'stick for cleaning one's teeth,' *chop box* 'food box,' *go-slow* 'traffic jam,' *motor park* 'bus and taxi station,' *been-to, beer parlour, cash madam* 'wealthy woman,' *long leg* 'use of undue influence to reach a goal'; *enstool/destool* (following Bokamba 1992:136–7, this "exhibits the rich derivational morphology that is so characteristic of African languages"), *practicalize*; hybrid compounds: *egusi soup, pounded yam*; conversion: *He naked himself, He pregnated her, She jealoused her sister, Horn before overtaking, He offed the light, The food doesn't ready*;
- phraseology: *off-head* 'from memory,' *take the light* 'make a power cut,' *social wake-keeping* 'feasting, drumming and dancing after a burial,' *bad eggs of the society, national cake, societal ills, if care is not taken, naming ceremony, roam the streets, second burial, tight friend* 'close friend,' *next tomorrow* 'day after tomorrow';
- semantic change: *balance* 'change,' *gallops* 'potholes,' *father* 'father or any of his brothers,' *globe* 'electric bulb,' *corner* 'bend in a road,' *locate* 'assign (a teacher) to a school or town,' *land* 'finish one's speech,' *environment* 'neighborhood,' *wet* 'water (flowers),' *exercise* 'action, event,' *drop* 'longest distance in a taxi for the minimum fare'; etc.

5.12.4   Where to from here?

All the above evidence indicates that English in Nigeria has progressed deeply into phase 3, has nativized strongly, and is still gaining ground at a rapid pace. The obvious follow-up question is therefore whether there are signs that the country is moving on into phase 4. I believe that a number of such indicators can be identified, though somewhat shakily; i.e. endonormative stabilization has not yet been reached but it may be just around the corner.

A preliminary question, important for identity definitions and the potential of symbolizing them, is of course whether political stabilization has been reached. Certainly so in the sense of "self-dependence," though an affirmative answer is not that secure when it comes to nation building and the issue of national unity versus tribal rivalries. More than three decades after the bitter and devastating Civil War which followed the secession of Biafra, progress has been made but it would be exaggerated to claim that national unity and stability have been achieved.

The acceptance of a local standard form of English has been called for frequently and has been the subject of a long and ongoing debate amongst Nigerian linguists and educators. In this respect, the country is far more advanced than any other country in East or West Africa (Schmied 1991a:174). Banjo's pronouncement characterizes the most liberal position: "it is generally felt that the time is ripe for an endonormative model to replace the exonormative one for purposes of teaching in schools" (1997:86–7); for statements similar in spirit, at least by implication, see Jowitt (1991:35), Bamgbose (1996:370), Udofot (2003a), and Alo and Mesthrie (2004:814). It is interesting to see that a "native," i.e. British, accent is no longer really aimed at, as it is seen as "affected and un-Nigerian" (Jowitt 1991:40) or "affected and arrogant" (Gut 2004:817). And there are the voices of those who, like the journalist Adadayo Ojo in 1986, see Nigerian English evolving as an "indigenous national language in the absence of an indigenous lingua franca" (quoted from Jowitt 1991:34). But obviously there is also the conservative position of those who consider Nigerian English inferior and would tend to avoid Nigerianisms once these are pointed out to them (Jowitt 1991:28), and in the educational arena such voices still have the say, with very limited concessions. Guidelines by the West African Examinations Council, for instance, permit Standard English as used by educated African speakers, which, however, in practice means little more than that a tightly circumscribed set of African lexis is deemed permissible (Jowitt 1991:31). The situation is summed up as follows:

the question of whether a Nigerian English exists should by now have become a non-issue; and the desirability of its existence, once accepted, seems like many truths to be so obvious as not to need restatement. It has to be frequently restated because of the need to correct entrenched misconceptions at both the academic and the popular level. (Jowitt 1991:35)

It remains to be seen whether Udofot is right in suggesting that "despite protests and legislations to the contrary, [English] is gradually being consciously and unconsciously groomed as the possible neutral language of unity" (2005:1).

Interestingly enough, despite its overt stigma Nigerian Pidgin also keeps surfacing in this quest for a possible future national language, having "attained a degree of respectability even in the popular mind" (Jowitt 1991:14; see also Simire 2004:139). Faraclas (1991:511) argues:

As long as NP [Nigerian Pidgin] is not accorded the place it deserves in Nigerian education, an invaluable tool for the teaching of English will continue to lie wasted and unused. Official recognition should be extended to NP as a major Nigerian language. A standard scientific orthography should be adopted to facilitate its use in written communication.

One component of phase 4 is already reality in Nigeria: Nigerian Pidgin and English have gained respectability by having been employed in literary creativity, reflecting the African experience. This applies to a range of literary productions extending from Nobel Prize winner Wole Soyinka via highly respected authors like Amos Tutuola, Chinua Achebe, who reflected explicitly on his use of an Africanized English, or Ken Saro-Wiwa, to products with a stronger local impact like the so-called Onitsha Market Literature (Jowitt 1991:30; Egbe 1996:128).

What is missing, however, is the stabilization of a more homogeneous concept of a Standard Nigerian English, i.e. an explicit codification. Jowitt, whose 1991 book comes closest to an authoritative description of Nigerian English, explicitly calls for a language academy to monitor its development and to define indigenous standards (35). Similarly, Nigerian Pidgin would have to undergo further development and codification, especially with respect to an accepted spelling system as called for in the above quotation from Faraclas, before it could ever adopt a more formalized role in society. Agheyisi (1988:237) recommends "the Delta variety, especially as spoken in Warri and Sapele, [which] already enjoys wide recognition among NPE [Nigerian Pidgin English] speakers as the purest and most internally resourceful variety of the language." For that to happen, however, a fundamental reversal of official language attitudes and language policy would be required. Whatever the future of English in Nigeria holds in store, this will be an exciting process to observe.

5.13   Cameroon

Due to their geographical proximity and partially shared history, especially in the early phase, the evolution of English in Cameroon is somewhat similar to the Nigerian process. While Nigeria was exclusively British in her colonial days, however, substantial differences in Cameroon can be explained by the country's earlier colonization by the Germans and the colonization of the southern and eastern (greater) parts of its territory by the French after World War I. It is especially marked by the heritage of the latter, resulting in the predominance of French on the national level and a much less prominent role of English and Pidgin in the country. In fact, the ongoing competition with French, in which English has definitely been losing ground, suggests that strictly speaking the evolutionary trends described in the Dynamic Model operate fully only in the Anglophone, Northwest and Southwest provinces. Chumbow and Simo Bobda (1996) explicitly apply a life cycle model to Cameroon; I adopt the phase delimitations which they propose.

Cameroon as a polity goes back no further than 1884. Before that date, the region shared coastal trade contacts and, beginning in 1844 in Bimbia near Douala, missionary activities with other West African coastal regions. At that time, the British practically controlled the coast of present-day Cameroon. However, they refrained from getting involved more deeply, and by the time they decided to accept formal authority in the region the Germans had forestalled them and signed a contract with the indigenous kings Bell and Akwa. Hence, from 1884 to 1919 Cameroon was a German protectorate. The Germans established plantations near the coast and gradually penetrated into the hinterlands. They were mainly interested in commercial exploitation, not in any kind of serious colonization; the number of administrators they sent remained small.[39]

While there is no reason to assume that the original identities of the persons involved in early contacts were substantially modified, a basically positive attitude on the side of the indigenous populations toward the British may be deduced from the fact that in 1879 and 1881 the local kings explicitly sent petitions to the Queen requesting formal annexation, asking for "English laws in our towns" and "an English Government here" (quoted from Schmied 1991a:10–1; see Todd 1982a:6; Chumbow and Simo Bobda 1996:403).

As elsewhere in the region, by the late nineteenth century Pidgin English and English had been firmly established. Trading activities and missionary schools brought early bilingualism involving Pidgin and English, respectively. While some of the missionaries attempted to study and employ indigenous languages, in practice they mostly used Pidgin, which turned out to be most effective, and taught Standard English. There was also a small number of English-medium schools, "highly regarded by Cameroonians" (Todd 1982a:9). The Germans discouraged formal education in English but did nothing to impose their own language. In fact, they found Pidgin English useful themselves for evangelization and administration, so in reality the Pidgin and also English continued to thrive and spread during those years. In particular, the plantations which they established fermented further uses of Pidgin as a lingua franca among a multiethnic workforce, and these workers then took the language into the hinterlands when they returned home. As is typical of a trade colony, pidginization and the spread of the pidgin are thus the most important linguistic effects of this phase.

Similarly to Tanzania, phase 2 began when in 1919 a part of Cameroon was mandated to Britain by the League of Nations, a relationship which practically continued after World War II under a UN Trusteeship. However, this pertains to only about a fifth of the country, a region in the west and northwest, adjacent to Nigeria, then called "British Cameroons." The vast majority of the region, however, went to France, under the same terms. Both colonial powers installed their own administrative structures

and institutions and imposed their language, a process which institutionalized a linguistic and cultural cleavage into "Francophones" and
"Anglophones" which strongly preoccupies Cameroon to the present day.
While the French installed a strictly centralized, Paris-oriented system and
ultimately succeeded in acculturating and Frenchifying the country, British
Cameroons was essentially treated like an annex to Nigeria, from where it
was administered – it had no capital, no separate administration, and no
budget of its own (Wolf 2001:100). The principle of indirect rule relied more
strongly on traditional power structures in society. State-supported English
education was institutionalized, but only in the elitist form familiar from
other colonies. The prestige which English enjoyed, indicating attitudes and
identities in the IDG strand, can be deduced from the fact that many pupils
changed from Basel missions, supportive of vernacular education, to other
mission stations where English was taught (Wolf 2001:89). Thus, the overall
attitude of the British toward their Cameroons possession, and, as far as we
can judge, the identity definitions of the parties involved during that period
were not that dissimilar from the situation in Tanzania, except in one
important respect owing to its vicinity to Nigeria, which nurtured the
development of Pidgin.

In theory, the British only wished to encourage vernacular primary
education and institutionalized English as a medium of instruction from
standard 5 onwards. In practice, however, this policy was frequently
undermined by the lack of qualified teachers and by the local demand
for the acquisition of English which led to the adoption of English as the
medium of education from the first grade of primary school starting in the
1950s (Todd 1982a:10). Secondary education, first offered in Nigeria only,
was established gradually, and the quality of English was regarded as high
(1982a:11), with an exonormative orientation (Schmied 1991a:11). This
has to be qualified, however, given that school enrollment was generally
low and secondary education was accessible to only a tiny minority of the
population. But basically during that phase "English became the language
of education and administration" (Chumbow and Simo Bobda 1996:405),
and the number of English schools rose (405–6).

The spread of the Pidgin continued vividly, promoted by the prestige
accorded to English, with a clear division of labor between the two: English
for scholastic and formal purposes, Pidgin for informal everyday
interactions.

Missionaries and administrators normally spoke English, ... but switched to
Pidgin when their interlocutors (church-members, house-servants, or others)
could not speak English. Teachers and pupils spoke English in class, but once
outside they usually switched to Pidgin; even in the classroom Pidgin was not
totally absent." (Chumbow and Simo Bobda 1996:408)

Pidgin English was diffusing further as a lingua franca also in the French-administered part of Cameroon – not as vigorously as in the British one but persistently, primarily in cities, like in Douala (where it had always been important).

In addition to the ongoing expansion of the pidgin, words were borrowed from the IDG strand, more so into Pidgin than into standard English, although the line of distinction cannot be drawn clearly. Borrowings into English include *fon* 'chief,' *nchinda* 'spokesman of the chief,' or *ashu* 'edible paste'; other words are more characteristic of the Pidgin, e.g. *mengwin* 'locusts,' *mboh* 'groundnut paste,' *nkang* 'maize drink,' *wahala* 'trouble,' *ngondere* 'young woman,' *mukala* 'white man,' *mbanya* 'co-wife' (Todd 1982a, 1982b, Ayafor 2004).

As elsewhere in Africa, the dawning of independence after World War II caused a reversal of the policy and attitude, with the aim of modernizing the territory ruled by the British. This transition triggered phase 3. Increased efforts were invested into the education and development of British Cameroons. The number of schools multiplied, and government activity was supported by the ongoing work of missionaries.[40] In 1960 French Cameroons became independent. One year later, in a referendum in the British part the population could decide between being merged with Nigeria or joining Cameroon. While a northern region voted in favor of Nigeria, Southern British Cameroons, now the two south-western provinces, decided in favor of reunification with French Cameroon (perhaps surprisingly so) to form the new "Federal Republic of Cameroon."[41]

In this new political entity, English remained the language of administration and education in the Anglophone zone, with French occupying the same role in the much larger part of the country. In 1972 the federation was considered strong enough to be transformed into a united, officially bilingual state, the "United Republic of Cameroon," in which both English and French were (theoretically) accepted as official languages everywhere, on equal terms.[42] In practice, however, it turned out that the regional autonomy of the federation to some extent had been a protective shield, a period during which the predominance of French was not felt to be overwhelming. To the Anglophones, who have felt discriminated against, this situation has been a constant source of discontent and grievance to the present day. It is frequently stated that this conflict is not exclusively a linguistic but rather a cultural one, with institutions and organizational principles inherited from the British colonial days being threatened and in some cases replaced by French-derived conventions. The situation was epitomized in another highly symbolic step: in 1982 the word "United" was dropped from the country's official name, thus attributing it the

designation which the French part had had on its own before the reunification, viz. Republic of Cameroon/République du Cameroun. Anglophones
have regarded this step as a "breach to the 1972 Constitution" and as a
forceful "assimilation of the minority" (Chumbow and Simo Bobda
1996:404). Furthermore, economic and political ties with France remain
strong. The relationship is probably not quite that clear-cut – some of
the British legacy has been successfully preserved, and, interestingly
enough, in "a remarkable foreign policy move in the direction of the
English-speaking world" (Wolf 2001:147), Cameroon recently joined the
Commonwealth, but the basic tension remains and can be felt very
strongly. Kouega (2002:112) rightly observes a "one-way expansion of
bilingualism, with speakers of English operating increasingly or fully
in French, but their French-speaking counterparts remaining largely
monolingual."

This situation has generated a rather unusual situation with respect to
the identity construction of a substantial proportion of Cameroon's population: it is based upon a postcolonial, second-language construct rather
than traditional ethnic alignments (Chumbow and Simo Bobda 1996:425;
Wolf 2001:46) Therefore, for this group the English language assumes an
important symbolic function as an identity carrier.

Thus, in the Anglophone provinces the functions of English and Pidgin
are manifold, and generally comparable to their uses in Nigeria. English
predominates in administration, education, the media, and generally in
primarily urban and formal domains and interethnic communication;
Pidgin complements it in informal settings and situations of social proximity. For more precise documentations of domains and speaker numbers,
see Chumbow and Simo Bobda (1996:417–20), Kouega (2002), and
Schröder (2003); the results can be summarized by stating that almost
everybody there commands Pidgin, and more than half of the urban
population speak Standard English. Pidgin is widely considered as a
form of English, and it is encroaching upon traditional domains of
Standard English (Simo Bobda and Wolf 2003:107).

Attitudes toward English are thoroughly positive, with English being "a
symbol of in-group solidarity" for Anglophones (Wolf 2001:231). Pidgin
profits from being widely considered English, and outside formal spheres it
enjoys covert prestige (164). Pidgin and also English are far from homogeneous and come in several shades and variants, adjusted to the "myriad of
real-life encounters of persons with different mother tongues in all kinds of
situations" (Wolf 2001:154). In terms of both functional distribution and
structural properties, the difference between the two is straightforward at
the top and bottom ends of the sociostylistic continuum but gets blurred in
the middle ranges, where one borrows from the other and speakers slip

between relatively more casual and more distanced modes, depending upon the demands of the situation. Wolf sees them on a continuum, finding little sense in attempts at separating them and arguing that this position is in line with the local practice of using *English* as a cover term for both (2001:187, 196). The structural gap between them is clearly shrinking (Simo Bobda and Wolf 2003:101, 113). Most recently, this was documented by Ngefac and Sala (2006), who compared Gilbert Schneider's Cameroon Pidgin data from the 1960s with corresponding present-day forms and found that many basilectal Pidgin forms have disappeared and that Standard English has been exerting a strong influence on Pidgin English.

Ongoing nativization is not only reflected by a growing range of uses and structural properties of both English and Pidgin but also, as in Nigeria, by the emergence of substantial numbers of mother-tongue speakers. Figures from Koenig et al.'s 1980s survey of five Anglophone towns show that between 19 and 31 percent of all children acquire Cameroonian Pidgin and up to 7 percent Cameroonian English as their first languages (quoted from Chumbow and Simo Bobda 1996:419). A 1998 survey by D'Epie yielded similar figures: up to 25 percent L1 speakers of Pidgin and 1–13 percent L1 speakers of English (quoted from Simo Bobda and Wolf 2003:105). Notably, comparable proportions, which may result from immigration from the Anglophone region, are reported for "Francophone" cities like Douala (10/6 percent, respectively) and Yaounde (15/8 percent). These figures may include cases where Pidgin and English are "co-L1s," but there is also a noteworthy proportion of children who do not learn an autochthonous African language at all (up to 16 percent; Wolf 2001:192).

In the Francophone region Pidgin English has retained its strong position as a lingua franca from the early colonial days, though it competes with other lingua francas and carries no symbolic meaning (Todd 1982a:19–21; Wolf 2001:155–63). Standard English is taught as a second language in secondary education, though the outcome is far from an effective bilingualism (or multilingualism, including African vernaculars; see Wolf 2001:170–6).

Despite this perplexing growth of both Pidgin and English in Cameroon, however, it is noteworthy that the position of authorities and educators remains decidedly conservative: Pidgin English is officially not tolerated at all in the classroom, and the orientation of English teaching remains fully exonormative (Todd 1982a:12; Wolf 2001:204–6; Ngefac 2001). There is even a mild form of a complaint tradition, lamenting falling standards of English and blaming Pidgin as a scapegoat (Schröder 2003:55).

Of course, nativization has also affected the structure of English. The distinctive phonology of English is described by Simo Bobda (2004), that

of Cameroonian Pidgin by Menang (2004). Considering complex vocabulary, we find compounding (e.g. *head tie / tie head* 'scarf,' *cry day* 'wake,
funeral rites'; mainly in Pidgin: *born-house* 'ceremony to celebrate the birth
of a child,' *follow-back* 'younger brother / sister,' *chopchia* 'successor, lit.
eat chair,' *high-up* 'proud,' *bigman for work* 'boss'), hybrid compounds
(e.g. *fufu corn* 'corn flour,' *mimbo-haus* 'bar'), phraseologisms (e.g. *move
with* 'go out with,' *be in state* 'pregnant,' *give kola* 'give a bribe,' *not so*,
make mouth 'brag,' *morning time* 'morning,' *I beg* 'please'), and semantic
modifications (e.g. *bending corners* 'sharp bends,' *woman's belly* 'large bag
(jocular),' *stranger* 'guest').[43] French influence upon the vocabulary and
pronunciation of English and Pidgin, an ADS effect, has also been noted
(e.g. *mandat* 'money order,' *concours* 'competitive exam,' *charged* 'busy,'
manifestation 'public demonstration,' *advance de solde* 'advance pay').
Syntactic innovations characteristic of structural nativization include
modifications of verb complementation like an extended set of verbs
which take *that*-causes (including *phone, insult*, and *mock*, each comple-
mented by a direct object followed by a *that*–clause) or constructions with
dative copy pronouns: *I am going me away, We are sitting us down*
(Mbangwana 2004).

   The highly complex and multilingual situation in Cameroon has produced a phenomenon that has been observed in similar forms elsewhere in
association with nativizing PCEs: a highly mixed code used primarily by
urban youths, associated with solidarity and an appreciation of cultural
hybridity. In Cameroon it is called 'Camfranglais," consisting of French,
English, Pidgin, and indigenous elements. Reportedly, it is in use "mainly
for relaxed and informal conversation among francophone youth"
(Schröder 2003:89; see also Menang 2004:906), comparable to what
Pidgin English means to young Anglophones.

   Thus, Cameroonian English has moved on into phase 3, especially in
the Anglophone region, but it seems barred from making further progress
by the overwhelming competition of French and by the fact that the region
where it really thrives lacks statehood and thus the option of an independent identity symbolized by the language. English is under pressure,
from Pidgin in the Anglophone part and from French elsewhere.[44]
Cameroonian Pidgin, on the other hand, is going strong in its grassroots
development, certainly with a qualitative difference between the two
parts of the country but basically almost everywhere. It has been suggested
as a candidate for a national language, being indigenous, widely
understood, and structurally close to the vernaculars (Todd 1982a:25;
Chumbow and Simo Bobda 1996:419; Schröder 2003:196–243; Simo
Bobda and Wolf 2003), but it lacks codification, and at present it is hard
to see how it should overcome its strong overt stigmatization.

5.14   Barbados

As was pointed out in section 3.3.3, Caribbean Creoles share a number of historical and structural properties which distinguish them from many other cases of emerging PCEs. They typically originate from plantation settlement colonies to which African slaves were transported and in which creoles emerged. One important consequence of this scenario is the fact that the linguistic processes typical of phases 2 and 3 practically fall together and structural nativization occurs earlier than elsewhere. This section focuses on Barbados, with occasional outlooks on the wider Caribbean context (see Map 5.8).

5.14.1   Phase 1 (1627–ca. 1650)

When the British settled Barbados in 1627, they found the island deserted by the Arawaks who had lived there in earlier times.[45] Phase 1 may be taken to coincide with Winford's (2000) pre-plantation period, 1627 to about 1650. This is identified as the "homestead" phase by Chaudenson (2001) and Mufwene (2004a:209), during which whites outnumbered black slaves and the contact between them was relatively close and constant. Relatively small-scale farm holdings produced tobacco and other crops.

Map 5.8: The Caribbean (Barbados and Jamaica)

The economy prospered, and the population multiplied, from 60 Europeans in 1627 to 1,800 in 1629 and 37,200 in 1642 (figures from Winford 2000:220). White settlers consisted of a minority of planters and their immediate dependents and a larger number of servants from England and, in relatively large numbers, Ireland and Scotland who came as indentured laborers for several years. African slaves were there from the very beginning as well, but they were outnumbered by whites (6,000 in 1642), and they lived in small farm dwellings in close proximity to Europeans, especially the servant laborers with whom they had to work the fields. Many of the bond servants stayed after they were freed, and sustained themselves as small-scale farmers, fishermen, retail merchants, laborers, and so on.

Interethnic contacts were common during this early phase, so it is uncontested that these were conditions favoring language shift and second-language acquisition rather than creolization. Women or children in the African community are not mentioned prior to 1640, so the English which the African newcomers acquired and spoke must have been a second-language variety, most likely with some transfer of native features and incomplete acquisition of the target language. Hence, in this scenario approximative acquisition of nonstandard English preceded creolization (Holm 1994b:328; Hickey 2004:327–8). Chaudenson's (2001) notion of "approximation of approximations" is seminal here (see Mufwene 2001b).

The target itself was not homogeneous either. European indentured servants came from a variety of regions in the British Isles, and given their social class background they certainly spoke nonstandard dialects. Some leveling and koinéization was going on (Roberts 1988b:112; Mufwene 2001b; Hickey 2004:336).

5.14.2   Phase 2/3 (ca. 1650–1961)

The onset of phase 2 can roughly be dated to the middle of the seventeenth century. By that time the small island had been filled with an English-speaking population, and large-scale British immigration discontinued, also because of fundamental changes in the British pattern of Caribbean colonization. In the 1640s the cultivation of sugar was introduced from Brazil, and as this proved much more lucrative than the earlier crops it soon revolutionized the economic basis and the social make-up of Barbados, with substantial effects for its linguistic situation. Planting sugar cane requires highly demanding labor for which large numbers of Africans were enslaved and imported. It also needs big plantations to be profitable, so many of the small-scale holdings of the first phase were bought out. Thus plantation sizes increased but the number of landowners decreased drastically: from over 11,000 in 1645 to ca. 745 in 1667 (Roy 1986:142). Of the former indentured servants, many lost their basis for living or sensed better opportunities elsewhere (like in Jamaica or the Carolinas), so they left Barbados in large numbers; the island's white population declined substantially between the 1650s and the 1680s. In contrast with many other Caribbean islands, however, a significant proportion of poor whites has always remained characteristic of the social make-up of Barbados (Roberts 1988:8); the percentage of whites never dropped below "14 percent at the height of plantation slavery" (Fields 1995:89). The mass importation of slaves and exodus of whites resulted in a drastic reversal of the demographic structure of the population in the second half of the seventeenth century. While in 1655 the number of whites still exceeded that of blacks (23,000 versus 20,000, respectively), by 1684 there were more than twice as many slaves as whites (ca. 46,600 vs. 20,000), and in 1780, at the peak of the plantation period, the proportion was 70,000 blacks to 17,000 whites (Winford 2000:220; Rickford and Handler 1994). By the early nineteenth century blacks made up about 80 percent of the overall population.

Phase 2, a stable colonial period, lasted remarkably long, from the late seventeenth to the mid-twentieth century. It seems that the changes that did occur during that period, including emancipation, did not substantially affect the conventional patterns of social life and communicative practice on the island (Rickford and Handler 1994:238). Labor was increasingly divided along racial lines, with Africans working the fields and Europeans making a living as overseers, artisans, and the like. Within the slave population a social stratification into field hands on the one hand and house servants and skilled workers on the other emerged: "bozal" slaves, newcomers from Africa, were typically forced into the former role and "creole," locally born slaves, stood a better chance of securing the latter status for themselves (Alleyne 1980:184–5). Unlike in other Caribbean islands, in Barbados from the eighteenth century childbirth became more important than slave importation to keep the number of slaves at the level demanded by the planters. It is noteworthy that from early on there was also a fairly numerous group of people of mixed ethnic descent who, in line with the local "color bar," tended to occupy an intermediate social status, being typically free and provided with some rudimentary education or vocational training (LePage and Tabouret-Keller 1985:48).

The end of the British slave trade in 1807 and the abolition of slavery in 1834/38[46] were legally important, but according to Alleyne (1980:186) most people of African descent stayed on the plantations and continued to labor as before. This may be due to the lack of alternatives, or to the fact that the post-emancipation period actually saw a labor surplus, commonly attributed to a high birth rate and a healthy climate (Roy 1986:143). The social system continued to be marked by a delicate but relatively stable balance of status assignments based on property and complexion (Roberts 1988:115). A somewhat different ethnographic situation applied in the cities, where Africans were fewer in number, metropolitan varieties were more widespread, and creole speech was introduced on a broader basis only after emancipation by some former slaves who chose to leave the plantations (Mufwene 2005a and p.c. 2006).

Indicators of a phase 3 on political terms came only deeply into the twentieth century, when the possibility of independence and democracy appeared on the horizon and blacks began to organize themselves politically: In 1938 Grantley Adams founded the Barbados Labour Party, and in 1951 adult suffrage was achieved.

Little evidence is available on social identities during this long period, but we may safely assume that group alignments and self-projections as well as the resulting sociolinguistic attitudes reflected the social history, power relationships and complex status assignments of the Barbadian community. Wealthy planters tended to send their sons (not usually their daughters) to England for education, and some remained involved in English affairs to a certain extent, though fundamentally their home was the Caribbean.[47]

Consequently, they were the only ones for whom a symbolic retention of an exonormative linguistic orientation mattered; most likely there was only "a tiny minority of upper-class whites speaking anything approaching standard English" (Holm 1994:335). Poor whites presumably did not care much about linguistic correctness but were occupied with defending their ethnically based status advantage against blacks.

Africans became more or less acculturated, involuntarily, to varying extents, depending upon their occupation and proximity to superior status carriers. It has been pointed out that "the system in Barbados was far more lenient" than elsewhere and "there was a close relationship between the slaves, especially the house slaves ... and their masters and mistresses" (Burrowes 1983:40). On the other hand, before emancipation there certainly was no way of ignoring the fundamentally inhumane status of slaves and the hostility, frustration, and suffering that it entailed. The history of the Caribbean records a long, though mostly (with the sole exception of Haiti) unsuccessful, series of slave revolts. It is quite indicative that the earliest plot occurred in 1657 but also that it was betrayed by Africans who apparently felt an obligation to remain loyal to whites (Cassidy 1986:198). Attitudes and behavioral patterns of blacks, including linguistic behavior, reflected their status and desired identification with other groups (Alleyne

1980:185). House servants presumably felt more closely bonded to the existing power structure and its representatives, but not necessarily so: "Not all domestics identified with the group of domestics (many slave revolts were led by domestics)" (185). The extreme oppression from which field hands suffered, and their lack of social interaction outside of their peers, resulted in "a strong ethnic identity" (220). This feeling of an ethno-social cleavage continued into the twentieth century, as indicated by the race riots of 1937.

The linguistic consequence of this situation amongst the Africans was creolization, a degree of language restructuring and innovation, significantly marked by grammatical substrate influences, considerably beyond similar processes in most other PCEs. This process set in after the homestead phase, when the number of Africans exceeded that of Europeans by far and access to the target language for the slaves thus became seriously restricted. More specifically, incoming new slaves most likely acquired their skills in the local language no longer from European native speakers but from contacts with other Africans who had acquired English (or the local form of it) earlier and with modifications, so a "founder effect" in Mufwene's sense (1996b, 2001b) certainly played a major role. For newly incoming slaves, the target of their language shift was not white people's English itself but rather an approximation of native speakers' ways of speaking as produced by earlier slaves, with quite some variability depending upon who a newcomer happened to be interacting with most. This situation constituted an ideal ground for restructuring, modification, and innovation; it is quite characteristic of the phase when homesteads rapidly expanded to become large plantations (Mufwene 1996b, 2001b, 2004b:209, Chaudenson 2001:138). This is not the place to discuss the structural characteristics of (Caribbean) creoles; they have been amply documented both in general (e.g. Holm 1988/89) and with respect to individual varieties (though a systematic overall survey of Barbadian Creole is still missing).

It is noteworthy, however, that many of the putatively characteristic features of creoles (preverbal markers for tense, modality, and aspect; specific copula variants according to following constituent; lack of inflectional morphology; conflation of pronoun forms for different functions and gender; complementizer usage of *say*; serial verbs; etc.) differ from the lexis – grammar interface that in other PCEs has been identified as a prime location of grammatical changes. The innovations resulting from creolization are more fundamental, affecting core features of the grammatical system like the categorization and marking of central grammatical categories.

Features which are considered distinctively Bajan (the local cover term which avoids the labels English or Creole) are listed in Burrowes (1983:40–44) and Roberts (1988:92–93) and discussed selectively in

Winford (2000), and Blake (2002). Blake (2004) surveys the pronunciation of Bajan and identifies three features as characteristic within the Caribbean: rhoticity, frequent uses of glottal stops, and a backed and raised realization of the PRICE vowel. On the lexical level, there is only a small number of direct loans from African languages (e.g. *pia(b) ba(h)* 'kind of herb,' *pampalam* 'fuss, confusion'; Holm 1994:358). New coinages of the expected types include calques (like *eye-water* 'tears,' *sweet mouth* 'flatter(er),' *big-eye* 'greedy,' and *have words* 'quarrel,' all of which are general Caribbean phrases), idioms (*to bad talk* 'malign,' *be own-way* 'headstrong, disobedient,' *like somebody bad* 'like somebody very much'), compounds (*golden-apple, increase-peas, slave-lizard*), semantic modifications (*talk* 'have personal or sexual relations,' *improvement* 'off-spring of livestock reared by a neighbor,' *skipper* 'boss, respectful form of address'), and newly coined phrasal verbs (e.g. *dark up* 'turn dark,' *drunk up* 'become intoxicated,' *hug up* 'embrace enthusiastically,' *wet up* 'soak') (Burrowes 1983:44; Allsopp 1996; Roberts 1988:93, 130; Holm 1994:361).

Bajan is known within the Caribbean to be a relatively "light" variety, not too distant from English, quite different from the radical basilects of Jamaica and Guyana, let alone Suriname.[48] This is usually explained by the relatively high proportion of whites and by the comparatively flat topography of the island, which does not allow for isolated, inaccessible communities, and by the country's fairly high level of education and literacy (Alleyne 1980:186; Burrowes 1983:39; Roberts 1998:14). How deeply creolized Bajan was in earlier centuries has been the subject of some controversy: Hancock (1980) suggested that it has always been a largely metropolitan, non-creole variety; Cassidy (1980, 1986) opposed; and Rickford and Handler (1994) and Fields (1995) presented textual evidence showing that some nineteenth-century texts in fact do contain stronger creole-like features than the present-day dialect. From the present perspective this is not of primary importance, however: depending upon sociolinguistic circumstances, the Dynamic Model allows for different degrees of nativization to the extent of full creolization.

One observation that is relevant for the applicability of the Dynamic Model, however, reflecting the fact that structural innovations proceed from the IDG (or in this case substrate) strand to socially proximate IDG strand members, is the fact that poor whites adopted features of black speech (see below, in section 5.15 on Jamaica, for evidence that this also affected higher-ranking speakers, especially females). Holm assumes: "The language of most local whites was probably increasingly influenced by Creole by the end of the seventeenth century" (1994:334–5; see Mühleisen 2002:63).

5.14.3   Phase 4 (1961–)

The current sociolinguistic dynamics of Bajan, to the extent that it is documented, suggests that the country has proceeded to phase 4; a number of features associated with endonormative stabilization can be identified. As was mentioned above, this process began before the mid-century, but it is probably best associated with the convenient cut-off dates of internal autonomy in 1961 and, most importantly, independence in 1966. Political power has now shifted to the black majority (of about 90 percent of the population), although the economic power still tends to rest in the hands of the minority of whites. Barbados has opened herself strongly to tourism, now a major source of her national income. This process exposes the people to different varieties of English, but it may be presumed that as elsewhere it also strengthens their indigenous identity and their dialect as a way of symbolizing it.

As elsewhere in the Caribbean, where independence has engendered a "growing sense of nationalism" (Winford 1991:578) and people are "becoming more positive about themselves and their heritage" (Roberts 1988:172), there is no doubt that a process of nation building has been successful and Barbadians now cherish their own nationhood, national identity, and shared culture (Blake 2004:498). This idea emphasizes cross-ethnic unity, symbolized most clearly by the "unofficial national slogan, 'All O' We Is One'" (2004:498; see Blake 2002). Whether this ideal conforms to a reality in which class and color divisions still play an important role is a different story, though. Divisions within the society are determined primarily by class boundaries associated with wealth, i.e. there is a cleavage between a small number of rich people (mostly whites) and the mass of people who are able to sustain themselves but do not have much property. In line with the overall ethnic composition of the society, most of these are black, but there is still a sizeable group of poor whites. Residual color boundaries are still there, but principally the identities of these two parties are not substantially different from each other, they socialize on a regular basis, and there are intermarriages (Roberts 1988:15). Blake (2002), based on ethnographic research in a small town on the east coast, describes the situation as such:

Although blacks and whites in the poor community of Fishtown go to school together, work together, drink together, and pray together, it appears that home time is spent apart, to the extent that it is rare to see blacks and whites sitting together or sharing meals in one another's homes. Whereas the poor blacks clearly identify with an African ancestry, the poor whites are more hesitant about their being descendants of the indentured servants, aware of the stigmatization and negative stereotypes ascribed to them. (8)

The gradual growing together of black and white Bajans is quite characteristic of the force of a core idea described in the Dynamic Model: despite different ethnic origins, people who live together in a nation for good are forced to get along respectfully with each other and to mutually align themselves. This socially cohesive force finds its symbolic reflection in the distinctive local language: "In the case of Barbados, I suggest that the negotiation of identity toward nationhood plays a part in the vernacular being used as an effective mode of communication by blacks and whites alike on radio, television and in print" (Blake 2002:23).

Of course, a Caribbean-accented form of standard English constitutes a class-marked local prestige variant, at least one bestowed with overt prestige. Devonish's statement, on the Caribbean in general, confirms that until independence an exonormative orientation prevailed but it also implies that this is no longer the case: "Until the period of independence beginning in the 1960s, the unquestioned target for English language usage in the Caribbean were models associated with Standard British English" (2003:160). Of course, English has prevailed as the official language, appropriate for political and formal discourse and associated with "a new political elite" (Devonish 1986:24), but even this situation seems to be changing: with the University of the West Indies having assumed a leadership role, the "third quarter of the century ... witnessed a gradual change in official policy toward the non-standard vernaculars" (Roberts 1988:172), and teachers now try to teach standard English without deliberately alienating children from their own home speech (173). Covert prestige rests clearly with the vernacular (Winford 1991:578; Blake 2002:23).

Though Creole has traditionally been associated with the black community, in Barbados it is a variety shared by black and white. Earlier work by Lilith Haynes (quoted from Blake 2004) suggested that whites also use creole features, albeit not to the same extent, and it was pointed out above that this accommodation process dates back many centuries. Blake's (2002) analysis of language use among poor blacks and whites in an east-coast village referred to above proves the strength of this alignment. She finds both blacks and whites using creole features, including copula absence and lack of past tense marking, in much the same way and with highly similar frequencies. In line with phase 4, this situation can be interpreted as a result of a homogenization process, possibly supported by the loss of erstwhile creole features (Rickford and Handler 1994, Fields 1995).

Another aspect of phase 4 that is clearly visible throughout the Caribbean is the growth of an indigenous literature that prides itself in local traditions and language. With respect to Barbados, names that come to mind are Kamau Brathwaite, George Lammin, and Timothy Calendar. It is noteworthy and significant that the local vernacular plays a primary role in this: "More and more Barbadian writers and poets are embracing Bajan dialect and incorporating it into their work to capture the true essence of the Barbadian experience."[49] For the Caribbean in general, the best-known names are probably Nobel Prize Laureates Derek Walcott and V.S. Naipaul. Representations of creole in Caribbean literature have changed their artistic function from "representing authenticity" in the beginning to "expressing authority" in the recent past (Mühleisen 2002: chapter 5).

Finally, from a pan-Caribbean perspective an important step toward codification has been done with the publication of the *Dictionary of Caribbean English Usage* (Allsopp 1996), explicitly motivated by the "need for a norm" (xix) which it intends to set. As Devonish (2003:160–1) points out, the Caribbean Lexicography Project from which this dictionary grew was deliberately set up in the aftermath of a few countries having gained political independence, in 1971, thus confirming the close causal connection between political self-determination and linguistic codification. An ongoing process toward codification also entails the development of an orthography for creole(s), "itself a site of negotiating competing views on the language" (Mühleisen 2002:215) for which various suggestions have been made.

5.15   Jamaica

Creolists and Caribbean linguists rate the language situation in Jamaica (Map 5.8) as quite different from the Barbadian one, because a much more radical creole basilect developed in Jamaica. In the light of the Dynamic Model, however, this difference is secondary, as the model allows for various degrees of IDG (or substrate) strand influence without invalidating the claims made for the overall evolutionary trends and goals. Both the discussion of section 3.3.3 and a few of the points regarding the Caribbean as a whole made above apply here as well. Again, phases 2 and 3 are treated jointly, as a core political feature of phase 2, a stable colonial status, coincides with the central linguistic component of phase 3, nativization, i.e. creolization.[50]

5.15.1   Phase 1 (1655–ca. 1690s)

Following the Arawaks, who had died out by about 1620, and defeating the Spanish, who had held the island for one and a half centuries, the British conquered Jamaica in 1655, and since then the island has been part of the English-speaking world. The new settlement built upon experiences and population influx from Barbados, Nevis, and elsewhere in the Caribbean, so sugar cultivation was introduced immediately, the settlement grew rapidly, and phase 1 was short. There was in fact a relatively brief homestead phase, during which the number of slaves was still small. Lalla and D'Costa (1990:17–8) quote a contemporary description of the rural Jelyar farm as a typical example: In 1669, the planter lived together with a mulatto wife, their two sons, a black grandmother, six slaves, and two whites: a servant and an overseer. But this demographic proportion was highly transient; by the late 1670s blacks outnumbered whites.

When the defeated Spanish left, some of their former slaves fled to the mountainous interior and set up independent communities. They formed the nucleus of the "maroons," who were later joined by runaway slaves (although in a treaty with the British in 1739 the maroons agreed not to support and integrate them any longer). The maroons defended their independence in two wars in the 1730s and 1790s. In the Jamaican mythology and identity construction they are important to the present day as defenders of black liberty and "custodians of African culture" (Patrick 2004:407), in cultural manifestations, and also language use.

The sociolinguistic settings and contact conditions of this very early phase are not documented in any detail, but most certainly conditions were unstable and highly variable. There were small farms of the type just described, followed by large plantations set up in the late eighteenth and early nineteenth centuries. Piracy was important in the island's early economy. There was also something like a vibrant and highly multilingual urban environment dominated by sailors, buccaneers, and traders, viz. the city of Port Royal, until the earthquake which destroyed it in 1692. There was a tremendous population influx: slaves from West Africa; sailors, soldiers, indentured laborers, convicts, merchants, etc. from the British Isles and from other Caribbean possessions (including Suriname) were seeking their fortune in Jamaica. It is clear that language contact was ubiquitous, but it is disputable which ingredients played a role, and to which extent: certainly various British dialects and African languages were involved, probably slightly older forms of Caribbean English, possibly pidgins which Africans may have acquired in West Africa or during the passage or developed on location.

A linguistic detail which reflects a characteristic structural effect of phase 1, if only marginally, is worth noting, namely traces of an indigenous (in the strict sense of the word) topography mediated via the Spanish: the island's name itself goes back to an Arawak word *Xaymaca* 'land of wood and waters,' and the small number of other surviving Arawak words documented includes further place names (*Linguanea*; *Mammee Bay*) and fauna terms (*iguana*; *hicatee* 'freshwater turtle') (D'Costa and Lalla 1989:2; Lalla and D'Costa 1990:11–3). Lexical heritage from the previous occupants, the Spanish, includes, in the domain of flora and fauna, the words / niizberi/ for a kind of tree (Lalla and D'Costa 1990:16) and *agouti* for a rodent as well as a few more place names (*Ocho Rios*; cf. *Spanish Town*) and words for objects and natural events like *savannah*, *hurricane*, and *cassava*, though these are widespread and not distinctively Jamaican.

5.15.2   Phase 2/3 (ca. 1690s–1962)

The subsequent phase, marked politically by a stable colonial status and linguistically by the emergence and evolution of Jamaican Creole, began late in the seventeenth century and can be taken to have lasted practically until independence in 1962. The slave population rose quickly, from about 9,500 or 55 percent of the total population in 1673 via 40,000 (85 percent) in 1693 to ca. 100,000 (91 percent) by 1739 (for precise statistics, see Lalla and D'Costa 1990:17; Holm 1994:341, Cassidy 1961:16). In comparison with Barbados, it is characteristic of Jamaica (and linguistically significant) that population growth and the demand for a growing labor force could not be upheld by natural reproduction but demanded a continuous importation of substantial numbers of African slaves until the end of the British slave trade in 1807 (actually, even in the mid-nineteenth century, after emancipation, thousands of new Africans arrived, then as contract laborers; see Alleyne 1988:42). Newly arriving Africans were usually assigned to experienced slaves for a "seasoning" period during which, we may safely assume, they were assimilated culturally and also linguistically (D'Costa and Lalla 1989:3). In the absence of any other means of social orientation, the pressure to quickly conform to local practice must have been strong.

Jamaica's sugar economy produced great wealth, though only the top echelons of a rigid social hierarchy, planters and big merchants, really profited from this revenue. Other whites around were servants, bookkeepers, overseers, artisans, shopkeepers, suppliers, smallholders, adventurers, soldiers, sailors, and privateers. There was also a constant demand for indentured laborers, who in many cases stayed as planters or merchants after their period of indenture (Cassidy 1961:13). During the eighteenth century a deliberate policy of bringing in British smallholders to counterbalance the ever-increasing number of Africans on the island was imposed (Christie 2003:8). Black ranks included domestic servants on top, a middle group of artisans, skilled foremen, cooks, drivers, sugar boilers, midwives, etc., and the mass of field hands at the bottom. The distinction between creole (locally born) and bozal (unseasoned African-born) slaves was perceived as important (Alleyne 1988:136). The middle ranks "mediated and dispensed authority and influence upward to the whites and downward to the black majority" (Lalla and D'Costa 1990:24). Slave life was cruel, especially for the field laborers. Running away, at first to join the maroons and later just to absent oneself from harsh plantation life for weeks or months, was a constant practice, though it was commonly followed by cruel punishments (1990:25). Not surprisingly, the history of Jamaica records a long series of minor and major slave uprisings, in addition to various forms of passive resistance. A growing intermediate group of mulattoes emerged during the eighteenth century, usually springing from unions of white fathers and black mothers. Many of them were freed and set up in small businesses by their fathers (1990:23). By the 1830s the number of these "browns" was estimated to be about 40,000 (92). Patrick states that "the 'black/brown' distinction remains a culturally relevant one today" (1999:25; see LePage and Tabouret-Keller 1985:48).

The abolitionist movement emerged since the 1770s, and it was locally fueled by growing missionary activity. Their thoughts and preachings, obviously unwelcome to the planters, were such that the 1831 slave rebellion, the largest in Jamaican history, became known as the "Baptist uprising." Parliamentary debate about this incident, however, triggered subsequent steps toward the liberation of slaves. The apprenticeship system, imposed in 1834, was practiced in such a cruel fashion, with the obvious intention of breaking the slaves' desire for freedom, that emancipation followed in 1838. In reality, however, conditions of life changed hardly at all thereafter, and the large sugar plantations continued to prescribe the patterns of everyday life. The ongoing hardship and injustice led to the Morant Bay rebellion of 1865, which brought some minor political changes (like the imposition of direct rule by the British Crown), though it is questionable whether it was just one more riot or, as some would make believe, a turning point in the country's political history.

A linguistically important consequence of emancipation was the gradual spread of education among former slaves. In practice, however, this was a slow and inefficient process, due to much absenteeism, inefficient teaching conditions and an emphasis on rote learning. By the 1960s only 4 percent of the population attended secondary schools (Christie 2003:12).

The composition of Jamaica's population also records a small adstrate component: apart from a small number of non-British Europeans, who came earlier and whose descendants tended to merge in invisibly, the nineteenth and twentieth centuries saw immigration by Indians, Chinese, Syrians and others. Apart from rather incidental contributions to the local lexicon and some cultural retention especially on the side of Indians these groups have largely joined the cultural and linguistic mainstream by today, unlike in Trinidad or Guyana.

The first half of the twentieth century brought small changes and an expansion of the outlook of some Jamaicans. External experiences through work abroad (for example in the building of the Panama canal) and through war participation introduced new ideas and a growing demand for social justice. Consequently, the island saw an emerging labor movement, the introduction of general suffrage in 1944, and the foundation of political parties. Furthermore, the demise of the sugar industry resulted in the growth of smallholdings and the production of other crops, like bananas. Still, no fundamental social upheavals occurred during all this period.

There is solid evidence that the identities of Jamaicans of all origins turned essentially native from early on. The exception may have been a small stratum of top-ranking whites, who still saw themselves primarily as Englishmen on foreign soil and who consequently sent their sons to England for education (where some remained, causing the phenomenon of absentee ownership of plantations; Lalla and D'Costa 1990:23). Among lower-ranking whites D'Costa and Lalla (1989) find some initial support for seeking relief from hardships "in the memories of a distant home and the hope of eventual return" (4), but it is clear that those who stayed soon developed a strong Jamaican identity (without renouncing their British ancestry):

During the eighteenth century, creole whites took on the split identity that has marked them ever since. Many looked outside for cultural models and worldly approbation, but many others firmly identified with Jamaica. ... local patriotism was so pronounced that on several occasions they attempted to exclude English-born persons from filling posts in the island ... [and refused] to be called Englishmen. (Lalla and D'Costa 1990:23)

Obviously, things were more complicated with the black population, who experienced the same conflict of identity but "in a different way" (1990:23). For them, the fundamental injustice and cruelty of the system of slavery and the existing cleavage clearly did not instill a desire to develop an "us" reading including their oppressors, and this antagonism is given expression by a long series of slave riots and acts of resistance. Certainly African loyalties remained and were constantly reinforced by new arrivals from Africa. On the other hand this was clearly a thing of the past, a dream, or even a projection to the afterworld in a "reunion through death" with the "true home" of ancestral spirits (D'Costa and Lalla 1989:4) – which may explain the importance and persistence of African funeral rites and related customs like the characteristic "ninth night" celebration. In reality, however, the only social network that offered comfort were fellow slaves, who were also fellow Jamaicans. So in addition to hostility, isolation, and depression that no doubt were also serious components of the slaves' psychological attitude, there are also some indications of loyalty and even local pride; a "black creole consciousness rose in rivalry to African identity" (Lalla and D'Costa 1990:25). For example, in a 1740 fragment we find a statement like "the Creol Negroes greatly value themselves for being born in the Island" (quoted from Lalla and D'Costa 1990:129). The most obvious indication of such an orientation is the widespread attitudes of old hands toward African newcomers, who they held "in the utmost contempt" and commonly derided as "salt-water Negroes" or "Guinea birds" (Cassidy 1961:18; Lalla and D'Costa 1990:25).

There is another detail, characteristic primarily of Jamaica within the Caribbean, which must have supported the perpetuation of alignments with the slaves' origins, namely the retention of traces of African languages, even outside of the maroon communities (1990:25). It is frequently argued that the incoming slaves were ethnically fairly homogeneous, largely consisting of Akan and Twi people. In contrast to the general assumption that slaveholders sought to mix their slave populations ethnically to avoid the danger of surreptitious communication (which no doubt also was a reality; see D'Costa and Lalla 1989:5) there are reports – marginally, quite clearly, but nevertheless – of traces of African languages being in use and pockets of African cultural rituals being practiced on Jamaican plantations (Alleyne 1988:120; Lalla and D'Costa 1990:2). For examples, Cassidy (1961) quotes a contemporary description of a Christmas celebration from as late as 1838: "The Mongolas, the Mandingoes, the Eboes, the Congoes, & c. & c., formed into exclusive groups, and each strove to be the loudest in their music and their songs, or rather yells, peculiar to their country" (18).

From a sociolinguistic perspective, language contact settings and patterns of language use have always been quite variable and complex and, for any individual, determined by social status and one's range of contacts. Blacks of intermediate social stance commanded mesolectal speech forms, and occasionally even acrolectal English (the best-known example being an eighteenth-century black poet by whom "literary English is fluently handled"; Lalla and D'Costa 1990:86). Conversely, the vast majority of field laborers spoke creole. An exonormative orientation was valid for top-ranking whites, supported by their English education and connections, but hardly anyone else (Holm 1994:335).

What is much more interesting, especially in the light of the Dynamic Model which maintains that IDG, or in this case substrate, strand speech starts to intrude into settlers' speech behavior, is the widely noted fact that whites also commanded and used the Creole (or some form of it) adopted from the blacks (1994:335; D'Costa and Lalla 1989:44). Typically, this influence dates back to early childhood years which the planter's offspring frequently spent in close contact with black children so that, according to a report from 1739, a boy "acquires their broken Way of talking" (quoted in Cassidy 1961:21; similarly Mühleisen 2002:63, quoting Long's report of 1774). Also, to some extent the use of Creole or local speech forms by whites was gendered, being more typical of women because they lacked education (2002:63; Lalla and D'Costa 1990:97). For example, in 1790 an observer reports: "The Creole language is not confined to the negroes. Many of the ladies … speak a sort of broken English," and he quotes "a lady" commenting on the fresh air by saying "him rail-y too fra-ish" (quoted from Cassidy 1961:23; see also Mühleisen 2002:62).

The linguistic acculturation process of blacks is neatly summarized by Cassidy as follows:

In sum it may be said that all Jamaica-born Negroes learned English, whether or not they kept up some part of Africa; that there were always great numbers of new-come Africans who, however, had good reason to learn English as well as the situation permitted; that their first models were not upper-class English, and that the chief models after the seventeenth century must have been the native Negroes rather than the whites. (1961:19)

The linguistic outcome of this contact situation is the genesis of Jamaican Creole. It is somewhat disputed when and how exactly creolization occurred in Jamaica (though in the present context this is only a secondary issue; see Patrick 2004:409; Lalla and D'Costa 1990:16). Most likely its roots were laid late in the seventeenth century, with black population figures multiplying in proportion to whites. According to the evidence provided by Lalla and D'Costa (1990), some key features were in place by the mid-eighteenth century, while others emerge only in texts of the nineteenth century (Patrick 2004:407). It is generally agreed that the demographic proportions, the constant influx of Africans, and the fact that their target was the speech of other slaves produced a comparatively basilectal creole.

Although the process of creolization is qualitatively different from and more radical in its effects than the restructuring that leads to structural nativization of PCEs elsewhere, some of the grammatical features associated with the latter process can be observed in Jamaica as well. Modifications of verb complementation include the transitive use of *care* (instead of *care for*; Christie 2003:15), the fact that some verbs allow a bare infinitive rather than the marker *to*, e.g. *Him start tell*, and also the fact that the default infinitive marker is *fi*, derived from *for* rather than *to* (Patrick 2004).[51]

Lexical creativity manifests itself in much the same way as in other PCEs; the following categories are noteworthy:[52]

- indigenous, i.e. African, loans, covering to a considerable extent the domains of fauna, flora, food, and other cultural practices (*ackee*, the 'national fruit,' *fufu* 'mashed starch-vegetables,' *nyam* 'food,' *susu* 'whisper,' *mumu* 'mute person, idiot,' *chaka-chaka* 'disorderly,' *anancy* 'spider,' *obeah* 'black magic,' *dopi* 'spirit,' *doti* 'earth,' *bammy* 'cassava bread,' *backra* 'white man,' *busha* 'overseer,' *yaba* 'clay pot,' *John Canoe* 'masked dancer,' *nana* 'grandmother') and a few ADS loans (*daru* 'rum,' used among Indians);
- compounds, including some calques (e.g. *garden egg* 'egg plant, or aubergine,' *bush man, brown rat, galley-wasp* 'lizard-like animal,' *hard-back* 'beetles,' *hand middle* 'palm,' *fresh fish* vs. *salt fish, fine voice* 'high-pitched voice,' *dead stranger* 'perfect stranger,' *tall hair* 'long hair');
- hybrid formations (*macca-fat, obeah man, ground-anancy*);
- derivations (*grudgefulness, stupidness, upliftment*);
- semantic modifications (*dandelion, cherry, pear, apple, robin, crow, dumpling* – all used for different objects than their European counterparts; *brass* 'penny,' *hand* 'hand and arm,' *foot* 'foot and leg,' etc.).

5.15.3   Phase 4 (1962–)

The period after World War II opened Jamaica to the modern age. It brought socioeconomic diversification (reducing the formerly automatic link between race and class), democratization, and urbanization (resulting in the tremendous growth of Kingston; Patrick 1999:26). Independence in 1962 engendered a "growing sense of nationalism" (Winford 1991:578). A process of cultural nation-building was initiated, symbolized by the national motto proclaimed at that time, "Out of Many One People." The process was meant to instill pride in the nation's African heritage and its distinctive cultural manifestations, like Reggae music – and slowly (because of the resistance instilled by the exonormative and "complaint" traditions) but gradually, language has become a part of this process. The outcome of this sociopolitical development is a pan-ethnic, distinctively Jamaican identity, which, given the sociodemographic conditions, must incorporate rural and lower-class traditions and habits. Identity building, set against a pan-Caribbean background (LePage and Tabouret-Keller 1985:75), has become "an important issue" (Lawton 1982:268).

However, this new "very strong love and promotion of things Jamaican and Jamaican Creole" also has had to meet with resistance, a conservatism which is becoming increasingly residual but which still represents "a very vocal anti-creole element in the society" (Roberts 1988:22). This position can be taken to be Jamaica's equivalent to the complaint tradition. The view that Jamaican Creole is no more than a bastardized, corrupt form of English, to be avoided and eradicated at all cost, is deeply rooted as a "linguistic ideology" (Devonish and Harry 2004:450; see also Winford 1991:578; Christie 2003:4, 35–7; Patrick 2004:408).

English is the nation's official language and, of course, the language of formal and official domains. A few decades ago I might have added the adjective "public" to this list, but this is no longer exclusively so. An exonormative orientation prevailed until the 1960s (Devonish 2003:160), but since then this attitude has slowly crumbled away. In theory, "English" as the target of teaching still means "British English,"[53] though in practice, as used in official contexts by educated speakers, it implies in speech an educated Caribbean accent (as described by Devonish and Harry 2004, for instance) and in writing an unmarked grammatical common core interspersed with lexical Jamaicanisms. Standard English is "still expected in the conduct of government business, in the law courts, the schools, the mass media, in religious worship and in all the other contexts where written language is required" (Christie 2003:2).

For most Jamaicans this kind of standard English is primarily imposed by the education system but not transmitted outside of school, and a full command of it indicates an upper-class, elitist status (Devonish 1986:24). Christie observes that "more than half of the children in today's high schools lack adequate exposure to Standard English on entering school and never achieve satisfactory command of it" (2003:40; similarly Winford 1991:568). However, this tension between expectations and reality is triggering slight changes of attitudes and policies even in the educational arena: recently even the Minister of Education publicly considered the possibility of using "the dialect" in schools to help children to make progress, and demanded respect for both English and Creole (Christie 2003:36).

In reality, what most Jamaicans grow up with and what is most widely audible in public is a mesolectal form of Jamaican Creole, with a lot of variation toward and away from the standard or basilectal ends, depending upon the social relationship between the interlocutors and the formality of the situation.[54] For the last few decades, this variety has made major inroads into semi-formal and formal contexts from which is was absolutely banned until the onset of phase 4 – a strong pull toward an implicit endonormative orientation is now perceivable. This change results simply from the force of the realities of language use, from the fact that for the vast majority of speakers Jamaican Creole is not only the variety they grow up with but also "a valuable symbol of Jamaican identity" (Christie

2003:27; see also Patrick 2004:407). Members of all social classes use it "in moments of relaxation, as a vehicle for the expression of emotion [and] the description of personal experiences" (Christie 2003:2). Christie (2003) introduces an interesting, finely graded distinction: while Jamaican English is a "sign" of Jamaican identity, only Jamaican Creole is a "symbol" of it (63).

Thus, Jamaican Creole has definitely acquired new prestige (Mühleisen 2002), changing from covert to overt, and there has also been a "gradual change in official policy," dated by Roberts to the third quarter of the twentieth century (1988:172). Politicians now use it, at least intermittently, in order not to distance themselves from their audience and electorate. How drastic this change has been becomes audible in comparison with the official independence broadcast of 1962, in which Jamaica's cultural heritage was celebrated in Standard British English with a near-RP accent (Mair 2002:33). Just ten years later, however, Prime Minister Michael Manley used basilectal creole in his election campaign (Sand 1999:74). Nowadays, it is almost mandatory for politicians to symbolically signal their solidarity with the masses by switching to Creole. For example, in 2001 the Prime Minister used some Creole in his speech on the eve of the election (Christie 2003:4). Alleyne (1980:222) observed Creole in use in headlines of campaigns for voter enumeration launched by the Electoral Office, and in radio commercials and the talk of disc jockeys. Some Creole has also made it into the law courts, though it is not officially recognized there (Devonish 1986:29–31).

A similar situation obtains in the media landscape. A few decades ago Creole was tolerated only marginally, e.g. in humorous cartoons in the *Gleaner*. Today, however, to varying degrees it can be used to discuss serious issues. It is regularly audible on the radio (1986:34; Sand 1999), e.g. in phone-in programs,[55] and it comes up (though usually still as a noticeable code-switch) in other contexts, internet postings, and the like. Shields-Brodber (1997) claims that "the diglossia of the past ... is being steadily eroded, as Jamaican Creole ... gradually usurps the functions of the 'High' (H) language" (57). She documents uses of Creole in new, formal contexts on a broad basis, proclaims the "marginalization" (57) and "dethronement" (64) of English, and goes so far as to project a "requiem for standard English in Jamaica." Mair (2002:39) considers this "premature," mainly because very little Creole is yet visible in written texts. Christie, however, surmises that the regularity with which some Creole forms now occur in newspapers "suggests that they could one day be part of the norm" (2003:18).

The strongest indicator of an endonormative orientation being "just around the corner" is a recent political initiative to bestow Jamaican

Creole with constitutional recognition: "only in the 21st century has the Jamaican government seriously begun to explore language planning and recognition of JamC as a national language" (Patrick 2004:408). In December 2001 the "Joint Select Committee of the Charter of Rights Bill" set up an agency "to formally propose and standardize the existing system for writing Patois" in parliament, with the intention of supplementing the Constitution with a clause to rule out discrimination on the grounds of language (Christie 2003:6). This also entails the promotion of literacy in Creole (61). As a member of this committee, Devonish (2003) discusses the background and the political ramifications of this proposal.[56]

However, in order to possibly gain official acceptance Jamaican Creole would not only need to undergo elaboration and status planning (Devonish 1983, 1986; Winford 1991:597), but it also has to overcome another serious obstacle, viz. its lack of an accepted orthography. While this step toward codification remains a problem, there is a strong awareness of it, and it has been tackled repeatedly (Mühleisen 2002:185–98). Amongst linguists, a transliteration system proposed by Cassidy has gained wide recognition while in public writing conventions culled from literary dialect prevail. In terms of symbolic value and user-friendliness, there are pros and cons associated with both options. The issue is problematic because it is fraught with symbolic meaning, with codification being "itself a site of negotiating competing views on the language" (Mühleisen 2002:215).

Lexical codification, on the other hand, has already been achieved. In addition to Allsopp's (1996) *Dictionary of Caribbean English Usage*, mentioned earlier (see Devonish 2003:160–2), with the work by Cassidy and LePage (1980) a thorough historical and philological dictionary covering the Jamaican lexis is available. Devonish's call for an institute in charge of the development and codification of Caribbean Creole (1983) is noteworthy but seems to have vanished without effect.

Another indicator of the growing acceptance of Jamaican Creole is its common use in serious literature, also essentially a phenomenon of the post-emancipation period. Historically speaking, Lalla (2005) shows how the function of Creole in Jamaican literature has proceeded from a "ventriloquist phase" through "censorship" and "alternation" phases to a current "expansion" phase in which Creole can also be the narrator's code, and implies "authority, authenticity and autonomy." Louise Bennett's poetry, tying in with an African-derived oral tradition, is credited with having had a major influence on the recognition of indigenous language use as a serious poetic device. Other authors who come to mind in this context are the novelists Orlando Patterson and Trevor Rhone, playwright Dennis Scott, and the poet Mervyn Morris.

Schneider and Wagner (2006) document how sophisticated and sociolinguistically convincing the manipulation of different styles in the mouths of different characters in Thelwell's novel *The Harder They Come* is. Accepting a slightly expanded notion of literary creativity, Reggae lyrics provide a fine example of the artistic expressivity of Jamaican language, and Bob Marley's songs have given the variety global visibility. In general, there is a wide array of language-based musical and popular art deriving from Jamaica, some having achieved international renown, ranging from earlier, more conventional songs by Harry Belafonte to the work of the dub poet Mutabaruka.

Finally, one feature is observable in Jamaican language use which seems to be foreshadowing phase 5 already, namely initial diversification. As Mufwene (2004a:208) also observed, Jamaican Creole is "not only still thriving but also developing more divergent varieties." The best-known example is "Dread Talk," the distinctive language of the Rastafarians (Pollard 1983, 1986; Alleyne 1988:146–8, 151; Christie 2003:34). Another case in point is Speaky-Spoky, a stylistic variant described by Patrick (1997, 1999:277–8). In the absence of substantial homogenization in the previous phase, however, this aspect should not be overestimated.

5.16   Canada

The focus of this section's discussion will be on the evolution of a distinctive variety of English in mainland Canada (Map 5.9). There are two important processes in early Canadian history which, in order not to bleach the notion, are best taken not as manifestations but as precursors of phase 1.[57]

One is the settlement of the island of Newfoundland. British presence on this island goes back to Cabot's landing in 1497. However, its history remained quite distinct from that of "mainland" Canada for a long time. Newfoundland's population mostly stems from two massive IDG settler streams, the first coming from south-west England in the sixteenth century (together with Portuguese fishermen), and the second from Ireland in the eighteenth. Both have shaped the island's marine-based culture and her dialect to the present day. Perhaps even more importantly in the Canadian context, Newfoundland was not a location where the American "Loyalists" of the late eighteenth century ended up, so there are different founder populations, and the connections between the north-eastern off-shore island and the mainland were weak for a long time. Newfoundland remained a colony of its own and joined the Canadian federation only in 1949. Hence, in the following discussion I will largely exclude this island.

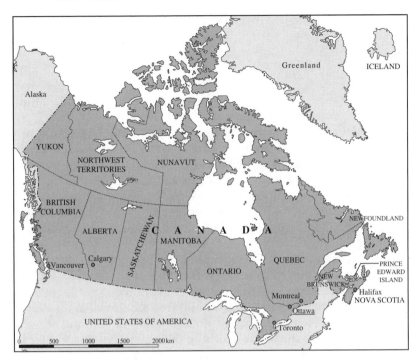

Map 5.9: Canada

Secondly, French settlement in the territories of "la Nouvelle France" preceded the British history by more than a century, and, unlike, for instance, early Spanish activity in Jamaica, it has left important permanent traces in Canada's official bilingualism and francophone regions. Of course, the French colonists were settlers like, later, the English-speaking ones, but their continuous development was interrupted or at least severely hampered by their loss of power. In the course of time what was left of this early French period had to struggle for and find a role in an English-centered society, much like other minority groups. Thus, in the light of the Dynamic Model focusing upon English they are best treated as an important ADS strand, though one that antedates the evolution of English itself. A few interesting consequences have resulted from this peculiar constellation. First, specific identity relationships and a special kind of bilingualism, backed by high demographic proportions and the reputation of a respected language and history, emerged. Secondly, some of the earliest characteristics of the Dynamic Model, especially those having to do with STL – IDG contacts, involved the French as agents of a STL strand, and the British, who came later, could build upon or inherit patterns which had developed earlier.

5.16.1   Phase 1 (1713–1812)

During the seventeenth century there were short periods when the British had a hold on eastern Canada, but essentially the region was French. Phase 1 of British Canada began with the Treaty of Utrecht of 1713, when France surrendered Acadie, the southern part of Nova Scotia. French settlers continued to dominate the shorelines in the new English colony, however, until ongoing distrust in their loyalty caused the British to expel them during the French and Indian War (1754–63). At the end of this war, in the Treaty of Paris in 1763, France had to cede all of her North American possessions, and immigration from New England to the north was encouraged.

Soon these early British immigrants were followed by a numerically large group who became more important than any other for the future development of Canada and for the discursive construction of its history in particular:[58] Americans who remained loyal to the Crown in the War of Independence. They are usually divided into the "United Empire Loyalists" who left the thirteen colonies prior to 1783, when the Treaty of Paris recognized the independence of the young United States and established the remaining colonies as British North America, and the "Late Loyalists," who followed thereafter and early into the nineteenth century. The Loyalists constitute a classic case of a "founder population" in Mufwene's sense: it is generally argued that due to their large numbers, their cultural significance and the fact that in many districts they were "the first settled population" (Chambers 1997:389) they set the standards (and developed early, informal linguistic norms) to which later immigrant groups had to adjust. During that period they populated eastern Canada up as far as Quebec and Ontario (then divided into Upper and Lower Canada), next to the remaining and later some returning French speakers.

No doubt the identity of the Loyalists was decidedly British-oriented – that, after all, was what motivated them to leave the US and move north. Of course, there was language contact with the indigenous population, although by the time the British arrived on the scene they had already been diminished due to European diseases, and their impact was weakened by military defeats.[59] Many native tribes got involved in the conflicts between European powers, and sided with one of them. The Iroquois, for instance, fought the Americans in the War of Independence, and their defeat, with the British, contributed to the opening of their traditional lands in the interior to European settlement (Bailey 1982:141).

The following structural effects of phase 1 can all be observed. Mackey (1998) attests that "the mixture of their [the colonists'] dialects gradually resulted in a common language, less dialectal than those of Europe" (26; similarly Chambers 2004a:224), though I am not aware of a detailed study of koinéization from that period. Despite restricted contacts and native linguistic influence otherwise, the topography is strongly indigenous: four out of ten provinces, four of the five Great Lakes, four capital cities including the national capital, and "many lakes and rivers and thousands of city, town and local names" are Native in origin (Orkin 1970:170), e.g. *Abitibi, Chinguacousy, Chiputneticook, Kakbeky, Kikkertaksoak, Kouchibougwack, Manawagonish, Manitoba, Memphremagog, Niagara, Ontario, Opinipiwan, Passamaquoddy, Pugwash, Temiskaming, Wetaskiwin, Yukon,* and so on (170–1, 189–90). In addition, there is a fair selection of French-derived place names, e.g. *Boissevain, Deux Rivières, Portage la Prairie, Souris* (Bailey 1982:139; Orkin 1970:176–7).

5.16.2 Phase 2 (1812–1867)

After the War of 1812, which settled the relationship between the United States and Britain (and her remaining North American colonies) and inspired renewed patriotic sentiments among the citizens of British North America, a stable colonial period lasted for more than half a century. This period was characterized by another wave of population influx, mainly from the British Isles: despite the overt pro-British attitude of the Loyalists, the government distrusted their American origins, and attempted to balance their impact by promoting immigration by "genuinely" British people.

Identities in the STL strand oscillated between a firm allegiance to the mother country and a "growing sense of national unity among the new Canadians," who combined their American origin with self-images as "keepers of the true Loyalist faith" (Bailey 1982:144). In the early nineteenth century, a contemporary observer thus saw "a national character in the process of formation" (quoted from Bailey 1982:157). In this construction, Canadians have accepted their binary roots but have readjusted their respective weights, having "created for themselves a sense of their past that reduces Yankee influence and asserts kinship with Great Britain." (150; Avis 1973:53) While overt prestige was assigned to educated English accents (Bailey 1982:155, Chambers 1997:392) and things British in general (Chambers 2004a:232), local speechways tended to be construed as inferior ("slovenly pronunciation, slack articulation, flat voices, and Yankee barbarisms"; Avis 1973:42; see also Chambers 1993:24). However, for the majority of settlers, down-to-earth working people struggling to survive and develop their communities, such an orientation had little practical value.

242 Countries along the cycle: case studies

Contemporary visitors confirm that accents from all corners of the British Isles could be heard in Canada during that period (Orkin 1970:13), but the children of these immigrants readily adopted the accent of their peers, following the model set by the Loyalists (Chambers 1991:91, 2004a:226–8).[60]

Relationships with non-British residents were distant to terse but operative as required by the circumstances, grounded in a clear power relationship (confirmed, for instance, by the unsuccessful rebellions of 1837 and 1838 led by Francophones in Upper and Lower Canada). By the end of this period persons with British ancestry outnumbered the French by a ratio of about 2:1 (Mackey 1998:23). Indians were decimated, outnumbered, subdued, and separated in reserves, and some of their children forced into white residential schools (Mackey 1998:17–8). Intermarriages did occur but usually required a cultural shift of the minority partner. As the case of the Michifs (from French *Métis*), a truly biracial community set in present-day Manitoba whose language is a mixture of Cree and French, suggests, the French tended to be more receptive and tolerant to native cultural input.

The demographic developments of this period presumably laid the foundations for the character of the Canadian English variety, most prominently its accent, to the present day: it "shows the effect of a standard Southern British superstratum having been imposed on a North American variety" and consequently "varies between standard British and American forms on a long list of variables concerning phonemic incidence, morphosyntax, lexicon, and general usage" (Boberg 2004a:355).

In line with the structural characteristics of phase 2 of the Dynamic Model, "[i]ndigenous plants and animals usually kept their native names, such as *tobacco, potato, tamarack, skunk, raccoon, beaver, grizzly* (bear), *moose*, and *caribou*" (Chambers 1997:386 – though not all of these examples are distinctively Canadian). Many of these words were mediated and phonetically modified through French contacts. Further examples include the following, with dates of first attestations where available (Orkin 1970:66–89, 196–202; Avis et al. 1967): *wapiti* (1824), *namaycush* 'kind of fish' (1787), *tuladi* 'lake trout,' *ouananiche* 'freshwater salmon' (1787), *muskellunge* 'kind of pike,' *hackmatack* 'coniferous tree' (ca. 1805), *pembina* 'highbush cranberry' (1760). There are also words for local objects and customs, including *pemmican* 'kind of food mixed of meat and fat' (1743), *komatik* 'Eskimo sledge,' *muskeg* 'type of wet soil,' *toboggan* 'type of sledge' (1691), *wendigo* 'mythical being' (1830), *chicamin* 'money.'

5.16.3   Phase 3 (1867–ca. 1910s)

After some two decades of political activities toward a federation of the British colonies in North America, the British North America Act (or

"Constitution Act") of 1867 established the Dominion of Canada as a self-governing political entity, thus terminating the colonial phase in the strict sense, although close cultural and also legal ties with Britain remained in effect. Thus, the doors were opened toward the country's independent development, including the issues of cultural and linguistic orientation. At the same time, the 1848–9 establishment of the Pacific colonies of British Columbia and Vancouver Island and the 1868 purchase of Rupert's Land and the North-Western Territory from the Hudson Bay Company (Mackey 1998:30) opened the lands west of Ontario for further settlement and expanded the country's territorial base quite substantially. One prerequisite for this extension was the settling of the border conflict with the US, with both countries agreeing upon the 49th parallel as the national boundary in 1818 and 1846 (for Oregon) – disregarding the presence and claims of indigenous peoples in this area. Of course, this did not prevent intensive north–south exchange and also migration across the border, so to ensure a primarily Canadian rather than American character and orientation of the Canadian West, great pains were taken to strengthen east – west connections (most importantly through the construction of the Canadian Pacific Railway, completed in 1885) and to encourage westward migration from an Ontario population base. In the 1870s and 1880s Manitoba was settled, though the expansion met with strong resistance by the Michifs. Some twenty years later, Alberta and Saskatchewan followed.

The identity of Canadians of European descent (except for the French Canadians, who kept fighting for their cultural independence) was always deadlocked between their British–Loyalist roots and American origins, respectively. They were "conditioned from infancy to think of themselves as citizens of a country of uncertain identity" (Frye, quoted from Bailey 1982:156). On the one hand, it seems unlikely that they were interested in mimicking British models (156); on the other, they definitely wanted to set themselves off from the United States, as indicated by the deliberate strategy of attracting Canadian, not American, settlement to the West.[61] But then, an independent Canadian self-confidence was only in the process of emergence in the early dominion period, with the country just "speedily approaching puberty in her drive toward nationhood and . . . beginning to exercise her independence" (Chambers 1993:24). The struggle for which components would be recognized as essential ingredients of an evolving Canadian identity was fierce. The IDG strand was denied such a status, as is indicated, for instance, by the fate of the Michifs. Despite the fact that in the beginning they made up ten thousand out of eleven thousand inhabitants of Manitoba, the 1870 constitution of the new province declared only English and French as official languages (Mackey 1998:30). With their strong base in Quebec, the French fared somewhat better, although in the late nineteenth and early twentieth centuries some provinces denied a legal status to their language (30).

Dialect contact between various styles and varieties of English as well as language contact between English, French, and indigenous languages continued, and gradually this mixture produced Canadian English. Its written standard deliberately cherished its mixed markers as "tokens of linguistic independence," like *tire centre* (Bailey 1982:150). On the spoken level, the same mixture from British and American ingredients can be found, both in the standard accent and in colloquial dialects. It is indicative that the term "Canadian English" itself originated shortly before the onset of phase 3 as dated here, namely in 1857, in an article by a certain Rev. Geiki – and it is also not surprising that, like many other contemporary statements of a similar persuasion, it was meant derogatorily, scorning the "corruptions" of the new mode of speaking (Chambers 2004a:230).

Linguistically speaking, Canadian English is thus marked by very few distinctive features of its own but rather by its unique combination of linguistic components. Its most characteristic, and readily audible, pronunciation feature, of uncertain origin (Chambers 1998a:262), is "Canadian Raising," a raised central onset in the /aɪ/ and /aʊ/ phonemes before voiceless consonants, i.e. *about* is pronounced [ə'bəʊt] and *night* is [nəɪt]. For other features of the Canadian accent, see Boberg (2004a) and also Avis (1973:64–5). The Canadian lexis includes types of elements found in other PCEs as well, including loans from indigenous languages (*pesogan* 'dried fungus used as punk,' *mocock* 'container made of birchbark') and the French adstrate (*lacrosse, portage, rapids*), compounds (*sessional indemnity, baby bonus, home-and-school club, chuck wagon, blue line, remittance man*) and hybrid compounds (*Winnipeg couch, pembina cart*), new meanings (*reeve* 'chairman of a village,' *riding* 'subdivision of a county,' *shoot* 'falls, rapids') and other coinages, like *mountie* (Avis 1973:65–7; Orkin 1970:68–88; Avis et al. 1967). Little evidence is available on grammatical features, but the most distinctive of all, and a well-known marker, is a lexicogrammatical element, the invariant tag *eh*. A notable syntactic transfer feature from French, an adstrate, is the noun-modifier order in some names, e.g. of the Great Lakes (*Lake Superior, Lake Ontario*, etc.), and also in "government-created names", e.g. *Parks Canada, Air Canada* (Bailey 1982:162). Another feature that is reported to be characteristically Canadian is its high variability: where other varieties, e.g. American English, have one word or option, Canadians may freely choose from a wide range of alternatives (Chambers 1998a:269).

5.16.4   Phase 4 (ca. 1920–ca. 1970)

With the Dominion status still fresh and the settlement of new provinces in the West to be shouldered, the young Canadian nation was still very much in the making, busy with defining her external boundaries, both in a literal and in a transferred sense. Like in Australia and New Zealand, however, the participation of Canadian troops in World War I, painful as it must have been, marked a new status of nationhood, and introduced a period of fierce nationalism and endonormative stabilization which lasted well into the social upheavals and reorientations that the 1960s brought in many western countries. Politically, these developments are encapsulated in the 1931 Statute of Westminster, which bestowed full legislative equality (and ultimate independence, as it were) upon the Dominion. According to Chambers, the years between the 1920s and the 1970s were "peak years" of a "rabid Canadian nationalism," producing "all the iconic events historians point to as emblems of nationalism," including economic protectionism, political alliances, celebrated sports victories, and symbolic acts like the "unfurling of the national flag in 1965" (1998a:270).[62] An important legal step marking this national independence is the Canadian Citizenship Act of 1947, which for the first time created a new Canadian citizenship independent of the British one. Further symbolic emblems of this newly won national orientation are a new national anthem (in 1967) and the maple leaf flag (in 1968), both replacing the corresponding British symbols.

Not surprisingly, this growing national orientation translated into "a growing sense of Canadian identity," dated by Boberg to "the decades after the Second World War" (2004a:355), and this, in turn, had direct consequences for the symbolic role of language. An endonormative linguistic orientation is claimed to have been a direct consequence of the political nationalism of this era: "The autonomy of standard CE appears to have arisen naturally and subconsciously as the medium for this heady nationalistic thrust" (Chambers 1998a:270). Avis (1973:57) dates this new public interest in Canadian English to the 1960s. While clearly the facts, the intermediate position of Canadian English between British and American norms, had not changed, the emphasis in the national discourse on Canadian language usage was laid on "a small but significant set of features that are uniquely Canadian" (Boberg 2004a:355). Kurath's work for the Linguistic Atlas of the United States and Canada conducted in the 1930s confirmed that this attitude reflects the sentiments of not only scholars and intellectuals but also ordinary people: his informants "prefer what they regard as their own Canadian speech, i.e. the speech of the old Loyalist families" (Bailey 1982:145). Boberg's statement, backed by solid research, sounds programmatic: "at a time when so many other differences have fallen prey to continental cultural convergence, the sound of Canadian English will be closely bound up with Canadians' sense of their national identity for many generations to come" (2004a:364; see also Bailey 1982:168).

Hence, phase 4 was clearly reached now: by this time, Canadian English was fully accepted, endorsed, and appreciated as the nationally appropriate way of speaking. The major sociolinguistic and structural characteristics of phase 4 can clearly be identified in Canadian English: literary creativity, homogeneity, and codification.

It is now generally accepted (against occasional views to the contrary) that a distinctively Canadian literature exists. An early precursor was Thomas Chandler Haliburton, who in his Sam Slick stories in *The Clockmaker* contrasted "Yankee" and Nova Scotian perspectives on life. Well-known modern authors, many of whom address the issue of a Canadian identity, include Robertson Davies, Timothy Findley, and Booker Prize winners Margaret Atwood, Michael Ondaatje, and Yann Martel.

Similarly to Australia, Canada is one of those countries where the high degree of linguistic homogeneity across thousands of miles has continued to surprise observers, commentators, and analysts.[63] Here are three characteristic statements:

- In Canada, the accents of second-generation middle-class anglophones from Halifax or Ottawa or Winnipeg or Edmonton are indistinguishable. (Chambers 1998a:254)

- Canadian English is remarkably homogeneous from one end of the country to the other. This is particularly true in the broad stretch of territory extending almost 3,000 miles (4,500 km) from Ottawa and Kingston, Ontario, in the east, to Vancouver and Victoria, British Columbia, in the west, including all the major cities of central and western Canada ... one type of English, with minor regional variations, is spoken across most of the country, and central and western Canadians are generally incapable of guessing each other's regional origins on the basis of accent or dialect. (Boberg 2004a:352–3)

- [A] general characteristic of Canadian English is its relative homogeneity. To a large extent, a single type of English is spoken across the 3,000 miles from Vancouver, British Columbia, to Ottawa, Ontario. (Labov et al. 2006:217)

Similar observations can be found elsewhere, e.g. Avis (1973:50), Chambers (1991:91, 1997:385), and Brinton and Fee (2001:422). Clarke's (1993) collection also provides strong support for the ongoing trend toward homogeneity: evidence is presented for similar sound changes going on from Ontario to the Pacific coast, like the fronting and non-raising of /aʊ/ diphthongs or the retraction of /æ/. This homogeneity is usually interpreted as the product of both the similarity of the founding populations (Chambers 1991:99) and a strong pressure on newcomers to accommodate to existing linguistic norms which ultimately appear to go back to the Loyalists (Bailey 1982:156–7). It is noteworthy that this need to conform to a national norm has also affected Newfoundland English after the island joined the Federation: a gradual adoption of general Canadian features in this former enclave has been reported (Chambers 1991:92).

A direct consequence of the national reorientation up to the 1960s was an important step toward an independent codification of Canadian English: according to Boberg (2004a:355), this was the direct motivation for the compilation of the *Dictionary of Canadian English on Historical Principles* (Avis et al. 1967) which, like comparable dictionaries in Australia or New Zealand, served as a milestone of linguistic independence. Other Canadian dictionaries followed, some of them smaller spin-offs directed at a wider audience, like the *Concise Dictionary of Canadianisms* of 1973. Barber (2001) describes interesting reactions to the *Canadian Oxford Dictionary* of 1992. These range from residuals of conservative attitudes (like the question whether someone working for Oxford University Press shouldn't rather be interested in "proper English, not Canadian English") via requests for "sexy Canadianisms" to, ultimately, the following, telling assessment:

The Canadian public embraced the dictionary enthusiastically ... For them the dictionary was tangible proof that Canadians are a distinct people, no longer subjugated (or so we would hope) to the dominant powers of Britain or the United States. (285)

Altogether, the late twentieth century produced as many as six dictionaries and four usage guides and style books (Brinton and Fee 2001:424) – a strong indicator of the importance of and interest in codification in that period.

5.16.5   Phase 5 (ca. 1970–)

Beginning in the last third of the twentieth century, Canada has left this particular form of a nationalistic orientation behind and, consequently, the country has moved on into phase 5 in the Dynamic Model. Formally, all remaining legislative ties with and dependencies upon Britain were removed by the Canada Act, and as part of it the Constitution Act, of 1982. Politically, the country redefined herself as an immigrant nation par excellence. Unlike earlier waves of immigration with a predominantly European base, the second half of the twentieth century saw a massive population influx from Latin America and Asia (Boberg 2004a:354). As this movement was directed primarily toward the big cities, substantial ethnic enclaves have emerged in Toronto, Vancouver, and other metropolitan areas.

More than most other countries in the world, Canada has accepted immigration as a part of her national identity – an attitude which was perhaps prepared and backed by the country's earlier intermediate stance between two looming national models. Officially, the cultural contribution of immigrants is cherished, and they are encouraged to maintain their roots and also their "heritage languages" (Mackey 1998:26) in addition to adjusting to Canadian surroundings. A 1977 government document entitled "A national understanding" explicitly states:

rejection of uniformity ... constitutes the most authentic and widely shared experience of Canadians. The affirmation and preservation of differences ... has consumed the minds and hearts of Canadians all through their history. It is the Canadian response to the question of identity. Our unity ... arises from the determination to preserve the identity of each of us. (quoted in Chambers 1991:101)

This attitude favoring cultural diversity is apparently not only promoted by the authorities but also widely supported in the population (Berry 1998). Thus, Mackey notes: "As the twentieth century draws to a close a new concept of Canada is in the making" (1998:35).

This reorientation has also had an important effect on the assessment of the contribution of the IDG strand to Canada's history and identity. The "post-colonial myth of 'two founding peoples'," the French and the British, is "no longer politically tenable" today (Mackey 1998:35). As in Australia, Aboriginal rights and the recognition of land claims and demands for self-government have become an important issue on the political and judicial agenda, although there is still a long way to go, and there is no way of making historical injustice undone. Changes of self-designations "symbolise a total rejection of colonialism" (Barber 2001:292): the "shift from *Eskimo* to *Inuit* about 25 years ago" (288), the spelling change from *Micmac* to *Mi'kmaq*, and similar modifications among many of Canada's native groups (288). Another consequence is a renewed influx and acceptance of words for Aboriginal cultural realities. Barber regards these developments as the "result of a more inclusive post-colonial mentality" (293) – a statement which, in a nutshell, rephrases a core idea of the Dynamic Model.

A similarly complex situation, also indicative of a trend toward fragmentation, obtains with respect to the country's original ADS community, the French Canadians. Actually, it has been argued that "the francophone – anglophone debate has in fact acted as a catalyst for broader discussions" and for the fact that "all group affiliations and all identities ... are now in a state of flux" (Edwards 1998:2–3). Since the Official Languages Act of 1969 English and French enjoy an equal status on the national level, and all government postings have to be bilingual. In practice, however, the concept of French – English bilingualism seems to be making little if any progress. 83 percent of the population of Quebec use French as a home language. Outside of Quebec (and a few neighboring parts of Ontario and New Brunswick which are truly bilingual), however, French is not seriously rooted in Canadian usage at all. The continuing cleavage between the two population groups found its political expression in two referenda aiming at independence of the French Canadian region in the late twentieth century. Both were turned down, but the last one, in 1995, only by a very narrow margin of 49.7 percent vs. 48.5 percent in favor of independence (Edwards 1998:2). When French Canadians speak English at all,[64] they use a distinctive variety which "shows French influence on a few variables" (Boberg 2004b:189). While this English contributes to the diversification of Canadian English, it is unlikely to become a symbol of group identity, as this function is strictly reserved to Canadian French.

Thus, the sociolinguistic situation of present-day Canada is marked by changes, realignments, and diversification. An important vowel change, called "Canadian Shift," marked by lowering and backing of high and mid-high short vowels, has been progressing in recent decades (Boberg 2004a:361; Labov et al. 2006:130–2); it is not clear as yet whether it will qualify as a new marker of a pan-Canadian identity. Research on ongoing changes has identified the demise of earlier Briticisms (Chambers 2004a) and, especially among the young, also the gradual weakening or even disappearance of traditional markers of Canadian English, including Canadian Raising and the word *chesterfield* 'sofa.' This evolution has been at the expense of the gradually encroaching Americanisms (Chambers 1991:93, 101; 1998a; 1998b:269; Boberg 2004a:355). At the same time, however, new features are gaining ground. Most importantly, current changes in Canadian English are moving toward the birth of new dialects, as is characteristic of phase 5: "diversification ... lies ahead" (Chambers 1998a:171). This includes both social (i.e. ethnic) and regional variation.

An important sociolinguistic consequence of the large-scale immigration discussed earlier, a side effect of which has been a high degree of linguistic tolerance (Chambers 1991:101), is the emergence of strongly visible bicultural and bilingual urban groupings of their own. The second and third generations of these immigrant groups have been moving toward the adoption of Canadian English and ultimately language shift, though so far the degree of retention of the erstwhile native languages is still high. Not surprisingly, given the size and the independent status of these communities, their English shows signs of transfer and thus forms which are developing into ethnic markers in the Canadian context. It is expected that these markers will persist and thus result in new ethnic dialects, i.e. one form of fragmentation within Canadian English (Chambers 1998a:271).

Another type of dialect birth and fragmentation, also in line with observations made elsewhere in phase 5, is the fact that the stunning supraregional homogeneity of Canadian English seems on the point of breaking down, and new regional dialect distinctions are emerging. Chambers (1991:99) hypothesizes: "In the course of time, one might expect that regionalisms will accumulate, ultimately diversifying Canadian urban accents." Some of these emerging regional markers are worked out by Boberg (2004a:360) and Labov et al. (2006:220–4).

Many of these phenomena, however, can be observed most extensively in the oldest and best researched postcolonial variety of all: American English. This is also the form of English on which, apart from the British source variety itself, most research has been conducted. However, varieties of American English have usually not been viewed as a postcolonial variety, and no theoretically informed history of the language has been written so far. Thus, this is what we will turn to in chapter 6.

6   The cycle in hindsight: the emergence of American English

It is not customary to view American English as one of the "New" or Postcolonial Englishes. It is typically regarded as an "old," established, "Inner Circle" variety, one of the world's two major "reference accents" – quite unlike the newly emerging varieties discussed in chapter 5. However, such a perspective may be misguided simply by the fact that American English originated considerably earlier than these other varieties. On second thoughts, it cannot be denied that it emerged very much like the Englishes of Australia, New Zealand, and South Africa did much later, and the difference to other PCEs is essentially one of colonization type and of a more prolonged time depth, not a matter of principle.[1] English-speaking North America started out as Britain's first overseas colonial offspring, and the early American settlers met with indigenous people and had to deal with them in much the same way British expatriates did in many locations around the globe centuries later. The fundamental similarities may have been obscured by the remarkable political and economic success of the United States in the twentieth century that turned her into a global superpower. Basically, however, as I will show momentarily, American English has proceeded along the same developmental cycle as the others.

American English thus provides an almost unique opportunity to observe the entire developmental cycle in hindsight, as it were. Hence, after briefly pointing out the specifics of the American situation in contrast with other Englishes in the next few paragraphs, in this chapter I will go through the five developmental phases and their constituent properties as applied to American English. It will be shown that the components of the Dynamic Model can be identified quite accurately.

In comparison with other PCEs, the emergence of American English has been characterized by a few distinctive traits. Firstly, as just stated, the time depth is considerably greater – with a span of almost four hundred years it is about twice as long as that of many other major varieties in the antipodes, Asia, and Africa. Secondly, and perhaps most characteristically, the role of the IDG strand is quite different from most other colonies, perhaps with the exception of Australia. American English has evolved as the model case of a settlement colony dialect. The impact of the native American peoples upon the evolving national language and culture has remained fairly restricted, and the characteristic intertwining of the English and indigenous cultures has barely happened. Compensating for this, adstrate influences have come to be extremely important and characteristic, in quantitative and also qualitative terms. This concerns not only the multiplicity of immigrant groups from a variety of European countries but also, and perhaps most importantly, the people of African descent, even if their coming to the North American soil happened forcedly. In addition, Hispanic population groups from various origins as well as, later, Asians have been absorbed while retaining some degree of ethnolinguistic distinctiveness. Overall, the social and linguistic relationship between the STL strand, i.e. the long-dominant Anglocentric culture and speech habits, on the one hand, and the combined IDG and ADS strands on the other has worked out in a fashion not too dissimilar to STL – IDG relations elsewhere. A consequence of this is the third characteristic, namely the fact that diversification in phase 5 very strongly, though not exclusively, moves along ethnic lines of division.

Finally, the amount of internal homogeneity observed within American speechways needs to be assessed relative to the sheer geographical size of both the original colonial region and the fully settled continent in the end. The physical extension of the newly settled region is so vast that it precluded regular contacts between all regions and major groups, at least in the early phases when the means of transportation available were still rather poor, so some internal differentiation clearly has always existed in American English. On the other hand, one issue to be discussed will be the country's widely observed linguistic homogeneity. Also, for specific historical reasons in their respective homelands, many settlers and adstrate groups tended to come in waves, with shared origins and largely shared destinations, and this joint migration pattern of large groups and also entire families has accounted for some degree of homogeneity within certain regions, settled roughly at the same time by people similar in origin and social characteristics (thus reducing the range of factors to be considered in their specific "contact equations," and the set of features available in their regional "feature pools"). So homogeneity in the US needs to be judged on two levels, the national one (in the early phase with respect to comparisons to British dialectal diversity, and today with an eye on notions such as "General American" or "network English") and the regional or ethnic one (take, for instance, the conceptualizations of a distinctive "Appalachian English" or of a non-regional, nationwide, and

relatively uniform urban African-American Vernacular English, henceforth "AAVE").

The same need to distinguish a national from a regional perspective
holds true for the identification and dating of the different phases of
the developmental cycle as well – a fact which is not surprising given the
vastness of the territory and the historical extension of the expansion of
English settlement across some two and a half centuries. Consequently, the
initial phases in particular proceeded much earlier along the east coast
than in the west, where the onset of the Anglicization process occurred
much later but also, linguistically speaking, on quite a different basis, to
some extent building upon prior developments in the older settlement
regions. Take, for example, the dawn of the nineteenth century: by that
time, as I will show, the former colony and now young nation along the
Atlantic Seaboard had evolved deeply into phase 3, about to proceed into
the next stage of endonormative orientation, while at the same time in the
regions further to the west, across the continent, the English language
hadn't been heard as yet. Thus in these regions phase 1 only started with
the Lewis and Clark expedition of 1804–6, while by the end of the same
century the Midwest and West had made up the east coast's head start to
achieve a relative unity from coast to coast in cultural and linguistic terms.[2]
In other words, we need to distinguish two distinct realizations of phase 1:
early in the seventeenth century along the east coast (and but little later in
the remaining parts of the thirteen original colonies), some two hundred
years later in the interior and western parts of the continent. Consequently,
phases 2 and 3 can be more clearly identified in the colonial regions, while
further to the west the development is characterized by a higher degree of
overlap and simultaneity of the characteristics of different phases.

An interesting and peculiar thread connects two individual groups in the
initial and the final phases of the evolutionary cycle, almost symbolically:
Sir Walter Raleigh's "Lost Colony" and the Lumbee Indian tribe of
today's Robeson County in North Carolina. In 1587 Raleigh established
the earliest English settlement in North America, on Roanoake Island off
the coast of North Carolina, but when the leader of the group left to
replenish low provisions and returned from England after two years, the
small colony of those who had been left behind had simply vanished
(Nichols 2003:42–4). But even though the group had disappeared without
any visible trace it did have a lasting impact on the identity construction of
the Lumbee Indians, who gave up their ancestral language so early that we
do not even know whether they were Algonquian, Iroquoian, or Siouan.
According to a theory popular among the Lumbee, the "lost colonists"
merged and blended their culture with a "Croatan" Indian tribe, and their
descendants migrated inland to resettle along the Lumber River. The

Lumbees do have a distinct ethnolinguistic identity, which is expressed by linguistic means. Their dialect has peculiar features on the levels of lexis (*Lum* 'Lumbee tribe member,' *ellick* 'coffee with sugar,' *on the swamp* 'in the neighborhood'), pronunciation (largely shared with other dialects of the south-eastern region), and syntax (with a perfect formed with *be* rather than *have*, as in *I'm been there*, or an inflected copula form: *how it bes*; Wolfram and Dannenberg 1999; Wolfram et al. 2002). They state that outside of Lumbee land they recognize each other by their speechways, and they are proud of that. And some of their pride as a group rests on their belief in their possible "Lost Colony" ancestry. As Wolfram et al. (2002:39) observe: "the connection between a distinct Native American group and a mysterious but celebrated British group shows how legend functions in the construction of identity."

6.1   "Assembled in America from various quarters":[3] Phase 1 (ca. 1587–1670)

6.1.1   Sociopolitical background

The earliest English expedition, with the aim of exploring the possibility of North American colonization, was launched in 1587, and, in fact, that occasion led to the very first instance of individual IDG strand bilingualism, as two young male natives were taken back to England for a year and most likely acquired some proficiency in English (Wolfram et al. 2002:36–7). Raleigh's colonization attempt of 1587, just mentioned, left no visible traces. Large-scale systematic settlement started soon thereafter, with the first English-speaking permanent settlers founding the South Atlantic colonies (beginning with Jamestown, Virginia, in 1607) and New England (where the Mayflower landed the Pilgrim Fathers in 1620, followed by numerically more important settlements during the following decade).

The Jamestown settlement marked a significant beginning but in itself it wasn't really thriving for a while: located in rather unhealthy marshland, initially it was not self-sufficient. A minor movement was the foundation of Maryland in the 1630s as a stronghold of religious tolerance. At the same time, tobacco farming became the region's economic basis, with the first African slaves having been imported as early as in 1619. In the 1640s the Chesapeake region received its substantial population influx of people who left a lasting impact, when the English Civil War caused Cavaliers, Royalists from southern and south-western England, to move to the area. These people, gentrified and conservative, also orientated toward England, founded what was to become the aristocratic southern planters' culture which later spread across the southern lowlands and dominated the region until the Civil War. Although influential, they were a minority in numbers – they were joined and followed by rural farmers and laborers from the same source regions, many of whom came as indentured servants and then stayed, occupying new lands and trying to make a living.

The Plymouth and Massachusetts Bay colonies were dominated by the Puritans, who insisted on severe and rather rigid religious principles as the basis of their social order. They were followed by about twenty thousand other religious dissenters, mostly well-educated middle-class people and also craftsmen from eastern England. These settlers then spread into other parts of New England, including Connecticut and today's New Hampshire. Providence, Rhode Island, was founded in 1636 by dissenters from the Bay Colony who favored a slightly more liberal society. A certain cultural cleavage between western and eastern New England soon emerged, with the western part being occupied by farmers while the east turned to the sea for its economic basis (which could imply anything from sustaining contacts with England to, later, large-scale whaling).

The mid-Atlantic region was contested between the English and the Dutch, who had founded New Amsterdam in 1624/25, but their influence soon vanished, and in the 1660s the English controlled New Jersey and exchanged their colony of Suriname against New Amsterdam, thereafter called New York. More importantly, however, political events in England, in a troubled mid-century marked by the upheavals of the English Civil War, continued to drive America's settlement history. Especially after the King's Restoration, Quakers and their sympathizers fled persecution by moving to North America, finding the middle Atlantic region their most suitable gateway. William Penn received a land grant in 1681, and Pennsylvania soon attracted mostly lower-middle-class people from all over England but predominantly from the north midlands. Immigrants spilled through mid-Atlantic ports into the interior to where unoccupied lands could still be found. The entry through Pennsylvania and drive onwards also characterized the fourth of the great waves of American in-migration identified by Fischer in his (1989) influential book *Albion's Seed* as the northerners. Most notably, this wave included the Scotch-Irish, descendants of migrants from Scotland to Northern Irelands during the "Ulster plantation" of the early seventeenth century. These settlers, primarily from the lower walks of life, started to come to America late in the seventeenth century well into the eighteenth, mostly for economic reasons. They moved on into the Great Valley of the Appalachian Mountains, where the landscape and the economic basis of mining and lumbering allowed the continuation of traditional lifestyles, and from West Virginia into northern Georgia they constituted the backbone of a conservative and somewhat secluded mountaineer culture, with later extensions into the Ozarks and parts of the south-west.

It was only after the end of the revolutionary war that English spread beyond the relatively narrow confines of the thirteen original colonies. Phase 1 began in inland regions with the expansion of the frontier, when an endless stream of settler groups rolled into the interior of the continent, continuously reducing the land allocated and left to Native Americans. In 1763 the outcome of the French and Indian War resulted in Britain's sovereignty of Canada and the land as far as the Mississippi (though the upheavals of the following decades delayed the actual exploration and settlement of that region). The Louisiana Purchase of 1803 doubled the land area of the United States, although it took decades for first explorers and then settlers to really take possession of this region, to give it a political organization as part of the US, and to transport and root the English language there, along overland trails that connected the staging areas of the east with expanding and open lands in the west. Florida was bought in 1819; English-language settlement of what now is Texas, then still Mexican territory, began in the 1820s. Roughly between the 1820s and the 1850s settlers from western New England and upstate New York populated the Great Lakes region. Western Georgia and further parts of the South were cleared for white settlement by the cruel acts of Jackson's presidency (see below). By mid-century, settlement, if only piecemeal, reached the Pacific Northwest, and the California gold rush of 1848/49 speeded up the Anglicization of the Pacific coast. The Gadsden purchase of 1854, bringing in parts of New Mexico and present-day Arizona, essentially completed the territorial expansion of the coherent landmass of the United States, with English as the language that diffused into formerly native lands, uninhabited regions, and Spanish-speaking areas, and effectively concluded phase 1 in North America (except for Alaska, purchased from Russia a little later).

In comparison with other PCEs, it is characteristic of the American version of the evolutionary process that the IDG strand has remained linguistically rather insignificant because of the cruel and tragic fate that Native American tribes faced whenever Anglo-American expansion encroached upon their traditional lands and lifestyles (see Nichols 2003). It is estimated that when the first settlers came up to 17 million Native Americans speaking up to 500 different languages were living on the North American continent (Romaine 2001); today, only 2.5 million Native Americans and fewer than 200 indigenous languages (most of which are seriously endangered) have survived. In the beginning the native peoples offered generous hospitality, but the tensions resulting from continuously rolling waves of newcomers and their hunger for land soon gave way to distance, isolation, and hostility. It may also have been a religiously motivated sense of cultural superiority that prevented many settlers from paying due respect to the native population and embarking on a relationship on roughly equal terms. Instead, Native Americans were driven off their traditional lands, and diminished by exposure to unknown germs. So the relationship between the STL and the IDG strands, while conforming to some characteristics of the Dynamic Model, essentially remained a rather one-sided affair.

On the other hand, adstrate groups played a major role in the evolution of American English. Some of these came from Europe as well – there were Swedes settling in Delaware in 1638; Dutch and French colonial endeavors resulted in early contacts; and Germans started to immigrate in the 1680s and constituted the largest non-English group along the frontier in later centuries, concentrating in certain areas like Wisconsin or the Texas hill country. The most important and numerically largest of the adstrate groups, however, were Africans, captured in their West African homelands and brought to North America, sometimes via the Caribbean, as slaves to work the Southern tobacco, sugar, rice, and later cotton plantations. The first twenty African slaves were sold by Dutch traders in Virginia in 1619, and the importation of slaves continued until both Congress and the British Parliament passed legislation banning the slave trade in 1807. Algeo (2001b:15) quotes a figure of an estimated 400,000 slaves having been imported into British North America during this period (which accounts for only about 4 percent of the overall slave transportation across the Atlantic, with the vast majority having been brought to Brazil, the Caribbean, and the Spanish possessions).

Another very important adstrate group was native speakers of Spanish. The Spaniards had held Florida and, most importantly, the entire Southwest until the US acquired these territories and English speakers moved in, causing early and long-term bilingualism and language contact. Immigration by Mexicans in large numbers has continued to the present day, has established the Mexican-Americans as an important population group (not only) in the Southwest, and has had noteworthy linguistic effects, to be discussed later. The twentieth century also saw the establishment of other groups with a Hispanic heritage, namely the Puerto Ricans (primarily in New York City) and the Cubans (in southern Florida).

6.1.2   Identity constructions

Individual and collective identities from the early colonial period are difficult to reconstruct, given that the limited seventeenth-century evidence that is available (in sermons, legal and historical texts, etc.) stems from a few elite members of society only and is not representative of the overall colonial population. In a settlement colony like North America we may safely assume that the vast majority of all immigrants came with the intention never to return to the "homeland." This does not apply to all of them, however – regular naval connections provided for some exchange in both directions, and some of the Puritans, for instance, actually did return during Oliver Cromwell's reign, when the political climate in England favored their cause. We may safely assume that the earliest generations of settlers from Britain simply perceived themselves as Englishmen living on foreign soil. During the nineteenth century the agents of westward expansion presumably saw themselves as frontiersmen and settlers, as Americans, and as heirs of their individual cultural and religious legacies, determined by their respective family histories.

Given what we know about early contacts, Native Americans offered hospitality first, but pretty soon they must have understood that white settlement endangered everything that was important to them – their lives, their sovereignty over their ancestral lands, their cultures and languages, their tribal integrity. They certainly felt themselves as the natural occupants of the land, threatened by the European invaders. Similarly, the fate and attitudes of enslaved Africans must have been desperate, deprived of human dignity and with no prospect of returning to their homelands. For later generations, born into slavery in the colonies, it may be presumed that the emotional attachment to Africa faded, but some of it must have been retained through the transmission of some cultural habits, perhaps some oral history, and also simply through the common bond of sharing the fate of life under slavery.

6.1.3   Sociolinguistic conditions

Relationships between the European newcomers and the Native Americans varied from friendly to hostile, but they were never very intimate. It all boiled down to the basic fact that the Europeans and the Natives were competing for land, and that the continuous flow of immigrants implied an ever-increasing demand for new lands. Land grants in Native American territory were a common reward for Revolutionary soldiers, for instance (Conklin and Lourie 1983:7). In the long run Native Americans were pushed to the west, not infrequently into regions occupied by other tribes hostile toward them.

Thus, the IDG strand in North America remained relatively weak. There was always some interethnic communication going on, required by the needs of trade and other negotiations, but it was never really extensive.

In line with the Dynamic Model, even during the very early phase some second-language acquisition of English occurred on an individual basis, resulting in the first bilingual speakers; and, alternatively, some Europeans showed some interest in the native languages (although, as is common in these situations, the burden of second-language acquisition was distributed extremely unevenly).

As far as we know, the earliest contacts were peaceful and relatively harmonious: the first settlers were "cheek by jowl" (Algeo 2001b:15) with some Native tribes, and the Natives helped them to survive, showed them places, and taught them how to set corn or how to catch fish.[4] It seems that rudimentary bits and pieces of English were picked up by the Natives quite rapidly. In fact, Allen Walker Read found compelling evidence that very soon the language was not only used for interethnic but also for intranative communication: in an 1838 reprint of an English explorer's report published in 1628 he found the following report:

the governor was at my house, and brought with him a savage, who lived not above seventy miles from the place which I have made choice of, who talking with another savage, they were glad to use broken English to express their mind to each other, not being able to understand one another in their language. (2002:26)

Interethnic contacts of the early colonization phase were usually mediated by linguistically skilled bilingual translators, so-called *linguisters* or *linguists*. Romaine (2001:158) tells the story of one of the earliest of these intermediaries, a Patuxet Indian named Squanto – a story which in many respects is reminiscent of Sydney's Aboriginal Bennelong, some 170 years later. Having been captured and exiled to England, he returned to Massachusetts to find his tribe exterminated by disease, so he joined another tribal group. William Bradford, in his *History of Plymouth Plantation*, records how "about 16th March [1621], a certain Indian came boldly among them and spoke to them in broken English, which they could well understand" (quoted from Romaine 2001:158). Subsequently he kept close contact with the whites and played a crucial role in their dealings with Natives. It is also noteworthy that, as was the case in many other communities in the first phase of the evolution of a PCE, this type of bilingualism not only served the colonists but was "beneficial to Squanto too. His access to the settlers enhanced his own power with people among whom his own status was marginal" (158). Such instances, then, must have been visible incentives for bilingualism to spread further. In many cases this led to a pidginized English used by Native Americans, attested widely from the beginning (e.g. Craig 1991; Romaine 2001:158–9). In the long run, and with tribal coherence increasingly threatened and disintegrating, it frequently led to language shift.

The burden of acquiring a second language rested primarily upon the Natives, but there were also some, if only occasional, instances of the reverse pattern as well. In Virginia, Thomas Heriot elicited a word list and prepared a dictionary of Algonquian (Romaine 2001:159). In 1643 Roger Williams, a founding father of American Baptism and of the state of Rhode Island, published his *Key Into the Language of the Indians of America*, an early dictionary. Missionary work like the activities described in the *Eliot Tract*, a series of documents from the mid-seventeenth century that include bible translations into Algonquian, provided for a certain degree of balanced language contact. William Penn claimed to have understood the Natives and marveled at the "sweetness or greatness, in accent and emphasis" of their words and names (quoted from Krapp 1925,1:175).

While the early phase of contact along the eastern seaboard happened relatively peacefully (relations between the Natives and the government in Pennsylvania were explicitly described as "favorable"; McDavid 1958:500), the extension of phase 1 into the west tended to result in much more violence and hostility, even outright massacres. The Iroquois in the Mohawk Valley and the Cherokee in western Georgia had for a long time prevented direct expansion into these directions. In 1828 Andrew Jackson gained the presidency as an explicit "Indian fighter." His "Indian Removal Act" of 1830 paved the way for the violent relocation of many Natives, especially in the South, to "Indian Territory," present-day Oklahoma. The Cherokees in particular suffered tremendously, and many did not survive the infamous "Trail of Tears." Later, many military incidents and Indian wars have passed into the history of the West. The construction of the transcontinental railroad increased the pressure upon the Natives, and for many Western tribes a fundamental component of their nomadic lifestyle was destroyed by the wanton killing of millions of buffalo in the early 1870s.

6.1.4   Linguistic effects

As a settlement colony, the early phase of American English was characterized primarily by koinéization. However, two qualifications are required at this point. First, I stated at the outset of this chapter that there were actually two "phase 1s" in America, English being brought first to the original colonies and only later to the interior and the West. In the same vein koinéization peaked twice, as it were: both among the early settlers (which resulted in British visitors' observations of uniformity in eighteenth-century American English) and during the settlement of the West (which resulted in the perception of midwestern English as "accentless" and idealizations like the one of "General American"). The distinction need not be overemphasized – wherever settler groups mixed, and that happened practically all the time, koinéization occurred, so in a sense it was an ongoing process for almost three centuries, but with two recognizable historical and regional peaks. Secondly, important as it certainly was – the notion of koinéization in the American context has always had to be taken with a pinch of salt. I will discuss the issue of the putative uniformity and homogeneity of American English later, in the context of phases 2 and 4, but it is quite clear that this never adequately described the situation in full. The history of American English has always been marked by a tension between centripetal forces, favoring uniformity, and centrifugal ones, strengthening linguistic diversity.

Using Mufwene's (2001b) metaphor, Kretzschmar (2004:258) describes colonial koinéization as follows:

Out of the pool of language characteristics available in each colony there emerged, within a few generations, the particular set of features that would form the characteristic speech of the colony. No colony sounded too much like any particular area of England because of the mixture of settlers, and for the same reason the different American colonies sounded more similar to each other than to the speech of the old country.

This description applies to all colonial settlements, but dialect mixture seems to have been strongest in Pennsylvania, where the Quakers themselves came from a wider range of regions than the Southern or New England settlers, and their tolerant and receptive attitude attracted many others from different quarters and backgrounds. This is the cradle of the North Midland dialect, arguably the most neutral accent and the source of today's "mainstream" inland – northern – western type of American English.

Conversely, less mixing implies less koinéization, or, to put it positively, where population groups which were relatively more homogeneous in origin stayed together there was a stronger chance for the retention of dialectal features peculiar to their respective source region. With respect to the early settlement phase in North America, this deserves to be discussed for the very earliest settlements, New England and the South, on the one hand and the Appalachian Mountains on the other.

As pointed out earlier, the settlers of tidewater Virginia and the Massachusetts colonies were relatively homogeneous in their regional and social origins, and also in their religious and cultural orientations. This applies in each of the two regions, but to a certain extent it also unites both of them: settlers came from southern parts of England and shared a middle- to upper-class background and a continuing attachment and some exchange with the home country. It is not a surprise, therefore, that (a) both regions, New England and the South, have produced the most distinctive dialects of American English to the present day, and (b) they share a number of conservative linguistic features with each other (but not with the Midland region which lies between them). The most significant example is the lack of rhoticity: as in southern England, a postvocalic /r/, in words like *car* or *card* is not pronounced in conservative New England and southern dialects (this has been shown to be changing among young urban speakers today). Another pronunciation feature shared by both southern England and these two American regions (traditional pronunciations, again) is the realization of a palatal glide after alveolars before /u:/, as in *tune, new, duke*, pronounced with /ju:/ as against northern and western US /u:/. There are also shared lexical forms, including *piazza* 'veranda,' *belly-girt/girth* 'band of harness around abdomen of a horse,' *spider* 'iron skillet,' *hog('s) head cheese, nor(th)easter* 'wind' (Carver 1987:132–5).

Similarly, the population of the Appalachian Mountains was relatively homogeneous in stock, made up primarily by the Scotch-Irish, and it is not surprising that cultural (e.g. musical traditions) and linguistic continuities with Ulster or, more generally, Ireland, Scotland, and northern England have been sought and, to a certain extent, also identified. It is methodologically difficult to really pin down such transmission without any doubt (see Montgomery 1989 for details), but there are a few linguistic forms for which such continuity seems documented strongly enough to be accepted. These include grammatical patterns like "positive *anymore*" meaning 'nowadays' (e.g. *Anymore them crows just come*) or the "Northern Subject Rule" (a tendency to use verbal -*s* after full noun phrase subjects only, e.g. *crows comes* but *they come*) as well as lexical items (*scope* 'large tract of land,' *discomfit* 'inconvenience,' *sop* 'gravy,' *sprangle* 'spread out') and collocational tendencies (*spend an opinion*) (Wolfram and Christian 1976; Montgomery 1989, 2004; Schneider 1994; Montgomery and Hall 2004).

As predicted by the Dynamic Model, IDG strand, i.e. Native American, toponyms were borrowed in large numbers and from the very beginning. Krapp explains: "In the earlier periods of American colonization, the attitude of the colonists toward Indian names seems to have been that such names might be retained as designations for natural features of the country, for rivers, hills, mountains, lakes and sometimes meadows" (1925, I:172). The state of *Massachusetts* and some towns there bear native names (*Natick*, 1763; *Marshpee*, 1763; *Monomoy*, 1678; *Cohasset*, 1770), although it has been pointed out that especially for towns in the east there also was a noticeable tendency to use names which sounded familiar (e.g. *New England* itself or *Plymouth*) or were explicitly programmatic (like *Providence*), and thus did not emphasize the exotic, threatening character of a strange land as did native names. Hence, only two of the states along the east coast have Native names (*Massachusetts* and *Connecticut*, named after the river). But even in the east, while there was a certain preference for towns and counties to be given English names, rivers, mountains, and other features of the landscape readily adopted Native toponyms (e.g. *Alleghany, Rappahannock, Shenandoah, Ogeechee, Chattahoochee*).

Later, with the westward expansion, the eastern reluctance to accept indigenous names for one's own place of living all but vanished. This is best illustrated by state names: both the newly settled states close to the original colonies (*Tennessee, Kentucky, Ohio, Illinois, Michigan*) and, even more so, a majority of the states further to the west (*Wisconsin, Iowa, Dakota, Mississippi, Missouri, Arkansas, ...*); altogether as many as twenty six out of the fifty states of the US have indigenous names. Of course, the same applies to the names of rivers (from which some state names are derived), mountains, and the like. Romaine (2001:166) estimates the number of rivers and streams with native names to be more than a thousand, not including further early borrowings which got lost again in the course of time. For cities, consider *Tallahassee, Chicago, Kalamazoo*, or *Milwaukee* as examples. Fittingly, Marckwardt (1958:154) summarizes this impact of Native American languages as follows: "the pervasiveness, the extent and the frequency of their influence upon our place names far exceeds their general effect upon the American lexicon."

Of course, the Indian place names, being long and phonetically complex in the ears of English speakers,[5] underwent all kinds of adjustment processes characteristic of borrowings in general. They were phonetically assimilated and simplified (for example, *Milwaukee* is supposed to be derived from *mahnah-wauk-seepe* 'council ground near a river'; Mencken 1963:644). Folk etymology transformed the names, sometimes beyond recognition (e.g., the Chippewa name *Kakakiwing* in Minnesota became *Crow Wing*; *Pootuppag* in Maryland became *Port Tobacco*; 1963:644). They entered English through other European languages, like native names along the St Lawrence and in the Great Lakes region transmitted through French, as, for instance, the pronunciation of *Illinois* shows (Krapp 1925,1:179–80). Their spelling was highly variable for a long time – we find forms such as *Illenois, Missorie, Chickaugo, Chatanuga* (Krapp 1925, I:340).

The special importance of adstrates in America is also illustrated by place names derived from such languages. This includes Dutch elements in the New York area (e.g. *Harlem, Yonkers, Flushing* [from *Vlissingen*], or *Staten Island*), French names along the earlier zones of contact and conflict (city names ending in *–ville*, like *Louisville, Greenville*, or the un-Germanic pattern with heads first and modifiers last in *Lake X*, e.g. *Lake Michigan*), and of course Spanish place names in *Florida* (including the state name itself) and the Southwest.

6.2   "English with great classical purity":[6] Phase 2 (ca. 1670–1773)

6.2.1   Sociopolitical background

The transition from phase 1 into phase 2 was not explicitly marked by any specific historical event. It can be assumed to have proceeded once the population of a given region reached a certain degree of stability, i.e. typically some decades or some two or three generations after the arrival of the earliest immigrants. On the eastern seaboard, typically royal charters (or "patents") were granted to the colonies stating their duties and privileges – these, perhaps, could be regarded as indicating formally the onset of phase 2 (e.g. Maryland 1632; Connecticut 1662; Carolina 1663). However, historically this is a highly complex topic, and as indicators these documents may be problematic, as both the dates and the legal provisions varied considerably from one region to another, depending upon when settlement began and how it evolved: a "Charter of New England" was already issued by King James I in 1620; the colony of New Haven had already reached a "Fundamental Agreement, or Original Constitution" in 1639; and the charter of Carolina predates the foundation of Charleston, SC, by six years. As a symbolic cut-off date, I choose 1670, the foundation year of this city, the last of the influential colonial towns.

What is important in the present context, however, is that the colonies (or provinces) stabilized and prospered, and a stable colonial status was sustained for more than a century. For generations they maintained relatively strong political and cultural ties with their mother country. This applies even more strongly to the upper-class Southern and New England colonists. The Virginia planters typically sent their sons to England for their education, where they were admitted to schools and universities, being Anglicans. Boston also maintained close bonds with the motherland (although this does not apply to its rural hinterland, detached from the sophistication and transatlantic orientation of the city).[7] Eastern New England in particular, with its important cultural centers, emphasized this orientation and has maintained some of its distinctiveness: through trade, whaling, and later early industrialization the region achieved economic prosperity, and those who had established themselves there saw little reason to leave, so linguistically and culturally the region was somewhat different from the rest of the US.

In the interior and the west, the pattern was similar, though, perhaps, dictated more strongly by down-to-earth living conditions behind the frontier and less by a strive for urban and cultural attainments. The waves of settlers who had followed the explorers and squatters built towns and churches and established schools and small businesses. In some cases they were still fighting the Native population, or defending themselves when the Natives reclaimed their lands; in other instances peaceful agreements were reached (but also frequently broken) and respectful, if distanced, relationships maintained.

New settlers continued to pour into the country, from Britain and elsewhere. In many cases specific historical incidents in Europe triggered mass emigrations, like those of Scots after the Highland clearings beginning in the mid-eighteenth century. The ADS strand grew in importance during this phase, in two different ways. In the South, African slaves were imported in increasingly large numbers throughout the eighteenth century. And in general, many European newcomers were of non-English stock. Before the Revolution, these numbers were still relatively small, although some compact groups left a significant cultural impact (e.g. German dissenters settling in the Susquehanna Valley of Pennsylvania). "With the opening of the Middle West to settlement, the trend was accelerated, the normal practice being the movement of the European group in the second or third wave behind the pioneers who had made the first clearings and displaced the Indians" (McDavid 1958:506). Germans, Scandinavians, and Slavs came in large numbers in the second half of the nineteenth century. "In some states – notably Wisconsin, Minnesota and the Dakotas – these waves of foreign settlement almost overwhelmed the older American stock. For example, in Wisconsin in 1910 more than half the population was of German birth or German parentage" (506).

6.2.2. Identity constructions

Identity writings during this phase can be expected to continue what was stated for phase 1, with experiences and contacts broadening for all parties involved. Upper- and middle-class English colonists saw themselves as English gentlemen living on foreign soil, and we may assume that the fact that they contributed substantially to England's political importance and economic welfare filled them with some pride. Their educational and legal systems copied the English model, which indicates their respect for and attachment to the mother country. At the same time, and more so away from the coast and among the less affluent, no doubt physical separation, intercultural contacts, and the frontier experience exerted their influence, strengthening a colonial identity as "English-plus."

In the IDG strand, increasing tensions and hostilities most likely strengthened distinct native identities while at the same time a wider

range of contacts may have weakened them. Again, it is difficult to generalize, and even to know, but there existed a range of relations and
attitudes, from pure resistance and isolation via various intermediate
stages of trying to get along with each other to the maintenance of reasonably friendly relations to conduct trade, negotiations, and so on, including
the conversion to Christianity (Nichols 2003:50–1).[8] Despite all unavoidable tensions it must have been clear to native tribes that somehow they
would have to deal with and accommodate the whites. And certainly this
gave a special status to those with a command of English.

Africans and their descendants must have oscillated between sheer
resistance (leading to occasional slave uprisings), the longing for freedom
(e.g. by running away, or also, exceptionally, by legal measures, as in the
famous Amistad case, filmed by Steven Spielberg), attempts at maintaining some cultural distinctiveness and African heritage, and the forces to
adjust, to carve out for themselves a bearable life pattern within the
insurmountable confines of the inherited slavery status.

Non-English-speaking immigrants usually had some very specific reason to leave their homelands – mostly, religious prosecution or economic
despair. They came to America for good, to evade that problem, although
they did carry with them their cultural and linguistic heritage, not necessarily wanting to reject their roots despite whatever their problem and
reason to emigrate was. So it may safely be presumed that their identity
was split between the desire to adjust and succeed in America as soon as
possible and their wish to preserve some of their cultural, religious, and
linguistic roots and traditions. In many cases, parochialism of settlement
patterns supported the retention of their national languages as community
vernaculars for some time, often into the twentieth century.

6.2.3   Sociolinguistic conditions

With respect to language attitudes, phase 2 in colonial America clearly
shows the expected exonormative orientation: "the British standard was
held up, on both sides of the Atlantic, as the defining variety of correct
English and exerted a powerful influence on Colonial English" (Algeo
2001b:19).[9] The fact that high-ranking young gentlemen from the colonies
tended to be educated in England certainly contributed to that attitude and
the retention of a close relationship. Some of the old-world prestige also fell
upon the speech of Boston, not only because of its wealth or the academic
reputation of Harvard (and, later, other New England schools and colleges)
but simply because it resembled polite southern British English, and once in
a while individual teachers and academics revived such an attitude in the
Middle West as well (McDavid 1958:502). Mencken (1963:57–61) shows

that this admiring attitude toward British English left a "formidable American fifth column" well into the nineteenth century in the form of the policing of American speech habits, with an English ideal in mind.

Given the but limited amount of contact between Europeans and Natives, Read rightly states "the fascinating American Indian languages cannot be put forward as a substratum, for the relatively small numbers of speakers never influenced American English except to provide a reservoir for items of vocabulary" (2002:25). But bilingualism among the Natives spread, and so did pidginization (Romaine 2001:158).

The evolution of English among the largest ADS community, African-Americans in the South, has long been disputed, with some scholars believing that isolation from Europeans soon resulted in the evolution of a creole language with strong retention of African elements (e.g. Dillard 1972; Rickford 1998) and others arguing for an essentially dialectal British, though conservative, character of earlier AAVE (Schneider 1989; Poplack 2000). Of the sociolinguistic framework which shaped this process we have a reasonably good understanding now; Winford (1997a) provides an excellent summary of demographic conditions by states (see also Mufwene 2000b, 2003a). The most central result is that the conditions of the acquisition of English by Africans and their offspring, and of the emergence of AAVE, were anything but uniform and varied widely, thus producing a range of different African-American speech varieties from the outset; in that respect the history of AAVE is comparable to that of white dialects of American English, which are also products of dialect and language contact (Mufwene 1996a, 2001b). During the early period (the homestead phase) the number of Africans was still restricted and they lived in close proximity to Europeans, so they had sufficient occasions for language contact and language acquisition in their dealings with their white speech models, mostly nonstandard English speakers. Following Mufwene's Founder Effect (1996b, 2001b), the varieties which these early speakers developed certainly were disproportionally influential in shaping subsequent versions of black dialects. Later, when the number of Africans in many localities increased dramatically, intra-ethnic communication among Africans in English presumably became more important than contacts with whites. In many instances not (exclusively) whites but other Africans, longer in residence (locally born and seasoned slaves), served as target models for the acquisition of English by new arrivals. Demographic ratios varied considerably. South Carolina was the only state in which African-Americans ever outnumbered whites significantly, especially on the coast. Elsewhere they were a minority, although on individual plantations blacks constituted a majority of the local speech community. On the other hand, it is well known that the stereotypical image of the large plantation, with hundreds of field hands who rarely interacted with whites except for an overseer, misrepresents the realities of the south-eastern states, where small-scale plantations with few slaves, and not infrequently their white owners working the fields as well, was the norm; if anything this image applies to the rice fields of South Carolina and possibly the late phase of slavery, cotton plantations in the Delta South of the nineteenth century. Also, there were substantial status differences within the African-American group correlating with speech opportunities and differences: house servants and also craftsmen had ample contact with whites, field hands less so, depending upon demographic proportions on a plantation.

It is unlikely that linguistic influences in black – white contacts were only monodirectional. Many whites, including those of higher status, had regular contact with African-Americans as well, especially during their childhood years when it was common for planters' children and future slaves to spend some time and play together. Many white children spent more time in the presence of black caregivers or "mammies" than with their own mothers. We have no immediate evidence of such contact effects, but linguists assume that black speech must have influenced Southern white speech patterns as well (Schneider 1989:37).

In sum, the available evidence suggests that there is room for lots of linguistic variability in earlier black – white sociolinguistic relations. Some African-Americans probably had extensive linguistic contacts with whites and sufficient occasion to acquire (nonstandard) English reasonably well; others had primarily intra-ethnic contacts and restricted access to European speech models. Winford (1997a) rightly characterizes earlier AAVE as an approximation (a notion introduced by Mufwene 1996b, following Chaudenson) and adoption of settler dialects, a process in its own right. Certainly, given the social conditions of slavery, there was room for the development and retention of ethnic speech markers, for the development of linguistic means to signal a non-white, and possibly subliminally counter-European, ethnolinguistic identity.

The situation was different for other adstrate groups. In rare cases like the one of the "Pennsylvania Dutch," if the respective groups were large enough and preferred an isolated lifestyle with a purely group-internal, usually religiously motivated focus, the mother tongue was deliberately retained (although even here English was adopted as a second language for outside contacts). Usually, however, non-English-speaking immigrants had to communicate with an English-speaking environment on a daily basis, for instance at the workplace, and they were also strongly motivated to integrate into their new host society. This implied acquiring the English of their surroundings. There are competing views of how rapid and effective this process was. A traditional account states that the first immigrant generation acquired English as a second language with an accent; the second, the first American-born, generation became fully bilingual and spoke English as fluently as their American peers; and the third generation tended to lose their grandparents' original language and to command it only passively and with limitations (Conklin and Lourie 1983). A slightly different perspective gaining ground nowadays, suggested by Harvard University's Longfellow Institute and publications resulting from this scholarly context, emphasizes enduring traces of bilingualism and multi-lingualism in American history and culture (Mufwene 2004b:210). A long-accepted, now problematized metaphor for this process of cultural and linguistic assimilation of (primarily) European immigrant groups has been that of the American society as a "melting pot" in which the original ingredients fused into a new, homogeneous unit. In this process an indivi-dual's ethnic heritage has tended to turn into a vague knowledge about a rather distant ancestry and possibly into folkloristic manifestations.

6.2.4 Linguistic effects

Linguistically speaking, all these developments resulted in the following effects: (1) as the outcome of koinéization, a remarkable degree of linguis-tic homogeneity in the colonies; (2) the emergence of lexical innovations, labeled "Americanisms," and, among these, (3) the borrowing of words for fauna and flora and indigenous cultural notions from the IDG stream; as well as (4) some lexical import from early adstrates.

Koinéization soon produced a linguistic effect which to outside observers appeared to be absolutely remarkable, both in a literal and in a figurative sense. It was customary for British visitors to the colonies to report on what they had found upon returning, and one of the most commonplace obser-vations in such travelers' reports, up until the time of the Revolution, concerned the unexpected "purity" and "uniformity" of English as spoken in the American colonies. Here are a few select quotations:

- the Planters, and even the Native Negroes generally talk good English without idiom or Tone (Hugh Jones, 1724; quoted in Read 1933:44)

- a striking similarity of speech universally prevails ... The language of the immediate descendants of such a promiscuous ancestry is perfectly uniform, and unadultered (William Eddis, 1770, quoted in Read 1933:44)

- Though the inhabitants of this Country are composed of different nations and different languages, yet it is very remarkable that they in general speak better English than the English do. No County or Colonial dialect is to be distinguished here, except it be the New Englanders (Nicholas Creswell, 1777, quoted in Read 1933:45)

- in North America there prevails not only ... the purest pronunciation of the English tongue ... but a perfect uniformity (Jonathan Boucher, 1777; quoted in Mencken 1963:403)

These statements, and similar ones, strongly testify to the impact koinéization had upon the evolution of American English. However, on closer inspection it is obvious that they all remain rather superficial – no linguistic details are described, and what "uniformity" really means to an outside observer is difficult to assess (it may simply indicate less diversity than found in Britain). The strongest version of the koinéization hypothesis has been put forward by Dillard (1975), who believes in a "full koiné stage ... reached in the middle of the eighteenth century" (50). After practically all dialectal differences had been wiped out, he suggests, the nineteenth century saw the renewed emergence of dialects as a result of contact with immigrant languages. Dillard's primary goal is to counter the dialectologists' tradition of tracing American dialectal features back to specific British dialects, as in Kurath (1965).

Montgomery (1996), in a focused discussion of the koinéization thesis, accepts that because of the fluid and dynamic situations in America, new-world dialects cannot be traced back directly to British ones, but refuses to take the commentators' statements at face value. He argues that full uniformity is "logically impossible" and that we do not know to what extent these travelers had contact with common people. Against Dillard, he points out evidence for the existence of socially stigmatized features and suspects that koinéization may have appeared stronger than it was in written records than in the vernaculars which have not come down to us. Also, regional rivalries between the colonies must have been reflected in speech differences. In sum, Montgomery concludes that "koinéization undoubtedly occurred in American English" (1996:230) but it "was only part of the picture, hardly encompassing all the internal and external dynamics" (2001:153).

Despite his strong views on the matter Dillard's timing fails to recognize what I have called the second wave of koinéization, dialect mixing and leveling during the westward expansion of the nineteenth century, even if a founder effect from the first wave may have prepared this process. We may safely assume that the situation then was similar to the colonial one, and that Montgomery's caveats also apply: no doubt the continuous mixing of settler streams resulted in further homogenization of dialects and ultimately in the commOn perception of a non-dialectal, relatively uniform type of American English outside of New England and the South,[10] but at the same time this mixing was not absolute, and clearly some cultural and linguistic peculiarities were retained. For example, McDavid (1958:484) warns that to a certain extent the westward expansion happened in horizontal bands, with less overlapping than is sometimes hypothesized.

It is actually conceivable that the notions of uniformity as applied during the colonial period and in the nineteenth century did not refer to the same variety. Westward expansion resulted in a dialect which in the twentieth century would be labeled "General American," characterized, for example, by rhoticity and glidelessness in words like *new* or *student*, an accent which conventionally is taken to be largely northern English in origin, transmitted through the Pennsylvania and North Midland regions and going back strongly to the last two of Fischer's (1989) immigrant waves. It is doubtful whether these features also characterized the colonial koiné, which is likely to have been shaped primarily by the earliest settler groups from southern England and the ones most influential along the east coast, the Southerners and New Englanders. Evidence for such an assumption is provided by Read (1938), who analyzed advertisements for runaway indentured servants who were frequently identified by their speech behavior. He finds that northern, Scottish, and Irish accents were frequently listed as distinguishing marks of these people, while no mention was made of southern or East Anglia accents, these, obviously, having been taken as something like "default" variants. Read concludes:

These advertisements tend to show that even by the middle years of the eighteenth century the speaking of English dialects and "broad" English was a noticeable deviation from the general body of American speech. Except for the East Anglians and the southeasterners, those who used the dialects could be identified by them. Thus in the colonial period American English had a consistency of its own, most closely approximating the type of the region around London. (1938:79)

On an individual basis Read's evidence makes it clear that koinéization and uniformity were only one side of the coin but that residual dialects were imported and could be identified in colonial America. On a community basis, the same point can be made by looking at some features shared by the New England and Southern dialects. Some of these were probably English innovations which the colonial American cities adopted from the cultural center of England, London. These are particularly interesting in the present context because such transmission signals the exonormative orientation of and the continuing impact of polite English speech upon these regions. The most interesting case in point is postvocalic /r/, a sound which was pronounced even in southern British English well into the eighteenth century and disappeared only then, as in modern RP. In other words, the r-lessness of New England and the South must have developed in America, modeling English linguistic fashion – a strong indication of the exonormative linguistic orientation of colonial America. Similarly,

Boston's "broad a" has been suggested to be a late adoption of a prestigious British innovation (Pyles 1952:55; Conklin and Lourie 1983:77–8; cf. Krapp 1925, II:79–80.).

As is characteristic of phase 2 of PCEs, however, there was also some innovation going on especially on the lexical level: the earliest and most classic of all "-isms," Americanisms, appear during that period. The first observations of lexical peculiarities used by the American settlers appear almost immediately: the American use of *maize* was recorded as early as 1621 by Alexander Gill, a London schoolmaster (Read 2002:8). In 1663 John Josselyn, a British traveler, observed the first known semantic innovation, finding that the Americans use *Ordinary* for a 'tavern,' a place for drinking, while in Britain the word denoted a place to get meals (Read 2002:9). By the eighteenth century the number of new words was large enough to be noted and commented upon fairly regularly (Read 1933:40). In 1781 John Whitherspoon, a clergyman who had signed the Declaration of Independence, deliberately coined the notion "Americanisms," in an article in the *Pennsylvania Weekly Advertiser*.

It is noteworthy (and in line with the exonormative orientation of the period) that Americanisms in those days were commonly equated with barbarisms – they tended to be evaluated negatively, as deviations from a British norm. This was also Witherspoon's attitude, who largely equated Americanisms with "improprieties and vulgarisms" (Mencken 1963:6). The tradition started with Francis Moore, a traveler, who in 1735 noted that "in barbarous English" the colonists call a river bank a *bluff* (Read 2002:10; for further examples see Mencken 1963:3–5, 17–25). Conservative Americans adopted this exonormative attitude, and some retained it for a long time: even the first dictionary of Americanisms, published by John Pickering in 1816, was meant as a collection of terms to avoid. On the other hand, such attacks also produced a countereffect: "The fact that Englishmen expressed disapproval of American lexical innovations helped to consolidate a sense of Americanness among the colonies" (Algeo 2001b:19).

An important segment of the new vocabulary items in America, also characteristic of this phase, is the contribution by the IDG strand, loan words from native languages. Again, the earliest ones date almost from the beginning of contacts: in 1608, in the Virginia colony, Captain John Smith recorded the word *raccoon*, which he spelled *rahaugcum* (Mencken 1963:110).[11] Semantically, native borrowings relate to what is to be expected. Native terms for fauna and flora reflect the fact that the colonists met with many plants and animals which were unfamiliar to them, so these objects were assumed to "have" a name which was borrowed, with the usual phonetic adjustments, into colonial English. Animal names from indigenous languages include *raccoon, opossum, moose, skunk, terrapin, woodchuck, chipmunk, caribou, menhaden,* and *muskellunge.* Words for flora include *hickory, catalpa, chinquapin, pecan, catawba, persimmon, sequoia,* and *squash* (see Marckwardt 1958:25). Of course, the colonists borrowed words for native customs and cultural artifacts as well: *canoe* (spelled *Kanoa* and defined as 'a boat hollowed out of a tree by fire and flintstones' when noted in 1621 by Gill; Read 2002:8), *moccasin, tomahawk, wigwam, teepee, squaw, wampum,* etc. Some cultural terms were also taken over as loan translations: *war dance, warpath, pipe of peace, Great Spirit, paleface, medicine man, big chief,* etc. (Pyles 1952; Mencken 1963; Cassidy and Hall 2001; Bailey 2004:6). It is noteworthy that the vast majority of native borrowings (not all of which survived until today) date from the early period, the seventeenth century (Romaine 2001:163–4). In contrast, the "Indians of the Far West added little to the American vocabulary" (Mencken 1963:189).

The special role of adstrates in American English is reflected by the fact that, similar to IDG strand lexical impact, there are also early borrowings from other contact languages. Among the oldest are Dutch words, from early contacts in the Hudson River area: *yankee, boss,* and *Santa Claus.* Irish Gaelic, preserved by some of the Scottish and Irish immigrants, is reported to have contributed *smithereens* and *shanty* (Wolfram and Shilling-Estes 1998:106).

On the state of the IDG and ADS strand Englishes of that period we have practically no direct evidence beyond the attestation of pidginized forms of English used by Native Americans. Linguistic evidence of AAVE takes us back into the mid-nineteenth century but not into the colonial period.

6.3 "That torrent of barbarous phraseology":[12] Phase 3 (ca. 1773–1828/1848)

6.3.1 Sociopolitical background

The British won the French and Indian War (1754–63) against the French and their allies, which gave them political sovereignty over all lands east of the Mississippi River and stopped French attempts at preventing the gradual penetration of the region west of the Appalachians by British colonists. This was the last war the colonies fought on the behalf of the motherland, but it seems that resentment was growing between the "polished" British troops and the supposedly undisciplined colonists (Algeo 2001b). The "Boston Massacre" of 1770, an incident in which five Boston men were killed by British soldiers and which was popularized by

Paul Revere's well-known engraving, brought the antagonism to light violently and had a forceful impact on the colonists' attitudes toward the British. A spirit of rebellion could be sensed in the following years. What made the balance tip toward independence, however, was the ensuing conflict over taxation. To cover the high expenses of colonial defense, Britain imposed new taxes on the colonies, which, however, opposed taxation without representation in the British Parliament. Some earlier and minor conflicts could be resolved, mostly by repealing the respective taxes, although relationships became increasingly strained. The British insisted on their privilege to tax goods imported to the colonies. What really spurred the colonists to action was when the British insisted upon a tax levied on tea, for which the struggling East India Company was given sole importation privileges.

This taxation act, both symbolic and effective, was an "Event X" for the colonists. It ultimately opened their eyes to the fact that for the British the colonies were no longer really a part of "us" but rather an "other" whose welfare was carefully balanced against the Company's economic situation and the financial interests of the mother country (and, in effect, given less weight). The following events culminated in the so-called "Boston Tea Party" of December 16, 1773, when colonists disguised as Natives threw shiploads of tea into Boston harbor.[13] Subsequently, punitive measures by London triggered the chain of events that ultimately, prepared significantly by Thomas Paine's pamphlet "Common Sense" of January 1776, caused the colonists to declare their Independence on July 4, 1776. As is well known and well documented, the Americans ultimately won the Revolutionary War and wrote and ratified their own Constitution.

It is noteworthy that the colonists did not set out to gain independence right at the outset, and of course there was a lot of internal tension about how to proceed; in fact, it is estimated that in 1776 a third of the population were loyalists to the British Crown (Mencken 1963:143). So the events of a few turbulent political years, perhaps just bringing to the surface diverging cultural orientations and interests of years before, resulted in identity realignments which forged a new nation.

The United States of America has been characterized by seemingly conflicting tendencies and orientations from the very beginning. Certainly a high degree of continuity with her British heritage prevailed and was deliberately upheld by many. At the same time, the new nation, sensing that they could not and should not compete with a millennium of traditions in Europe, deliberately defined itself as a nation starting afresh, emphasizing the vibrancy of nature rather than the weary staleness of nurture, and espousing political ideals derived from philosophers such as Jean-Jacques Rousseau and manifested in the ideals of the French

Revolution.[14] This fresh start as a defining criterion manifested itself not only in the American Revolution but also in the frontier experience, where new threats and options were always lurking just around the corner and settlers had but few traditions and little firm ground to rely on. So, in much the same way that the Revolution marked the onset of phase 3 along the East Coast, in the thirteen original colonies, westward expansion and the frontier spirit epitomized this phase in the second wave of bringing English to the continent, during the late eighteenth and nineteenth centuries in the Midwest and West, where no clear distinctions can be identified – local ones at best – between the first three phases of the Dynamic Model.

6.3.2 Identity constructions

No doubt Independence and the Revolutionary War led to a reorientation of the identity alignments of American colonists, the STL strand. Historians have labeled the following decades the "National" (or "Early Republic") period, with Americans emphasizing their cultural independence and innovativeness and discontinuity with their English heritage – they were bound to stay in North America as a nation, and stay on their own; they felt American now, no longer British. There are many attestations to this end, and, interestingly enough, they usually entail language use as a substantial part of cultural independence; e.g. "The Declaration of Independence and the rebellion against the mother country caused a great surge of linguistic and cultural patriotism" (Pyles 1952:72); or: "on this side of the ocean ... there was a widespread tendency to reject English precedent and authority altogether, in language no less than in government" (Mencken 1963:10). The close nexus between political events and linguistic developments (via identity rewritings), and the causal role of the former for the latter, are undisputed; I focus on this aspect in section 6.3.3.

It is hard to say anything of substance on identity patterns in the IDG strand at this stage (or in the African-American ADS strand, for that matter), and we should probably resist any temptation to reduce the plurality of attitudes and relationships that must have prevailed within these communities to any simple formula. During the colonial wars of the mid-eighteenth century native tribes associated themselves with both the British and the French, thus partly continuing tribal rivalries. Certainly they still considered themselves the traditional and rightful residents, but they were also definitely not blind to the fact that the period of their sole dominance and occupancy was irretrievably past.

European ADS strand members aligned themselves with the Americans, as described before.

6.3.3   Sociolinguistic conditions

The separation of the two nations in the late eighteenth century found its direct reflection in many voices calling for an explicit separation of the two languages, British and American; "the very notion of American English itself was strongly tied to nationalism" (Wolfram and Schilling-Estes 1998:18). The birth of American English as a concept and as a variety falls into that period: "In the third quarter of the eighteenth century Americans began to feel that their mother tongue was something near and intimate, the speech which gave to them a unity upon their American soil" (Krapp 1925,1:6). In the years and decades after the Revolution in America linguistic independence was very much a matter of public, educated discourse. For example, in 1784 Witherspoon, then President of Princeton, proclaimed: "being entirely separated from Britain, we shall find some center or standard of our own, and not be subject to that island" (quoted from Krapp 1925, I:47). Interestingly enough, some leading American politicians of the time had a stake in this (Krapp 1925; Mencken 1963; Read 2002).

In 1780 John Adams proposed an academy to establish an American standard language, a proposal which strongly reflects the spirit of the Age of Reason and Enlightenment in the European tradition, where language academies were either established or proposed in several countries. In America, the intention was also to "fix" and "improve" the language, but a new goal and idea was added: language development and standardization was regarded as a means of democratizing the country, with equal access to eloquence reflecting the ideal of human freedom and equality. Benjamin Franklin advocated a spelling reform for American English. Thomas Jefferson deliberately coined new words and seems to have taken pride in that (Wolfram and Schilling-Estes 1998:106), and believed in an explicit future separation of the two languages (Krapp 1925, I:10).

It is interesting to see how in many respects the issue of a distinct language was freighted, perhaps overburdened with symbolic meaning. A separate language was meant to reflect and embody the ideals of the young nation, from democratic equality (via equal access to public discourse) to the "fresh" and honest qualities of American culture. For this I find William Thornton's high-sounding statement quite indicative: "The American Language will thus be as distinct as the government, free from all follies of unphilosophical fashion, and resting upon truth as its only regulator" (1793; quoted from Fisher 2001:61).

The most fervent advocate of America's linguistic independence, however, was Noah Webster. His statements during this early phase were absolutely clear and determined: "in a course of time, a language in North

America, as different from the future language of England, as the modern Dutch, Danish and Swedish are from the German," he wrote in his *Dissertations on the English Language* of 1789 (quoted from Krapp 1925, I:9), or, in the same work, "several circumstances render a future separation of the American tongue from the English necessary and unavoidable" (quoted from Mencken 1963:15). On 21 July 1786 he gave a lecture in Boston entitled "Some Differences between the English and the Americans Considered. Corruption of Language in England. Reasons Why the English Should Not Be Standard, Either in Language or Manners" (quoted in Read 2002:58). Or, most explicitly: "as an independent nation, our honor requires us to have a system of our own, in language as well as government" (quoted in Wolfram and Schilling-Estes 1998:17). For a while, Noah Webster, with a group of followers in a Philological Society, promoted the creation of a new language, which he called "Federal English," an idea which also pursued the ideal of democratization, as this variety should be "accessible to every yeoman" (Krapp 1925, I:279). The campaign had few practical implications, however, and fell dormant fairly soon. Webster himself, despite all ardent rhetoric, apparently was pragmatic enough (and promoting his own interests) not to push such issues to an unrealistic degree, and his linguistic nationalism then reverted to the profitable follow-up activities of spelling reform and dictionary production, both of which will be discussed in later sections. The role of patriotism in this enterprise is nicely illustrated by the fact that he changed the title of the first part of his earlier *A Grammatical Institute of the English Language* ... to *American Spelling Book* in 1789.

However, "language attitudes in America have always been Janus-like" (Algeo 2001b:35), and hence we soon encounter the American version of the "complaint tradition," a continuing upholding of British speech norms as the only kind of real and good English.[15] This ambivalence has many faces. With respect to lexis, it shows in the evaluation of Americanisms as either innovations, expressions of a new, vigorous spirit, or corruptions, deviations from a norm which is held to be the only possible one. Similarly, and down to the present day, there is a tension between a pride in and love of creative language use, which frequently implies vernacular and expressive language, on the one hand and the emphasis on correct usage as proclaimed by dictionaries, usage guides, language authorities, and the proverbial schoolma'am on the other. In quantitative terms, however, nativization made the balance tip toward the former position. Americanisms were increasingly welcomed, and frontier speech was perceived as creatively powerful.

In the IDG and ADS strands contact with American English was ongoing and intensifying. Bilingualism became increasingly common, and language shift spread.

6.3.4   Linguistic effects

The consequence of these developments and attitudes was the emergence of American English as a distinct variety of the English language. Of course feature differences appeared earlier (from the very beginning, as was shown before) and have continued to emerge to the present day, but the period of structural nativization was the one during which effects inhibiting divergence disappeared and, in contrast, linguistic differences became actively promoted or at least positively evaluated. Westward expansion, then, brought an increasingly appreciative attitude toward down-to-earth speechways, and hence strengthened another powerful factor promoting linguistic nativization.[16] While of course British and American Englishes still have a lot in common and linguistic continuity has also been important, differences between the two major varieties of English kept increasing.

The major forces in promoting differentiation have been selective retention, internal innovation, and language contact. The role of isolated retention is disputed. Marckwardt (1958) suggested that many differences can be explained by "colonial lag," but Görlach (1991a) and others have shown that for many features this is not true. On the other hand, it is clear that American English owes many of its characteristics to its internal dynamics: words were coined afresh, sounds changed, or constructions were restructured and came to be used in their own, new ways. Contact effects became noticeable as well, first in certain ethnic or regional dialects; some of them diffused into and shaped mainstream American English.[17] No detailed history of American English with respect to structural details has been written as yet, but it is clear that these forces operated on all levels of language organization.

On the lexical level (see Cassidy and Hall 2001, Romaine 2001), borrowing primarily of culture-specific terms from IDG languages continued, though not to the same extent as before. Examples from that period include *tamarack, mugwump, cayuse, chipmunk, sequoia, quamash, calumet, medicine bag, lodgepole, bury the hatchet,* and *hogan.* The ADS strands continued to contribute to the American word stock. Similar to words from the IDG strand in this phase, loan words mostly reflect the original cultures of immigrant groups, pertaining to their traditional customs or foods. Examples include the following: from German *thickmilk* 'clabber,' *check* (from *Zeche*), *hamburger, pretzel,* or many compounds in *–fest*; from Italian *pizza, pasta, mafia, don,* and *capo*; from Polish *kielbasa*; from Spanish *burrito, chili, taco, bronco, corral,* or *canyon.* Words provided by African-Americans, presumably with African roots, are *gumbo, okra, pinders, goobers, cooter,* and *buckra.* The coining of other Americanisms continued, of course, including examples such as *know-how*, *land poor*, *know-nothing*, *filibuster*, *bushwhacker*, and the most successful Americanism of all, *OK*. Mencken (1963:149–51) considers "tall talk," impressively sounding new coinages of the post-Jackson era like *absquatulate* or *ring-tailed roarer*, distinctively American, especially Western.

In general, American English counts as highly creative and playful in its word formations and lexical creations (which is one characteristic element of PCEs in the phase of nativization). A case in point is the liberal American usage of conversion, a change of word classes without formal marking as in *to engineer, to stump, to bog, to style* (Mencken 1963:100).

As to phonology, relatively little is known on earlier American English. Historical records which do indicate or suggest local accents are scarce and difficult to interpret, so hardly any systematic analyses of such texts have been published. Krapp (1925, II) is a notable exception. Immigrant languages were usually overwhelmed and replaced by English but may have left traces "occasionally in a pronunciation" (McDavid 1958:527). It is likely that most of these were transient, but some may have been preserved as ethnic identity markers (see phase 5).

On the level of grammar, we find most of the differences and innovations, exactly as predicted by the Dynamic Model, at the lexicogrammatical interface, i.e. many words have developed new and distinctive grammatical patterns. Mencken (1963:7–54) provides a large number of examples showing that these processes had been in effect by about 1800. A classic example of a change of complementation patterns of verbs, the American use of *notify*, was scorned by Witherspoon in 1781: "In English . . . we do not *notify* the person of the thing, but *notify* the thing to the person." He also attacked (and thus testified to the regularity of) new prepositional uses, as in *I have been to Philadelphia* rather than *at* or *in*. Similarly, critical statements concerning *wait on* rather than *wait for* and word formation processes (*to utilize*), including conversion (*to spade*), date from 1801 and 1808, respectively. Witherspoon's list of detestable Americanisms includes another structural innovation, viz. a tendency to omit *to be* in constructions like *These things were ordered delivered to . . .* . Similarly, a British observer's account of 1807, stripped of its ideological facade, catalogues further characteristics of structural nativization: "a variety of new compounds and combinations of words, or roots of words . . . the perversion of a still greater number of English words from their proper use or signification . . . employing nouns substantive for verbs, for instance, and adjectives for substantives, &c" (quoted from Read 2002:61). Innovative phraseology is also well attested. Mencken (1963) quotes *to fill the bill, to back water, to make the fur fly, to handle with gloves,* and attributes these to "the national talent for condensing a complex thought ... into a vivid and arresting image" (156).

It is really interesting to note that while standard sources typically state that there are only few important and systematic grammatical differences between British and American English the list of lexicogrammatical peculiarities, testifying to the strength of structural nativization along this borderline, is almost endless. Here are a few more select examples (Mencken 1963; Butters 2001; Tottie 2002; Murray and Simon 2004):

- *different than* (vs. *from, to*)
- *have* in questions treated as a full verb: *Do you have* ... (vs. *Have you | Have you got* ...)
- the creation (or borrowing) of new second-person plural pronouns: *y'all, youse, you'uns, you guys*
- succinct substitutes for verb phrases via conversion: *to service* for *to give service, to intern* for *to serve as an intern, to style* ..., *to model* ...,
- double modals, esp. *might could* (Southern dialect)
- preference for clausal complementation of *like, hate* with *for* + subject: *I like for you to do it*
- "catenative semi-modal" *want to*: *You want to study harder or you'll fail*
- *Come, go, help* followed immediately by full verbs: *Come look at this; Go tell it* ...; *Help set the table.*
- phrasal verb differences: *want out* (vs. *want to go out*), *fill out* (vs. *fill in*)
- Uses of adjective forms without *–ly* as adverbs: *I sure do; real fast*
- *Hopefully* as a sentence adverb: *Hopefully he'll win.*
- *need, want, like* with past participles (Midland): *The car needs washed; The cat wants petted; The baby likes cuddled.*
- transitivity shifts (Appalachians, Midland): *He complained me off; holler him over.*

Structural contact effects, whereby certain syntactic patterns can be explained by constructions in ancestral languages, can primarily be observed in regional or ethnic varieties. In the IDG strand, Native Americans have been shown to use a disproportionally high percentage of predicates without past tense marking. The pattern can be traced back to the seventeenth and eighteenth centuries and is documented among a wide range of native groups today, and it may reflect the grammar of some native languages, although this seems difficult to generalize (Wolfram 1984). Wolfram and Shilling-Estes account for the article use in constructions like *He's in the hospital* in American English in general or *He's got the earache* in Appalachian English by possible impact of Irish Gaelic (1998:106). More generally, they suggest that the Upper Midwest "draws its distinctiveness, in part, from the numerous non-English-speaking Europeans who were among its earliest non-native inhabitants" (109). In south-eastern Pennsylvania loan syntax from German shows in *Are you going with*? (111); Butters (2001:330) ascribes a tendency to postpose direct objects (now rare) to the same source, as in *Throw Papa down the stairs his hat*.

A word is in order in the present context on spelling, a language level which normally is not considered particularly important or interesting but which has a special status in the comparison of British and American English. It is well known that there are a number of fairly consistent spelling differences (some are obligatory; others are strong tendencies): Americans write *honor* with *-or*, *standardize* with *-ize*, *center* with *-er*, *traveler* with one *l*, *dialog* with a final *-g*, and *defense* with *s* where British English has, respectively, *-our*, *-ise*, *-re*, *-ll-*, *-logue*, and *-ence* (*standardise*, *centre*, *traveller*, *dialogue*, and *defence*). What is different from other language levels is that these distinctions have not emerged as speech conventions but are products of deliberate language planning, a part of the nationalistic reorientation of the American language in the late eighteenth century. Many of them go back to Webster's proposals or his influence and were popularized through his "blue-backed speller." The most interesting aspect of all this is the symbolic significance that has been attributed to such spelling differences in public discourse. Spelling differences received a lot of attention during the discussions on refinement and reform of the eighteenth century, and in the late eighteenth century, essentially a pamphlet culture, spelling innovations became immediately visible in public texts and had thus a more conspicuous and provocative character than they would have today. Webster originally advocated Franklin's proposal to develop a phonetic spelling system and intended to present a new alphabet to Congress for approval (Krapp 1925, I:330–5), but the proposal received insufficient support, and so he soon gave up, presumably also recognizing that such a radically reformed spelling would not only impede access to earlier English writing but limit the sales prospects of his elementary books. So a few modifications had to suffice but were loaded with symbolic importance:

though American customs in spelling have never differed widely from British, such differences as have existed have nevertheless been treated as though they were matters of some moment, as though the Americans had really done something startling to spelling … the notion that American spelling is radical and revolutionary seems indeed to be mainly a survival from eighteenth and nineteenth century political feeling. (Krapp 1925, I:328)

In sum, during the nativization phase American English acquired a large number of linguistic innovations on all language levels. Actually, instructive as the above lists and examples are, I suspect they only capture part of the truth, which is even more complex: differences between varieties of English, British and American in the present case, not only consist of the ones frequently observed, documented and listed, but they encompass an infinitely larger set of habits and constructions which are hardly ever explicitly noted, most of which are associated with particular lexical items. An example which shows how subtle and manifold the differences are, from Algeo (1989), was discussed in section 4.2.1. This suggests that structural nativization operates inconspicuously but highly effectively, affecting frequencies and co-occurrence tendencies of individual words and constructions more than anything else. In other words, lists of features characteristic of varieties of English are likely to be but the tip of the iceberg.

6.4   "Our honor requires us to have a system of our own":[18] Phase 4 (1828/1848–1898)

6.4.1   Sociopolitical background

The first years and decades after Independence were still very much a period of transition and also instability: the young nation had to fight and recover from the Revolutionary War, to develop its political institutions, and simply to stabilize. Of course, nationalism was going strong, but that was only one side of the coin – many Americans who were hesitant or loyal to England needed to be won and integrated. According to Mencken, at the time of Jefferson's election to the presidency in 1800 "confidence in the solidarity and security of the new nation was still anything but universal. Democracy was still experimental, doubtful" (1963:144). However, two events of the early nineteenth century contributed a lot to the development of American self-confidence.

Lack of stability characterized the relationship with Britain, the former colonial power, as well. Simmering resentments, minor incidents, and a conflict over the land border with Canada led to the War of 1812, which lasted for two years. Some naval and land battles were fought, but neither side achieved anything of substance. An American invasion into Canada was stopped, and the British were ultimately defeated at New Orleans. So the end effect was very much a stalemate, but somehow, the war ultimately confirmed America's independence. It settled disputed issues and the relationship with Britain, which from then on developed into a special partnership grounded in a common history. And in America the War of 1812, sometimes explicitly labeled the "Second War for Independence," triggered a renewed wave of nationalism, based on the feeling of having really and fully achieved independence, once and for all.

Another turning point, which also symbolized a shift of power and cultural orientation from sophisticated east coast centers to the expanding settlements further west and the frontier, was the rise to the presidency of the "Indian fighter" and 1815 victor Andrew Jackson, elected in 1828:

Jackson was the archetype of the new American who appeared after 1814 – ignorant, pushful, impatient to restraint and precedent ... an Anglophobe in every fiber. He came from the extreme backwoods ... Thousands of other young Americans of the same sort were growing up at the same time. They swarmed across the mountains and down the great rivers, wrestling with the naked wilderness and setting up a casual, impromptu sort of civilization ... Schools were few and rudimentary; any effort to mimic the amenities of the East, or of the mother country, in manner or even in speech, met with instant derision. ... America began to stand for something new in the world. (Mencken 1963:144–5)

The growing self-confidence of the common American, symbolized by Jackson's success, translated into a new type of national self-dependence and a national pride based upon local, American, achievements, a solid basis for an endonormative orientation. Further events and changes contributed to this, like improved means of transportation (e.g. the opening of the Erie Canal, which made the Great Lakes region easily accessible to settlers via waterways, and later the railroad) or the establishment of a manufacturing economy in some cities. The fact that Jackson also acted decisively and mercilessly for the removal of the Natives does not appear to seriously overshadow his place in American history.

So the ground was laid for a rapid and effective settlement of the Midwest and West, and things developed vibrantly and sometimes violently there. National unity was also at stake because of the conflict over slavery (which on a deeper level was a product of the regional and economic diversification of the country, of the difference between a conservative and agricultural South and the more strongly urbanized and industrialized North). The Civil War was painful and left deep scars in the South in particular, where the "Yankees" were not welcome during the period of Reconstruction. Slaves were emancipated but denied equal citizenship by social segregation, poverty, the Jim Crow laws, and also physical violence.

The century proved to be important for the IDG and ADS strands as well. Indian Wars marked the conquest of the continent by white settlers, in addition to diplomatic efforts, trade relations, and coexistence, which at times led to assimilation. Early in the century the outcome of battles, like Tecumseh's defeat in 1811 or Jackson's victory against the Creeks in 1814, followed by the government's removal policy, cleared the region to the Mississippi for European settlement. After the mid-century the tribes of the West were gradually subjugated by negotiation or military force. President Grant's "peace policy" and several treaties of the late 1860s were unsuccessful in the long run. Between the 1860s and the 1880s, ending with the 1890 massacre of hundreds of Native Americans in Wounded Knee, a series of wars and battles against the Plains and western tribes forced them to accept life on reservations (Nichols 2003:126–44).

European immigrants continued to enter the United States in large numbers, mostly triggered by specific events at home. Millions of Irish came because of the potato famines in the 1830s and 1840s. Germans immigrated in even larger numbers around the mid-century, also because of the unsuccessful revolution in Germany. Italians followed after the 1860s, Scandinavians in the 1870s, Jews from central and eastern Europe after the 1880s. Asian immigration started with impoverished Chinese who were recruited as laborers in California and Hawaii, beginning in the 1850s. Many of them were employed in railroad construction.

Despite all turmoil and turbulence, however, the nineteenth century was a period during which the USA defined and consolidated herself as a nation. Roughly by the 1870s or 1880s some degree of national stability had been reached across most of the continental United States. The transitional phase of the Confederacy set aside, we see the emergence of a self-confident and unified nation, but also a nation which in this process of stabilization was very much preoccupied with herself. This period climaxed in the year 1898, when the United States as a strong nation turned outward and entered the world stage. The Spanish-American War gave the US control over Puerto Rico, Guam, and the Philippines, and thus resulted in the country's global military and political presence.

6.4.2   Identity constructions

In a sense, the nationalism of the immediate post-Independence period was still very much a sign of insecurity. America was independent and a union of states, but no doubt the emphasis on unity "was due in part to a fear of disunity which was quite natural in a young nation, particularly a federation of states" (Pyles 1952:70). Much of the discourse of that time is directed against the superiority of England – take the subtitle of Webster's 1786 lecture mentioned earlier, "Why the English Should Not Be Standard, Either in Language or Manners," as a case in point. That is not the same, however, as being confident in one's own status and abilities. It is predominantly after the turn of the nineteenth century that comparisons no longer boil down to denigrations of the other but build upon pride in oneself, in things American. Pyles dates this as follows: "The War of 1812 and the appearance on the American scene of the frontiersman – both in the flesh and as a national symbol – mark the beginnings of an indigenous psyche Americana" (1952:118). According to Mencken (1963), it was during the Jacksonian period that the "national feeling, long delayed in appearing, leaped into being at last in truly amazing vigor" (145). As always, this takes time and does not happen unanimously, so we do find both progressive voices fairly early and conservative ones late in time. Mencken himself, with his book with the programmatic title *The American Language* first published in 1919, counts as the last and most influential champion of American linguistic independence, perhaps the one who succeeded in bringing home the message to a wider audience.[19] It is fitting that in 1923 the state of Illinois formally enacted a Bill which states explicitly: "The official language of the State of Illinois shall be known hereafter as the 'American' language and not the 'English' language" (quoted from Mencken 1963:93).

The change of identities and perspectives is epitomized best by attitudes to local words in two collections of Americanisms. As late as in 1816 a conservative attitude can be heard in Pickering's *Vocabulary or Collection of Words and Phrases which have been supposed to be peculiar to the United States*, the first dictionary of Americanisms ever:

we should undoubtedly avoid all those words which are noticed by English authors of reputation as expressions with which *they are unacquainted* ... the very circumstances of their being thus noticed by well-educated *Englishmen* is a proof that they are not in use at this day in England, and, of course, ought not to be used elsewhere by those who would speak *correct English*. (quoted in Mencken 1963:58)

In stark contrast, Bartlett's dictionary of 1848 was no longer apologetic but "gloried in the newly developing American diction" (Read 2002:17), thus reflecting the now self-confident American attitude. Read remarks: "In those 32 years the American outlook had changed radically. ... Bartlett ... was entranced with the Davy Crockett material, and recorded his terms with approval" (17). Americans very much felt as members of a new and strong nation, conquering and then controlling an entire continent.

It is very much open to discussion to what extent this identity construction can be regarded as pan-ethnic – if so, then only to the extent that physical complexion allowed a group's merging into a white Anglo-dominated society. In the IDG strand instances of a high degree of assimilation via the adoption of the English language certainly also existed, but, as the Indian Wars of the century and many other cruel incidents make very clear, the Natives must have felt oppressed and threatened in their dignity and human existence; for many of them it is highly unlikely that they would have adopted a territory-based identity integrating the whites in any way. "Indian Boarding Schools" attempted to coerce them into integration; these programs did have the effect of turning many Natives fully bilingual but failed to assimilate them culturally, naturally enough – identities are deeply rooted components of one's self that must be constructed with conviction and in freedom, that cannot be forced upon anybody.[20] Certainly in the course of time some sort of integration proceeded among the Native Americans as well, but only to a certain extent and with grave mental reservations.

In the ADS strand, a similarly ambiguous but basically oppressed identity prevailed among African-Americans, most conspicuously in the South. Some of the slaves were treated relatively humanely, felt at home where they were, and identified more or less closely with their white surroundings (though it is difficult to say to what extent such behavior was a form of role-playing, wearing a mask). Certainly such an attitude could have been found more regularly among house slaves than among field hands. Statements of the type "Ole Massa treated us well" can be found in ex-slave narratives, representing a white, paternalistic perspective of historiography. However, they are characteristic of a distorted view backwards influenced by the difficult Restoration years when living conditions were harsh and former slaves sometimes viewed the antebellum period as a time when their basic needs were taken care of. Most likely, such statements capture no more than a tiny fraction of the truth: slaves were very much aware of their legal status and its potential consequences, even under the best of circumstances. Some attempted resistance; some ran away, if only "into the woods," for as long as they could survive and stay on their own. Many were involved in the turmoil of the Civil War, as soldiers on both sides and as victims of the economic decline of the South. Certainly Emancipation made a difference for their identities; certainly they had no other option than to feel as Americans and to try to get integrated into mainstream society; but progress in that respect was made only very slowly if at all.

The situation was radically different for ADS-strand immigrants from Europe, for whom, in the relative absence of physical or legal barriers, integration was a realistic prospect which they certainly were striving for. In religion and customs they did retain traces of their original cultural identities, but that was secondary to the desire of many to become Americans as fast as possible. These are the people for whom the melting-pot metaphor may have applied best: "nationalism encouraged newly arrived Europeans to think that they could participate fully in American life by adopting Anglo-Saxon virtues, including the English language" (Conklin and Lourie 1983:70).

6.4.3   Sociolinguistic conditions

The new national pride resulted in positive attitudes toward American ways of speaking, including, to some extent, vernacular forms. As was shown above, Americanisms were now cherished rather than scorned. We now get contemporary statements testifying to Americans' endonormative orientation. For instance, in 1833 James Boardman, a British traveler, notes that "Americans have ceased to look to England as their model" (Read 2002:62). In 1856 the President of Marietta College in Ohio pronounced: "London then is no standard for us. The pronunciation of this country will never be conformed to that of London" (quoted in Read 2002:74). The same applies to the "tall talk" of the West; indigenous linguistic creativity and local ways of speaking became a source of pride. Mencken argues that these patterns of language use also reached the political and literary arenas: "It was Abraham Lincoln, fresh from the Western wilds, who first made a deliberate effort to speak and write in the simple terms of everyday America. He did not succeed as thoroughly as Mark Twain did, but his effort had a long-reaching influence" (1963:201).

Several factors strengthened not only the independence but also the uniformity of American speech during that period. One was the settlement of the West and the resulting second, strong phase of koinéization, mentioned earlier. The other, the expansion of literacy, contributed to that effect. Webster's *American Spelling Book*, generally known as the "blue-backed speller," played a role in this which can hardly be overemphasized. It was distributed not only by schools but also via pedlars, who offered it along with molasses, whiskey, and gridirons (Krapp 1925,1:28), and it sold about a million copies a year in the 1820s. By 1865 it had reached a circulation of 42 million copies (339), and total sales are estimated to have been about a hundred million copies (Algeo 2001b:34). For many Americans the blue-backed speller was "their only and all-important text-book ... for the average American citizen, especially in the North and West, throughout at least three generations, Webster's spelling book was almost the solitary means of approach to the elements of literary culture" (Krapp 1925, I:339). It is no accident that part of the tremendous success of this book was due to the fact that the road to correct spelling and linguistic uniformity was again couched as a moral and political, even a national affair: it had the word *American* in its title, and later editions added a "'Moral Catechism' and a 'Federal Catechism', containing a short explanation of the Constitution of the United States and the principles of government" (336). McDavid offers a nice explanation:

In the absence of a well-defined elite ... it is not surprising that a citizen population that often sought salvation from the literal (though translated) message of the Bible should seek its path to education in the literal message of the school grammars, regardless of the discrepancies between grammatical rules and the actual language practices of the educated. In fact – for grammar as for morals – the greater the proportion of the erring, the greater the reward of the faithful. (1958:510–1)

Of course, all of this, in a country characterized by the coexistence of a multiplicity of opinions and positions, does not exclude the residual conservatism that is to be expected. One form of this attitude is a lingering admiration for British English as the only "pure" form of the language, "the true English standard."[21] Actually, the struggle toward endonormativity in America, against conservative voices, is quite similar to what we observe today in a number of PCEs. For others, it meant the scorning of vernacular forms as "rude" and "vulgar." Webster's *Grammar*, for instance, was attacked for "gaining our idiom from the mouths of the illiterate" (1807; quoted from Fisher 2001:67). A strongly prescriptively minded school tradition has preserved such attitudes to the present day, perhaps because "good usage" (i.e. conforming to certain prescriptive rules) was considered a sign of education and even intelligence, perhaps also because even a political dimension was attached to this issue. Pyles (1952) argues that America was particularly receptive to linguistic prescriptivism because "good usage" accessible to everyone without class boundaries reflected democratic ideals; "it became a patriotic duty to follow the precerpts of those who knew what language ought to be" (70). This is a remarkable union of intellectual strands: rationalism and nationalism meet to foster linguistic prescriptivism and uniformity.

As the pendulum swings back and forth, it is fitting and noteworthy that a purist, pro-English movement, which "seems to have got its chief support from schoolma'ams ... and ... Anglomaniacs" (Mencken 1963:198), gained momentum after the Civil War and in the 1870s and 1880s, after endonormative stabilization. A leading representative of this school of thought was Edward Gould, who in 1867 published a book entitled *Good English*.

Bailey (2006) documents very convincingly how the complaint tradition took the form of scorning local varieties of English in the Midwest. A letter to the editor printed in 1906 in the magazine *The Nation*, titled "Slovenly Speaking of English," provides a classic manifestation of the complaint tradition:

in Chicago ... he will find dozens of schools in which not one teacher is capable of setting an example of pure and beautiful speech. Let him visit, also, our great high schools ... he will find in each perhaps one or two noble women, bred back in old New England, who are really fit to carry the torch of enlightenment ... But the count has not reached ten righteous ones. (172–3)

A "Speech Movement," including a "Good Speech Week," was launched – which brings to mind Singapore's "Speak Good English Movement," two activities indicative of the same developmental stage! Bailey (2006:173–6) gives vivid descriptions of how children paraded with posters hailing "Mr. Good English" or in short theatrical scenes performed the denial of access for certain words to Webster's Dictionary. "Boy Scouts rousted

'Mr. Ain't' from Bad English town," and two girls, one neat, one untidy, carried posters saying "It is I" and "it is me," respectively. A pledge which the children had to give illustrates the intimate mingling of nationalism, morality, and language use:

American Speech Committee of the Chicago Women's Club Pledge for Children
   I love the United States of America. I love my country's flag. I love my country's language. I promise:
   1. That I will not dishonor my country's speech by leaving off the last syllables of words.
   2. That I will say a good American "yes" and "no" in place of an Indian grunt, "um-hum" and "nup-um" or a foreign "ya" or "yeh" and "nope."

Similar efforts to police and purify the English language in America have survived well into the twentieth century (Mencken 1963:59) and to the present day.

A typical indicator of the stage of having attained linguistic and cultural self-confidence, according to the Dynamic Model, is literary creativity in the new variety – in America, it also sets in during this period. In 1813 Jefferson still complained about the absence of literati, due to other "industrious pursuits" and "main businesses in life" (Mencken 1963:21). But the same decade saw a distinctive American literature awaking (21). Washington Irving and James Fenimore Cooper, among others, soon set a standard and became admired and influential American writers. Before long American English "began to leave its marks upon a distinctively national literature" (145), and the new national feeling produced a burgeoning and self-confident American literary scene (145–7). A substantial portion of this literature employs dialect, resting "upon a foundation of general informal colloquial speech" (Krapp 1925, I:243). Important and internationally renowned authors from that period include Ralph Waldo Emerson, Nathaniel Hawthorne, Henry Wadsworth Longfellow, Edgar Allan Poe, Henry David Thoreau, James Russell Lowell, Herman Melville, Walt Whitman, Emily Dickinson, and Mark Twain. Emerson's oration entitled "The American Scholar," given at Cambridge in 1837, is widely considered an important benchmark of the country's evolving cultural nationalism. Longfellow and other so-called "Fireside Poets" were probably most influential in the dissemination of a contemporary literature, being widely recited in public and in schools. "Sentimental fiction" with a strong moral undertone, like Harriet Beecher Stowe's novels, reached very high circulation figures.

6.4.4   Linguistic effects

As was implied in many of the above statements, after the National period, American English definitely stabilized, and part of that process concerns the fact that the homogeneity observed during the eighteenth century, documented above, lasted to a certain extent, and got reinforced during the second heightened phase of koinéization with westward migration (Algeo 2001b:36; Read 2002:24–5). Aware of the danger of diversification inherent in the national expansion, some statesmen and writers explicitly called for the preservation of uniformity (see Krapp 1925, I:16). Certainly Webster's "blue-backed speller," discussed above, went a long way in that direction, given its wide dissemination, its authoritative stance, and its singular role in giving access to literacy and an idea of a linguistic norm to many. In fact, in a later edition of 1843 Webster credits himself with having shaped or strongly influenced "the remarkable uniformity of pronunciation among the citizens of the United States" (Pyles 1952:82–3). Homogeneity was also promoted by social factors such as the lack of a single, dominant big city (comparable to London in England) and the more democratic structure of society, which was not classless but with substantially weaker class distinctions than in England. Certainly this has to be balanced against the undeniable truism that regional and social speech differences persisted as well – any other assumption would be unreasonable given the vastness of the country and the fragmentation of its society. But the basic fact that American English has been perceived as relatively homogeneous is equally correct. A number of statements from the nineteenth century confirm that this impression was alive and strong, for example:

- extensive as the country is, one uniform correctness obtains in speaking the English language (Horton James, 1847; quoted from Read 2002:64);
- there are fewer local peculiarities of form and articulation in our vast extent of territory than on the comparatively small soil of Britain ... English is more emphatically *one* in America (Marsh, *Lectures*, 1860; quoted from Krapp 1925, I:47).

Fundamentally, this assessment still holds, as McDavid observed in the mid-twentieth century: "To those familiar with the situation in European countries ... dialect differences in American English are rather small." (1958:482). Similarly, Pyles (1952) states "American English is characterized by a high degree of uniformity" (58); all existing variability "should not ... obscure the picture of an essentially homogeneous American English" (59). Of course there is a strong class dimension to this observation: "the most highly educated speakers in formal settings tend to suppress any linguistic features that they recognize as marked, i.e. regionally or socially identifiable" (Kretzschmar 2004:261). Hence, formal and educated American English appears and is rather homogeneous, while a lot of variation can be found underneath that surface.

The conceptualization of homogeneity in American English has found its best-known crystallization in the notion of "General American," which in many countries is used as an equivalent to RP, a label for a "default" form of American English. The meanings associated with this term vary greatly, but basically it denotes a speech that is neither recognizably from New England nor Southern. The term was used by Krapp (1925) and then popularized by John Kenyon, the phonetician, soon thereafter. Van Riper (1973) documents the various uses of the label from the 1920s to the 1960s but argues that because of its ambiguity and because it obscures existing dialect variability it should be discarded.

Finally, this is also the period when the codification of American English began. Webster's *Spelling Book* certainly paved the way toward codification as well, in addition to establishing its author as an authority on language matters. Other precursors include lists of Americanisms like Pickering's and an early *American Grammar* by Robert Ross, published as early as 1782 (Fisher 2001:61). But the real monument, the first standard reference work codifying the American vocabulary, was Noah Webster's *An American Dictionary of the English Language*, a work culminating his nationalistic pride and patriotism. It is a fitting coincidence that Webster's *Dictionary* was published in the year of Jackson's first election, 1828. In 1848 there followed Bartlett's *Dictionary of Americanisms, a Glossary of Words and Phrases usually regarded as peculiar to the United States*, with a thoroughly positive attitude toward Americanisms.

6.5 "We know just who we are by our language":[22] Phase 5 (1898–)

A note by Read (2002:30–1) illustrates very neatly the transition between phases 4 and 5 with respect to its ideological underpinnings:

> Those of us whose memories go back several decades recall the time when the term melting pot represented a high ideal in American culture ... [it] guided American thinking ... Its tendency was toward uniformity ... But in recent years our thinking has swung in a different direction, toward the recognition of diversity.

6.5.1 Sociopolitical background

The Spanish-American War of 1898, although insignificant in military terms, became "a turning point in the history of the country, directing the nation's attention outside its own borders to the world stage" (Algeo 2001b:37). In the twentieth century the United States of America became a global superpower, the economically strongest and politically most influential nation on earth, grounded in a strong military. Branches of big businesses and the model of American popular culture have diffused into the remotest localities conceivable. All of this is based on a democratic value system and an unbroken national self-confidence. At the same time, underneath the unifying national level, shared and accepted by most, an ongoing cultural fragmentation can be observed, and the once-mainstream "WASP" (White Anglo-Saxon Protestant) orientation is no longer unchallenged. For some ethnic minorities, notably African-Americans and Hispanic Americans, World War II was a turning point insofar as the fact that they fought for the country morally authorized them to demand and also fight for equal rights and their share of the national prosperity. The second half of the century has seen several processes of ethnic awakening and social diversification. To some extent these have been going hand in hand with a certain degree of segregation; many people tend to socialize primarily or exclusively with other members of their own ethnic or social group.

Early in the twentieth century African-Americans migrated to the industrial cities of the North in large numbers, in search of economically better lives after the large-scale breakdown of the plantation system and shortage of jobs in the South. In many cases this has resulted in housing segregation and the ghettoization of inner cities or other primarily "black" districts. Some Native Americans have assimilated to mainstream society and live in urban areas; many, however, continue to live on reservations, where problems with unemployment, educational failure, and alcoholism seem insurmountable. Hispanic Americans, especially Mexican-Americans, constitute an increasingly large percentage of the national population, due to high rates of birth and immigration. In many parts of the Southwest they are a majority today, and their representatives hold influential political offices. By now substantial communities of Hispanics can be found in many other parts of the country as well, however.[23] As is well known, these demographic changes, predicted to become even stronger in the future, have stirred political unrest and opposition with linguistic ramifications, like the "English-Only" movement (see Wiley 2004).

6.5.2.   Identity constructions

No doubt the national identity of Americans is a strong and unifying force. In addition, however, most Americans regard themselves as members of sub-national groups which are important for their lives and their identities. The international outlook which is a natural consequence of the nation's global role characterizes representatives of big business and an intellectual elite; the majority of the population, however, are more interested in local affairs, in their immediate environment. Many whites identify with their respective regions or other social groups, frequently including an association with the national origins of their ancestors if they are not Anglo-Saxons. For all other groups ethnicity tends to play a primary role.

The Civil Rights movement and events of the 1950s and 1960s, with leaders like Martin Luther King and slogans like "Black is beautiful," have instilled pride into the African-American community. By and large the situation of many African-Americans has improved, and many of them have risen to the middle class. At the same time a disproportional share of the homeless and poor in society are black, and the problems of urban ghettoes, including economic deprivation, violence and drug consumption, have not been solved. Hip-hop and rap have come to be artistic expressions of the African-American experience which have turned into influential cultural models in many countries. It is perfectly clear that African-Americans, young ones in particular, very strongly identify with their ethnicity. The impact of this factor may be stronger in urban contexts but it has been shown to be effective in rural surroundings as well.

Native Americans have also experienced an ethnic revival, which has definitely strengthened their identity as members of the "First Nations" peoples. Old traditions, including religious practices and attention to sacred sites, are being revitalized (to the extent possible), powwows have been held in increasingly large numbers, and so on (Nichols 2003). One aspect of this movement is the fight for Native American rights within the legal system, like court appeals to establish rights for Natives or legal procedures about Indian Trust beneficiaries and about gaming rights. It is noteworthy, however, that now this operates under the umbrella of the shared national identity. For example, one website states explicitly *"as American citizens*, we cannot be deprived of the land and resources we own" (indiantrust.com, accessed March 4, 2005; italics mine). Following Nichols (2003:231), "American society is more ready than ever to welcome [Native Americans] as one more ethnic group in the national social mix."

Mexican-Americans may have the strongest of all ethnic identities, backed by their respected Spanish heritage and reinforced by continuous contacts with and population influx from America's southern neighbor. On the other hand, within the United States many of them tend to suffer from a low status and a desperate economic situation, not infrequently as illegal immigrants or lowly paid migrant workers. So this group is carving out an identity niche between its Hispanic heritage and its American and English-speaking present and future. In the 1960s militant Mexican-Americans accepted the label "Chicano" as a term of ethnic affiliation and pride, and launched what has come to be known as the "Chicano Movement," demanding equal rights and opportunities and ultimately strengthening the ethnic group's identity.

Similar movements can be found elsewhere (the Cajun Renaissance, to be mentioned below, is another case in point), and most of them seem to have found some sort of a symbolic linguistic expression, as will be shown below. America's society is changing in some respects, and, as always in such situations, there is a struggle between conservative forces wishing to retain the traditional patterns and values in unmodified form and innovators who enforce cultural pluralism and a conceptualization of the US as a society of ethnic groups – which to a strong extent she is by now. The traditional "melting pot" metaphor has now given way to the "salad bowl" metaphor, in which rather than being blended to come out the same each of the ingredient groups of a complex society retains its individual cultural (and linguistic) characteristics. American society is being transformed into a multicultural mosaic, and this process is mirrored by the emergence of distinct varieties of English, each associated with different identities.

6.5.3   Sociolinguistic conditions and linguistic effects: a general survey

The history of research, as addressed by Wolfram and Schilling-Estes, mirrors linguistic developments themselves: "As the United States became securely independent, the focus changed from the relationship between American and British English to the diversity within American English itself" (1998:20). People socialize with their peers, so in many ethnic communities today we find strong in-group ties but relatively less outside communication. Of course this correlates with education and social class: upper-class members, the educated, and the highly mobile tend to have a supraregional orientation and hence a wider range of contacts, while as a rule of thumb a strongly local focus and an expressed in-group identity correlate with lower social status, as does strongly dialectal usage. The fact that there is an inverse correlation between social class membership and the strength of an individual's dialect is a sociolinguistic truism which of course applies in the present context as well. But the essential point is that after the national orientation of the eighteenth and nineteenth centuries with its concomitant tendency toward linguistic homogeneity, in the twentieth century we have experienced a tremendous dialect diversification as an expression of these newly emerging group identities and their associated patterns of communicative behavior. An insightful contemporary confirmation for this claim is provided by Sweet's observation of 1892: "American English itself is beginning to split up into dialects."[24]

Remarkably, all of this has been happening despite the fact that all the "official," overt linguistic prestige supports standard English. Educators and schoolma'ams, politicians and businesspeople emphasize the need to "speak good English" in order to succeed on the job market, and usage handbooks, dictionaries, and prescriptive language columns in news-papers are established propagators of "proper" speech. Nevertheless, many people, males in particular, do not seem to care as much as others think they should. Local dialect carries the covert prestige (Labov 1972; Chambers 2003:241–4) of real and honest life, down-to-earth values, a slightly subversive, anti-authoritarian spirit which is also deeply entrenched in the American national character, one of the country's many cultural ambiv-alences. Bailey's (2006) documentation of "Good English" movements in the Midwest contains a very nice illustration of the attraction which local dialects hold, in this case upon upper-class children. In a report to the "Chicago Women's Club" a member of an "American Speech Committee" complains:

Yet I know of a certain group of children in the most fashionable part of Chicago where the so-called *old* families of Chicago live. These children, fifty or sixty in number, never have had their speech affected by foreign-born children. They play in a private playground. They attend the best private schools in Chicago, where the teachers speak a most cultivated English. Most of the children have English or French governesses with excellent voices. Yet these children when they are together almost without exception try to talk as badly as they can. They try deliberately to mispronounce every word. They talk through their teeth – particularly the boys. Maybe they are imitating pirates. (174–5)

It is noteworthy that dialect diversification is strongest with social groups which are marginalized. On the one hand, this concerns ethnic minorities, like African-Americans and Chicanos. It is remarkable that after a language shift, having abandoned their ancestral language, these groups are adopting a distinct, new form of English:

The old ethnic ties found their linguistic expression in loyalty to a language other than that of the major society. The new ethnic identities rely on linguistic symbols to establish speech conventions that are significantly different. These symbols are much more than mere markers of identity. (Gumperz and Cook-Gumperz 1982:6)

On the other hand, groups whose identities are threatened somehow are the most fervent in expressing their identities by linguistic means. Examples, well known in sociolinguistics, include the islanders discussed below, whose traditional status and lifestyles are imperiled by recent social changes.

In a strictly linguistic perspective, it is interesting to observe that typi-cally only a relatively small number of features are selected as explicit identity markers. They can be from any language level (lexical, phono-logical, or grammatical), but the point is that typically the language system as a whole is not affected and remains similar to what it was like before or

296 The emergence of American English

what is used elsewhere. Certain features, however, are attributed special importance as identity markers in any given dialect. Frequently these features are not new but reallocated, "recycled" to specific uses, i.e. they gain in prominence and frequency, and are loaded with symbolic meaning. Which features are selected for such a purpose varies from one community to another, as will be shown below.

No doubt some forms of dialectal diversity have always existed in American English. In the light of the Dynamic Model, however, the point is that socially indicative dialectal diversity, an ethnic and regional fragmentation of the population along linguistic lines in perception and production, is essentially a product of the twentieth century, the phase after the post-national, endonormative stabilization period of the nineteenth century. Certainly there was some continuity of specific dialectal features transmitted from Britain to America, as suggested by Kurath (1965) and many others, but it is equally clear that there is no continuity of any individual dialect as a coherent system: the features brought over from Britain were whirled into the chaos of koinéization, dialect mixing, and feature competition in contact, and if they survived, they tended to come out with different roles and functions in the overall linguistic system, or systems of new dialects. In that sense, transported features were embryonic at best, no more (Gordon and Trudgill 1999). Certainly there is also some degree of continuity between present-day dialects and those of the nineteenth century and before, but the overall impression that we get from the historical record is quite clearly that in earlier periods dialect differences seem to have been less pronounced (with mixing and uniformity having been consistently observed and commented upon) and less strictly compartmentalized along specific local, regional, and ethnic lines. It was the twentieth century which despite seemingly leveling effects like an increase in mobility and supraregional communication, also via the mass media, saw the most explicit and systematic, socially motivated stage of dialect differentiation in American English. And this diversification happened because the various regional, social, and ethnic groups recognized the importance of carving out and signaling their own distinct identities against other such groups and also against an overarching nation which, while it is good to be a part of, is too big and too distant to be comforting and to offer the proximity and solidarity which humans require. I am of course not suggesting that this divergence has been a deliberate, conscious process; most of it operates subconsciously but nonetheless vigorously.

The following sections will illustrate these principles by looking into some of these newly emerging or strengthened dialects in turn. I will begin by discussing some regional varieties in the STL strand and will then comment on IDG and ADS strands' ethnic Englishes.

6.5.4 STL I: Signaling endangered local identities through language

The classic example of a study which documents the impact of speakers' identities upon linguistic form is Labov's investigation of the dialect of Martha's Vineyard island (1972; originally published in 1963). Labov found that islanders frequently use a centralized onset of the /aɪ/ and /aʊ/ diphthongs, i.e. they pronounce words like *right* and *house* with [əɪ] and [əʊ], respectively, and he attempted to find out why. By quantifying his data he determined that centralization characterizes primarily middle-aged fishermen in a specific region, Chilmark. These people are proud of their ancestral status on the island, which is threatened, however, by ever-increasing numbers of "summer people": tourists and new residents. For economic reasons they cannot reject these newcomers, so they use a symbolic linguistic means to demarcate themselves from them, to signal their genuinely local identity: "high centralization ... is closely correlated with expressions of strong resistance to the incursions of the summer people" (Labov 1972:28). Labov concludes: "the immediate meaning of this phonetic feature is 'Vineyarder'. When a man says [rɐɪt] or [hɐʊs], he is unconsciously establishing the fact that he belongs to the island: that he is one of the natives to whom the island really belongs" (Labov 1972:36).

Interestingly enough, this concerns both STL and ADS strands in ways predicted by the Dynamic Model. Young people of English descent show a weaker attachment to the island (with many of them going to college and seeking employment on the mainland) and, consequently, lower central-ization rates. Young islanders of Portuguese ancestry, however, who tend to remain on the island, strongly identify themselves with local life and thus assert this status by high centralization rates. This is quite unlike what is found in their parent generation, in which the Portuguese were denied full acceptance in the island society. Thus, with respect to the young Portuguese the threat from outside entails a redefinition of who is an ancestral, "real" islander on the side of the Chilmarkers to now include them as against the incoming "others," a redefinition of alignments and identities which finds symbolic linguistic expression.

A highly similar case was documented by Walt Wolfram and his research associates some thirty years later on the island of Ocracoke off the coast of North Carolina (e.g. Wolfram and Schilling-Estes 1996; 1997). The basic pattern is the same: an island community of long standing experiences a seasonal flood of visitors and an increasing number of new residents, which they cannot really resist and from which to a certain extent they benefit but who at the same time threaten their exclusive status as natives. The reaction is also very much the same, a strengthening of the traditional island dialect to set themselves off by symbolic means from the intruders. In this particular case the feature which is chosen to achieve this effect most evidently (there are others as well) is the backing of the /aɪ/ diphthong to [ɔɪ], a change which has earned the islanders the label *hoi toiders*. Interestingly enough, the same curvilinear age group can be observed, in addition to a gender bias: backed [ɔɪ] occurs most frequently with a middle-aged group of males called the "poker players." The explanation is clear and insightful: the old generation is not that strongly concerned about social changes any longer, because they are not directly affected nor exposed so strongly. The young generation does not share the "us" identity of islanders to the same extent, hoping to leave the island. So it is the middle generation who sense the threats of social changes most directly, and who are also most directly affected by them. Unlike earlier generations of males the "poker players" no longer generate the larger portion of family incomes (now tied to tourism) as fishermen, so for them using the strong elements of local dialect, almost like still owning a boat, is also a "symbolic projection of identity" (Wolfram and Schilling-Estes 1998), a means of asserting their special status as indigenous islanders.

6.5.5.   STL II: Southern English

In a broader perspective, the dialect of the American South, the strongest and best-known regional variety in the US, illustrates our topic equally well: "Southerners have long viewed their dialect as a strong marker of regional identity and often as a source of cultural pride" (Wolfram and Schilling-Estes 1998:115; see Nagle and Sanders 2003). Popular and traditional views hold Southern English, at least rural and conservative forms, to be equal to "Elizabethan" or "Shakespearean" English (see Schneider 2003b for documentation). However, the importance of directly transmitted British dialect features is actually considerably smaller than is conventionally assumed. In a detailed comparison of British and US Southern dialect features, Schneider (2004c) showed that on the lexical level, no more than about a quarter of all dialect words in Southern English are British retentions; on the grammatical level, except for non-standard structures widespread in practically all dialects of England, distinctively US Southern structures are mostly innovations; and for pronunciation idiosyncratic similarities but no direct transmission patterns could be documented.

Against received wisdom, Guy Bailey (1997) proposed a radically new view, based on very strong evidence which led to the conclusion that "innovation and change, rather than preservation and stability, may well be the most important factors in the development of [Southern American English]" (Tillery and Bailey 2003:159). He claims that present-day

Southern English as spoken in urban communities essentially goes back to not earlier than the post-Reconstruction period, the last quarter of the nineteenth century and thereafter. Somewhat similar to the cases of Martha's Vineyard and Ocracoke discussed before, this was a period of crisis and change for Southerners, with their traditions being disrupted after the defeat in the Civil War and the social changes resulting from it, including the presence of an increasingly large numbers of incoming "Yankees." According to Tillery and Bailey (2003:164), a second period during which changes in Southern English gathered momentum, caused by dialect contact through urbanization, was the time around World War II.

Linguistically speaking, this period of turmoil and change during which the linguistic expression of a new, modern Southern identity was shaped, affected both "Traditional" and "New" Southern features (a distinction proposed by Schneider 2004c to reconcile the conflicting views). Features of Traditional Southern, associated with a rural, antebellum culture, have become archaic or have largely disappeared, including non-rhotic pronunciation, the retention of /j/ in *new* etc., intrusive /r/ (as in *Warshington*), the common use of verbal *–s* in persons other than the third singular, and preverbal *a-* (*he's a-comin'*). Conversely, a number of innovative features symbolizing the "New South" have come to be regularly used, especially among the urban young: rhoticity, /j/-dropping, the laxing of tense vowels (leading to homophony of *fill-feel* and *full-fool*), the *pin/pen* merger, /aɪ/ monophthongization and other vocalic changes as part of the "Southern Shift" (Labov 1994), inceptive *get to/got to*, the second plural pronoun *y'all*, double modals, and *fixin' to*. Wolfram and Schilling-Estes confirm that *"fixin' to* carries strong symbolic meaning as a marker of a regional identity" (1998:115) – and other features do so as well, we may add. Bernstein (2006) documents highly subtle social meanings attributed to /aɪ/ monophthongization in different phonetic environments (see 4.2.3).

6.5.6. STL III: the Northern Cities Shift

Another striking example of twentieth-century dialect diversification in the US is the so-called "Northern Cities Shift" (NCS), a clockwise rotation of checked (tense, or "short") vowels in cities of the Northeast and the Great Lakes region studied by Labov and his team (Labov, Ash and Boberg 2006; Labov 1994, esp. 177–201; Gordon 2004). It is noteworthy that the NCS is "a fairly recent addition to the speech of the Inland north" (Gordon 2004:296). Dialect geographers noted precursor phenomena in the 1930s, and the earliest traces of the shift were found in a few individuals born late in the nineteenth century (Gordon 2001:25, 29–32), but the pattern itself was observed for the first time in the 1960s, and "it underwent a great expansion, geographically and phonologically, in the second half of the twentieth century" (Gordon 2004:296). Hence, the NCS constitutes another strong example of a phase 5 diversification process of new American dialects associated with a distinctive region. According to Wolfram and Schilling-Estes, recent research suggests that the differences "may actually be intensifying rather than weakening" (1998:120). It has been shown to be spreading in a cascade-like fashion from big cities like Rochester, Syracuse, Buffalo, Cleveland, Detroit, Chicago, and Milwaukee to smaller cities and towns, where people begin to adopt the image of urban modernity that is subconsciously signaled by it (see Gordon 2001, esp. 177–8). An interesting case study of how the NCS spreads in rural Michigan and how its adoption is steered by group alignments and local identity projections in different social groups was reported earlier, in 4.2.3.

6.5.7   ADS I: ethnic speech forms in European-American groups

In the European ADS strands, the effects of the "melting pot" accommodation forces and the adoption of English by the second generation have largely prevented strong linguistic markers of traditional alignments, but some distinguishing tendencies can be observed nevertheless. Even in his classic study of New York City pronunciation, Labov (1966:198–212) observed that Jewish and Italian New Yorkers differ from others in some pronunciation details: Italians use higher realizations of what Labov calls the (eh) variable (in *bad, bag, ask*, etc.) and more stops in words spelled with *th*-, while Jewish speakers tend to have higher variants of (oh), i.e. the vowel in *caught, talk, dog*, etc., differences which Labov tentatively attributed to "the possibility of influences from the structures of the Italian and Yiddish vowel systems" (1966:210).

Another interesting case of an identity-driven ethnic pronunciation among a European ADS group is attested by Nagy and Roberts (2004:278) for people of French lineage in New Hampshire: they variably omit word-initial *h*- but also insert an *h*- before vowels, as in [oli hɛndʒl aɪ] 'Holy Angel High.' The authors comment: "Interestingly, several of these speakers are monolingual Anglophones, so this is not a case of mother tongue interference in a second language, but rather a marking of cultural identity."

My final example of how European-American ADS groups have retained and re-emphasized a small amount of ethnolinguistic distinctiveness relates to a group that is traditionally considered as fully merged: Americans of Swedish ancestry. In a detailed long-term study of elderly Swedish Americans in a rural and an urban community, Karstadt (2003) shows how the sustained contact between both languages, even if they are typologically similar, has produced both a hybrid mix sometimes labeled *Swenglish* or *Svengelska* and "Swedish-influenced linguistic variants that are re-cycled in English conversations" (217). It is documented that the immigrant variety employs relatively fewer, and fewer types of, relative clauses and relative markers and hypercorrectly overuses certain pragmatic particles (like *you know, well, so, ja*). By using specific linguistic identity markers including Swedish lexical items and some nonstandard phonology, Karstadt hypothesizes, some Swedish-Americans "are symbolically converging toward their parents' and grandparents' generations which represent pioneer values" (231). The recycling of linguistic forms to gain symbolic function is nicely illustrated by the fact that in the Swedish-American community widespread nonstandard pronunciations (like *tink* and *dat*, or *vas* for "was") fulfill this function: "the identity markers are not *Swedish* items *per se*, but correspond to phonetic substitutions that Swedish L2 speakers of English typically make" (231). Similarly to what we have observed in other communities, speakers use their "Swedish-influenced English to highlight their social identity" (iv).

6.5.8   The IGD strand: Native American English(es)

Relatively less research has been carried out into the English spoken by Native Americans, mostly called American-Indian English (Bartelt et al. 1982; Craig 1991; Leap 1977, 1993; see also Wolfram 1984; Rowicka 2005). Three fourths of all Native Americans today speak English, as their only language or alongside their ancestral tongue, and many of them speak a distinctive variety (Leap 1993:17). Various hypotheses have been forwarded as to possible origins of Native American English. Multi-tribal boarding schools by the Bureau of Indian Affairs, established toward the end of the nineteenth and early twentieth centuries,[25] as well as "Indian Territory" contacts and reservation life may have fostered some mutual alignments beyond transfer effects and tribal boundaries.

However, Native American English is not a single, coherent entity. Quite a number of the contributions in Leap (1977) document variation by tribal background on the levels of phonology and grammar. Leap (1993) explicitly asserts that no uniform "American Indian English" exists or is on the rise, and he shows how both accents and grammatical properties are marked by ethnic transfer features, thus varying from one tribe to another. Chapter 2 of his book (44–89) surveys phonological, syntactic, and also semantic phenomena documented in Native American English varieties, and the following chapters explicitly set out to prove the importance of ancestral language traditions in shaping specific features. Native

American English is probably best seen as a plurality of dialects which are historically and typologically related even if ethnically marked and distinct from each other. This diversity reflects the fact that Native Americans have never constituted an ethnolinguistically homogeneous group.[26] However, the basic fact that new forms of English have sprung in these contexts as well and that these forms of English also have socially indicative functions is undisputed. For example, Conklin and Lourie note on Cherokees living in Los Angeles:

> Like other English-speaking Indians, the urban Cherokees employ a variety of English unique to their tribe. Even those who have no knowledge of the tribal language use nonstandard phonology and grammatical structures which derive from the ancestral tongue. (1983:201–2)

American-Indian English convincingly illustrates the fact that varieties are not only characterized by sounds and structures but that, in addition, "discourse conventions tend to persist and to be taken over into the group's use of the majority language" (Gumperz and Cook-Gumperz 1982:6). For example, unlike Anglos, Navajos do not find lengthy pauses in conversations embarrassing, and therefore they do not avoid them (as Tony Hillerman's highly successful novels frequently assert; see also Leap 1993:87–9). Lakota English has a topic–comment structure which appears to reflect ancestral language transfer (Craig 1991:28). Leap's examples of "verbal imagery" (1993:78–80) are illuminating. They include "naming practices, euphemisms and slang, 'sacred' vs. 'secular' meanings, and strategies for identifying prominent features of the natural environment and social life" (78) and pragmatics, like the cooperative nature of American-Indian English discourse.

The ethnic revival of roughly the last third of the twentieth century resulted in a reassertion of Indian rights, tribal empowerment and a renewed emphasis on native languages and cultures, in many cases as elements in school curricula catered specifically for Native Americans (Conklin and Lourie 1983:8; see the Native American Languages Acts of 1990 and 1992). With many ancestral language traditions having been lost, Native American English also assumes some symbolic importance: "Indian English fluency becomes a highly valued social skill, and the nonstandard features of the Indian English conversation have an even greater cultural significance for their speakers" (Leap 1993:3). It is possible that these developments have consequences for the overall positioning of Native American English(es). It has occasionally been suggested that pan-tribal features may be emerging, but this is disputed (Craig 1991; Rowicka 2005). Rowicka (2005) hypothesizes that the replacement of voiceless stops, particularly /t/, by a glottal stop may be a case in point; earlier research (e.g. Wolfram 1984; Leap 1993) identified unmarked tense in verbs as a possible candidate. Further possibilities include missing plural marking, nonstandard prepositional usage, and pronoun deletion (Leap 1993). In any case, there is definitely a perception of distinctly Native American ways of speaking which are socially adequate in in-group situations; "talking like a cowboy" or "using the big man's English" is scorned in the community (Leap 1993:169). English as spoken in "Indian country" is assuming identity-carrying functions; in many situations it is the Natives' "code-of-choice when making particular statements, if not for the discourse as a whole" (Leap 1993:175). In many contexts it has replaced ancestral language traditions and assumed their former social functions.

6.5.9   ADS II: African-American English

In the mid-twentieth century the Civil Rights Movement, followed by affirmative action, achieved improvements in the lives of many African-Americans, beginning with the desegregation of schools and leading to the rise of an African-American middle class. These social changes should have resulted in an increasing integration of African-Americans into the mainstream of American culture, socially as well as linguistically. On the other hand, in practice ongoing segregation, housing and job discrimination, and but limited success of educational efforts in association with reduced public funding have resulted in the opposite effect for many members of the African-American community. In the mid-1980s William Labov and Guy Bailey and their respective research teams submitted what has come to be known as the "divergence hypothesis," arguing that the dialectal gap between the races is actually increasing rather than decreasing (Bailey and Maynor 1987, 1989). A heated debate followed, and the last two decades have seen some investigations of the thesis, with mixed results. While it is clear that the notion of divergence fails to adequately capture the entire story and in some respects black and white Englishes are indeed converging as well, it cannot be denied that there is some truth to it: there are a few linguistic developments in the African-American community which are separating it increasingly from white speech forms (Mufwene 2001a:319). There is also no doubt that the driving force behind such developments is the case projected by the Dynamic Model: "A socio-psychological corollary would be the heightened awareness of African-American cultural identity and the function of a distinctive dialect in maintaining this cohesive identity" (Wolfram and Schilling-Estes 1998:179).

The features which increasingly separate black from white speakers are both phonological and syntactic in nature. African-Americans do not

304 The emergence of American English

participate at all in vocalic changes which are spreading vigorously among white speakers, so that the difference between them, of course, increases (Labov 2001:506). Their dialect also continues to be non-rhotic, while even in formerly non-rhotic dialect regions like the South, rhoticity has been spreading rapidly among young whites. One of the most consistent syntactic innovations, documented convincingly by Bailey and Maynor (1987, 1989), is the use of an invariant *be* followed by a verbal *-ing* form to express habitual actions, as in *We be taking spelling tests* 'We regularly take ...' Today this pattern is regularly used especially amongst young urban males (amply demonstrated, for instance, in the well-known movie *Boyz N the Hood*). Other grammatical innovations are reminiscent of creole preverbal markers, like *come* expressing indignation and *steady* expressing persistence, or a functional split of *be, been,* and *be done* as aspectual markers (Labov 1998; Green 2002). Finally, another feature that has emerged and spread rapidly only after World War II in AAVE (and that has come to be discovered and studied only recently) is "innovative *had* + past participle," the use of what appears to be a past perfect to signal simple past time, as in *he had lied* 'he lied' (Cukor-Avila 2001).

What all of this boils down to is that during the last few decades distinctly African-American ways of speaking have evolved, and this change is psychologically motivated: "there seems to be a growing sense of linguistic solidarity and identity among African-Americans that serves to unify AAVE in different locales" (Wolfram and Schilling-Estes 1998:180). Of course not all African-Americans speak alike, and the 1970s suggestion of a nationally uniform black dialect in its strong form would no longer be upheld today, but on the other hand it is perfectly clear that a novel sense of distinctly African-American ways of speaking, of signaling ethnic identity by select speech forms, has emerged. Even isolated individuals, like the only black family on the island of Ocracoke, or communities, like remote Hyde County, North Carolina, participate in the nationally shared trajectory of change (Wolfram and Thomas 2002). As Wolfram and Schilling-Estes (1998:181) observe, "we postulate that identification with an increasingly coherent nationwide African-American culture plays a large role in the adoption of AAVE features by the younger speakers in this rural community." In line with phase 5, African-Americans and whites have developed "separate, though related, ethnolinguistic identities" (Mufwene 2001a:319).

6.5.10   ADS III: Chicano English and other Hispanic varieties

For Mexican-Americans in the Southwest, Spanish remains a vital language, but with the increasing integration of Hispanics into the mainstream of society English has become the language of choice more and more commonly. "Many third-generation Chicanos, especially those who have moved into the middle class, have abandoned Spanish altogether" (Conklin and Lourie 1983:191). However, this is a Spanish-influenced variety of English – even Chicanos who are monolingual English speakers sound as if they had "a Spanish accent." The Chicano Movement has forged the label "Chicano" into a positively valued ethnic identity label, and Chicano English, even if it is disparaged by outsiders and educators, has come to be accepted as a symbolic representation of this identity. Features characteristic of this variety, possibly to be accounted for as transfer from Spanish, include a distinctive intonation contour; specific discourse markers; pronunciation details like confusion of /tʃ/ and /ʃ/, a tendency to devoice /z/, or the merger of /i/ and /ɪ/; and grammatical peculiarities like a tag *no*, specific preposition and modal uses, and zero-subject pronouns. For further details, see e.g. the sophisticated documentations by Penfield and Ornstein-Galicia (1985), Fought (2003), Santa Ana and Bayley (2004), and Bayley and Santa Ana (2004). Despite conservative myths that surround the variety and misguide its perceptions outside the community there is no doubt today that Chicano English is a vigorously evolving ethnic identity marker.

A similar process of a positive re-interpretation as a signal of social identity seems to be affecting Puerto Rican English in New York City. Adolescent peer group orientations and ethnic identities are signaled by the adoption of select phonological features, like monophthongal realizations of /eɪ/ and /oʊ/ and "light" realizations of the lateral /l/ in onset positions (Slomanson and Newman 2004).

It is noteworthy that the Hispanic varieties of English also illustrate the close relationship between IDG and various ADS strands. Chicanos have adopted some Native American influences in their speech (Conklin and Lourie 1983:185), and Puerto Ricans have borrowed features from African-American English in Harlem (Wolfram 1974; Slomanson and Newman 2004:205) – processes which derive from the close mutual associations of these groups, respectively, and indicate their equality in terms of social status and alignments as against the STL strand, the white community.

6.5.11. *ADS IV: Cajun English*

New Orleans was founded by the French in 1717, but Louisiana received its most significant population influx after 1765 with the arrival of the Acadians from eastern Canada. A brief interlude of formally Spanish possession after the French and Indian War left hardly any traces.

American in-migration in larger numbers started in the nineteenth century, gradually resulting in bilingualism. French remained the language of the home and the playground, however. It was only the twentieth century with its profound social changes, including men serving in the military, which caused an older generation of Cajuns to reject their ancestral language. However, an outcome of that process of bilingualism and language shift was the emergence of an ethnically distinctive new variety of English, known as Cajun English (Dubois and Horvath 2004).

Dubois and Horvath (2004) argue convincingly that Cajun English cannot be accounted for solely as a product of French interference; rather, it has also been shaped by social attitudes within the community. Beginning in the 1960s, the wholesale abandonment of the people's original culture was stopped in a process called the "Cajun Renaissance," which has strengthened historical and ethnic pride in a community which was about to give up its cultural distinctiveness together with its former language. With French being no longer sufficiently available to the younger generations, a specific form of English was chosen and further developed to signal their identity:

> CajVE represents an innovation from within the Cajun community so that some of the Cajun variants which began in the accented speech of the oldest of the speakers in our sample have either been passed on to the next generation of speakers or have been *recycled as markers of social identity* by the youngest speakers (399; my emphasis).

Cajun English is marked (amongst other things) by a strong tendency to delete final consonants (not only in clusters), by glide reduction in diphthongs, by a lack of aspiration of word-initial stops, and by "heavy nasalization" of both vowels and consonants. The social significance of the dialect is determined by generational differences in attitudes: the older generation initiated the process of language shift, using French-accented second-language English; the middle generation, attempting to join the mainstream of society, abandoned French altogether; but the young generation, proud to be Cajuns again, is the one that now senses the loss of their heritage and recycles their grandparents' way of speaking English into a distinctive identity marker.

6.5.12   ADS V: Hawaiian Creole

Another convincing example of a novel twentieth-century variety blossoming as a marker of social identity and diversification is the creole of Hawai'i, locally known as Pidgin, which "serves as a sign of ethnic and peer-group solidarity among teenagers, particularly young men" (Conklin and Lourie 1983:218) and enjoys strong covert prestige (S. J. Roberts 2000:273–4). The history and origins of this variety have been the subject of some debate (see, for example, Bickerton 1981 and S. J. Roberts 1998), but that is not our concern here. A highly readable account of the dialect's historical evolution and its distinctive features is provided by Sakoda and Siegel (2003). Mufwene (2005a:155–61) suggests that the evolutionary process in Hawai'i was unique in some respects. What is important in the present context is that Pidgin has turned into "an important badge of local identity – i.e., the language of people born and bred in Hawai'i, especially ethnic Hawaiians and descendants of plantation laborers" (Sakoda and Siegel 2003:18; see also Siegel 2005:152). Pidgin is not for *haoles*; it inspires pride in those who belong to the islands.

6.5.13   ADS VI: Asian Englishes

In the twentieth century the mid-nineteenth century Chinese immigrants were followed by many other Asian groups in larger numbers, mostly as a consequence of political events: Japanese, Koreans, Filipinos, Vietnamese, Cambodians, and others (Conklin and Lourie 1983). There has been a strong tendency for these groups to form tightly knit communities, and many of them have shifted to English – conditions which should favor the emergence of ethnic varieties. On the other hand, the Asians' strong commitment to education and social advancement may undermine such tendencies, promoting the acquisition of a standard accent instead. Wolfram and Schilling-Estes observe that "Vietnamese English, with roots in the extensive migration of Vietnamese into the US following the fall of Saigon in the mid-1970s, has become a recognized variety, characterized by features such as the use of unmarked past tense forms" (1998:114).[27] Whether Asian Englishes in the US will be emerging as social varieties remains to be seen; this will depend on whether Asian communities are big enough to develop and maintain ethnic features and whether the next generations will be integrated in the mainstream.

6.6   Summary and outlook

A lot of evidence has been accumulated showing how during phase 5, in the twentieth century, the linguistic landscape of American English has continued to diversify, and how because of new social alignments and identities a host of new varieties have emerged or intensified their distinctive features. I have demonstrated that the Dynamic Model fits the emergence of American English remarkably well. The similarities with what has been stated about other PCEs in earlier chapters are all too obvious: the relocation of English and gradual separation from the homeland; the explosion of linguistic nationalism as a consequence of an explicit "Event X," fostering linguistic nativization strongly (though the process as such certainly was going on long before and after this incident); endless discussions on which English is the "better," the more refined, and so on. Perhaps unlike other PCEs, and despite ongoing insecurity and struggling, American English soon developed the self-confidence to counter British linguistic hegemony, but the process as such seems to have been pretty much the same as in other locations. And, of course, as was shown in the last sections, American English has already come full circle, experiencing a fragmentation into new regional and social identity carriers.

What does the future hold in store? In a recent programmatic essay, Tillery, Bailey, and Wikle (2004) identify three major demographic changes of the recent past that they regard as the main driving forces of ongoing linguistic changes and the main challenges to a modern discipline of dialectology: continued urbanization, expanding migration, and ethnic diversification. They observe what they call the balkanization of the population: within a state and within a metropolis members of ethnic groups stick together – Caucasians in the suburbs, African-Americans and other minorities in the inner cities or ethnic quarters – so that a spatial reorganization and fragmentation of population groups substantially enhances group-internal linguistic processes, to the effect of new dialect formation. The ongoing diversification of American English, consonant with phase 5, is to be recognized as a truism, and is likely to continue.

7   Conclusion

At the end of this survey, it is time to recapitulate, to focus upon general insights which can be drawn from the above applications of the Dynamic Model to PCEs. It will be helpful to start with a final, brief glimpse at a specific case study where the principles postulated so far are manifested in quite an indicative fashion. LePage and Tabouret-Keller (1985), whose claim that language use constitutes "acts of identity" has obviously been highly influential not only in creole studies but also on the present volume, primarily discuss Caribbean creoles to drive home their message; but they also build an implicit bridge to a similar understanding of PCEs, namely by citing the case of the acculturation of the Chinese communities in Malaysia and Singapore (176–7). The Chinese, they argue, have always looked back culturally to China, but "today pressures are strong for them to adopt in one case a Malaysian, and in the other a Singaporean, identity." The younger generation is "perhaps faute de mieux … perhaps out of a genuine sense of identity, accepting that they must be Malaysians or Singaporeans first and 'Chinese' second, while continuing to want economic advancement." In both cases this reorientation has resulted in similar sociolinguistic situations, attitudes, and structural effects: code-mixing has grown in importance, and indigenous vernacular norms in English have emerged and become popular. These local, emergent varieties have been rejected vigorously by the authorities, the official gatekeepers of linguistic propriety, but this opposition has not prevented them from spreading more widely. The authors' concluding assessment envisions their further growth in importance:

> These vernacular norms are not yet highly focussed; they are quite diffuse … Nevertheless, all linguistic history tells us that more focussed local vernacular norms will emerge through close daily interaction and similar processes … and that these will become the target varieties. (176–7)

In a nutshell, as it were, this illustrative case and the points made here exemplify some central aspects of the Dynamic Model.

One simple but strong conclusion to be drawn from the facts discussed in the earlier chapters is that the Dynamic Model works. Give or take adjustments required by differences in time and place, unique historical circumstances, and colonization types, its core ideas have been found to be applicable across many different countries, varieties, and contexts, all around the globe and through several centuries of colonial and post-colonial history. Granted, all kinds of sociolinguistic and structural differences between individual PCEs have also been observed, some more and others less substantial, and how much weight is attributed to these is a matter of assessment and purpose. The Dynamic Model highlights commonalities. As in any case of model-making, the emphasis is on shared attributes believed to be important, abstracting from a complex reality. It is remarkable, however, that these common, underlying traits do exist, contrary to expectation and irrespective of differences in external history and setting. Despite all abstraction and observable variations, the Dynamic Model is grounded in and grasps important facets of sociopsychological, sociolinguistic, and structural reality in language evolution.

Unavoidably, like all far-reaching claims, models, being abstractions, meet with certain difficulties when faced with the messy realities of real-life situations. This observation corresponds to Thomason's (2001) assessment concerning the generalizability of language contact typologies: they apply to a far-reaching extent and describe a wide range of cases, but there are typically also exceptions and idiosyncratic instances. The features listed in chapter 3, of the cycle's individual phases, clearly cannot be regarded as a checklist of "necessary and sufficient conditions," but they work well when interpreted as characteristic properties. It is useful to put such features together, even if in reality categories are frequently fudged. In individual cases not all features listed for a given phase were found to apply, though many of them typically did. We also encountered cases where features associated with subsequent phases coexisted, thus implying transition periods. New features and developments take time to develop and spread in a society, especially since populations are not internally homogeneous, and in all processes of change old phenomena lag behind with conservative subgroups. Some of the constituent elements of the five phases may evolve independently of each other and concurrently, so it is to be expected to find phases overlapping.

Of the various factors influencing the applicability of the model, two have been found to be particularly important and fundamental in the shaping of distinctively local circumstances.

One is demography, the relative proportion between STL and IDG (and in some cases also ADS) stream members who interact at any given point in time. Of course, this is also a dynamic relationship, changing in different phases of any country's history, and it tends to correlate strongly with colonization types as discussed in 3.3.5. A wide range of parameter settings has been observed, largely extending along a cline between two extreme points. On the one hand, for example in exploitation colonies in Africa and Asia, the STL strand was always limited in size and almost completely removed with independence; on the other, primarily in settlement colonies in North America and Australasia, the IDG strand was marginalized and almost excluded from serious participation in the process of carving out a new culture and language. In both types of cases, however, the entire range of contributing effects has always been present, and the roles of the erstwhile weaker one – supporting English in the former, indigenous languages in the latter – have actually been strengthened in the recent past, thus contributing to the characteristic linguistic hybridity of the outcome.

The other factor is a society's primary motivation for the use of English, the role which the language has assumed in a given community. As a tendency, its evolution has been most vigorous if it was adopted as a means of community solidarity. This process usually works subconsciously, and it entails covert prestige for indigenous varieties of English, typically even against the official promotion of a formal (and often external) norm. Alternatively, in many communities English has been adopted primarily for utilitarian motives, as a stepping stone toward economic prosperity and social advancement. In these cases the strive toward English tends to be relatively weaker (but persistent nevertheless), and more explicitly directed toward overt and officially promoted target norms.

Many other factors have been found to contribute to any particular evolutionary process and to direct its outcomes. Thus, bits and pieces of the components of the Dynamic Model may be missing in individual instances, or they may be realized with different degrees of intensity, or occur earlier or later than in the typical case. Nevertheless, the basic principles remain valid: human beings of different origins who stay together need to get along with each other, and therefore they will accommodate in the long run; and they are likely to give expression to this convergence by linguistic means.

One aspect of the Dynamic Model which is particularly noteworthy (and, I maintain, valuable) is the fact that it provides a coherent roof for different types of varieties, including native-language English, second-language usage, and English-lexifier pidgins and creoles. Traditionally, these language types have been viewed independently of each other. As was pointed out in chapter 3, the firm distinction between English on the one hand and pidgins and creoles on the other has been rejected by a few scholars in recent years, though in general it still dominates creole theory and is upheld by many creolists. The distinction between L1s and L2s is still generally accepted and has not been seriously challenged (unlike the native-speaker status on an idiolectal basis). I am not saying that these categories should be given up – they surface in the case studies above as well, in the form of internal modifications of the Dynamic Model, e.g. different weights of STL vs. IDG impact, respectively, different degrees of restructuring, and variation in the timing of the process of nativization. More importantly, however, this book has shown that these distinctions represent not independent categories but differences of degree only, and that the underlying force of identity-driven accommodation uniformly underlies all of these language types.

In a sense, insisting on this unity and equality is in line with efforts to view PCEs not as inferior deviations from an external norm but rather to promote them as language varieties on a par with the "major" national varieties of English. Hence, with others, I argue that "indigenized varieties ... are as legitimate offspring of English as the varieties said to be 'native' and ... spoken in former settlement colonies" (Mufwene 2004b:205). This position is also supported by the realities in many of the countries discussed earlier, where such distinctions are explicitly blurred. Nigeria is a case in point: in this country it would be futile to look for a clear boundary between English as an L1, as an L2, and Pidgin English (and also between Pidgin, as a second language, and Creole, when defined as a child's mother tongue or L1, for that matter).

Taken together, the case studies and applications have confirmed the relevance of the theoretical foundations outlined in chapter 3, the theories of identity, contact, and accommodation, and the validity of the associations between these theories which have been tied together. In line with recent sociolinguistic thinking, the evolution of PCEs has been portrayed as a function of sociopolitically driven identity reconstructions of all parties involved in a colonization process. It has thereby been regarded as a special type of contact-induced language change, closely related to and encompassing the genesis of pidgin and creole languages, from which it cannot be distinguished in principle (Thomason and Kaufman 1988; Thomason 2001; Neumann-Holzschuh and Schneider 2000; Mufwene 2001b). In a cline of increasing degrees of intensity of contact and increasingly far-reaching types of borrowing and restructuring, as postulated by Thomason and Kaufman (1988), PCEs therefore cover the range from language shift with moderate to heavy interference to pidginization/creolization. Finally, the progressively growing linguistic convergence between speakers in extended contact situations postulated by accommodation theory (Giles 1984; Thomason 2001:142–6; Trudgill 1986), initiated by cooperative speakers who gradually approximate each other's speech forms to be maximally successful in their communication and to gain each other's approval, has also been documented in the case studies. Given the above frameworks, I postulate that the study of PCEs can make important contributions to the theories of language variation and change. PCEs are "young" varieties, in many cases still caught in the middle of evolutionary, productive processes, so in-depth investigations of ongoing changes in these communities promise to yield fundamentally important insights.

In comparison with earlier models of PCEs as outlined in chapter 2, the Dynamic Model offers several innovative qualities and advantages. First, it is holistic in imposing an overarching and unifying perspective, as against the static and individualizing typologies of earlier approaches. It thus reinterprets isolated observations and case studies as situated in a coherent framework, relating them to each other and to relevant linguistic theories in a systematic fashion. Secondly, it adds an essential dynamic dimension to earlier static classifications, regarding differences between varieties of English as instantiations of characteristic phases of an under-lyingly uniform process. The postulation of this single evolutionary process underneath what we see emerging at various locations independently of each other all around the globe is a provocative, innovative assertion in itself. Thirdly, the model adopts the speech community rather than the nation-state as its sociolinguistic unit of description. By distinguishing between STL and IDG strands and by allowing for speech differences between ethnic, social and regional communities, it is thus descriptively more adequate and can be more finely tuned and adjusted than the ENL – ESL – EFL or Three Circles models, which overlook intra-national differentiation.

Fourthly, and perhaps most interestingly, to some extent the model implies predictive power – again, a strong claim but at the same time a most interesting quality required of good science. This implication seems natural at first sight: the claim that in a cyclic and dynamic model any entity has reached stage n almost automatically entails the assumption that at any future point in time it is likely to proceed to stage $n + 1$. However, Mufwene warns us that such an assumption would be misleading:

At least according to Stephen Jay Gould no theory of evolution is expected to be predictive, because there are so many variables to grasp. Theories of evolution are turned to the past, not the future. They cannot be predictive, to the extent that every new situation may highlight a factor that is more significant there than elsewhere. (p.c. 2005)

This ties in with the observations concerning the potential effects of "catastrophic" events redirecting the putatively "natural," expected course of history. The expectation of a quasi-linear linguistic evolution operates only under the default assumption that social history will hold no major surprises. As Thomason and Kaufmann stated, "the history of a language is a function of the history of its speakers" (1988:4; see also Thomason 2001:77), and the fate of humans, as individuals and as communities, can be anticipated with hope and expectation but is by its very nature ultimately unpredictable.

Furthermore, there is an aspect of the sequential linearity of the Dynamic Model that also has an immensely practical consequence to it, connecting the framework with applied linguistics, namely its association of norm questions with certain developmental stages. The claim that at a certain evolutionary stage a community is likely to switch from an exonormative to an endonormative orientation may have serious implications for future language and educational policies in many countries (and in others, which have moved beyond that point, the effects of this reorientation have shown in the recent past). If generally accepted, this sequentiality can contribute to the reconsideration and repositioning of postulated norms of correctness in the usage of English in different nations. Irrespective of a linguist's strive for descriptiveness, norms are required as guidelines in certain spheres of society, e.g. language teaching and formal public discourse, to name but two of the most important ones. But which linguistic norm to accept and adopt is a difficult decision and a painful process for many countries, also because issues of linguistic correctness not infrequently function as scapegoats to camouflage power relationships. It is important for a society to understand that linguistic norms are not absolute but rather, as the Dynamic Model implies, they change, and they vary from one context to another. Today's norms may not be tomorrow's usage any longer. It is absolutely necessary to develop some tolerance toward such changes – they are not "for the worse," as conservative language observers tend to suggest.

Also, an awareness is needed of the fact that within a society a variety of competing norm orientations is likely to exist, including the difference between a written standard and a spoken vernacular, and the competition between "overt" prestige and "covert" solidarity norms. While overt norms, usually proclaimed by authorized institutions, attract almost all the attention in public discourse, covert norms, which result from the implicit competition and selection processes which always take place during communicative acts of speakers, are in fact more powerful. In the long run, any speech community will and any society needs to define its own norms of acceptance, as the Dynamic Model implies in positing the ultimate victory of endonormative orientations.

One issue that is frequently raised by conservative forces as a counter-argument against proposals to adopt an endonormative orientation is the goal of achieving international intelligibility. This concern should not be underestimated: for the welfare of any nation it is important to train scientists and executives who are able to communicate in international settings. However, the argument should not be misused to conceal fundamentally conservative attitudes, behind which there may be lurking a desire not to question power inequalities in a society. In comparison, consider the fact that in ENL/"Inner Circle" countries so-called "intelligibility" is not normally adduced as an argument against local vernaculars. Nobody has ever accused a Yorkshire farmer, a Devon fisherman, or a Southern US cotton picker of speaking a variety that is not internationally intelligible (and this could certainly be stated about these dialects). I argue that their situation is not fundamentally different from that of a Singaporean hawker, an African taxi driver, or a rural Jamaican dweller. Whoever needs to be "internationally intelligible" (including these persons if their social contacts happen to shape up in such a way) is likely to acquire this skill before too long. Besides, it is only fair to require some effort to understand others also from British or American native speakers and from visitors to any society. Kembo Sure gets this idea to the point: "multiple standards of English around the world will not necessarily foster intercultural misunderstanding, but on the contrary, it would enhance mutual respect and increase intercultural interaction" (2004:101). Adjustment and accommodation will work here as well – human beings are remarkably adaptable. A situation in which a local variety is used to express local solidarity and a standard form, closer to international conventions, is preferred for formal situations and community – external contacts can be labeled "bidialectal diglossia." This is what can be found in many "Inner Circle" countries, and I argue that such code distributions are likely to emerge in PCEs as well. To quote Kembo Sure once again:

variations (lexical, semantic and discoursal) are not insuperable difficulties; with positive attitudes, encounter with those differences becomes only a challenge that is quickly overcome; they finally become such a small price to pay for cross-cultural tolerance and appreciation of differences. (2004:113)

This development corresponds with what Crystal has called the "centripetal and centrifugal forces" operating on English (2004:36). It also relates to the functionalization of sociostylistic distinctions: "the gap between standard and nonstandard Englishes is likely to widen, with both domains expressing distinct and complementary functions of intelligibility and identity respectively" (Crystal in Watts and Trudgill 2002:242). Clearly a common core of English, largely shared by educated speakers who operate in cross-regional and international contexts, is likely to prevail, with limited tolerable variation. This set of shared features will be found especially on the levels of grammar and, to some extent, lexis, and more explicitly in writing than in speech. Conversely, however, many studies, including the present one, have made it clear that some degree of fragmentation of English, the emergence of local vernaculars utilized to encode subtle social messages, is going on at the same time. The notion of English as a "glocal" language, a term borrowed from Pakir (1999) and a nice blend of the global and the local, encapsulates this process quite pointedly.

It should not, however, be forgotten that all of this is embedded in the context of bilingualism and multilingualism on a national and international scale. While the Dynamic Model entails that English is likely to evolve and expand along certain characteristic paths in societies where it has been implanted, it does not imply that English will be becoming the sole language, or even the main language, in any of the countries where the dynamic cycle is operating. The parameters of the model have been found to be working convincingly in bi- and multilingual societies (e.g. India, South Africa or Kenya), and in many instances it has been observed that nativized and localized forms of English coexist alongside indigenous languages. If that is the case both types of varieties can either share the functions of communicating within narrow social confines and of projecting group identities, or they can adopt complementary symbolic roles in a society. Not infrequently, in informal situations different linguistic choices, from localized forms of English to local languages, are available (Platt, Weber, and Ho 1984:146).

In fact, (local) English and indigenous languages may not only exist side by side but also get inherently intertwined, mixed up with each other. One of the most interesting, and perhaps most surprising, findings of the present survey has been the importance of language mixing, the widespread and firm grounding of mixed codes as positively evaluated expressions of hybrid identities. Some of these varieties have apparently crystallized and gained perceptual unity to the extent of having been given names (e.g. Taglish, Sheng, or Camfranglais); others thrive without such holistic conceptualization, as in Malaysia. All seem to be innovative and rather recent phenomena, having grown mainly among the young in multicultural, typically urban settings. These mixed codes are reminiscent of bilingual mixed languages described, for example, by Thomason (2001:196–221), which are also primarily carriers of hybrid identities. Thus, they should be an interesting and challenging object of future comparative investigations. It will be exciting to observe which cultural and linguistic manifestations of hybridity in culturally and linguistically complex settings will be generated in the future. Important as it may be, in many countries and communities English is but one player in a kaleidoscope of available choices for linguistic expression.

Overall, thus, the emergence of PCEs reflects a delicate balance between forces of divergence and forces of convergence which characterize both human interaction and language use in general, a balance which needs to be continuously readjusted. The crystallization of new varieties is here understood as ultimately a process of convergence, both social and linguistic. Viewed in this perspective, in a sense the core idea of the Dynamic Model is a deeply humane, if a little optimistic, motif: people who live together for good, will need to socialize and adjust to each other. Sadly enough, as reality keeps teaching us, this principle does not prevent misuse of power, inequality, hostility, and conflict, but it suggests (as perhaps the social history of modern societies over the last few centuries may imply) that improvement can be hoped for. On the other hand, the model also accounts for sociolinguistic fragmentation and the birth of new dialects. Fragmentation derives from restricted mutual interaction, either because of social detachment or because of demographic density. Perhaps there is a built-in limit to the size of human communities of whatever organizational structure: when they get too big to be surveyable, to be acceptable as a comforting social unit, then there is a tendency for them to break up into smaller, more manageable parties. In any case shared linguistic features and choices reflect social contact and collaboration; varying features and differences in usage signal distancing, lack of interaction, or social discontinuity. But as humans need social organization to survive and to feel comfortable, cooperative principles stand a good chance of winning out in the long run. This is what the Dynamic Model also entails: linguistic accommodation, as encoded in the emergence of PCEs, reflects regular interactions between human beings which are based on receptive attitudes toward each other. The glocalization of English will continue.

Notes

NOTES ON CHAPTER 1

1. A useful and concise timeline of the global spread of English is available in McArthur (2002:453–65) and in Hickey (2004b:621–6). The history of the British Empire is authoritatively discussed in Lloyd (1984). Rubal-Lopez (1996) provides a recent, statistically based documentation of the ongoing spread of English that also looks into causes of this process. The volume by Fishman, Conrad & Rubal-Lopez (1996) continues this saga in a most impressive fashion by tracing the fate, and in most cases the further expansion and growth, of English in many countries around and after the end of the colonial period.
2. In that respect it has clearly been informed and influenced by the uniformitarian hypothesis proposed in Mufwene (2001b) and expanded in Mufwene (2005a, 2005b).
3. I adopt a cyclic line of thinking that was suggested for the study of pidgin languages by Hall (1962) and later Mühlhäusler (1986), and applied to "New Englishes" originally by Moag (1992; first published in 1982).

NOTES ON CHAPTER 2

1. Gupta (1994) introduced the notion of "English as a Dominant Language" (EDL) to account for such situations.
2. In the framework suggested by Melchers & Shaw (2003:30), and with these authors, I would regard myself as a "liberal" by conviction.

NOTES ON CHAPTER 3

1. Of course, expressing one's identity is not the only factor which drives the selection of linguistic choices.
2. In later publications (e.g. 2004b) Mufwene emphasizes the distinction between plantation and non-plantation colonies more explicitly, and he also points out that plantation contexts in the Caribbean, in Melanesia and in Hawai'i were quite different from each other (2005a).
3. Trudgill (2004:28) points out that this principle of "talk-like-the-others-talk" represents the linguistic application of a more fundamental biological principle, a universal and presumably innate "tendency to 'behavioural co-ordination'."
4. In a postcolonial framework, this model can be regarded as a process of overcoming the "othering" which is typical of the colonization situation.

318

5. For an earlier, comparable model, similar in some respects though different in others and considerably more constrained in its applicability, see Moag (1992) in relationship to the situation in Fiji. Moag distinguishes four overlapping phases, called "transportation," "indigenization," "expansion in use and function," and "institutionalization," sometimes followed by a fifth phase, "restriction of use and function." Perhaps the most important difference between Moag's idea and the present model is that he believes that in the end English typically tends to revert to a foreign-language status. However, the alternative outcome of "English inexorably becoming a native language in some societies" is also envisioned as a possibility (247).

   Schmied (1991a:194–7) adjusts Moag's model to the African situation, suggesting (after "contact," "institutionalization" and "expansion") a decision stage, in which either "recognition" leads to "adoption" or "repression" results in "de-institutionalization." Schmied's model, which otherwise is not worked out in detail, is more closely related to the present one by suggesting that English may survive and that different speeds and stages can be observed in different nations (197).

   For similar adoptions of cyclic models to individual PCEs, see Chumbow & Simo Bobda (1996) with reference to Cameroon & Llamzon (1986) on the Philippines.

6. In this respect I am in line with postcolonial theory, which emphasizes the need to give the same dignity to the perspective of the original inhabitants of an area as to that of the dominant group (Loomba 1998): they need to be regarded as co-agents in a historical (and discursive) process.

7. Obviously, this is more characteristic of rural locations than of urban centers, especially new foundations. Also, the privilege of bestowing names upon natural phenomena is not a value-neutral linguistic process but an expression of power. It is interesting to note that after independence in some instances this former power was explicitly renounced and its reversal symbolized by removing colonial names and replacing them by indigenous ones. For example, in India, former *Bombay* became *Mumbai*, *Calcutta* was changed to *Kolkata*, and *Madras* was replaced by *Chennai*; in Malaysia, *Kota Kinabalu* was chosen over *Jesselton*; in Zimbabwe, *Salisbury* became *Harare*, and in South Africa, *Tshwane* is under discussion as a new name for *Pretoria*.

8. Interestingly enough, more than a millennium earlier we find the same pattern operating in a totally different colonization situation and culture but in much the same way, namely with respect to Celtic place names in Britain being taken over into the emerging Old English language of the Anglo-Saxon invaders who had come from the European continent (e.g. *Kent, York, Thames, Dover, Duncombe, Huntspill*) – with very few other linguistic traces of the pre-Germanic Celts left in English.

9. In addition, of course, each community creates and gives names of its own, after old and familiar places, striking landscape formations, noteworthy people, memorable incidents, and so on; see Mühlhäusler (2002).

10. Fauna and flora terms are more characteristic of settlement colonies, where the settlers are more directly exposed to nature, whereas in trade and exploitation colonies terms for local customs and culture, like kinds of food, are more readily integrated.

11. Cf. Gordon & Deverson (1998:108): "Emerging colonial accents were felt to be a threat to good English, and much fruitless effort was expended in attempting to eradicate them, in New Zealand and elsewhere."

12. Cf. Trudgill's statement: "the sorts of prescriptivists who write letters to the newspapers today are atypical, small in number and totally without influence" (2004:154).

13. For example, with respect to Nigerian English Jowitt (1991:107) explicitly observes that "it is not easy in many cases to decide whether a non-Standard form demands consideration under 'syntax and morphology' or under 'lexis'."

14. Compare, for example, the amount of integration and acceptance of their heritage of Maoris in New Zealand with that of the Natives (or "First Nations") in North America. In the latter case, the creation of reservations must have been an important ecological factor (Mufwene, p.c. 2005).

15. Literary creativity in new varieties of English is also listed as an element characteristic of what Moag (1992:241) calls "institutionalization." More extensive treatment of the topic is provided in Platt, Weber, & Ho (1984:ch. 11) and in Part IV of Kachru (1992). Kachru (1994:528–33) illustrates it with respect to South Asian English, and Görlach (1991b:22–3) discusses it as a feature of PCEs.

16. Trudgill also observes that "extreme ... uniformity appears to be quite typical of the initial stages of mixed, colonial varieties" (1986:145), citing Australia and Canada as examples.

17. See LePage & Tabouret-Keller: "within any society linguistic groupings will develop and focussing will take place within them which may well lead to stereotypes about language coming into being which become reified, institutionalized and totemized and again extraordinarily tenacious" (1985:249).

18. This is confirmed by Thomason's observation that "the linguistic predictions are the same for all instances of imperfect group learning of a TL [target language] regardless of whether or not actual shift has occurred" (2001:74).

19. These groups are to be distinguished from the (primarily English-speaking) indentured laborers of the earlier and middle colonial phases who came, for example, to North America and the Caribbean and became an important part of the founder population and the STL strand.

20. In the same vein, Winford (2003:256) places both intermediate and radical creoles and "highly indigenized" as well as "somewhat indigenized" varieties on a "continuum of outcomes of language shift." Mesthrie (1996) explicitly compares the features of South African Indian English to those of creoles, thus suggesting a relationship between the two categories.

21. See also Mufwene (2000a, 2001b). With respect to the Caribbean, the autonomy of creoles is frequently asserted (Winford 1991:569; Devonish 2003), but there are also more moderate voices. For example, Roberts (1988b) talks of "Creole English" rather than "English Creole" (50), and Winford (2000:217) holds that "there is a sense in which they [the so-called "intermediate" creoles] might be regarded as restructured versions of English, French, etc."

22. Postcolonial theory tends to view this involvement highly critically: "colonial regimes achieved domination through creating partial consent, or involving the colonized peoples in creating the states and regimes which oppressed them" (Loomba 1998:31).

23. A substrate hypothesis to account for the differentiation of the Romance languages was first proposed in the nineteenth century by Ascoli, and has been disputed ever since (Kontzi 1978).

24. For some earlier and recent statements of this analogy, see Burchfield (1985:160), McArthur (1998:187–8, 204), Crystal (2004:31–7) and, applying it to pidgins and creoles, Mufwene (2004b:212–5; 2005a:106–11) and Gilbert (2005:168). Joseph (2004:148) argues, for instance, that "the status of Hong Kong English today is somewhat comparable to that of 'bad Latin' in the later Middle Ages."

25. However, Herman (1996) observes "a sort of conscious consecration of the new linguistic situation" (378) roughly in the eighth century – a state which may roughly correspond to the recognition of an endonormative reality. Similarly, as Janson (1991) shows, a change of linguistic perception was accompanied by a change of metalinguistic awareness possibly triggered by specific political causes, with new names being chosen to differentiate the Romance vernaculars from Latin.

26. Scholarship has primarily been concerned with the issue of when, not why, Romance languages branched off from Vulgar Latin (see Kontzi 1978, a collection of classic articles; Wright 1991; Herman 1996).

NOTES ON CHAPTER 4

1. For the representation of vowels I am adopting the system of "lexical sets" developed by Wells (1982), so the words set in SMALL CAPITALS are meant to identify their nuclear vowel types.

2. Labov (2001) provides a thorough documentation of the social characteristics of individuals whom he has identified as "leaders of linguistic change."

3. This observation has an important pedagogical consequence as well: it implies that in addition to the putatively "correct" usage of a community there are usually also many other ways of expressing the same idea which to the insider may sound unusual, strange, even mistaken, and which are judged unacceptable – but without really being ungrammatical. The label of "insider," of course, sidesteps using the disputed term "native speaker" and leads us to the question of the "ownership" of World Englishes, frequently raised by Kachru (e.g. 1986) and others.

4. For example, the voiced palato-alveolar fricative /ʒ/, originally found only in French loan words, was readily adopted into the Early Modern English sound system because there was already another palato-alveolar fricative, voiceless /ʃ/, and all other fricatives also come in voiced–voiceless pairs.

5. To quote another example from the history of English: the loss of word-final-*e* in late Middle English entailed the disappearance of the marker of dative case in many nouns (e.g. *sone* 'son (dat.)' → *son*, homophonous with the nominative form), and this, in turn, strengthened the need to syntactically mark the beneficiary role by a construction with *to* (e.g. *to the son*).

6. A special, though highly controversial, application of this factor is Lass' (1987) notion of "swamping" which claims that south-eastern English forms tend to prevail.

NOTES ON CHAPTER 5

1. In this region, there is a strong demand for English in Japan, China, and other countries as well, and a lot has been written on pedagogical aspects and implications of the attraction that English holds in these Asian countries. However, so far in all these countries English remains a foreign language, no claims as to a change in status from EFL to ESL have been made, and English has not embarked on the process described in the Dynamic Model. It will be an interesting question for future research to observe if, and if so how and under which circumstances, a nation might move from an "Expanding Circle" to an "Outer Circle" status, though at present such a move, outside of a postcolonial history, seems highly unlikely.
2. The title of Tent (2000a) is potentially misleading here, but it refers to the collection of local lexis without implying work on a dictionary near at hand.
3. For a comprehensive survey of the growth and composition of Australia's population to the present day, see Leitner (2004a:45–86). In general, Leitner (2004a, 2004b) provides a rich discussion of the evolution, social setting, and properties of varieties of Australian English, mainly from a language-contact perspective.
4. There is an ongoing discussion on where and how Australian English origi- nated (in Britain or in the antipodes; if the former, in London or in East Anglia; for a summary, see Gordon et al. 2004:81–4); recent evidence strongly supports the local-origin hypothesis (Trudgill, p.c. 2005). The essential point in the present context, that mixing did occur, is uncontroversial (Kiesling 2004).
5. In the northern region, two creoles, Kriol and Broken, have developed. In the present context I am disregarding them, however, as their segregation, resulting in marked structural divergence, has caused a largely independent evolutionary process, with little interaction with the overall emergence of Australian English.
6. Currently Pam Peters and Peter Collins are preparing a monograph on gram- matical phenomena in Australian English for the *Varieties of English Around the World* book series.
7. See the project's website at http://www.abc.net.au/wordmap/ (accessed in April 2006).
8. This, obviously, is a general pattern, arguably corresponding to what Freud called the "narcissism of small differences": "members of a national commun- ity simultaneously construct the distinctions between themselves and other nations, most notably when the other nationality is believed to exhibit traits similar to those of one's own nationality" (Wodak et al. 1999:4). We will be encountering it again later, for instance when talking about Canadians' atti- tude toward the US.
9. These findings have also resulted in the rejection of earlier single-origin theo- ries which had assumed that New Zealand English was essentially a product of transported accents from Australia, or also from parts of southeastern England like London or East Anglia (Gordon et al. 2004:66–77, 219–35; Gordon & Trudgill 2004; Gordon & Sudbury 2002:79). Trudgill (2004) argues that this process must have happened "deterministically," i.e. that, given certain processes of dialect mixing, the output was fully dependent upon the

constituent factors of the contact situation. For an in-depth discussion of and a thorough reaction to the issues involved, see Mufwene (2006).

10. Of course, the fact should not be ignored that this leaves more than half of the population without a knowledge of English. Especially in the lower economic sectors substantial segments of society function wholly without English.

11. Thompson (2003) provides an extremely detailed and lively account not only of the activities of the Thomasites but also of the history and current language situation of the Philippines in general, focusing upon conditions of language use in specific situations (e.g. media consumption, religion, and interpersonal relations, both in urban areas and in rural regions) and upon the importance of language mixing in particular. For further historical surveys, see Sibayan & Gonzalez (1996) and Gonzalez (1997, 2004). It is noteworthy that the American strategy of "lifting" and educating as much of the population as was possible was quite the opposite of the usual British colonial procedure of training just a small elite to help them control the masses.

12. For surveys of the transportation of English to and the spread of the language in Malaysia, see Platt, Weber, & Ho (1983), Asmah (2000), Gill (2002a), and Nair-Venugopal (2000).

13. Today their descendants constitute about 30 percent and 10 percent of the population, respectively (Baskaran 2004a:1034).

14. The tensions can be sensed reading Gill (2002a), a book which strongly advocates upholding high standards of Malaysian English for the Malaysian business community and for the population at large.

15. I ventured to predict earlier, in a BBC interview now published in part in Elmes (2001:117), that in the long run Singapore might turn out to be a largely English-speaking country. It is also indicative that Foley (2001) promotes the use of first-language rather than second-language teaching methods for the teaching of English in Singapore, based on estimates that over 50 percent of all children start nursery school able to speak English (Gupta 1994).

16. It has also had the strange side effect that in Singapore's official political discourse English is not regarded as a "mother tongue" (this label being reserved for Asian languages) even if it is spoken natively by many Singaporeans, including the group called Eurasians. Wee (2002; 2004b:1019–21) shows how the notion of "mother tongue" in Singapore has been politicized as an element in a strategy of handling interethnic relations by the government – hence its paradoxical denial of such a status to Eurasians despite the fact that English is clearly both their first and their dominant, and in many cases their only, language. See Gupta (1999:116–7).

17. For a discussion of the situation in the Tamil community, see Saravanan (1994), esp. the figures on p. 177. For the Malay context, see Bibi (1994), also including some statistics showing a similar trend (211, 219). Gupta (1994 and p.c. 2002) suggests the Census results are actually misleading in that they under-report the spread of English as a second language in in-household interactions.

18. Some structures have been shown to be modeled strongly upon Chinese patterns (e.g. Alsagoff, Bao, & Wee 1998). However, Mufwene (p.c. 2006) suggests that due to a founder effect a strong Malay influence may have affected this variety.

19. In contrast, Ansaldo (2004) suggests that the seeds for the typological distinctiveness of colloquial Singaporean English were laid considerably earlier. He views it as "a language that has developed from 20th century colonial English restructured through contact with predominantly Trade (or Bazaar) Malay and Hokkien, and possibly Cantonese" (145). Winford (2003:245–7) classifies Singapore Colloquial English as a fossilized interlanguage, with a Chinese substratum.

20. Wee (1998) and Tan (2001) provide systematic surveys of the processes effective in the nativization of the lexis of Singaporean English.

21. This paraphrases a statement by a business executive in a TV interview that I heard.

22. Brutt-Griffler (2002:39–48) shows that this policy was far from an attempt at imposing English as an imperial language upon Indians; quite to the contrary, its intention was to contain access to the language within a rigid class stratification, employed to the advantage of British administrative and economic needs.

23. Verma (1982) actually uses "Swadeshi English" as an idiosyncratic synonym for "Indian English."

24. Krishnaswamy & Burde actually doubt whether such a national identity really exists. In their view, "one is a Bengali or Punjabi or Tamilian while in India; only when one goes outside India, he/she becomes an 'Indian' because the outside world and the passport say so. No one in India feels he/she is an Indian . . . the notion 'nation-India' is insecure" (1998:63).

25. For useful general surveys of the history of English in South Africa, see Lanham (1982, 1996), Branford (1994), Mesthrie (2002d), Kamwangamalu (2002b), and Lass (2004).

26. In comparison, it is estimated that almost all Indians and 83 percent of Afrikaners spoke English late in the twentieth century (Lanham 1982:338).

27. For white SAfE, see Bowerman (2004a, 2004b), Lass (2004:374–82); for Cape Flats English, see Malan (1996), Finn (2004), McCormick (2004) and, on Afrikaans English, Watermeyer (1996); for Indian English, see Mesthrie (1992, 1996, 2004b, 2004c); and for black SAfE see Gough (1996:59–65), de Klerk & Gough (2002:360–5), van Rooy (2004), and Mesthrie (2004a).

28. According to the 1996 Census the proportion of English first-language speakers amongst black South Africans is 0.4 percent (Gordon & Sudbury 2002:73).

29. For surveys of the history of English in Kenya, and East Africa in general, see Hancock & Angogo (1982), Schmied (1991a, 2004b), Mazrui & Mazrui (1996), Skandera (2003), Mwangi (2003), and Michieka (2005).

30. Many of them came from South Africa after the troubled years of the Boer Wars, a fact which explains "a more or less discernible substratum of South African English phonology" in East African English (Hancock & Angogo 1982:312).

31. Actually, there were also substantial numbers of non-British European immigrants, but their impact on the overall language evolution is negligible. Also, thousands of Indians came, mainly to work on the construction of the railways. Their descendants have maintained a strong degree of cultural and ethnolinguistic integrity, and they speak a recognizable variety of English. They

constitute an ADS group with a certain degree of distinctiveness, but due to restricted numbers they have never been linguistically influential.

32. The history, status and properties of English in Tanzania are covered extensively in Schmied (1985, 1991a, 2004b), Abdulaziz (1991), Kanyoro (1991), Yahya-Othman & Batibo (1996), and Mafu (2003).

33. By 1910 the number of mission schools in Yorubaland alone was 129, though the north, being Muslim territory, was much slower in that respect, with the first one, in Kano, founded as late as in 1909 (Jibril 1982:74).

34. For in-depth accounts of Nigerian English and its history, see Jowitt (1991), Bokamba (1991), Bamgbose (1992, 1996), Gut (2004), and Alo & Mesthrie (2004). Primary sources on Nigerian Pidgin include Egbokhare (3003), Faraclas (2004), Elugbe (2004), and Deuber (2005).

35. Mufwene (2004b:211) points out that in Africa cities functioned much like sugar cane and rice plantations in Atlantic and Indian Ocean plantation colonies, generating ethnolinguistically heterogeneous contact settings and thus contributing to the obliteration of ethnic boundaries and the loss of ethnic languages.

36. In Nigeria, the year 1947 is also associated with the foundation of the All-Nigeria Legislative Assembly, which increased contacts between the north and the south (Gut 2004:818).

37. It is also noteworthy that in this quotation Nigerian Pidgin is explicitly classified as an indigenous African language. A good reason for this is that it evolved from the earlier, non-scholastic introduction of nonstandard English to West Africa, it indigenized earlier, and it is more deeply entrenched in the population than Nigerian English is (Mufwene, p.c. 2006).

38. The phonology of Nigerian English and Pidgin is described in Todd (1982b), Jowitt (1991), Jibril (1991), Gut (2004, 2005), and Elugbe (2004). For discussions of grammatical phenomena, see Jibril (1982), Jowitt (1991); Bokamba (1991, 1992), Banjo (1997), Alo and Mesthrie (2004), Faraclas (2004); for further lexical documentation, see Jibril (1982), Todd (1982b), Jowitt (1991), Bokamba (1991).

39. For surveys of the linguistic history of Cameroon, see Todd (1982a), Chumbow & Simo Bobda (1996), Wolf (2001) and Menang (2004).

40. "The Catholics opened English schools in every village, as one Basel missionary put it, and the Basel mission had to accommodate to the popularity of this language" (Wolf 2001:91).

41. Wolf (2001) provides a detailed discussion of the political background and likely causes behind this decision and of its consequences in the early years of a united country. The outcome of the plebiscite was probably determined by the force of the "Kamerun Idea" of a uniform nation imbued by the Germans, by discontent with the situation in Nigeria, and by UN measures (100).

42. To an outside observer, the formal uses of the terms "Anglophone," "Francophone" and "bilingual" in the Cameroonian context are stunning, because they slight the indigenous languages and the fact that of course the vast majority of the population is primarily "Afrophone." Given the high degree of multilingualism and the linguistic fragmentation of the country, however, indigenous languages are weak, both as regional lingua francas and, even more so, in the political arena. If nothing else, the terms are

indicative of the deep cultural and linguistic penetration of Cameroon by its former colonial powers.

43. See Todd (1982a:15–17, 1982b:288–289); Chumbow & Simo Bobda (1996:420–423), Schröder (2003:55–56); Ayafor (2004).

44. Just as a tiny indicator, I was surprised to find that the form to apply for a visitor's visa distributed by the Cameroonian embassy in Germany is in French only, not in English. On the other hand, it is repeatedly stated (Yaoundé, p. c. May 2006) that francophones increasingly seek an anglo-phone education for their children to improve their employability and to make closer connections with the international world of business, science, and technology possible – a trend which, if it stabilizes on a broader basis, may have important consequences for the future make-up of the country's linguistic landscape.

45. The most comprehensive discussion of the history of Bajan to date can be found in Winford (2000). Other useful sources include LePage and Tabouret-Keller (1985:36–45), Roy (1986), Roberts (1988b), Holm (1986, 1994), Rickford & Handler (1994), Blake (2002, 2004), and Hickey (2004).

46. Legally, slaves were emancipated in 1834 but forced into a so-called "inden-tured apprenticeship" which was discontinued in 1838.

47. Roberts (1998a:27) quotes an early 19th century statement which projects identities of that period as genuinely and exclusively Barbadian, marked by pride in the island and epitomized in the "common expression, 'neither Charib nor Creole, but true Barbadian' " or the "adage 'What would poor old England do, were Barbados to forsake her?'." Interestingly enough, the author adds: "The pride attaching to this sentiment . . . has diffused itself even to the negroes, who now loudly echo the boastful term, – "me Badian!"

48. Alleyne (1980) states that "Bajan is a regional nonstandard variety of English" (182), and Winford (2000) classifies it as an "intermediate" creole. Schneider (1990), investigating the possible "semi-creole" status of a number of Caribbean varieties on a comparative basis, concludes that on account of its features it "deserves to be called a creole" (104). See also Roberts (1988:111); Winford (1991:569); Blake (2004:501); Hickey (2004:334–6).

49. http://barbados.allinfoabout.com/literature.html, accessed 16 March, 2006.

50. The linguistic and social history of Jamaica is documented and discussed authoritatively by Lalla & D'Costa (1990), backed by their accompanying text collection (D'Costa & Lalla 1989). Other useful sources include Cassidy (1961; with a focus on lexis), Alleyne (1988, also 1980), Roberts (1988), Holm (1994), Winford (1997b), Christie (2003), and Patrick (2004).

51. For an authoritative description of the phonologies of both Jamaican English and Jamaican Creole, see Devonish & Harry (2004); other sources include Alleyne (1980, emphasizing African continuities), Cassidy (1961:26–48), Lawton (1982:255–8), Lalla & D'Costa (1990:47–67, aiming at a diachronic reconstruction), and Christie (2003:14–5). The grammar of Jamaican Creole is surveyed in Patrick (2004), Cassidy (1961:49–73), Bailey (1966) and Christie (2003:30–3).

52. Sources: Cassidy (1961); Cassidy & LePage (1980); LePage & Tabouret-Keller (1985:20); Alleyne (1988:145); Christie (2003:8–10).

53. A new Caribbean Examinations Council, set up after independence and authorized to make decisions in 1979, promoted Caribbean contents in exams but has upheld the linguistic target model of British Standard English (Sand 1999:71; LePage & Tabouret-Keller 1985:69).

54. In Creole studies a lively debate has been going on how to best model this situation, with the traditional model of a one-dimensional "post-creole continuum" as first submitted by DeCamp (1971) increasingly being challenged. LePage & Tabouret-Keller (1985) suggested an influential multidimensional model, assuming that speakers actively manipulate choices as determined by a complex array of factors. Winford (1997b) opted for a "co-existent systems" approach, i.e. he views the situation as diglossic, with the mesolect to be accounted for as essentially a mixture between the two distinct (though idealized) systems at the end points of the cline (see also Devonish & Harry 2004; Alleyne 1988:137). In contrast, Patrick (1999, 2004) analyzes the mesolect as a system in its own right and upholds a moderate version of the continuum model. For our present context this theoretical issue is of secondary importance only.

55. Internet radio makes it possible for me to listen to precisely such a program on a station called Power 106 FM while I am writing this from afar, in Germany; and I suppose with a little patience a reader with online access should be able to verify this statement and tune in to Jamaican sounds.

56. Devonish's discussion includes a linguistically interesting elaboration on the issue of regarding Jamaican Creole as a separate language. He shows that for the initiative to politically succeed it is necessary to assert its status as a language, a position with which he strongly sympathizes anyhow. However, the author also knows and makes it clear that the entire issue is futile: as a linguistic expert he "had earlier declared that it was not possible, on linguistic grounds, to assign languagehood to any language variety" (2003:174).

57. My selective survey of Canada's linguistic history is indebted to Avis (1973), Bailey (1982), Chambers (1991, 1993, 1997, 1998a, 2004b), Mackey (1998), Brinton & Fee (2001), and Boberg (2004a).

58. Bailey states: "Since modern Canadians discern the virtues of probity and patriotism in these Loyalists, there is a tendency to overestimate their numbers and influence" (1982:140; see also 142).

59. Prior to the British period, the profitable fur trade had caused the most intensive contacts between trappers and natives. The French had maintained even more intensive ties with the IDG population, including attempts not only to proselytize them but even to Gallicize them to a certain extent. Adjustment operated the other way around as well: it was reported that it was not uncommon for French youths to live with the natives, learn their languages, act as cultural and commercial go-betweens, and become wealthy pelt traders (Mackey 1998:16).

60. A minority view on the origins of Canadian English, voiced primarily by M.H. Scargill, holds that the impact of Loyalists seems to have been exaggerated and that of the British immigrants of that period must have been greater than is traditionally assumed, simply due to their large numbers (see Boberg 2004a:354).

61. As Barber (2001) has observed most pointedly, this attitude marks the "tortured" Canadian psyche to the present day: "one thing that unites almost all Canadians is the desire to show to the world that they are most emphatically *not Americans!*" (293).

62. For the time being, however, this process excluded two areas with a long-standing "national consciousness" (Chambers 1991:89) of their own, namely Quebec, separated by its French heritage and orientation, and Newfoundland, which joined the Canadian Federation in 1949.

63. Again, this excludes the historically distinct pockets of Newfoundland and Quebec, and sometimes also the maritime provinces where the greater historical depth and localised settlement patterns have left some regional distinctness.

64. When I spent an extended period of time with a group of French Canadians a few years ago, I was struck by the fact that the majority knew little or no English at all.

NOTES ON CHAPTER 6

1. Whether postcolonial theories and perspectives can be applied to the history of North America as well is disputed (Loomba 1998:19).

2. Algeo (2001a) is the most useful discussion of America's settlement history with an eye to linguistic consequences. Other important sources include Mencken (1963), Krapp (1925), Pyles (1952), McDavid (1958), Conklin & Lourie (1983), and Wolfram & Schilling-Estes (1998).

3. David Ramsay, London, in 1791; quoted in Read (1933:46).

4. This is commemorated in American folk lore most clearly in the story of Pocahontas, the daughter of Powhatan, the chief who controlled Chesapeake Bay when English colonists of the Virginia Company landed and built James Fort, later Jamestown. That Pocahontas saved the colonists from starving to death during their first winter and that she actually married a colonist later seem to be historically authentic incidents, for all we know, and they may be indicative of the relationships between Europeans and Natives in the beginning – as are reports of skirmishes with local tribes (Nichols 2003:44–5).

5. For example, Mencken (1963:645) quotes the towns *Anasagunticook, Mattawamkeag, Oquossoc,* and *Wytopitlock* and the lakes of *Unsuntabunt* and *Mattagomosis* in Maine.

6. James Adams, 1799; quoted from Read (2002:56).

7. In 1764–65 Lord Adam Jones, a traveler from Scotland, noted that Boston "is more like an English Old Town than any in America, – the Language and manner of the people, very much resemble the old Country, and all the Neighbouring lands and Villages, carry with them the same Idea" (quoted in Read 1933:44).

8. A well-known and illustrative case in point from the eighteenth century is the converted Native American Samson Occom (1723–92), who combined missionary activity, including teaching and writing, with advocacy for Native rights. In the early nineteenth century the continuation of such a pattern is exemplified by the work and writings of William Apess (1798–1839).

9. In the same vein, Cassidy & Hall (2001:188) observe: "The American colonists a generation or two later [after Shakespeare], especially their leaders, tacitly

acknowledged the prestige of standard English centered in London." For similar statements, see Krapp (1925, II:31), Pyles (1952:57), Conklin & Lourie (1983:76), and Wolfram & Schilling-Estes (1998:206).

10. Statements similar to the ones on colonial uniformity can be found for that period as well, e.g. "extensive as the country is, one uniform correctness obtains in speaking the English language" (Horton James, 1847; quoted from Read 2002:64). In fact, the koinéization process was perceived as recent by James Fenimore Cooper: "The distinctions in speech between New England and New York, or Pennsylvania, or any other State . . . were far greater twenty years ago than they are now" (1828; quoted Krapp 1925, I:14)

11. Even earlier records of individual words used by Native Americans (though not yet to be classified as loans) can be found in Thomas Harriot's *A Briefe and True Report of the New Found Land of Virginia* of 1588, as well as in some Spanish explorers' texts, e.g. by Cabeza de Vaca.

12. From an article in the *Annual Review*, 1808; quoted from Read (2002:60).

13. Initiating the Revolution, this is the date which I choose to represent the onset of phase 3. Possible alternatives would be the Great Awakening of the 1750s and 1760s, the end of the French and Indian War, in 1763, or the Boston Massacre of 1770.

14. American writing of the 1780s and 1790s eulogized this attitude as the "glorious contrast."

15. See Fisher (2001:67) or Pyles (1952:73): "To many, however, 'pure English' continued to mean simply British English."

16. See Mencken (1963:148): "From 1814 to 1861 the influence of the great open spaces was immediate and enormous, and during those gay and hopeful and melodramatic days all the traditional characteristics of American English were developed – its disdain of all scholastic rules and precedents, its tendency toward bold and often bizarre tropes, its rough humors . . . its love of neologisms for their own sake" (148).

17. It is noteworthy in the present context that the equivalence between what here is called the IDG and ADS strands is seen also by McDavid: "Each of the foreign languages brought to the United States by immigrants, and even each of the surviving American Indian languages, has its own peculiar history in this generally one-sided history of conflict between languages" (1958:528).

18. Noah Webster, 1789, quoted in Wolfram & Schilling-Estes (1998:18). I take this phase to have started in the East in the year which marks both Jackson's election and the publication of Webster's *Dictionary*, and in the West with the California gold rush, and to have lasted until the Spanish-American War, when the US hits the world scene. Alternative beginning and end dates in this case would be the War of 1812–15, introducing the period of national stability, and the Civil War of 1861–5, which threatened that stability.

19. Read (2002:19) believes that until Mencken many Americans "still felt inferior to Englishmen in their language."

20. For a first-hand illustration and reflection of these issues, see the autobiographic writings by Getrude Bonnin/Zitkala Sha (her self-adopted Lakota name; 1876–1938).

21. Charles Bristed, American *littérateur*, 1855; quoted in Read (2002:75); for further documentation, see Pyles (1952:73, 97), Mencken (1963:408–13), or Fisher (2001:66–7).

22. Hayes Alan Locklear, Lumbee artist, quoted from Wolfram et al. (2002:1)

23. An unexpected and interesting example is the case of Dalton, Georgia, where in recent years large numbers of Spanish-speaking in-migrants have been attracted by jobs offered in the local carpet industry. Their linguistic accommodation is being investigated by Ellen Johnson.

24. Quoted from Krapp (1925, I:46). Interestingly, Krapp, lacking modern sociolinguistic insights, rejects Sweet's view, confidently postulating the British-only origin of dialect diversity in American English.

25. Malancon & Malancon (1977) discuss the educational policies employed and some linguistic features documented at one of these boarding schools. In some respects, these off-reservation institutions are reminiscent of missionary schools and interethnic educational institutions in other emerging PCEs, e.g. in Malaysia, and they may have had similar effects, spreading proficiency in English and unifying some varietal choices.

26. Mufwene (p.c. 2005) points out that unlike African-Americans they have never integrated among themselves as a non-English group, and he hypothesizes that unless such an integration process is going on now their linguistic assimilation will be similar to that of European Americans.

27. Vietnamese English has also found an interesting literary representation in William Hart's novel *Never Fade Away* (2002).

References

Abdulaziz, Mohamed M. H. 1991. "East Africa (Tanzania and Kenya)." In Cheshire, ed. 1991: 391–401.

Adegbite, Wale. 2004. "Enlightenment and attitudes of the Nigerian elite on the roles of languages in Nigeria." In Muthwii & Kioko, eds. 2004: 89–100.

Agheyisi, Rebecca N. 1988. "The standardization of Nigerian Pidgin English." *English World-Wide* 9: 227–41.

Aitchison, Jean. 1991. *Language Change: Progress or Decay?* Cambridge: Cambridge University Press. 2nd edn.

Algeo, John. 1989. "Queuing and other idiosyncracies." *World Englishes* 8: 157–63.

Algeo, John, ed. 2001a. *The Cambridge History of the English Language*. Vol. VI: *English in North America*. Cambridge: Cambridge University Press.

Algeo, John. 2001b. "External history." In Algeo, ed. 2001a: 1–58.

Alo, M. A., and Rajend Mesthrie. 2004. "Nigerian English: morphology and syntax." In Kortmann et al., eds. 2004: 813–27.

Alleyne, Mervyn C. 1980. *Comparative Afro-American. An Historical–Comparative Study of English-Based Afro-American Dialects of the New World*. Ann Arbor: Karoma.

1988. *Roots of Jamaican Culture*. London: Pluto.

Allsopp, Richard, ed. 1996. *Dictionary of Caribbean English Usage*. Oxford: Oxford University Press.

Alsagoff, Lubna. 2001. "Tense and aspect in Singapore English." In Ooi, ed. 2001: 79–88.

Alsagoff, Lubna, and Ho Chee Lick. 1998a. "The grammar of Singapore English." In Foley et al., 1998: 127–51.

1998b. "The relative clause in colloquial Singapore English." *World Englishes* 17: 127–38.

Alsagoff, Lubna, Bao Zhiming and Lionel Wee. 1998. "Why you talk like that?: the pragmatics of a why construction in Singapore English." *English World-Wide* 19: 247–60.

Ansaldo, Umberto. 2004. "The evolution of Singapore English. Finding the matrix." In Lim, ed. 2004: 127–49.

Anvil-Macquarie Dictionary of Philippine English for High School. 2000. Pasig City: Anvil Publishing.

Arends, Jacques, 1993. "Towards a gradualist model of creolization." In Francis Byrne & John Holm, eds. *Atlantic Meets Pacific*. Amsterdam, Philadelphia: Benjamins, 371–80.

Arends, Jacques, Pieter Muysken, and Norval Smith, eds. 1995. *Pidgins and Creoles: An Introduction*. Amsterdam, Philadelphia: Benjamins.

Ashcroft, Bill, Gareth Griffiths, and Helen Tiffin. 2002. *The Empire Writes Back*. 2nd edn London: Routledge.

Asmah, Haji Omar. 1996. "Post-imperial English in Malaysia." In Fishman et al., eds. 1996: 513–55.

    2000. "From imperialism to Malaysianization: a discussion of the path taken by English towards becoming a Malaysian language." In Halimah & Ng, eds. 2000: 12–21.

Australian Government Publishing Service. 1988. *Style Manual for Authors, Editors and Printers*. 4th edn Canberra: AGPS.

Avis, Walter S. 1973. "The English language in Canada." In Thomas A. Sebeok, ed. *Current Trends in Linguistics*. Vol. X: *Linguistics in North America*. The Hague: Mouton, 40–74.

Avis, Walter S., Patrick D. Drysdale, Robert J. Gregg, Victoria E. Neufeldt, and Matthew H. Scargill. 1967. *A Dictionary of Canadian English on Historical Principles*. Toronto: Gage.

Ayafor, Miriam. 2004. "Cameroon Pidgin English (Kamtok): morphology and syntax." In Kortmann et al., eds. 2004: 909–28.

Bailey, Beryl Loftman. 1966. *Jamaican Creole Syntax: A Transformational Approach*. Cambridge: Cambridge University Press.

Bailey, Charles-James. 1974. *Variation and Linguistic Theory*. Arlington, VA: Center for Appled Linguistics.

Bailey, Guy. 1997. "When did Southern English begin?" In Schneider, ed. 1997, I: 255–75.

Bailey, Guy, and Natalie Maynor. 1987. "Decreolization?" *Language in Society* 16, 449–73.

    1989. "The divergence controversy." *American Speech* 64: 12–39.

Bailey, Richard W. 1982. "The English language in Canada." In Bailey & Görlach, eds. 1982: 134–76.

    1996. "Attitudes toward English: the future of English in South Asia." In Baumgardner, ed. 1996: 40–52.

    2004. "American English: its origins and history." In Finegan & Rickford, eds. 2004: 3–17.

    2006. "Standardizing the Heartland." In Murray & Simon, eds. 2006: 165–78.

Bailey, Richard W., and Manfred Görlach, eds. 1982. *English as a World Language*. Ann Arbor: University of Michigan Press.

Baker, Philip. 2000. "Theories of creolization and the degree and nature of restructuring." In Neumann-Holzschuh & Schneider, eds. 2000: 41–63.

Baker, Sidney J. 1978. *The Australian Language*. 3rd edn Milson's Point, NSW: Currawong Press.

Baldauf, Scott. 2004. "A Hindi-English jumble, spoken by 350 million." *The Christian Science Monitor*, Nov. 23. csmonitor.com/2004/1123/p01s03-wosc.html.

Bamgbose, Ayo. 1992. "Standard Nigerian English: Issues of identification." In Kachru, ed. 1992: 148–61.

    1996. "Post-imperial English in Nigeria 1940–1990." In Fishman et al., eds. 1996: 357–72.

Banjo, Ayo. 1997. "Aspects of the syntax of Nigerian English." In Schneider, ed. 1997, II: 85–95.

Bao, Zhiming. 1998. "The sounds of Singapore English." In Foley et al., 1998: 152–74.

Bao, Zhiming, and Hong Huaqing. 2006. "Diglossia and register variation in Singapore English." *World Englishes* 25: 105–14.

Bao, Zhiming, and Lionel Wee. 1998. "*Until* in Singapore English." *World Englishes* 17: 31–41.

1999. "The passive in Singapore English." *World Englishes* 18: 1–11.

Barber, Katherine. 2001. "Neither Uncle Sam nor John Bull: Canadian English comes of age." In Moore, ed. 2001c: 284–96.

Bartelt, H. Guillermo, Susan Penfield-Jasper and Baters Hoffer, eds. 1982. *Essays in Native American English*. San Antonio: Trinity University Press.

Baskaran, Loga. 2004a. "Malaysian English: morphology and syntax." In Kortmann et al., eds. 2004: 1073–85.

2004b. "Malaysian English: phonology." In Schneider et al., eds. 2004: 1034–46.

Baskaran, Loga Mahesan. 2005. *A Malaysian English Primer. Aspects of Malaysian English Features*. Kuala Lumpur: University of Malaya Press.

Bauer, Laurie. 1994. "English in New Zealand." In Burchfield, ed. 1994: 382–429.

1997. "Attempting to trace Scottish influence on New Zealand English." In Schneider, ed. 1997, II: 257–72.

2002. *An Introduction to International Varieties of English*. Edinburgh: Edinburgh University Press.

Bauer, Laurie, and Winifred Bauer. 2002. "Can we watch regional dialects developing in colonial English? The case of New Zealand." *English World-Wide* 23: 169–93.

Bauer, Laurie, and Paul Warren. 2004. "New Zealand English: phonology." In Schneider et al., eds. 2004: 580–602.

Baumgardner, Robert J., ed. 1996. *South Asian English. Structure, Use, and Users*. Urbana, Chicago: University of Illinois Press.

Baumgardner, Robert J. 1998. "Word-formation in Pakistani English." *English World-Wide* 19: 205–46.

Bautista, Maria Lourdes S., ed. 1997a. *English Is an Asian Language: The Philippine Context. Proceedings of the Conference Held in Manila on August 2–3, 1996*. Sydney: Macquarie Library Ltd.

Bautista, Maria Lourdes S. 1997b. "The lexicon of Philippine English." In Bautista, ed. 1997: 49–72.

2000. "The grammatical features of educated Philippine English." In Bautista, Llamzon, & Sibayan, eds. 2000: 146–58.

Bautista, Maria Lourdes S., and Kingsley Bolton, eds. 2004. "Philippine English: tensions and transitions." Special Issue of *World Englishes* 23: 1.

Bautista, Maria Lourdes S., Teodoro A. Llamzon, and Bonifacio P. Sibayan, eds. 2000. *Parangal cang Brother Andrew. Festschrift for Andrew Gonzalez on His Sixtieth Birthday*. Manila: Linguistic Society of the Philippines.

Bayley, Robert, and Otto Santa Ana. 2004. "Chicano English: morphology and syntax." In Kortmann et al., eds. 2004: 374–90.

Bell, Allan. 2000. "Maori and Pakeha English: a case study." In Bell & Kuiper, eds. 2000: 221–48.

Bell, Allan, and Janet Holmes. 1991. "New Zealand." In Cheshire, ed. 1991: 153–68.
Bell, Allan, and Janet Holmes, eds. 1990. *New Zealand Ways of Speaking English.* Clevedon, Philadelphia: Multilingual Matters.
Bell, Allan, and Koenraad Kuiper, eds. 2000. *New Zealand English.* Amsterdam, Philadelphia: Benjamins.
Benson, Phil. 2000. "Hong Kong words: variation and context." In Bolton, ed., 2000a: 373–80.
Bernstein, Cynthia. 2006. "Drawing out the /ai/: dialect boundaries and /ai/ variation." In Murray & Simon, eds. 2006: 209–32.
Berry, John. 1998. "Official multiculturalism." In Edwards, ed. 1998: 84–101.
Bhatt, Rakesh M. 2004. "Indian English: syntax." In Kortmann et al., eds. 2004: 1016–30.
Biber, Douglas, Stig Johansson, Geoffrey Leech, Susan Conrad, and Edward Finegan. 1999. *Longman Grammar of Spoken and Written English.* Harlow: Longman.
Bibi Jan Mohd Ayyub. 1994. "Language issues in the Malay community." In Gopinathan et al., eds. 1994: 205–30.
Bickerton, Derek. 1981. *Roots of Language.* Ann Arbor: Karoma.
Biermeier, Thomas. 2007. "Word formation in New Englishes." PhD dissertation, University of Regensburg.
Blair, David, and Peter Collins, eds. 2001. *English in Australia.* Amsterdam, Philadelphia: Benjamins.
Blake, Renée. 2002. "Not as clear as black and white: a study of race, class and language in a Barbados community." Unpubl. ms., New York University.
   2004. "Bajan: phonology." In Schneider et al., eds. 2004: 501–7.
Blevins, Juliette. 2006. "New perspectives on English sound patterns: 'natural' and 'unnatural' in evolutionary phonology." *Journal of English Linguistics* 34: 6–25.
Boberg, Charles. 2004a. "English in Canada: phonology." In Schneider et al., eds. 2004: 351–65.
   2004b. "The dialect topography of Montreal." *English World-Wide* 25: 171–98.
Bokamba, Eyamba G. 1991. "West Africa." In Cheshire, ed. 1991: 493–508.
   1992. "The Africanization of English." In Kachru, ed. 1992: 125–47.
Bolton, Kingsley, ed. 2000a. *Hong Kong English: Autonomy and Creativity.* Special Issue of *World Englishes* 19:3. Published as a book 2002, Aberdeen: Hong Kong University Press.
Bolton, Kingsley. 2000b. "Hong Kong English, Philippine English, and the future of Asian Englishes." In Bautista, Llamzon, & Sibayan, eds. 2000: 93–114.
   2000c. "The sociolinguistics of Hong Kong English and the space for Hong Kong English." In Bolton, ed. 2000a: 265–85.
   2003. *Chinese Englishes. A Sociolinguistic History.* Cambridge: Cambridge University Press.
Bolton, Kingsley, and Susan Butler. 2004. "Dictionaries and the stratification of vocabulary: towards a new lexicography for Philippine English." In Bautista & Bolton, eds. 2004: 91–112.
Bolton, Kingsley, and Braj B. Kachru, eds. 2006. *World Englishes.* 6 vols. Oxford, New York: Routledge.

Bolton, Kingsley, and Shirley Lim. 2000. "Futures for Hong Kong English." In Bolton, ed. 2000a: 429–43.

Bowerman, Sean. 2004a. "White South African English: morphology and syntax." In Kortmann et al., eds. 2004: 948–61.

2004b. "White South African English: phonology." In Schneider et al., eds. 2004: 931–42.

Bradley, David. 1989. "Regional dialects in Australian English phonology." In Collins & Blair, eds. 1989: 260–70.

2004. "Regional characteristics of Australian English: phonology." In Schneider et al., eds. 2004: 645–55.

Bradley, David, and Maya Bradley. 2001. "Changing attitudes to Australian English." In Blair & Collins, eds. 2001: 271–85.

Branford, William. 1994. "South African English." In Burchfield, ed. 1994: 430–96.

1996. "English in South Africa: a preliminary overview." In de Klerk, ed. 1996: 35–51.

Branford, Jean, with William Branford. 1991. *A Dictionary of South African English.* Cape Town: Oxford University Press.

Brinton, Laurel J., and Margery Fee. 2001. "Canadian English." In Algeo, ed. 2001a: 422–40.

Brutt-Griffler, Janina. 2002. *World English. A Study of its Development.* Clevedon: Multilingual Matters.

Bryant, Pauline. 1989. "Regional variation in the Australian English lexicon." In Collins & Blair, eds. 1989: 301–14.

1997. "A dialect survey of the lexicon of Australian English." *English World-Wide* 18: 211–41.

Burchfield, Robert. 1985. *The English Language.* Oxford: Oxford University Press.

Burchfield, Robert, ed. 1994. *The Cambridge History of the English Language.* Vol. V. *English in Britain and Overseas: Origins and Development.* Cambridge: Cambridge University Press.

Buregeya, Alfred. 2006. "Grammatical features of Kenyan English and the extent of their acceptability." *English World-Wide* 27: 199–216.

Burrowes, Audrey. 1983. "Barbadian Creole: its social history and structure." In Carrington, ed. 1983: 38–45.

Butler, Susan, 1997. "Corpus of English in Southeast Asia: implications for a regional dictionary." In Bautista, ed. 1997: 103–24.

Butters, Ronald R. 2001. "Grammatical structure." In Algeo, ed. 2001a: 325–39.

Carrington, Lawrence, ed. 1983. *Studies in Caribbean Language.* St. Augustine: Society for Caribbean Linguistics.

Carver, Craig. 1987. *American Regional Dialects: A Word Geography.* Ann Arbor: University of Michigan Press.

Cassidy, Frederic G. 1961. *Jamaica Talk. Three Hundred Years of the English Language in Jamaica.* London: Macmillan.

1980. "The place of Gullah." *American Speech* 55: 3–16.

1986. "Barbadian Creole – possibility and probability." *American Speech* 61: 195–205.

Cassidy, Frederic G. and Joan Houston Hall. 2001. "*Americanisms.*" In Algeo, ed. 2001a: 184–218.

Cassidy, Frederic G., and Robert B. LePage. 1980. *Dictionary of Jamaican English.* [1st edn 1967.] Cambridge: Cambridge University Press.

Chambers, J. K. 1991. "Canada." In Cheshire, ed. 1991: 89–107.

1993. "'Lawless and vulgar innovations': Victorian views of Canadian English." In Clarke, ed. 1993: 1–26.

1997. "The development of Canadian English." *Moderna Språk* 91: 3–15. Quoted from Bolton & Kachru, eds. 2006, Vol. I: 383–95.

1998a. "English: Canadian varieties." In Edwards, ed. 1998: 252–72.

1998b. "Social embedding of changes in progress." *Journal of English Linguistics* 26: 5–36.

1999. "Converging features in the Englishes of North America." *Cuadernos de Filología Inglesa* 8: 117–27.

2003. *Sociolinguistic Theory.* 2nd edn Malden, MA, Oxford: Blackwell.

2004a. "'Canadian dainty': the rise and fall of Briticisms in Canada." In Hickey, ed. 2004b: 224–41.

2004b. "Dynamic typology and vernacular universals." In Bernd Kortmann, ed. 2004. *Dialectology Meets Typology.* Berlin, New York: Mouton, 127–45.

Chambers, J. K., and Peter Trudgill. 1998. *Dialectology.* 2nd edn Cambridge: Cambridge University Press.

Chambers, J. K., Peter Trudgill, and Natalie Schilling-Estes, eds. 2002. *The Handbook of Language Variation and Change.* Malden, MA, Oxford: Blackwell.

Chaudenson, Robert. 2001. *Creolization of Language and Culture.* Revised in collaboration with Salikoko S. Mufwene. London, New York: Routledge.

Cheshire, Jenny, ed. 1991. *English around the World. Sociolinguistic Perspectives.* Cambridge: Cambridge University Press.

Chng, Huang Hoon. 2003. "'You see me no up': Is Singlish a problem?" *Language Problems and Language Planning* 27: 45–62.

Christie, Pauline. 2003. *Language in Jamaica.* Kingston: Arawak.

Chumbow, Beban Sammy, and Augustin Simo Bobda. 1996. "The life cycle of post-imperial English in Cameroon." In Fishman et al., eds. 1996: 401–29.

Clarke, Sandra, ed. 1993. *Focus on Canada.* Amsterdam, Philadelphia: Benjamins.

Clyne, Michael. 2003. *Dynamics of Language Contact. English and Immigrant Languages.* Cambridge: Cambridge University Press.

Clyne, Michael, Edna Eisikovits, and Laura Tollfree. 2000. "Ethnic varieties of Australian English." In Blair & Collins, eds. 2000: 223–38.

Coetzee-van Rooy, Susan, and Bertus van Rooy. 2005. "South African English: labels, comprehensibility, and status." *World Englishes* 24: 1–19.

Collins, Peter C. 2005. "The modals of necessity and obligation in Australian English and other Englishes." *English World-Wide* 26: 249–73.

Collins, Peter, and David Blair, eds. 1989. *Australian English: The Language of a New Society.* St. Lucia, Queensland: University of Queensland Press.

Collins, Peter, and David Blair. 2001. "Language and identity in Australia." In Blair & Collins, eds. 2001: 1–13.

Collins, Peter, and Pam Peters. 2004. "Australian English: morphology and syntax." In Kortmann et al., eds. 2004: 593–610.

Conklin, Nancy Faires, and Margaret A. Lourie. 1983. *A Host of Tongues. Language Communities in the United States.* New York: Free Press, Macmillan.

Conrad, Andrew W. 1996. "The international role of English: the state of the discussion." In Fishman et al., eds. 1996: 13–36.

Craig, Beth. 1991. "American Indian English." *English World-Wide* 12: 25–61.

Croft, William. 2000. *Explaining Language Change. An Evolutionary Approach.* Harlow: Pearson.

Crystal, David. 1997. *English as a Global Language.* Cambridge: Cambridge University Press.

2004. *The Language Revolution.* Cambridge, Malden: Polity Press.

Cukor-Avila, Patricia, 2001. "Co-existing grammars: the relationship between the evolution of African American and White Vernacular English in the South." In Lanehart, ed. 2001: 93–127.

Dako, Kari. 2001. "Ghanaianisms: towards a semantic and formal classification." *English World-Wide* 22: 23–53.

David, Maya Khemlani. 2000. "The language of Malaysian youth – an exploratory study." In Halimah & Ng, eds. 2000: 64–72.

Davis, Lawrence M. 1983. *English Dialectology: An Introduction.* Tuscaloosa, AL: University of Alabama Press.

Dayag, Danilo T., and J. Stephen Quakenbush, eds. 2005. *Linguistics and Language Education in the Philippines and Beyond. A Festschrift in Honor of Ma. Lourdes S. Bautista.* Manila: Linguistic Society of the Philippines.

D'Costa, Jean, and Barbara Lalla, eds. 1989.*Voices in Exile. Jamaican Texts of the 18th and 19th Centuries.* Tuscaloosa: University of Alabama Press.

DeGraff, Michel. 2003. "Against creole exceptionalism." *Language* 79: 391–410.

de Klerk, Vivian, ed. 1996. *Focus on South Africa.* Amsterdam, Philadelphia: Benjamins.

de Klerk, Vivian. 1997. "Encounters with English over three generations in a Xhosa family: for better or for worse?" In Schneider, ed. 1997, II: 97–118.

1999. "Black South African English: where to from here?" *World Englishes* 18: 311–24.

2003. "Towards a norm in South African Englishes: the case for Xhosa English." *World Englishes* 22: 463–81.

2005. "Expressing levels of intensity in Xhosa English." *English World-Wide* 26: 77–95.

de Klerk, Vivan, and Gary P. Barkhuizen. 1998. "English in the South African defence force: a case study of 6SAI." *English World-Wide* 19: 33–60.

de Klerk, Vivian, and David Gough. 2002. "Black South African English." In Mesthrie, ed. 2002c: 356–78.

DeCamp, David. 1971. "Toward a generative analysis of a post-creole speech continuum." In Dell Hymes, ed. *Pidginization and Creolization of Languages.* Bloomington, London: Indiana University Press, 349–70.

Delbridge, Arthur. 2001. "Lexicography and national identity: the Australian experience." In Blair & Collins, eds. 2001: 303–16.

Delbridge, Arthur, John R. L. Bernard, David Blair, William S. Ramson, and Susan Butler. 1981. *The Macquarie Dictionary.* Sydney: Macquarie Library.

Deterding, David. 2005. "Emergent patterns in the vowels of Singapore English." *English World-Wide* 26: 179–97.

338   References

Deuber, Dagmar. 2002. "'First year of nation's return to government of make you talk your own make I talk my own': Anglicisms versus pidginization in news translations into Nigerian Pidgin." *English World-Wide* 23: 195–222.

2005. *Nigerian Pidgin in Lagos. Language Contact, Variation and Change in an African Urban Setting.* London: Battlebridge.

Devonish, Hubert. 1983. "Towards the establishment of an Institute for Creole Language Standardisation and Development in the Caribbean." In Carrington, ed. 1983: 300–16.

1986. "The decay of neo-colonial official language policies. The case of the English-lexicon creoles of the Commonwealth Caribbean." In Görlach & Holm, eds. 1986: 23–51.

2003. "Language advocacy and 'conquest' diglossia in the 'Anglophone' Caribbean." In Mair, ed. 2003: 157–77.

Devonish, Hubert, and Otelemate Harry. 2004. "Jamaican Creole and Jamaican English: phonology." In Schneider et al., eds. 2004: 450–80.

Dillard, Joey L. 1972. *Black English. Its History and Usage in the United States.* New York: Random House.

1975. *All-American English: A History of the English Language in America.* New York: Random House.

Dubois, Sylvie, and Barbara M. Horvath. "Cajun Vernacular English: phonology." In Schneider et al., eds. 2004: 407–16.

Edwards, John, ed. 1998. *Language in Canada.* Cambridge: Cambridge University Press.

Eckert, Penelope. 2000. *Linguistic Variation as Social Practice. The Linguistic Construction of Identity in Belten High.* Malden, MA, Oxford: Blackwell.

Egbe, Daniel. 1996. "Semantics and the question of competence in English." *Lagos Notes and Records* 7: 115–26.

Egbokhare, Francis O. 2003. "The story of a language: Nigerian Pidgin in spatiotemporal, social and linguistic context." In Lucko et al., eds. 2003: 21–40.

Elmes, Simon. 2001. *The Routes of English 4.* London: BBC Adult Learning.

Elugbe, Ben. 2004. "Nigerian Pidgin English: phonology." In Schneider et al., eds. 2004: 831–41.

Evans, Betsy E., Rika Ito, Jamila Jones and Dennis R. Preston. 2006. "How to get to be one kind of Midwesterner: accommodation to the Northern Cities Shift." In Murray & Simon, eds. 2006: 179–97.

Evans, Stephen. 2000. "Hong Kong's new English language policy in education." *World Englishes* 19: 185–204.

Faraclas, Nicholas. 1991. "The pronoun system of Nigerian Pidgin: a preliminary study." In Cheshire, ed. 1991: 509–18.

2004. "Nigerian Pidgin English: morphology and syntax." In Kortmann et al., eds. 2004: 828–53.

Faraclas, Nicholas, Lourdes Gonzalez, Migdalia Medina and Wendell Villanueva Reyes. 2006. "Ritualized insults and the African diaspora: *Sounding* in African American Vernacular English and *Wording* in Nigerian Pidgin." In Mühleisen and Migge, eds. 2006: 45–72.

Ferguson, Charles A. 1996. "English in South Asia: imperialist legacy and regional asset." In Baumgardner, ed. 1996: 29–39.

Fields, Linda. 1995. "Early Bajan: creole or non-creole?" In Arends, ed. 1995: 89–111.

Finegan, Edward, and John R. Rickford, eds. 2004. *Language in the USA. Themes for the Twenty-first Century*. Cambridge: Cambridge University Press.

Finn, Peter. 2004. "Cape Flats English: phonology." In Schneider et al., eds. 2004: 964–84.

Fischer, David Hackett. 1989. *Albion's Seed: Four British Folkways in America*. Oxford, New York: Oxford University Press.

Fisher, John Hurt. 2001. "British and American, continuity and divergence." In Algeo, ed. 2001a: 59–85.

Fishman, Joshua A. 1972. *The Sociology of Language. An Interdisciplinary Social Science Approach to Language in Society*. Rowley, MA: Newbury House.

Fishman, Joshua A., Andrew W. Conrad and Alma Rubal-Lopez, eds. 1996. *Post-Imperial English: Status Change in Former British and American Colonies 1940–1990*. Berlin, New York: Mouton de Gruyter.

Foley, Joseph A. 1998. "Code-switching and learning among young children in Singapore." *International Journal of the Sociology of Language* 130: 129–50.

2001. "Is English a first or second language in Singapore?" In Ooi, ed. 2001: 12–32.

Foley, Joseph, ed. 1988. *New Englishes. The Case of Singapore*. Singapore: Singapore University Press.

Foley, Joseph A., et al. 1998. *English in New Cultural Contexts: Reflections from Singapore*. Oxford, Singapore: Oxford University Press.

Fought, Carmen. 2003. *Chicano English in Context*. Houndmills, New York: Palgrave Macmillan.

Francis, W. Nelson. 1983. *Dialectology: An Introduction*. New York: Longman.

Gargesh, Ravinder. 2004. "Indian English: phonology." In Schneider et al., eds. 2004: 992–1002.

Gerritsen, Marinel, and Dieter Stein, eds. 1992. *Internal and External Factors in Syntactic Change*. Berlin, New York: Mouton de Gruyter.

Gilbert, Glenn. 2005. "The Journal of Pidgin and Creole Languages and the Society for Pidgin and Creole Linguistics, in retrospect." *Journal of Pidgin and Creole Languages* 20: 167–74.

Giles, Howard. 1984. *The Dynamics of Speech Accommodation*. (International Journal of the Sociology of Language 46.) Berlin, New York: Mouton de Gruyter.

Gill, Saran Kaur. 1999. "Standards and linguistic realities of English in the Malaysian workplace." *World Englishes* 18: 215–31.

2002a. *International Communication: English Language Challenges for Malaysia*. Serdang: Universiti Putra Malaysia.

2002b. "Language policy and English language standards in Malaysia: nationalism versus pragmatism." *Journal of Asia-Pacific Communication* 12,1: 95–115.

Gisborne, Nikolas. 2000. "Relative clauses in Hong Kong English." In Bolton, ed. 2000a: 357–71.

Goebl, Hans, Peter H. Nelde, Zdenek Starý, and Wolfgang Wölck, eds. 1996/97. *Kontaktlinguistik/Contact Linguistics/Linguistique de contact. An International Handbook of Contemporary Research.* 2 vols. Berlin, New York: de Gruyter.

Goldberg, Adele E. 1995. *Constructions: A Construction Grammar Approach to Argument Structure.* Chicago: University of Chicago Press.

Gonzales, Andrew. 1982. "English in the Philippines." In Pride, ed. 1982: 211–26.

1983. "When does an error become a feature of Philippine English?" In Noss, ed. 1983: 150–72.

1997. "The history of English in the Philippines." In Bautista, ed. 1997: 25–40.

2004. "The social dimension of Philippine English." In Bautista & Bolton, eds. 2004: 7–16.

2005. "Distinctive grammatical features of Philippine literature in English: influencing or influenced?" In Dayag & Quakenbush, eds. 2005: 15–26.

Gopinathan, S., Anne Pakir, Ho Wah Kam, and Vanithamani Saravanan, eds. 1994. *Language, Society and Education in Singapore: Issues and Trends.* Singapore: Times Academic Press.

Gordon, Elizabeth. 1998. "The origins of New Zealand speech: the limits of recovering historical information from written records." *English World-Wide* 19: 61–85.

Gordon, Elizabeth, and Marcia Abell. 1990. "'This objectionable colonial dialect': historical and contemporary attitudes to New Zealand speech." In Bell & Holmes, eds. 1990: 21–48.

Gordon, Elizabeth, and Tony Deverson. 1998. *New Zealand English and English in New Zealand.* Auckland: New House.

Gordon, Elizabeth, and Margaret Maclagan. 2004. "Regional and social differences in New Zealand: phonology." In Schneider et al., eds. 2004: 603–13.

Gordon, Elizabeth, and Andrea Sudbury. 2002. "The history of southern hemisphere Englishes." In Watts & Trudgill, eds. 2002: 67–86.

Gordon, Elizabeth, and Peter Trudgill. 1999. "Shades of things to come: Embryonic variants in New Zealand English." *English World-Wide* 20: 111–24.

2004. "English input to New Zealand." In Hickey, ed. 2004b: 440–55.

Gordon, Elizabeth, Lyle Campbell, Jennifer Hay, Margaret Maclagan, Andrea Sudbury, and Peter Trudgill. 2004. *New Zealand English: Its Origins and Evolution.* Cambridge: Cambridge University Press.

Gordon, Matthew J. 2001. *Small-Town Values and Big-City Vowels: A Study of the Northern Cities Shift in Michigan.* Raleigh, NC: Duke University Press for the American Dialect Society.

2004. "New York, Philadelphia, and other northern cities: phonology." In Schneider et al., eds. 2004: 282–99.

Görlach, Manfred. 1991a. "Colonial lag? The alleged conservative character of American English and other 'colonial' varieties." In M. Görlach, *Englishes.* Amsterdam, Philadelphia: Benjamins, 90–107.

1991b. "English as a world language – the state of the art." In M. Görlach, *Englishes.* Amsterdam, Philadelphia: Benjamins, 10–35.

1995a. "Dictionaries of transplanted Englishes." In M. Görlach, *More Englishes.* Amsterdam, Philadelphia: Benjamins, 124–63.

1995b. "Word-formation and the ENL: ESL: EFL distinction." In M. Görlach, *More Englishes*. Amsterdam, Philadelphia: Benjamins, 61–92.

1998. "Recent dictionaries of varieties of English." In M. Görlach, *Even More Englishes*. Amsterdam, Philadelphia: Benjamins, 152–86.

Görlach, Manfred, and John A. Holm, eds. 1986. *Focus on the Caribbean*. Amsterdam, Philadelphia: Benjamins.

Gough, David. 1996. "Black English in South Africa." In de Klerk, ed. 1996: 53–77.

Green, Lisa J. 2002. *African American English. A Linguistic Introduction*. Cambridge: Cambridge University Press.

Greenbaum, Sidney, ed. 1996a. *Comparing English Worldwide. The International Corpus of English*. Oxford: Clarendon.

Greenbaum, Sidney. 1996b. "Introducing ICE." In Greenbaum, ed. 1996a: 3–12.

Grolier International Dictionary. World English in an Asian Context. 2000. Macquarie University, NSW: The Macquarie Library.

Gumperz, John J., ed. 1982. *Language and Social Identity*. Cambridge: Cambridge University Press.

Gumperz, John J., and Jenny Cook-Gumperz, 1982. "Introduction: language and the communication of social identity." In Gumperz, ed. 1982: 1–21.

Gupta, Anthea Fraser. 1988. "A standard for written Singapore English?" In Foley, ed. 1988: 27–50.

1994. *The Step-Tongue: Children's English in Singapore*. Clevedon: Multilingual Matters.

1996. "English and empire: teaching English in nineteenth-century India." In Neil Mercer and Joan Swann, eds. *Learning English: Development and Diversity*. London, New York: Open University, 188–94.

1997. "Colonisation, migration, and functions of English." In Schneider, ed. 1997, I: 47–58.

1999. "The situation of English in Singapore." In Foley et al., eds. 1999: 106–26. Repr. in Bolton & Kachru, eds. 2006, vol. II: 369–89.

Gupta, R. S. 2001. "English in post-colonial India. An appraisal." In Moore, ed. 2001c: 148–64.

Gut, Ulrike. 2004. "Nigerian English: phonology." In Schneider et al., eds. 2004: 813–30.

2005. "Nigerian English prosody." *English World-Wide* 26: 153–77.

Guy, Gregory R. 1991. "Australia." In Cheshire, ed. 1991: 213–26.

Halimah, Mohd Said and Ng Keat Siew, eds. 2000. *English Is An Asian Language: The Malaysian Context*. Kuala Lumpur: Persatuan Bahasa Moden Malaysia and Sydney: Macquarie Library.

Hall, Robert A. 1962. "The life cycle of pidgin languages." *Lingua* 11: 151–6.

Hancock, Ian F. 1980. "Gullah and Barbadian – origins and relationships." *American Speech* 55: 17–35.

Hancock, Ian F., and Rachel Angogo. 1982. "English in East Africa." In Bailey and Görlach, eds. 1982: 306–23.

Hart, William. 2002. *Never Fade Away*. Santa Barbara: Fithian Press.

Hazen, Kirk. 2002. "Identity and language variation in a rural community." *Language* 78: 240–57.

Heine, Bernd, and Tania Kuteva. 2005. *Language Contact and Grammatical Change*. Cambridge: Cambridge University Press.

Herman, Jószef. 1996. "The end of the history of Latin." *Romance Philology* 49: 364–82.

Hickey, Raymond. 2004a. "English dialect input to the Caribbean." In Hickey, ed. 2004b: 326–59.

Hickey, Raymond, ed. 2004b. *Legacies of Colonial English: Studies in Transported Dialects*. Cambridge: Cambridge University Press.

Hock, Hans Henrich and Brian D. Joseph. 1996. *Language History, Language Change, and Language Relationship. An Introduction to Historical and Comparative Linguistics*. Berlin, New York: Mouton de Gruyter.

Holm, John. 1986. "The spread of English in the Caribbean area." In Görlach & Holm, eds. 1986: 1–22.

1988/89. *Pidgins and Creoles*. Vol. I: *Theory and Structure*. Vol. II: *Reference Survey*. Cambridge: Cambridge University Press.

1994. "English in the Caribbean". In Burchfield, ed. 1994: 328–81.

2004. *Languages in Contact. The Partial Restructuring of Vernaculars*. Cambridge: Cambridge University Press.

Hopper, Paul J., and Elizabeth Closs Traugott. 1993. *Grammaticalization*. Cambridge: Cambridge University Press.

Horvath, Barbara M. 1985. *Variation in Australian English: The Sociolects of Sydney*. Cambridge: Cambridge University Press.

2004. "Australian English: phonology." In Schneider et al., eds. 2004: 625–44.

Horvath, Barbara M. and Ronald J. Horvath. 1997. "The geolinguistics of a sound change in progress: /l/ vocalization in Australia." In Miriam Meyerhoff, Charles Boberg, and Stephanie Strassel, eds. *Working Papers in Linguistics: A Selection of Papers from NWAVE 25*. Philadelphia: University of Pennsylvania, 105–24.

2001. "The geolinguistics of short a in Australian English." In Blair & Collins, eds. 2001: 341–56.

Huber, Magnus. 1999. *Ghanaian Pidgin English in its West African Context*. Amsterdam, Philadelphia: Benjamins.

Hung, Tony T. N. 2000. "Towards a phonology of Hong Kong English". In Bolton, ed. 2000a: 337–56.

Hundt, Marianne, 1998. *New Zealand English Grammar: Fact or Fiction? A Corpus-based Study in Morphosyntactic Variation*. Amsterdam, Philadelphia: Benjamins.

Hundt, Marianne, Jennifer Hay, and Elizabeth Gordon. 2004. "New Zealand English: morphosyntax." In Kortmann et al., eds. 2004: 560–92.

Hyland, Ken. 1997. "Language attitudes at the handover: communication and identity in 1997 Hong Kong." *English World-Wide* 18: 191–210.

Igboanusi, Herbert. 2002. *A Dictionary of Nigerian English Usage*. Ibadan: Enicrownfit.

Janson, Tore. 1991. "Language change and metalinguistic change: Latin to Romance and other cases." In Wright, ed. 1991: 19–28.

Jauncey, Dorothy. 2004. *South Australian Words. From Bardi-Grubs to Frog Cakes*. South Melbourne: Oxford University Press.

Jeffery, Chris, and Bertus van Rooy. 2004. "Emphasizer *now* in colloquial South African English." *World Englishes* 23: 269–80.

Jenkins, Richard. 1996. *Social Identity*. London: Routledge.

Jernudd, Björn. 2003. "Development of national language and mangement of English in East and Southeast Asia." In Humphrey Tonkin and Timothy Regan, eds., *Language in the 21st Century*. Amsterdam, Philadelphia: Benjamins, 59–66.

Jibril, Munzali. 1982. "Nigerian English: an introduction." In Pride, ed. 1982: 73–84.

1991. "The sociolinguistics of prepositional usage in Nigerian English." In Cheshire, ed. 1991: 519–37.

Joseph, John E. 2004. *Language and Identity. National, Ethnic, Religious*. Houndmills: Palgrave Macmillan.

Jowitt, David. 1991. *Nigerian English Usage. An Introduction*. Ikeja: Longman Nigeria.

Kachru, Braj B. 1983. *The Indianization of English. The English Language in India*. Delhi, Oxford: Oxford University Press.

1985. "Standards, codification and sociolinguistic realism: the English language in the outer circle." In Randolph Quirk and Henry G. Widdowson, eds. *English in the World: Teaching and Learning the Language and Literatures*. Cambridge: Cambridge University Press & The British Council, 11–30.

1986. *The Alchemy of English: The Spread, Functions, and Models of Non-native Englishes*. Urbana, Chicago: University of Illinois Press.

Kachru, Braj B., ed. 1992. *The Other Tongue: English across Cultures*. 2nd edn Urbana, Chicago: University of Illinois Press.

Kachru, Braj B. 1994. "English in South Asia." In Burchfield, ed. 1994: 497–553.

1997. "English as an Asian language." In Bautista, ed. 1997: 1–23.

Kamwangamalu, Nkonko M., ed. 2000. *Language and Ethnicity in the New South Africa*. (IJSL 144) Berlin, New York: Mouton de Gruyter.

2002a. "English in South Africa: at the millennium: challenges and prospects." *World Englishes* 21: 161–3.

2002b. "The social history of English in South Africa." *World Englishes* 21: 1–8.

2003. "When $2 + 9 = 1$: English and the politics of language planning in a multi-lingual society: South Africa." In Mair, ed. 2003: 235–46.

Kanyoro, Musimbi R. A. 1991. "The politics of the English language in Kenya and Tanzania." In Cheshire, ed. 1991: 402–19.

Karstadt, Angela. 2003. *Tracking Swedish-American English. A Longitudinal Study of Linguistic Variation and Identity*. Uppsala: Uppsala University Library.

Keller, Rudolf. 1994. *On Language Change. The Invisible Hand in Language*. London: Routledge.

Kembo Sure. 1991. "Language functions and language attitudes in Kenya." *English World-Wide* 12: 245–60.

2003. "The democratization of language policy. A cultural linguistic analysis of the status of English in Kenya." In Mair, ed. 2003: 247–65.

2004. "Establishing a national standard and English language curriculum change in Kenya." In Muthwii & Kioko, eds. 2004: 101–15.

Kerswill, Paul, and Ann Williams. 2000. "Creating a new town koiné: children and language change in Milton Keynes." *Language in Society* 29: 65–115.

Kiesling, Scott. 2004. "English input to Australia." In Hickey, ed. 2004b: 418–39.
    2005. "Variation, stance, and style. Word-final -er, high rising tone, and ethnicity in Australian English." *English World-Wide* 26: 1–42.
Kioko, Angelina Nduku, and Margaret Jepkirui Muthwii. 2004. "English variety for the public domain in Kenya: speakers' attitudes and views." In Muthwii & Kioko, eds. 2004: 34–49.
Kontzi, Reinhold, ed. 1978. *Zur Entstehung der romanischen Sprachen*. Darmstadt: Wissenschaftliche Buchgemeinschaft.
Kortmann, Bernd, and Benedikt Szmrecsanyi. 2004. "Global synopsis: morphological and syntactic variation in English." In Kortmann et al., eds. 2004: 1142–202.
Kortmann, Bernd, Kate Burridge, Rajend Mesthrie, Edgar W. Schneider and Clive Upton, eds. 2004. *A Handbook of Varieties of English*. Vol. II: *Morphology and Syntax*. Berlin, New York: Mouton de Gruyter.
Kouega, Jean-Paul. 2002. "Uses of English in Southern British Cameroons." *English World-Wide* 23: 93–113.
Krapp, George P. 1925. *The English Language in America*. 2 vols. New York: Century.
Kretzschmar, William. 2004. "Standard American English pronunciation." In Schneider et al., eds. 2004: 257–69.
Krishnamurti, Bh. 1990. "The regional language vis-à-vis English as the medium of instruction in higher education: the Indian dilemma." In Debi Prasanna Pattanayak, ed. *Multilingualism in India*. Clevedon: Multilingual Matters, 15–24.
Krishnaswamy, N., and Archana S. Burde. 1998. *The Politics of Indians' English. Linguistic Colonialism and the Expanding English Empire*. Delhi: Oxford University Press.
Kroskrity, Paul V. 2001. "Identity." In Alessandro Duranti, ed. *Key Terms in Language and Culture*. Malden, MA, Oxford: Blackwell, 106–9.
Kuiper, Koenraad, and Allan Bell. 2000. "New Zealand and New Zealand English." In Bell & Kuiper, eds. 2000: 11–22.
Kurath, Hans. 1965. "Some aspects of Atlantic seaboard English considered in their connections with British English." In *Communications et Rapports du Premier Congrès de Dialectologie Generale, Troisième Partie*. Louvain: Centre Internationale de Dialectologie Génèrale, 236–40.
Labov, William. 1966. *The Social Stratification of English in New York City*. 3rd printing 1982. Washington, DC: Center for Applied Linguistics.
    1972. *Sociolinguistic Patterns*. Oxford: Blackwell.
    1994. *Principles of Linguistic Change*. Vol. I: *Internal Factors*. Cambridge, MA, Oxford: Blackwell.
    1998. "Co-existent systems in African-American vernacular English." In Mufwene et al., eds. 1998: 110–53.
    2001. *Principles of Linguistic Change*. Vol. II: *Social Factors*. Malden, MA, Oxford: Blackwell.
Labov, William, Sharon Ash and Charles Boberg. 2006. *The Atlas of North American English. Phonetics, Phonology and Sound Change*. Berlin, New York: Mouton de Gruyter.

Lalla, Barbara. 2005. "Creole and respec' in the development of Jamaican literary discourse." *Journal of Pidgin and Creole Languages* 20: 53–84.

Lalla, Barbara, and Jean D'Costa. 1990. *Language in Exile. Three Hundred Years of Jamaican Creole.* Tuscaloosa, London: University of Alabama Press.

Lanehart, Sonja, ed. 2001. *Sociocultural and Historical Contexts of African American English.* Amsterdam, Philadelphia: Benjamins.

Lanham, L. W. 1982. "English in South Africa." In Bailey & Görlach, eds. 1982: 324–52.

  1996. "A history of English in South Africa." In de Klerk, ed. 1996: 19–34.

Lass, Roger. 1987. "Where do extraterritorial Englishes come from? Dialect input and recodification in tranported Englishes." In Sylvia Adamson et al., eds. *Papers from the Fifth International Conference on English Historical Linguistics.* Amsterdam, Philadelphia: Benjamins, 245–80.

  1990. "How to do things with junk: exaptation in language evolution." *Journal of Linguistics* 26: 79–102.

  2004. "South African English." In Hickey, ed. 2004b: 363–86.

Lawton, David L. 1982. "English in the Caribbean." In Bailey & Görlach eds. 1982: 251–80.

Leap, William L. 1993. *American Indian English.* Salt Lake City: University of Utah Press.

Leap, William L., ed. 1977. *Studies in Southwestern Indian English.* San Antonio: Trinity University.

Leitner, Gerhard. 2004a. *Australia's Many Voices. Australian English – The National Language.* Berlin, New York: Mouton de Gruyter.

  2004b. *Australia's Many Voices. Ethnic Englishes, Indigenous and Migrant Languages. Policy and Education.* Berlin, New York: Mouton de Gruyter.

LePage, Robert B., and Andrée Tabouret-Keller. 1985. *Acts of Identity: Creole-based Approaches to Language and Ethnicity.* Cambridge: Cambridge University Press.

Li, David C. S. 1999. "The functions and status of English in Hong Kong: a post-1997 update." *English World-Wide* 20: 67–110.

Lim, Choon Yeoh, and Lionel Wee. 2001. "Reduplication in Singapore English." In Ooi, ed. 2001: 89–101.

Lim, Lisa. 2001. "Ethnic group varieties of Singapore English: melody or harmony?" In Ooi, ed. 2001: 53–68.

Lim, Lisa, ed. 2004. *Singapore English. A Grammatical Description.* Amsterdam, Philadelphia: Benjamins.

Llamzon, Teodoro A. 1986. "Life cycle of New Englishes: restriction phase of Filipino English." *English World-Wide* 7: 101–25.

  1997. "The phonology of Philippine English." In Bautista, ed. 1997: 41–8.

  2000. "Philippine English revisited." In Bautista et al., eds. 2000: 138–45.

Lloyd, T. O. 1984. *The British Empire 1558–1983.* Oxford: Oxford University Press.

Loomba, Ania. 1998. *Colonialism/Postcolonialism.* London, New York: Routledge.

Low Ee Ling and Adam Brown. 2005. *English in Singapore. An Introduction.* Singapore: McGraw-Hill.

Lowenberg, Peter. 1991. "Variation in Malaysian English: the pragmatics of languages in contect". In Cheshire, ed. 1991: 364–75.

Lucko, Peter. 2003. "Is English a 'killer language'?" In Lucko et al., eds. 2003: 151–65.

Lucko, Peter, Lothar Peter and Hans-Georg Wolf, eds. 2003. *Studies in African Varieties of English*. Frankfurt a.M.: Peter Lang.

Luke, Kwang-Kwong, and Jack C. Richards. 1982. "English in Hong Kong: functions and status." *English World-Wide* 3: 47–64.

Macalister, John. 2006. "The Maori presence in the New Zealand lexicon, 1850–2000: Evidence from a corpus-based study." *English World-Wide* 27: 1–24.

Mackey, William F. 1998. "The foundations." In Edwards, ed. 1998: 13–35.

Macquarie Junior Dictionary. World English – Asian Context. 1999. Macquarie University, NSW: Macquarie Library.

Mafeni, Bernard. "Nigerian Pidgin." In Spencer, ed. 1971a: 95–112.

Mafu, Safari T. A. 2003. "Postcolonial language planning in Tanzania: what are the difficulties and what is the way out?" In Mair, ed. 2003: 267–78.

Mahboob, Ahmar. 2004. "Pakistani English: morphology and syntax." In Kortmann et al., eds. 2004: 1045–57.

Mair, Christian. 2002. "Creolisms in an emergent standard: written English in Jamaica." *English World-Wide* 23: 31–58.

Mair, Christian, ed. 2003. *The Politics of English as a World Language. New Horizons in Postcolonial Cultural Studies*. Amsterdam, New York: Rodopi.

Malan, Karen. 1996. "Cape Flats English." In de Klerk, ed. 1996: 125–48.

Malancon, Richard, and Mary Jo Malancon. 1977. "Indian English at Haskell Institute, 1915." In Leap, ed. 1977: 141–53.

Malcolm, Ian G. 1995. *Language and Communication Enhancement for Two-way Education*. Perth: Edith Cowan University and Education Department of Western Australia.

2001. "Two-way English and the bicultural experience." In Moore, ed. 2001c: 219–40.

2004a. "Australian creoles and Aboriginal English: morphology and syntax." In Kortmann et al., eds. 2004: 657–681.

2004b. "Australian creoles and Aboriginal English: phonetics and phonology." In Schneider et al., eds. 2004: 656–70.

Malcolm, Ian, and Marek M. Koscielecki. 1997. *Aboriginality and English. Report to the Australian Research Council*. Perth: Center for Applied Language and Literacy Research, Edith Cowan University.

Malcolm, Ian G. and Judith Rochecouste. 2000. "Event and story schemas in Australian Aboriginal English discourse." *English World-Wide* 21: 261–89.

Marckwardt, Albert H. 1958. *American English*. New York: Oxford University Press.

Marti, Roland. 1993. "Slovakisch und Čechisch vs. Čechoslovakisch; Serbokroatisch vs. Kroatisch und Serbisch." In Karl Gutschmidt et al., eds. *Slavistische Studien zum XI. internationalen Slavistenkongress in Bratislava*. Köln: Böhlau, 289–325.

Mathews, Mitford M. 1951. *A Dictionary of Americanisms on Historical Principles*. Chicago: University of Chicago Press.

Mazrui, Alamin M. and Ali A. Mazrui. 1996. "A tale of two Englishes: the imperial language in post-colonial Kenya and Uganda." In Fishman et al., eds. 1996: 271–302.

Mbangwana, Paul. 2004. "Cameroon English: morphology and syntax." In Kortmann et al., eds. 2004: 898–908.

McArthur, Tom. 1998. *The English Languages*. Cambridge: Cambridge University Press.

2002. *Oxford Guide to World English*. Oxford: Oxford University Press.

McCormick, Kay. 1995. "Code-switching, code-mixing and convergence in Cape Town." In Mesthrie, ed. 1995: 193–208.

2004. "Cape Flats English: morphology and syntax." In Kortmann et al., eds. 2004: 993–1005.

McDavid, Raven I., Jr. 1958. "The dialects of American English." In W. Nelson Francis, *The Structure of American English*. New York: Ronald, 480–543.

McMahon, Aril. 1994. *Understanding Language Change*. Cambridge: Cambridge University Press.

McWhorter, John. 2000. "Defining 'creole' as a synchronic term." In Neumann-Holzschuh & Schneider, eds. 2000: 85–123.

Mehrotra, Raja Ram. 1998. *Indian English. Texts and Interpretation*. Amsterdam, Philadelphia: Benjamins.

Melchers, Gunnel, and Philip Shaw. 2003. *World Englishes. An Introduction*. London: Arnold.

Menang, Thaddeus. 2004. "Cameroon Pidgin English (Kamtok): phonology." In Schneider et al., eds. 2004: 902–17.

Mencken, H. L. 1963 [1919]. *The American Language. An Inquiry into the Development of English in the United States*. One-volume abridged ed. by Raven I. McDavid, Jr. New York: Alfred Knopf. Repr. 1982.

Merican, Fadillah. 2000. "Going native and staying strong: Malaysian fiction in English." In Halimah & Ng, eds. 2000: 107–24.

Mesthrie, Rajend. 1992. *English in Language Shift. The History, Structure and Sociolinguistics of South African Indian English*. Cambridge: Cambridge University Press.

Mesthrie, Rajend, ed. 1995. *Language and Social History. Studies in South African Sociolinguistics*. Cape Town, Johannesburg: David Philip.

Mesthrie, Rajend. 1996. "Language contact, transmission, shift: South African Indian English." In de Klerk, ed. 1996: 79–98.

2002a. "Building a new dialect: South African Indian English and the history of Englishes." In Watts & Trudgill, eds. 2002: 111–33.

2002b. "From first language to second language: Indian South African English." In Mesthrie, ed. 2002c: 339–55.

Mesthrie, Rajend, ed. 2002c. *Language in South Africa*. Cambridge: Cambridge University Press.

Mesthrie, Rajend. 2002d. "South Africa: a sociolinguistic overview." In Mesthrie, ed. 2002c: 11–26.

2004a. "Black South African English: morphology and syntax." In Kortmann et al., eds. 2004: 962–73.

2004b. "Indian South African English: morphology and syntax." In Kortmann et al., eds. 2004: 974–92.

2004c. "Indian South African English: phonology." In Schneider et al., eds. 2004: 953–63.

2006. "Anti-deletions in an L2 grammar: a study of Black South African English mesolect." *English World-Wide* 27: 111–45.

Michieka, Martha Moraa. 2005. "English in Kenya: a sociolinguistic profile." *World Englishes* 24: 173–86.

Milroy, James, and Lesley Milroy. 1985. *Authority in Language*. London: Routledge.

Milroy, Leslie. 2002. "Social networks." In Chambers, Trudgill, and Schilling-Estes, eds. 2002: 549–72.

Mitchell, Alexander G. and Arthur Delbridge. 1965. *The Speech of Australian Adolescents: A Survey*. Sydney: Angus & Robertson.

Mittmann, Brigitta. 2004. *Mehrwort-Cluster in der englischen Alltagskonversation. Unterschiede zwischen britischem und amerikanischem gesprochenem Englisch als Indikatoren für den präfabrizierten Charakter der Sprache*. Tübingen: Narr.

Moag, Rodney F. 1992. "The life cycle of non-native Englishes: a case study." In Kachru, ed. 1992: 233–52.

Montgomery, Michael. 1989. "Exploring the roots of Appalachian English." *English World-Wide* 10: 227–78.

1996. "Was colonial American English a koiné?" In Juhani Klemola, Merja Kytö and Matti Rissanen, eds. *Speech Past and Present: Studies in English Dialectology in Memory of Ossi Ihalainen*. Frankfurt a.M.: Peter Lang, 213–35.

2001. "British and American antecedents." In Algeo, ed. 2001a: 86–153.

2004. "Appalachian English: morphology and syntax." In Kortmann et al., eds. 2004: 245–80.

Montgomery, Michael, and Joseph S. Hall. 2004. *Dictionary of Smoky Mountain English*. Knoxville: University of Tennessee Press.

Moore, Bruce. 2001a. "Australian English and indigenous voices." In Blair & Collins, eds. 2001: 133–49.

2001b. "Australian English: Australian identity." In Moore, ed. 2001c: 44–58.

Moore, Bruce, ed. 2001c. *"Who's Centric Now?" The Present State of Post-Colonial Englishes*. South Melbourne: Oxford University Press.

Morais, Elaine. 2000. "Talking in English but thinking like a Malaysian: insights from a car assembly plant." In Halimah & Ng 2000: 90–106.

2001. "Lectal varieties of Malaysian English." In Ooi, ed. 2001: 33–52.

Mufwene, Salikoko S. 1986. "The universalist and substrate hypotheses complement one another." In Muysken & Smith, eds. 1986: 129–62.

Mufwene, Salikoko S., ed. 1993. *Africanisms in Afro-American Language Varieties*. Athens, London: University of Georgia Press.

Mufwene, Salikoko S. 1996a. "The development of American Englishes: some questions from a creole genesis perspective." In Edgar W. Schneider, ed., *Focus on the USA*. Amsterdam, Philadelphia: Benjamins, 231–64.

1996b. "The Founder Principle in creole genesis." *Diachronica* 13: 83–134.

2000a. "Creolization is a social, not a structural, process." In Neumann-Holzschuh & Schneider, eds. 2000: 65–84.

2000b. "Some sociohistorical inferences about the development of African American English." In Poplack, ed. 2000: 233–63.

2001a. "African-American English." In Algeo, ed. 2001a: 291–324.

2001b. *The Ecology of Language Evolution.* Cambridge: Cambridge University Press.

2003a. "Genetic linguistics and genetic creolistics: a response to Sarah G. Thomason's 'Creoles and genetic relationship'." *Journal of Pidgin and Creole Languages* 18: 273–88.

2003b. "The shared ancestry of African-American and American White Southern Englishes: some speculations dictated by history." In Nagle & Sanders, eds. 2003: 64–81.

2004a. "Gullah: morphology and syntax." In Kortmann et al., eds. 2004: 356–73.

2004b. "Language birth and death." *Annual Review of Anthropology* 33: 201–22.

2005a. *Créoles, écologies sociale, évolution linguistique.* Paris: Harmattan.

2005b. "Language evolution: the population genetics way." In Günther Hauska, ed. *Gene, Sprachen und ihre Evolution.* Regensburg: Universitätsverlag Regensburg, 30–52.

2006. "The comparability of new-dialect formation and creole development." *World Englishes* 25: 177–86.

Mufwene, Salikoko S., John R. Rickford, Guy Bailey, and John Baugh, eds. 1998. *African-American English: Structure, History and Use.* London, New York: Routledge.

Mugler, France, and Jan Tent. 1998. "Some aspects of language use and attitudes in Fiji." In Jan Tent and France Mugler, eds. *SICOL: Proceedings of the Second International Conference on Oceanic Linguistics.* Vol. I: *Language Contact.* (Pacific Linguistics C-141) Canberra: Australian National University: 109–34.

2004. "Fiji English: morphology and syntax." In Kortmann et al., eds. 2004: 770–88.

Mühleisen, Susanne. 2002. *Creole Discourse. Exploring Prestige Formation and Change across Caribbean English-Lexicon Creoles.* Amsterdam, Philadelphia: Benjamins.

Mühleisen, Susanne, and Bettina Migge, eds. 2005. *Politeness and Face in Caribbean Creoles.* Amsterdam, Philadelphia: Benjamins.

Mühlhäusler, Peter. 1986. *Pidgin and Creole Linguistics.* Oxford: Blackwell.

2002. "Changing names for a changing landscape: the case of Norfolk Island." *English World-Wide* 23: 59–91.

Mukherjee, Joybrato, and Sebastian Hoffmann. 2006. "Describing verb-complementational profiles of New Englishes: a pilot study of Indian English." *English World-Wide* 27: 147–73.

Murray, Sarah. 2002. "Language issues in South African education: an overview." In Mesthrie, ed. 2002c: 434–48.

Murray, Thomas, and Beth Lee Simon. 2004. "Colloquial American English: grammatical features." In Kortmann et al., eds. 2004: 221–44.

Murray, Thomas, and Beth Lee Simon, eds. 2006. *Language Variation and Change in the American Midland: A New Look at "Heartland" English.* Amsterdam, Philadelphia: Benjamins.

Muthwii, Margaret Jepkirui, and Angelina Nduku Kioko, eds. 2004. *New Language Bearings in Africa. A Fresh Quest.* Clevedon: Multilingual Matters.

Muysken, Pieter, and Norval Smith, eds. 1986. *Substrata versus Universals in Creole Genesis.* Amsterdam, Philadelphia: Benjamins.

Mwangi, Serah. 2003. *Prepositions in Kenyan English*. Aachen: Shaker.

Nagle, Stephen J., and Sara L. Sanders, eds. 2003. *English in the Southern United States*. Cambridge: Cambridge University Press.

Nagy, Naomi, and Julie Roberts. 2004. "New England: phonology." In Schneider et al., eds. 2004: 270–81.

Nair-Venugopal, Shanta. 2000. *Language Choice and Communication in Malaysian Business*. Bangi: Penerbit Universiti Kebangsaan Malaysia.

Nelson, Gerald. 2005. "Expressing future time in Philippine English." In Dayak & Quakenbush, eds. 2005: 41–59.

Neumann-Holzschuh, Ingrid, and Edgar W. Schneider, eds. 2000. *Degrees of Restructuring in Creole Languages*. Amsterdam, Philadelphia: Benjamins.

Newbrook, Mark. 1997. "Malaysian English: Status, norms, some grammatical and lexical features." In Schneider, ed. 1997, II: 229–56.

  2001. "Syntactic features and norms in Australian English." In Blair & Collins, eds. 2001: 113–32.

Ngefac, Aloysius. 2001. "Extra-linguistic correlates of Cameroon English phonology." PhD dissertation, University of Yaounde I.

Ngefac, Aloysius, and Bonaventure M. Sala. 2006. "Cameroon Pidgin and Cameroon English at a confluence: a real-time investigation." *English World-Wide* 27: 217–27.

Nichols, Roger L. 2003. *American Indians in U.S. History*. Norman: University of Oklahoma Press.

Nihalani, Paroo, R. K. Tongue, Priya Hosali, and Jonathan Crowther. 2004. *Indian and British English. A Handbook of Usage and Pronunciation*. 2nd edn. New Delhi: Oxford University Press.

Norton, Bonny. 2000. *Identity and Language Learning: Gender, Ethnicity and Educational Change*. Harlow: Longman.

Noss, R. B., ed. 1983. *Varieties of English in Southeast Asia*. Singapore: Singapore University Press for SEAMEO Regional Language Centre.

Olavarria de Ersson, Eugenia, and Philip Shaw. 2003. "Verb complementation patterns in Indian Standard English." *English World-Wide* 24: 137–61.

Ooi, Vincent B. Y., ed. 2001. *Evolving Identities. The English Language in Singapore and Malaysia*. Singapore: Times Academic Press.

Orkin, Mark M. 1970. *Speaking Canadian English*. Toronto: General Publishing.

Orsman, Harry. 1997. *A Dictionary of New Zealand English on Historical Principles*. Auckland: Oxford University Press.

Orsman, Elizabeth, and Harry Orsman. 1994. *The New Zealand Dictionary*. Educational Edition. Takapuna: New House.

Pakir, Anne. 1991. "The range and depth of English-knowing bilinguals in Singapore." *World Englishes* 10: 167–79.

Pakir, Anne, ed. 1993. *The English Language in Singapore: Standards and Norms*. Singapore: Singapore Association for Applied Linguistics.

Pakir, Anne. 1994. "English in Singapore: the codification of competing norms." In Gopinathan et al., eds. 1994: 92–118.

  1999. "English as a glocal Language: implications for English language teaching world-wide." Paper presented at International Association of Teachers of English as a Foreign Language (IATEFL) 1999, Edinburgh.

2001. "The voices of English-knowing bilinguals and the emergence of new epicentres." In Ooi, ed. 2001: 1–11.

Patrick, Peter. 1997. "Style and register in Jamaican Patwa." In Schneider, ed., 1997, II: 41–55.

1999. *Urban Jamaican Creole. Variation in the Mesolect.* Amsterdam, Philadelphia: Benjamins.

2004. "Jamaican Creole: morphology and syntax." In Kortmann et al., eds. 2004: 407–38.

Paul, Premila. 2003. "The master's language and its Indian uses." In Mair, ed. 2003: 359–65.

Pawley, Andrew. 2004. "Australian Vernacular English: some grammatical characteristics." In Kortmann et al., eds. 2004: 611–42.

Peeters, Bert. 2004. "Tall poppies and egalitarianism in Australian discourse: From key word to cultural value." *English World-Wide* 25: 1–25.

Penfield, Joyce, and Jacob L. Ornstein-Galicia. 1985. *Chicano English: An Ethnic Contact Dialect.* Amsterdam, Philadelphia: Benjamins.

Peng, Long, and Jane Setter. 2000. "The emergence of systematicity in the English pronunciations of two Cantonese-speaking adults in Hong Kong." *English World-Wide* 21: 81–108.

Pennycook, Alastair. 1998. *English and the Discourses of Colonialism.* London, New York: Routledge.

Peters, Pam. 1995. *The Cambridge Australian English Style Guide.* Cambridge, New York, Melbourne: Cambridge University Press.

Phillipson, Robert. 1992. *Linguistic Imperialism.* Oxford: Oxford University Press.

Platt, John, and Heidi Weber. 1980. *English in Singapore and Malaysia: Status, Features, Functions.* Kuala Lumpur: Oxford University Press.

Platt, John, Heidi Weber, and Mian Lian Ho. 1983. *Singapore and Malaysia.* (Varieties of English Around the World T1). Amsterdam, Philadelphia: Benjamins.

1984. *The New Englishes.* London: Routledge & Kegan Paul.

Pollard, Velma. 1983. "The social history of Dread Talk." In Carrington, ed. 1983: 46–62.

1986. "Innovation in Jamaican Creole. The speech of Rastafari." In Görlach & Holm, eds. 1986: 157–66.

Poplack, Shana, ed. 2000. *The English History of African American English.* Malden, Oxford: Blackwell.

Prendergast, David. 1998. "Views on Englishes. A talk with Braj B. Kachru, Salikoko Mufwene, Rajendra Singh, Loreto Todd and Peter Trudgill." *Links & Letters* 5: 225–41.

Pride, John, ed. 1982. *New Englishes.* Rowley, London, Tokyo: Newbury House.

Pyles, Thomas. 1952. *Words and Ways of American English.* London: Melrose.

Quinn, Heidi. 2000. "Variation in New Zealand English syntax and morphology." In Bell & Kuiper, eds. 2000: 173–97.

Quirk, Randolph, Sidney Greenbaum, Geoffrey Leech and Jan Svartvik. 1985. *A Comprehensive Grammar of the English Language.* London, New York: Longman.

Rajadurai, Joanne. 2004. "The faces and facets of English in Malaysia." *English Today 80* 20: 54–8.

Ramson, W. S. 1966. *Australian English: An Historical Study of the Vocabulary 1788–1898.* Canberra: Australian National University Press.

Ramson, W. S., ed. 1988. *The Australian National Dictionary.* Melbourne: Oxford University Press.

Read, Allen Walker. 1933. "British recognition of American speech in the eighteenth century." *Dialect Notes* 6: 313–34. Quoted from reprint in Read 2002: 37–54.

1938. "The assimilation of the speech of British immigrants in colonial America." *Journal of English and Germanic Philology* 37: 70–9.

2002. *Milestones in the History of English in America.* Edited by Richard W. Bailey. (PADS 86) Durham, NC: Duke University Press for the American Dialect Society.

Reaser, Jeffrey, and Benjamin Torbert. 2004. "Bahamian English: morphology and syntax." In Kortmann et al., eds. 2004: 391–406.

Richards, Kel. 2005. *Word Map.* Sydney: ABC Books.

Rickford, John R. 1987. *Dimensions of a Creole Continuum. History, Texts, and Linguistic Analysis of Guyanese Creole.* Stanford: Stanford University Press.

1998. *African American Vernacular English.* Malden, Oxford: Blackwell.

Rickford, John R. and Jerome S. Handler. 1994. "Textual evidence on the nature of early Barbadian speech, 1676–1835." *Journal of Pidgin and Creole Languages* 9: 221–55.

Richards, Jack C., ed. 1979. *New Varieties of English: Issues and Approaches.* Singapore: SEAMEO Regional Language Centre.

Roberts, Peter A. 1998a. "The fabric of Barbadian English." In Pauline Christie, Barbara Lalla, Velma Pollard, and Lawrence Carrington, eds. *Studies in Caribbean Language II.* St. Augustine: Society for Caribbean Linguistics, 13–33.

1988b. *West Indians and Their Language.* Cambridge: Cambridge University Press.

Roberts, Sarah Julianne. 1998. "The role of diffusion in the genesis of Hawaiian creole." *Language* 74: 1–38.

2000. "Nativisation and genesis of Hawaiian Creole." In John McWhorter, ed. *Language Change and Language Contact in Pidgins and Creoles.* Amsterdam, Philadelphia: Benjamins, 257–300.

Romaine, Suzanne. 2001. "Contact with other languages." In Algeo, ed. 2001a: 154–83.

Rowicka, Grazyna J. 2005. "American Indian English: the Quinault case." *English World-Wide* 26: 301–24.

Roy, John D. 1986. "The structure of tense and aspect in Barbadian English Creole." In Görlach & Holm, eds. 1986: 141–56.

Rubal-Lopez, Alma. 1996. "The ongoing spread of English: a comparative analysis of former Anglo-American colonies with non-colonies." In Fishman et al., eds. 1996: 37–82.

Rubdy, Rani. 2001. "Creative destruction: Singapore's Speak Good English Movement." *World Englishes* 20: 341–55.

Sahgal, Anju. 1991. "Patterns of language use in a bilingual setting in India." In Cheshire, ed. 1991: 299–307.

Sakoda, Kent, and Jeff Siegel. 2003. *Pidgin Grammar. An Introduction to the Creole Language of Hawai'i.* Honolulu: Bess Press.

Salleh, Habibah. 2000. "Which English? And, does it matter?" In Halimah & Ng, eds. 2000: 57–63.

Sand, Andrea. 1999. *Linguistic Variation in Jamaica. A Corpus-Based Study of Radio and Newspaper Usage.* Tübingen: Gunter Narr.

Santa Ana, Otto, and Robert Bayley. 2004. "Chicano English: phonology." In Schneider et al., eds. 2004: 417–34.

Saravanan, Vanithamani. 1994. "Language maintenance and language shift in the Tamil community." In Gopinathan et al., eds. 1994: 175–204.

Schäfer, Ronald P., and Francis O. Egbokhare. 1999. "English and the pace of endangerment in Nigeria." *World Englishes* 18: 381–91.

Schmied, Josef J. 1985. *Englisch in Tansania. Sozio- und interlinguistische Probleme.* Heidelberg: Groos.

1991a. *English in Africa: An Introduction.* London, New York: Longman.

1991b. "National and subnational features in Kenyan English." In Cheshire, ed. 1991: 420–32.

2004a. "East African English (Kenya, Uganda, Tanzania): morphology and syntax." In Kortmann et al., eds. 2004: 929–47.

2004b. "East African English (Kenya, Uganda, Tanzania): phonology." In Schneider et al., eds. 2004: 918–30.

Schneider, Edgar W. 1989. *American Earlier Black English. Morphological and Syntactic Variables.* Tuscaloosa: University of Alabama Press.

1990. "The cline of creoleness in English-oriented creoles and semi-creoles of the Caribbean." *English World-Wide* 11: 79–113.

1994. "Appalachian mountain vocabulary: its character, sources, and distinctiveness." In Wolfgang Viereck, ed., *Proceedings of the International Congress of Dialectologists Bamberg 1990.* Stuttgart: Steiner, Vol. III: 498–512.

Schneider, Edgar W. ed. 1997. *Englishes Around the World.* Vol. I: *General Studies, British Isles, North America.* Vol. II: *Caribbean, Africa, Asia, Australasia. Studies in Honour of Manfred Görlach.* Amsterdam, Philadelphia: Benjamins.

Schneider, Edgar W. 1999. "Notes on Singaporean English." In Uwe Carls and Peter Lucko, eds. *Form, Function and Variation in English. Studies in Honour of Klaus Hansen.* Frankfurt a.M.: Peter Lang, 193–205.

2000a. "Corpus linguistics in the Asian context: exemplary studies of the Kolhapur corpus of Indian English." In Bautista, Llamzon, & Sibayan, eds. 2000: 115–37.

2000b. "Feature diffusion vs. contact effects in the evolution of New Englishes: a typological case study of negation patterns." *English World-Wide* 21: 201–30.

2000c. "From region to class to identity: 'Show me how you speak, and I'll tell you who you are'?" *American Speech* 75: 359–61.

2003a. "Evolutionary patterns of New Englishes and the special case of Malaysian English." *Asian Englishes* 6: 44–63.

2003b. "Shakespeare in the coves and hollows? Toward a history of Southern English." In Nagle & Sanders, eds. 2003: 17–35.

2003c. "The dynamics of New Englishes: from identity construction to dialect birth." *Language* 79: 233–81.

2004a. "Global synopsis: phonetic and phonological variation in English world-wide." In Schneider et al., eds. 2004: 1111–30.

2004b. "How to trace structural nativization: particle verbs in world Englishes." *World Englishes* 23: 227–49.

2004c. "The English dialect heritage of the Southern United States." In Hickey, ed. 2004b: 262–309.

2005a. "Cataloguing the pronunciation variants of world-wide English." Paper presented to the Twelfth International Congress on Methods in Dialectology, Moncton, Canada, August.

2005b. "The subjunctive in Philippine English." In Dayag & Quakenbush, eds. 2005: 27–40.

Schneider, Edgar W., and Christian Wagner. 2006. "The variability of literary dialect in Jamaican Creole: Thelwell's *The Harder They Come.*" *Journal of Pidgin and Creole Languages* 21: 45–95.

Schneider, Edgar W., Kate Burridge, Bernd Kortmann, Rajend Mesthrie, and Clive Upton, eds. 2004. *A Handbook of Varieties of English.* Vol. I: *Phonology.* Berlin, New York: Mouton de Gruyter.

Schreier, Daniel. 2003. "Insularity and linguistic endemicity." *Journal of English Linguistics* 31: 249–72.

2005. *Consonant Change in English Worldwide. Synchrony Meets Diachrony.* Houndmills, New York: Palgrave Macmillan.

Schröder, Anne. 2003. *Status, Functions, and Prospects of Pidgin English. An Empirical Approach to Language Dynamics in Cameroon.* Tübingen: Gunter Narr.

Schumann, John H. 1978. "The acculturation model for second-language acquisition." In Rosario C. Gringas, ed. *Second Language Acquisition and Foreign Language Teaching.* Washington, DC: Center for Applied Linguistics, 27–50.

Sharma, Devyani. 2001. "The pluperfect in native and non-native English: a comparative corpus study." *Language Variation and Change* 13: 343–73.

Shastri, S. V. 1996. "Using computer corpora in the description of language with special reference to complementation in Indian English." In Baumgardner, ed. 1996: 70–81.

Shields-Brodber, Kathryn. 1997. "Requiem for English in an 'English-speaking' community: the case of Jamaica." In Schneider, ed. 1997, II: 57–67.

Sibayan, Bonifacio P., and Andrew Gonzalez. 1996. "Post-imperial English in the Philippines." In Fishman et al., eds. 1996: 139–72.

Siegel, Jeff. 1987. *Language Contact in a Plantation Environment. A Sociolinguistic History of Fiji.* Cambridge: Cambridge University Press.

1991. "Variation in Fiji English." In Cheshire, ed. 1991: 664–74.

2005. "Creolization outside creolistics." *Journal of Pidgin and Creole Linguistics* 20: 141–67.

Silva, Penny. 1997. "The lexis of South African English: reflections of a multilingual society." In Schneider, ed. 1997, II: 159–76.

2001. "South African English: politics and the sense of place." In Moore, ed. 2001c: 82–94.

Silva, Penny, Wendy Dore, Dorothea Mantzel, Colin Muller, and Madeleine Wright., eds. 1996. *A Dictionary of South African English on Historical Principles.* Oxford: Oxford University Press.

Simire, G. O. 2004. "Developing and promoting multilingualism in public life and society in Nigeria." In Muthwii & Kioko, eds. 2004: 135–47.

Simo Bobda, Augustin. 2003. "The formation of regional and national features in African English pronunciation: an exploration of some non-interference factors." *English World-Wide* 24: 17–42.

2004. "Cameroon English: phonology." In Schneider et al., eds. 2004: 885–901.

Simo Bobda, Augustin, and Hans-Georg Wolf. 2003. "Pidgin English in Cameroon in the new millenium." In Lucko, Peter, & Wolf, eds. 2003: 101–17.

Singapore Census of Population 2000. http://www.singstat.gov.sg/C2000/census.html

Singh, Rajendra, ed. 1998. *The Native Speaker: Multilingual Perspectives.* New Delhi, Thousand Oaks, London: Sage.

Singler, John Victor. 2004. "Liberan Settler English: morphology and syntax." In Kortmann et al., eds. 2004: 879–97.

Skandera, Paul. 1999. "What do we *really* know about Kenyan English? A pilot study in research methodology." *English World-Wide* 20: 217–36.

2003. *Drawing a Map of Africa. Idiom in Kenyan English.* Tübingen: Gunter Narr.

Slabbert, Sarah, and Rosalie Finlayson. 2000. " 'I'm a cleva!': the linguistic makeup of identity in a South African urban environment." In Kamwangamalu, ed. 2000: 119–36.

Slomanson, Peter A., and Michael Newman. 2004. "Peer group identification and variation in New York Latino laterals." *English World-Wide* 25: 199–216.

Smith, Geoff. 2004. "Tok Pisin: morphology and syntax." In Kortmann et al., eds. 2004: 720–41.

Spencer, John, ed. 1971a. *The English Language in West Africa.* London: Longman.

Spencer, John. 1971b. "West Africa and the English language." In Spencer, ed. 1971a: 1–34.

Sridhar, Kamal K. 1991. "Speech acts in a indigenised variety: sociocultural values and language variation." In Cheshire, ed. 1991: 308–18.

Sridhar, S. N. 1996. "Toward a syntax of South Asian English: defining the lectal range." In Baumgardner, ed. 1996: 55–69.

Starks, Donna. 2000. "Distinct, but not too distinct: gender and ethnicity as determinants of (s) fronting in four Auckland communities." *English World-Wide* 21: 291–304.

Strevens, Peter. 1972. *British and American English.* London: Macmillan.

Stubbe, Maria, and Janet Holmes. 2000. "Talking Maori or Pakeha in English: signalling identity in discourse." In Bell & Kuiper, eds. 2000: 249–78.

Talib, Ismail S. 1998. "Singaporean literature in English." In Foley et al. 1998: 270–86.

2002. *The Language of Postcolonial Literatures. An Introduction.* London, New York: Routledge.

Tan, Hwee Hwee. 2002. "A war of words over 'Singlish'." *Time Asia* 160.3, July 29.

Tan, Peter K. W. 2001. "*Melaka or Malacca; Kallang or Care-Lang*: Lexical innovation and nativisation in Malaysian and Singaporean English." In Ooi, ed. 2001: 140–67.

Tay, Mary. 1982. "The phonology of educated Singapore English." *English World-Wide* 3: 135–45.

Tay, Mary W. J. and Anthea Fraser Gupta. 1983. "Towards a description of Standard Singaporean English." In Noss, ed. 1983: 173–89.

Tayao, Ma. Lourdes G. 2004. "Philippine English: phonology." In Schneider et al., eds. 2004: 1047–59.

Tent, Jan. 2000a. "English lexicography in Fiji." *English Today 63*, 16,3: 22–8.

   2000b. "The dynamics of Fiji English: a study of its use, users and features." PhD dissertation, University of Otago.

   2001a. "A profile of the Fiji English lexis." *English World-Wide* 22: 209–45.

   2001b. "The current status of English in Fiji." In Moore, ed. 2001c: 241–68.

   2001c. "Yod deletion in Fiji English: phonological shibboleth or L2 English?" *Language Variation and Change* 13: 161–91.

Tent, Jan, and France Mugler. 1996. "Why a Fiji corpus?" In Greenbaum, ed. 1996a: 249–61.

   2004. "Fiji English: phonology." In Schneider et al., eds. 2004: 750–79.

Thomason, Sarah G. 2001. *Language Contact: An Introduction.* Washington, DC: Georgetown University Press.

Thomason, Sarah G., ed. 1997. *Contact Languages. A Wider Perspective.* Amsterdam, Philadelphia: Benjamins.

Thomason, Sarah Grey, and Terrence Kaufman. 1988. *Language Contact, Creolization and Genetic Linguistics.* Berkeley, Los Angeles: University of California Press.

Thompson, Roger M. 2003. *Filipino English and Taglish. Language Switching from Multiple Perspectives.* Amsterdam, Philadelphia: Benjamins.

Tickoo, Makhan L. 1996. "Fifty years of English in Singapore: all gains, (a) few losses?" In Fishman et al., eds. 1996: 431–55.

Tillery, Jan, and Guy Bailey. 2003. "Urbanization and the evolution of Southern American English." In Nagle & Sanders, eds. 2003: 159–72.

Tillery, Jan, Guy Bailey, and Tom Wikle. 2004. "Demographic change and American dialectology in the twenty-first century." *American Speech* 79: 227–49.

Times-Chambers Essential English Dictionary. 1997. 2nd edn. Singapore: Federal Publications.

Todd, Loreto. 1982a. *Cameroon.* (Varieties of English Around the World. T1) Heidelberg: Groos.

   1982b. "The English language in West Africa." In Bailey & Görlach, eds. 1982: 281–305.

Tongue, R. K. 1974. *The English of Singapore and Malaysia.* Singapore, Kuala Lumpur, Hong Kong: Eastern Universities Press.

Tottie, Gunnel. 2002. *An Introduction to American English.* Malden, Oxford: Blackwell.

Trudgill, Peter. 1986. *Dialects in Contact.* Oxford, New York: Blackwell.

   1987. *Sociolinguistics. An Introduction to Language and Society.* Harmondsworth: Penguin.

   2004. *New-Dialect Formation. The Inevitability of Colonial Englishes.* Edinburgh: Edinburgh University Press.

Trudgill, Peter, and Jean Hannah. 2002. *International English. A Guide to Varieties of Standard English*. 4th edn. London: Arnold.

Trudgill, Peter, Elizabeth Gordon, Gillian Lewis, and Margaret Maclagan. 2000. "Determinism in new-dialect formation and the genesis of New Zealand English." *Journal of Linguistics* 36: 299–318.

Trudgill, Peter, Margaret Maclagan, and Gillian Lewis. 2003. "Linguistic archeology: the Scottish input to New Zealand English phonology." *Journal of English Linguistics* 31: 103–24.

Tsui, Amy B. M., and David Bunton. 2000. "The discourse and attitudes of English language teachers in Hong Kong." In Bolton, ed. 2000a: 287–303.

Times-Chambers Essential English Dictionary. 1997. Singapore: Federal Publications & Edinburgh: Chambers Harrap.

Turner, George W. 1966. *The English Language in Australia and New Zealand*. London: Longmans.

1994. "English in Australia." In Burchfield, ed. 1994: 277–327.

Udofot, Inyang M. 2003a. "Nativisation of the English language in Nigeria: a cultural and linguistic renaissance." *Journal of Nigerian English and Literature* 4: 42–52.

2003b. "Stress and rhythm in the Nigerian accent of English: a preliminary investigation." *English World-Wide* 24: 201–20.

2005. "Emergent trends in English usage in Nigeria." Paper given to the 22nd Annual Conference of the Nigeria English Studies Association.

Upton, Clive. 2004. "Received Pronunciation." In Schneider et al., eds. 2004: 217–30.

van der Walt, Johann L. and Bertus van Rooy. 2002. "Towards a norm in South African Englishes." *World Englishes* 21: 113–28.

van Riper, William R. 1973. "General American: an ambiguity." In Harald Scholler and J. Reidy, eds. *From Lexicography and Dialect Geography. Festgabe für Hans Kurath*. Wiesbaden: Steiner, 232–42.

van Rooy, Bertus. 2004. "Black South African English: phonology." In Schneider et al., eds. 2004: 943–52.

Verma, Shivendra Kishore. 1982. "Swadeshi English: form and function." In Pride, ed. 1982, 174–87.

Warren, Paul, and Laurie Bauer. 2004. "Maori English: phonology." In Schneider et al., eds. 2004: 614–24.

Watermeyer, Susan. 1996. "Afrikaans English." In de Klerk, ed. 1996: 99–124.

Watts, Richard, and Peter Trudgill, eds. 2002. *Alternative Histories of English*. London, New York: Routledge.

Wee, Lionel. 1998. "The lexicon of Singapore English." In Foley et al., 1998: 175–200.

2002. "When English is not a mother tongue: Linguistic ownership and the Eurasian community in Singapore." *Journal of Multilingual and Multicultural Development* 23: 282–95.

2003. "The birth of a particle: *know* in Singapore English." *World Englishes* 22: 5–13.

2004a. "Singapore English: morphology and syntax." In Kortmann et al., eds. 2004: 1058–72.

2004b. "Singapore English: phonology." In Schneider et al., eds. 2004: 1016–33.

Weinreich, Uriel, William Labov, and Marvin Herzog. 1968. "Empirical foundations for a theory of language change." In Winfred P. Lehmann and Yakov Malkiel, eds. *Directions for Historical Linguistics. A Symposium.* Austin: University of Texas Press: 95–188.

Wells, John. 1982. *Accents of English.* 3 vols. Cambridge: Cambridge University Press.

Wiley, Terrence G. 2004. "Language planning, language policy, and the English-Only movement." In Finegan & Rickford, eds. 2004: 319–38.

Williams, Jessica. 1987. "Non-native varieties of English: a special case of language acquisition." *English World-Wide* 8: 161–99.

Wiltshire, Caroline. 2005. "The 'Indian English' of Tibeto-Burman language speakers." *English World-Wide* 26: 275–300.

Winer, Lise. 1993. *Trinidad and Tobago.* (VEAW T6) Amsterdam, Philadelphia: Benjamins.

Winford, Donald. 1991. "The Caribbean." In Cheshire, ed. 1991: 565–84.

1997a. "On the origins of African American Vernacular English – a creolist perspective. Part I: The sociohistorical background." *Diachronica* 14: 305–44.

1997b. "Re-examining Caribbean English creole continua." *World Englishes* 16: 233–79.

2000. " 'Intermediate' creoles and degrees of change in creole formation: the case of Bajan." In Neumann-Holzschuh & Schneider, eds. 2000: 215–46.

2003. *An Introduction to Contact Linguistics.* Malden, MA, Oxford: Blackwell.

Wodak, Ruth, Rudolf de Cillia, Martin Reisigl, and Karin Liebhart. 1999. *The Discoursive Construction of National Identity.* Edinburgh: Edinburgh University Press.

Wolf, Hans-Georg. 2001. *English in Cameroon.* Berlin, New York: Mouton de Gruyter.

Wolfram, Walt. 1974. *Sociolinguistic Aspects of Assimilation: Puerto Rican English in New York City.* Washington, DC: Center for Applied Linguistics.

1984. "Unmarked tense in American Indian English." *American Speech* 59: 31–50.

Wolfram, Walt, and Donna Christian. 1976. *Appalachian Speech.* Arlington, VA: Center for Applied Linguistics.

Wolfram, Walt, and Clare Dannenberg. 1999. "Dialect identity in a tri-ethnic context: the case of Lumbee American Indian English." *English World-Wide* 20: 179–216.

Wolfram, Walt, Clare Dannenberg, Stanley Knick, and Linda Oxendine. 2002. *Fine in the World: Lumbee Language in Time and Place.* Raleigh, NC: North Carolina State University, Human Extension/Publications.

Wolfram, Walt, and Natalie Schilling-Estes. 1996. "Dialect change and maintenance in a post-insular community." In Edgar W. Schneider, ed. *Focus on the USA.* Amsterdam, Philadelphia: Benjamins, 103–48.

1997. *Hoi Toide on the Outer Banks. The Story of the Ocracoke Brogue.* Chapel Hill, London: University of North Carolina Press.

1998. *American English. Dialects and Variation.* Malden, MA, Oxford: Blackwell.

Wolfram, Walt, and Erik Thomas. 2002. *The Development of African American English*. Oxford, Malden: Blackwell.

Woodward, Kathryn. 1997. "Concepts of identity and difference." In Kathryn Woodward, ed. 1997. *Identity and Difference*. London, Thousand Oaks, New Delhi: Sage.

Wright, Roger, ed. 1991. *Latin and the Romance Languages in the Early Middle Ages*. London, New York: Routledge

Yadurajan, K-S. 2001. *Current English. A Guide for the User of English in India*. New Delhi: Oxford University Press.

Yahya-Othman, Saida, and Herman Batibo. 1996. "The swinging pendulum: English in Tanzania 1940–1990." In Fishman et al., eds. 1996: 373–400.

Yule, Henry, and A. C. Burnell. 1886. *Hobson-Jobson. A Glossary of Colloquial Anglo-Indian Words and Phrases, and of Kindred Terms, Etymological, Historical, Geographical, and Discursive*. Repr. 1986. London, New York: Routledge & Kegan Paul.

Zuengler, Jane E. 1982. "Kenyan English." In Braj B. Kachru, ed. *The Other Tongue. English Across Cultures*. Urbana: University of Illinois Press, 112–24.

Zuraidah, Mohd Don. 2000. "Malay + English → a Malay variety of English vowels and accent." In Halimah & Ng, eds. 2000: 35–45.

Index of authors

Algeo, John. 91–2, 257, 259, 266, 272, 273, 277, 282, 287, 290, 291
Alleyne, Mervyn. 221, 222, 224, 229, 230, 232, 236, 238
Allsopp, Richard. 52, 224, 227, 237
Alsagoff, Lubna. 159
Ansaldo, Umberto. 161
Arends, Jacques. 10, 60

Bailey, Guy. 298–9, 303, 304, 308
Bailey, Richard. 168, 240, 241, 243, 244, 245–6, 247, 273, 288, 295
Bamgbose, Ayo. 202, 204, 205, 206, 207, 208, 209, 211
Bao, Zhiming. 158, 159
Baskaran, Loga. 151, 152
Bauer, Laurie. 10, 54, 71, 127, 128, 129, 130, 132–3
Baumgardner, Robert. 46, 80
Bautista, Maria Lourdes. 142, 143
Bell, Allan. 10, 131, 132, 133
Boberg, Charles. 242, 244, 245, 246, 247, 248, 249, 250, 256, 299
Bokamba, Eyamba. 204, 205, 208, 209, 210
Bolton, Kingsley. 11, 48, 135, 136, 137, 138, 139, 140, 142, 143
Butler, Susan. 125–6, 135, 140, 142, 143, 172
Butters, Ronald. 280, 281

Cassidy, Frederic. 222, 224, 229, 232, 233, 237, 273, 278
Clarke, Sandra. 246
Clyne, Michael. 126
Chambers, J.K. 9, 10, 18, 84, 103, 240, 241–2, 243, 244, 245, 246, 247, 249–50, 295
Collins, Peter. 92, 93, 119, 122, 125, 127
Crystal, David. 1, 19, 48, 321 n. 24

de Klerk, Vivian. 83, 179, 183, 185, 186, 187, 188
Delbridge, Arthur. 19, 52, 119, 125, 126

Deterding, David. 105, 159
Deuber, Dagmar. 67, 201, 202, 205, 206, 208, 209
Devonish, Hubert. 61, 63, 226, 227, 235, 236, 237

Faraclas, Nicholas. 205, 206, 208, 211, 212
Fishman, Joshua. 10, 318 n. 1
Foley, Joseph. 156, 157, 160

Gill, Saran Kaur. 147, 148, 149, 150, 151, 153
Gonzalez, Andrew. 140, 141, 143
Gordon, Elizabeth. 10, 49, 93, 94, 119, 124, 127, 128–33, 180, 187, 296
Görlach, Manfred. 2, 13, 80, 278, 320 n. 15
Gumperz, John. 26, 42, 47, 55, 295, 302
Gupta, Anthea Fraser. 25, 37, 65, 66, 154, 318 n. 1
Gut, Ulrike. 200, 201, 202, 205, 211

Hickey, Raymond. 3, 71, 101, 220
Horvath, Barbara. 10, 122, 125, 126, 306
Huber, Magnus. 10, 201, 202, 203
Hundt, Marianne. 43, 46, 130
Hung, Tony. 138

Igboanusi, Herbert. 88, 202, 204

Jibril, Munzali. 208, 209
Jowitt, David. 201, 202, 205, 206, 207, 209, 211–12

Kachru, Braj. 3, 11, 13, 14, 17, 19, 29, 44, 71, 80, 94, 95, 161, 163, 164, 165, 166, 168, 169, 170, 171, 172, 320 n. 15
Kamwangamalu, Nkonko. 186
Kembo Sure. 191, 194–5, 196, 315
Kortmann, Bernd. 72, 84, 85
Krapp, George P. 260, 262, 263, 272, 276, 277, 279, 281, 287, 289, 290, 291

Kretzschmar, William. 261, 290
Krishnaswamy, N. 161, 163, 164, 166–7, 172

Labov, William. 10, 18, 27, 95, 97, 109, 246–7, 249, 250, 295, 297, 299, 300, 303, 304, 321 n. 2
Lalla, Barbara. 228, 229, 230, 231–3, 237
Lanham, L.W. 175, 176, 177, 179, 180–1, 182, 183, 188
Lass, Roger. 106
Leap, William. 301, 302–3
Leitner, Gerhard. 119, 120–1, 122, 123, 124, 125, 129
LePage, Robert. 26, 28, 156, 221, 230, 234, 237, 309, 320 n. 17, 327 n. 54
Lim, Lisa. 83, 154, 158, 159, 161
Llamzon, Teodoro. 142, 143, 144, 319 n. 5
Low, Ee Ling. 154, 158, 159, 160, 161

Mair, Christian. 63, 236
Malcolm, Ian. 103, 119, 120, 122, 124
Marckwardt, Albert. 263, 273, 278
Mazrui, A. 189, 191, 194, 197
Mbangwana, Paul. 103, 218
McArthur, Tom. 12, 318 n. 1, 321 n. 24
McDavid, Raven. 260, 265, 266, 270, 279, 287, 290
McWhorter, John. 11
Mehrotra, Raja Ram. 161, 163, 164, 165, 167, 168, 170, 172
Melchers, Gunnel. 14, 20, 71, 318 n. 2
Mencken, H.L. 263, 266, 270, 272, 273, 274, 275, 276, 277, 279, 280, 282, 283, 284, 285, 287, 288, 289
Mesthrie, Rajend. 87, 90, 94, 176, 179, 182, 183, 186, 187, 189, 211, 320 n. 20, 324 n. 27
Milroy, Leslie. 43, 53
Moag, Rodney. 116, 144, 318 n. 3
Montgomery, Michael. 262, 270
Moore, Bruce. 121, 123, 124–5
Mufwene, Salikoko S. 4, 11, 19, 21, 22, 22–4, 25, 29, 58, 60, 63, 65, 94, 105, 107, 110–11, 112, 145, 153, 156, 219, 220, 222, 223, 240, 261, 267, 268, 269, 303, 304, 307, 312, 313, 318 n. 2, 320 nn. 14, 21, 321 n. 24, 323 nn. 9, 18, 325 nn. 35, 37, 330 n. 26
Muckherjee, Joybrato. 87, 93, 170
Mugler, France. 105, 106, 114, 116, 117
Mühleisen, Susanne. 47, 61, 224, 227, 233, 236, 237
Mühlhäusler, Peter. 64, 318 n. 3, 319 n. 9

Nelson, Gerald. 142
Nihalani, Paroo. 168, 172

Ooi, Vincent. 160
Orsman, Harry. 132

Pakir, Anne. 156, 157, 160, 161, 316
Patrick, Peter. 10, 105, 228, 230, 233, 234, 235, 236, 237, 238
Pennycook, Alastair. 19
Peters, Pam. 122, 125
Phillipson, Robert. 19
Platt, John. 3, 10, 29, 47, 71, 72, 83, 142, 144, 158, 161, 316, 320 n. 15
Pride, John. 3
Pyles, Thomas. 272, 273, 275, 284, 288, 290

Ramson, W. S. 39, 121, 125
Read, Allen Walker. 259, 267, 269, 271, 272, 273, 276, 277, 279, 285, 287, 290, 291
Rickford, John. 10, 221, 224, 226, 267
Roberts, Peter. 220, 221, 222, 223, 224, 225, 226, 235, 236
Roberts, Sarah. 307
Romaine, Suzanne. 256, 259–60, 263, 267, 273, 278

Schmied, Josef. 102, 192, 193, 194, 195, 196, 197, 198, 199, 211, 213, 214, 319 n. 5
Schneider, Edgar W. 10, 11, 23, 26, 47, 48, 54, 58, 60, 72, 73, 74, 86, 92, 93, 142, 150, 151, 169, 237, 262, 267, 268, 298, 299, 312, 326 n. 48
Schreier, Daniel. 109, 111
Schröder, Anne. 216, 217, 218
Shastri, S.V. 170
Shaw, Phillip. 14, 20, 71, 87, 88, 92, 93, 170, 318 n. 2
Shields-Brodber, Kathryn. 63, 236
Siegel, Jeff. 37, 59, 61, 111, 114, 115–16, 117, 307
Silva, Penny. 178, 181, 186, 187, 188
Simo Bobda, Augustin. 101, 212, 213, 214, 216, 217, 218

Talib, Ismail. 50, 160
Tan, Peter. 158
Tent, Jan. 46, 47, 105, 106, 114, 115, 116, 117
Thomason, Sarah G. 11, 21, 23, 24, 27, 29, 40, 44, 45, 48, 57, 60, 310, 312, 314, 316, 320 n. 18
Thompson, Roger. 48, 64, 140, 141, 142, 143
Todd, Loreto. 202, 208, 213, 214, 215, 217, 218
Tottie, Gunnel. 280
Trudgill, Peter. 9, 10, 35, 54, 71, 72, 73, 103, 107, 109, 119, 124, 127, 132, 296, 312, 318 n. 3, 320 nn. 12, 16, 322 n. 9
Turner, George W. 118, 119, 120, 121, 122

Udofot, Inyang. 205, 206, 207, 209, 211

van Rooy, Bertus. 184

Webster, Noah. 276–7, 281, 284, 287, 290, 291
Wee, Lionel. 106, 154, 158, 159
Wiltshire, Caroline. 78, 168

Winford, Donald. 10, 11, 21, 27, 48, 58, 60, 61, 219, 220, 221, 223, 225, 226, 235, 267, 268, 320 nn. 20, 21, 324 n. 19, 326 nn. 45, 48, 327 n. 54
Wolf, Hans-Georg. 201, 214, 216–17, 218
Wolfram, Walt. 27, 254, 262, 273, 276, 277, 280, 294, 297–8, 299, 300, 301, 303, 304, 305, 307

Index of subjects

Aboriginal 12, 35, 42, 119, 120, 121–2, 123,
  124, 127, 259
  English 73, 103, 122, 126
  place names 36, 120
accommodation 5, 6, 8, 21, 27, 32, 33, 35, 42,
  45, 53, 61, 62, 95–6, 99, 187, 226, 247,
  311, 312–13, 315, 317, 318 n. 3
adjective 84, 169, 280
adstrate 24, 58–60, 115, 126, 133, 145, 146–7,
  179, 180, 218, 230–1, 239, 252, 257,
  263, 268, 273, 275, 277, 278, 284, 286,
  297, 300
adverb 84, 184, 280
African-American 27, 96, 254, 257, 258,
  265, 266, 267–8, 275, 286,
  292, 293
  English 83, 273, 278, 303–4, 305
American English 7, 9, 73, 82, 91–2, 96, 105,
  107, 142, 251–308
Americanism 39, 249, 272–3, 277, 278–9,
  285, 291
aspect 84, 118, 223, 304
attitude, language 23, 31, 33, 42, 43, 48, 50,
  57, 64, 65, 69, 94, 95–6, 111, 125, 136,
  187, 194, 199, 205, 206–7, 216, 235,
  277, 285, 286
Australia 7, 11, 12, 25, 33, 42, 48, 49, 51,
  52, 65, 67, 94, 118–27, 245,
  248, 252
  English 10, 35, 46, 82, 84, 85, 320 n. 16
  ethnic differentiation 55, 59
  regional differentiation 5, 9
  social variation 19
  see also Aboriginal

Bahamas 84, 103
Barbados 63–4, 66, 219–27, 228, 229
bilingualism 22, 34, 38, 47, 55, 62, 64, 116,
  121, 135, 136–7, 141, 146, 149, 154,
  157, 163, 164, 165, 167, 177, 180, 191,
  198, 201, 216, 239, 249, 259, 267, 269,
  277, 285, 306, 316

borrowing, of words 5, 22, 27, 36, 39, 42, 58,
  78–80, 107, 169, 192, 195, 198, 215,
  224, 244
  of cultural terms 39, 44, 79–80, 117, 121,
  129, 135, 138, 140, 147, 152, 155, 165,
  181, 192, 203, 234, 242, 248, 273, 278,
  319 n. 10
  of fauna and flora words 39, 79, 117, 121,
  129, 135, 140, 147, 155, 165, 181, 192,
  203, 228, 234, 242, 272–3, 319 n. 10

Cajun 55, 294, 305–6
Cameroon 212–18, 316, 319 n. 5
  English 72, 81, 84, 103
  Pidgin 67, 107, 213, 214–15, 216–17, 218
Canada 52, 55, 238–50, 256, 282
  English 5, 103, 320 n. 16
  French Canadians 12, 58, 239–40, 242,
  243–4, 248–9, 327 n. 59
Caribbean 3, 4, 9, 10, 11, 13, 40, 47, 52, 61,
  62, 64, 68, 72, 73, 84, 85, 107, 219–38,
  320 n. 21
Chinese 59, 115, 116, 133, 135, 136, 137, 138,
  139, 145, 146–7, 149, 153–4, 155, 156,
  157, 158, 159, 230, 284, 307, 309
code-switching 22, 40, 47, 107, 138, 236
codification 14, 48, 52, 124–5, 131–2, 143,
  152, 153, 161, 172, 188, 212, 218, 227,
  237, 247, 291
cognition 98, 99, 104, 122
collocation 46, 81, 87–8, 92, 94, 152, 170,
  262, 282
colonial lag 278
colonization types 6, 7, 24–5, 29, 42, 45, 49,
  61, 62, 65–7, 197, 311, 318 n. 2
  exploitation 35, 38, 64, 85, 95, 101, 163
  plantation 40, 67
  settlement 35, 67, 71, 101, 258, 319 n. 10
  trade 35, 36, 38, 101, 145, 163, 213
complaint tradition 5, 18–19, 43, 50, 69, 94,
  108, 130, 137, 141, 151, 158, 168, 183,
  194, 209, 217, 234, 235, 277, 288–9

complementation, of verbs 5, 46–7, 86, 87,
    88, 151, 160, 170, 184, 196, 199, 209,
    218, 233, 279, 280
consonant cluster reduction 74, 77–8,
    151, 158
construction 88, 92, 282
contract laborers 34, 59–60, 66, 154
corpus linguistics 11
creole 7, 8, 10–11, 23, 24, 108, 311, 312
    African-American 267, 304
    Barbadian 226
    Caribbean 219
    Hawai'an 306
    Jamaican 227, 229, 233, 234, 235–8
    Nigerian 312
creolization 10–11, 22, 25, 40, 60–4, 208, 220,
    223, 227, 233, 312
critical linguistics/Critical Discourse
    Analysis 11, 14, 19

death, of languages 22, 42
demography 23, 25, 59, 60, 65, 66, 99, 110,
    115–16, 117, 221, 224, 228, 233, 239,
    242, 267–8, 292, 310, 317
dialect emergence 5, 125–6, 132–3, 308,
    316, 317
dialect contact 4, 23, 32, 34, 99, 100, 108–9,
    119, 154, 163, 178, 261, 299
dialect geography, see regional variation
dictionary 11, 52, 124–5, 126, 132, 143, 153,
    161, 172, 181, 188, 227, 237, 247, 272,
    277, 291, 295
differentiation (phase 5) 6, 30, 32, 52–5, 65,
    118, 125–7, 132–3, 161, 238, 247–50,
    252, 291–307
diglossia 10, 205, 236, 315
discourse marker 47, 98, 106, 159, 301, 305
drift 89–90, 98
Dutch 3, 175, 176, 177, 178, 255, 257,
    263, 273
Dynamic Model 5, 6–7, 21, 25–6, 27, 28–55,
    57, 58, 59–64, 68, 70, 81, 83, 139, 143,
    174, 175, 176, 224, 226, 227, 239,
    248, 296, 297, 303, 307, 309–10,
    313–14, 317

ecology 4, 6, 21, 22–3, 31, 34, 40, 60, 62, 66,
    71, 112
EFL (English as a Foreign Language) 12, 13,
    19, 313
elite, English as a language of an 24, 25, 34,
    37, 38, 45, 51, 64, 66, 73, 95, 115, 135,
    141, 142, 143, 146, 150, 154, 165, 177,
    179, 193, 198, 201, 202, 204, 205, 214,
    226, 235

Empire, British 1, 41, 318 n. 1
endonormative stabilization (phase 4) 6, 32,
    48–52, 65, 68, 122–5, 131–2, 143, 159,
    160–1, 171–2, 185–8, 210–12, 225–7,
    234–8, 245–7, 282–91
endonormativity 6, 50, 63, 94, 122, 124,
    132, 143, 152–3, 160–1, 171, 187,
    194–5, 196, 211, 235, 236, 253, 283,
    287, 288, 314
English World-Wide 2–3
Englishes, as a term 3
ENL (English as a Native Language) 12, 13,
    14, 17, 19, 31, 174, 311, 313, 315
ESL (English as a Second Language) 12, 13,
    17, 19, 31, 73, 78, 167, 174, 216, 311,
    312, 313
ethnolect 32, 49, 51, 54–5, 60, 116, 120, 122,
    126, 133, 174, 183–4, 250, 252, 254,
    302, 307
Event X 49, 122–3, 131, 132, 185, 274, 308
exaptation 106
exonormative stabilization (phase 2) 6, 32,
    36–40, 62, 63, 64, 65, 66, 79, 115–17,
    120–1, 128–9, 133, 135, 140, 145, 153,
    154–5, 163–5, 178–81, 191–2, 197–8,
    201–3, 213–15, 219, 220–2, 229–32,
    241–2, 253, 264–73
exonormativity 5, 38, 43, 135, 137, 150, 154,
    160, 165, 168, 180, 182, 194, 202, 214,
    217, 222, 226, 232, 234, 235, 266–7,
    271, 272, 277, 288, 314

feature pool 21, 22, 23, 27, 60, 85, 89, 99, 252,
    261, 296
Fiji 37, 114–18, 133, 319 n. 5
    English 44, 46, 47, 80, 82, 85, 98, 105, 106
foundation (phase 1) 6, 32, 33–6, 62, 64,
    65, 108, 114–15, 118–20, 127–8,
    133–5, 140, 144–5, 153–5, 162–3,
    175–8, 189–91, 197, 199–201,
    212–13, 219–20, 227–9, 240–1,
    253, 254–64
founder effect 23, 58, 62, 63, 110–11, 127,
    129, 155, 176, 223, 240, 267, 270,
    320 n. 19
French 3, 69, 175, 212, 213–14, 215–16, 217,
    218, 241, 244, 257, 263, 273, 275, 300,
    305–6, 320 n. 21
fricative 73, 158, 169

General American 252, 271, 291
German 197, 198, 212, 213, 257, 265, 268,
    278, 281, 284
Ghana 12, 67, 80, 82, 84, 107
glocalization 316, 317

grammar (morphology, syntax) 6, 8, 9, 10,
    17, 39, 40, 44, 46, 50, 52, 54, 61, 72,
    82–5, 125, 138, 151, 159–60, 169–70,
    187, 196, 262, 279–81, 304, 316
grammar-lexis interface 46, 81, 83, 86–8, 92,
    108, 117–18, 122, 131, 138, 142, 151,
    159, 170, 184, 196, 209–10, 223, 244,
    279, 280, 320 n. 13
grammaticalization 105, 106, 108, 118, 142
Guyana 10, 59, 224, 231

Hawai'i 59, 66, 284, 306–7, 318 n. 2
Hispanic Americans 55, 257, 292, 293, 304–5
homogeneity, of speech 5, 30, 35, 51, 54, 65,
    124, 131, 161, 172, 187, 188, 196, 226,
    246–7, 250, 252–3, 269–70, 271, 287,
    288, 290–1, 329 n. 10
Hong Kong 12, 48, 133–9
    English 50, 321 n. 24
hybridity 24, 202, 301, 311
    cultural 6, 50, 193, 218
    of identity 28, 29, 37, 53, 142, 184, 185, 316
    in compounds 80, 81, 117, 130, 138,
        152, 159, 169, 184, 195, 210, 218,
        234, 244

idiom 46, 142, 224
India 4, 12, 17, 25, 33, 50, 59, 94, 101, 144,
    161–73, 192, 319 n. 7
    English 47, 73, 78, 80–1, 82, 83, 84, 85, 87,
        89, 92, 101
Indian diaspora
    in Fiji 114, 115–16, 117
    in Guyana 231
    in Kenya 324 n. 31
    in Jamaica 230, 234
    in Malaysia 144, 145, 146, 147, 149
    in South Africa 179, 180, 182, 183,
        186, 187
    in Trinidad 60, 231
innovation 40, 43, 44, 45, 50, 83, 85–6, 88, 96,
    99, 101, 102–7, 109–10, 117, 159, 223,
    272, 278, 281, 298, 304, 306
intelligibility 2, 61, 103, 156, 208, 315
International Association of World
    Englishes (IAWE) 3
International Corpus of English (ICE) 80,
    93, 142
Ireland/Irish 98, 101, 119, 120, 154, 238, 262,
    271, 273, 284
Italian 126, 278, 284, 300

Jamaica 25, 221, 224, 227–38, 315
    Creole 7, 10, 63, 107, 224
    English 73

Kenya 80–1, 83, 86, 189–97, 316
koinéization 18, 23, 27, 35, 45, 51, 59, 65,
    103, 109, 115, 119, 128, 163, 177–8,
    191, 220, 241, 260–1, 269, 287, 290,
    296, 329 n. 10
Krio 201, 202

Latin 68–9
law, English as the language of 12, 36,
    116, 168, 191, 193, 201, 205,
    235, 236
lexicography, see dictionary
lexis 6, 8, 17, 39, 44, 46, 50, 54, 78–82, 272,
    312, 316
    regional 9
lingua franca 1, 35, 67, 115, 116, 137, 186,
    196, 217
literacy 65, 224, 237, 287
literature, written in Postcolonial Englishes
    4–5, 50, 124, 143, 153, 160, 161, 172,
    188, 196, 212, 226–7, 237–8, 246, 289,
    320 n. 15
loan words, see borrowing

Malaysia 14, 38, 48, 52, 58, 101, 144–53, 309,
    316, 319 n. 7, 330 n. 25
    endoglossic language policy 1, 58, 140
    English 73, 82, 85, 95, 102, 155
Maori 36, 42, 65, 127, 128, 129, 130, 131,
    320 n. 14
    English 73, 98, 133
markedness 104, 109, 111
media, English as a language of 1, 12, 67, 68,
    116, 141, 142–3, 149, 168, 205, 216,
    235, 236
methodology 6, 10
missionary 24, 34, 35, 36, 114, 115, 120,
    128, 135, 146, 162, 163, 177, 179,
    189, 197, 198, 200, 201, 213, 214,
    215, 230, 260
mixing, of languages 21, 22, 27, 46, 47–8,
    107, 138–9, 142–3, 152, 170–1, 184–5,
    196, 209, 218, 309, 316
modal verb 83, 92, 280, 299, 305
mother country 5, 37, 40–1, 43, 48–9, 66,
    122–3, 131, 241, 264, 265, 273,
    274, 283
mother tongue, see native speakers
multilingualism 10, 12, 13, 22, 25, 55, 126,
    149, 152, 156, 174, 175, 177, 179, 188,
    196, 217, 316

nation building 4, 6, 16, 49, 51, 63, 121, 155,
    171, 185, 196, 210, 225, 234, 243, 245,
    274, 275, 284

Native Americans 12, 36, 42, 252, 253–4, 256–7, 258–60, 265–6, 275, 277, 283–4, 285–6, 292, 293, 305, 320 n. 14
English 280, 301–3
pidgin English 259, 273
native speakers 14, 17, 167, 312
of English emerging in postcolonial countries 2, 12–13, 19, 67, 95, 149, 157, 188, 194, 207–8, 217, 323 n. 16
nativization (phase 3) 6, 32, 40–8, 62, 64, 66, 81, 117–18, 121–2, 129–31, 135–9, 140–3, 148–52, 155–60, 165–71, 181–5, 192–7, 198, 203, 204–10, 215–18, 219, 222–4, 232–4, 242–4, 253, 273–82
nativization, structural 5–6, 18, 31, 33, 39–40, 62, 63, 64, 85, 86, 108, 110, 151, 158, 169–70, 183–4, 195–6, 218, 278, 280, 282
negation 84, 101, 209–10
Newfoundland 238, 247
New Englishes, as a term 3
New Zealand 5, 10, 33, 42, 43, 48, 49, 55, 59, 65, 67, 127–33, 245
English 9, 35, 73, 81, 83, 84, 93, 98
see also Maori
Nigeria 7, 50, 83, 199–212, 214, 215, 216, 312
English 12, 13, 44, 83, 85
Pidgin 4, 67, 201, 202–3, 204, 205–7, 208–9, 211–12, 312
norm 5, 8, 16, 17–19, 32, 33, 38, 43, 44, 48, 50, 52, 58, 68, 92, 94, 160, 227, 290, 311, 312, 314
Northern Cities Shift (NCS) 96, 299–300

Pakistan 46, 80, 85, 105, 171
Papua New Guinea (Tok Pisin) 12, 64, 103, 106
passive 83, 159
pedagogy, language 2, 4, 10, 14, 16, 18, 29
Philippines, The 3, 48, 52, 58, 140–4, 316, 319 n. 5
English 64, 80–1, 83
phonology, see pronunciation
phrasal verb 47, 92–3, 118, 170, 196, 210, 224, 280
phraseology 46, 81, 94, 159, 170, 184, 195, 210, 279
pidgin 8, 10, 11, 40, 108, 311, 312
Aboriginal 120
American-Indian (Native) 259, 273
Cameroonian 67, 107, 213, 214–15, 216–17, 218
Chinese P. English 133, 135
Melanesian 115

Nigerian 201, 202–3, 204, 205–7, 208–9, 211–12, 312
West African P. English 10, 67, 201, 228
pidginization 35, 36, 64, 66–7, 267, 312
place names 35, 36, 39, 58, 79, 115, 120, 128, 135, 147, 155, 163, 178, 191, 228, 241, 262–4, 319 nn. 7, 8, 9
plantation 25, 34, 40, 60, 62, 63, 66, 189, 219, 268, 318 n. 2
plural 47, 83, 84, 85, 89, 102, 103, 105, 117, 138, 142, 151, 159, 169, 303
policy, language 2, 10, 14, 16, 18, 20
Portuguese 3, 69, 238, 297
Postcolonial Englishes, as a term 3
power 14, 16, 23, 24, 25, 28, 38, 40, 41, 43, 48, 53, 65, 66, 67, 99, 191, 201, 214, 222, 242, 283, 314, 315, 317, 319 n. 7
pragmatics 47, 122, 161, 169, 302
preposition 5, 46, 90, 142, 184, 196, 199, 209–10, 279, 303, 305
prestige 14, 18, 48, 64, 98, 99, 200, 236, 314
covert 48, 67, 111, 150, 188, 194, 207, 216, 226, 295, 307, 311
overt 226, 294
preverbal marker 118, 203, 223, 304
progressive 45, 47, 84, 85, 89, 151, 169, 184, 203
pronoun 84, 89, 103, 106, 117, 203, 223, 280, 299, 303, 305
pronunciation 6, 8, 9, 10, 17, 40, 44, 54, 71, 72–8, 125, 138, 142, 151, 158–9, 169, 196, 224, 244, 279, 301, 305, 306

question 84, 85, 105, 169

reallocation 54, 107, 109, 180, 296
reduplication 159, 169
regional variation 8, 9, 54, 125–6, 132–3, 168, 250, 298–300
regularization 89, 102, 103, 104
removal of English as a political goal 1, 12, 57–8, 141, 143–4, 147–8, 166, 197, 198, 199
restructuring 22, 23, 44, 60, 62, 63, 105, 107, 223, 233, 278, 312
revitalization, language 123, 293
Romance languages 6, 68, 69, 321 n. 23
RP (Received Pronunciation) 18, 73, 94, 102, 132, 187, 194, 202, 236, 271, 291

Scotch-Irish 255–6, 262
second-language acquisition 16, 22, 32, 34, 40, 42, 45, 57, 61, 63, 82, 87, 89, 220, 259

semantic shift 82, 117, 130, 138, 142, 152, 159, 169, 184, 195, 210, 218, 224, 234, 244
shift, language 5, 16, 32, 40, 42, 51, 61, 62, 63, 89, 116, 117, 118, 121, 126, 130, 157, 220, 249, 259, 277, 295, 306, 307, 312, 320 n. 20
simplification 74, 89, 102–4
Singapore 4, 10, 25, 33, 37, 52, 55, 153–61, 288, 309
 English 12, 13, 47, 61, 80–1, 83, 84, 92, 105–6
 Singlish 47, 94, 158, 159, 160, 315
slavery 20, 34, 59, 60, 61–2, 63, 66, 176, 219, 220, 221, 222–3, 228, 229, 230, 231–2, 254, 257, 258, 266, 283, 286
Slavic languages 68, 69–70, 278
social class variation 8, 9–10, 11, 17, 19, 43, 45, 51, 52, 53, 54, 64, 68, 72, 82, 96, 107, 111, 119–20, 126, 133, 168, 175–6, 180, 206, 290, 294
South Africa 3, 4, 13, 14, 25, 50, 54, 55, 58, 82, 130, 173–88, 319 n. 7
 Afrikaans English 174, 176, 183, 184
 Black English 73, 83, 90, 182–4, 188
 Cape Flats English 84, 177, 183, 184
 Indian English 73, 105, 179, 180, 182, 183, 184
 White English 45, 176, 178, 184
Spanish 3, 69, 142, 228–9, 256, 264, 278, 293, 304–5
spelling 212, 248, 263, 276, 277, 281, 287
Sri Lanka 13, 17, 83, 171
stop 73, 74, 98, 158, 169, 302

stress 73, 151, 158, 169
style 42, 50, 65, 72, 82–3, 92, 101, 107
subjunctive 142
substrate 10, 58, 60, 61, 62, 63, 68, 78, 82, 99, 151, 158, 159, 223, 321 n. 23
superstrate 10, 58, 60, 63, 99, 242
Suriname 224, 255
syllable-timing 73, 74, 158, 169

Tanzania 1, 58, 140, 189, 197–9, 213, 214
 English 81, 92
Three Circles model 13–14, 313, 315
tone 74
transfer 22, 40, 44, 45, 46, 74, 78, 82, 107, 108, 138, 158, 169, 184, 196, 220, 244, 250
Trinidad 10, 59, 60, 231

Uganda 189
universals, typological 10, 23, 60, 62

vowel 72–4, 76, 77, 93, 96, 97, 101–2, 105–6, 132, 151, 158–9, 224, 244, 246–7, 249, 297, 298, 299–300, 304, 305

word formation 46, 80–1, 117, 130, 138, 142, 152, 159, 169, 184, 195, 210, 218, 224, 234, 244, 279
World Englishes, as a discipline 2, 11–12
 journal 3
 as a term 3

Zimbabwe 319 n. 7